SHARON ZARDETTO AKER

The Macintosh Companion

THE BASICS AND BEYOND

ADDISON-WESLEY
PUBLISHING COMPANY, INC.

Reading, Massachusetts

Menlo Park, California

New York

Don Mills, Ontario

Wokingham, England

Amsterdam

Bonn

Sydney

Singapore

Tokyo

Madrid

San Juan

Paris

Seoul

Milan

Mexico City

Taipei

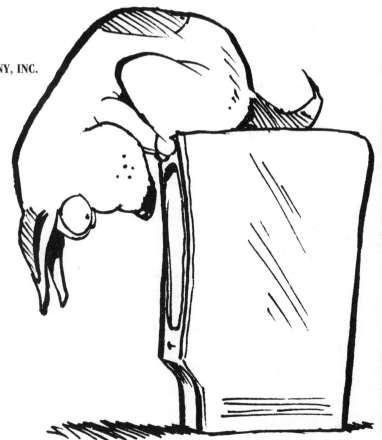

Library of Congress Cataloging-in-Publication Data

Aker, Sharon Zardetto.
    The Macintosh companion : the basics and beyond /Sharon Zardetto Aker.
        p.   cm.
    Includes index.
    ISBN 0-201-57754-2
    1. Macintosh (Computer).   I. Title.
QA76.8.M3A437   1991
005.265–dc20   91-18845
                                                                          CIP

Cover and text illustrations by Berkeley Breathed
Cover design by Hannus Design Associates and Jean Seal
Set in 11.5-point Garamond Book by ST Associates, Wakefield, MA

ISBN 0-201-57754-2
123456789-MW-9594939291
First printing, July 1991

A final one for the l. J. m. Thanks for everything.

Contents

Acknowledgments

I would like to thank:

At Addison-Wesley, Rachel Guichard and Joanne Clapp Fullagar for their skills in cajoling and coercing; and Tema Goodwin for her copyediting skills.

Technical reviewer and reader: Dr. Richard Wolfson
Technical editor: C.K. Haun
General answer men: Paul Snively, Rich Wolfson, Bill Hensler, Nick Lucia, and Mike Bielen

Some art in this book was provided by:

Dubl-Click Software
3-G Graphics
Carol Aiton, Parallax Design
Thaumaturge, Inc.
Claris, Inc.
Apple Computer, Inc.

Introduction

If you just bought a Macintosh, or if you've had one for a while and now you're ready to learn more about it, this book is for you.

The Mac is an elegant machine. It's so well-designed that you don't have to know a lot in order to start using it. But it's also a sophisticated machine, so the more you know, the more productive you can be.

Knowing "more" isn't just finding out the easiest, quickest, and best way of performing a specific operation. It also means understanding the basic Mac interface so you can find your way around in any program. It means being familiar with the power and capabilities of the system software Apple provides. And it means having a sense of what's going on "behind the scenes" so you can avoid common problems and troubleshoot the ones that do occur.

Throughout this book, it's assumed that you're using Apple's newest operating system, System 7. That means it's also assumed that you have, as a minimum hardware configuration, a Mac with a hard drive and 2 megabytes of RAM. (If you don't have System 7, or a hard drive, or 2M of memory, you can get any or all of them from your Apple dealer.)

ABOUT THIS BOOK . . .

The first section of this book combines theory and practice—starting with practice. Chapter 1 is for anyone who wants to just jump in and get started. It provides a step-by-step tour of the Mac interface and the Desktop. Even if you decide not to follow along on your Mac, the chapter will introduce you to all the basic concepts—and there are plenty of pictures so you'll know what everything should look like. Chapter 2 backtracks a little into theory, providing basic Macintosh and general computer terms you'll need.

The rest of the chapters in the book are grouped into related sections, and provide all the details on various topics, starting with the Mac interface and its ever-present Desktop, right through to trouble-shooting problems. Although sometimes the information in a chapter is based on something explained in an earlier one, you certainly don't have to read the book in order—you might, for instance, want to try out some desk accessories before you learn all the ins and outs of the Desktop.

Getting Started

Beginnings

ABOUT THIS CHAPTER

This chapter, with its "now do this" approach, introduces you to the basics of operating your Macintosh—from turning it on and handling icons and windows to using menu commands and dealing with dialog boxes.

When you see colored text, that's your signal to do something at the computer to turn theory into practice.

GETTING STARTED

Basics

So you've got (or you want to get) this terrific new machine with a great reputation for friendliness and you don't know exactly what to do with it, or how.

What, really, do you need to get started? Since this book assumes that you're running version 7.0 or later of Apple's System Software, the minimum requirements are:

- A Macintosh with at least 2 megabytes of memory (RAM) and either a built-in screen or a separate monitor. If you have a separate monitor, you need a cable and a video card that let you connect it to the computer.

- A keyboard and the connecting cable that comes with it.

- A mouse (it comes with every Macintosh model).

- An internal floppy disk drive and a hard drive, either internal or external. Blank floppy disks will come in handy for making backup copies of important files.

- The System Software that came with your Macintosh—version 7.0 or higher. (If you have a previous version of the System Software, you can get an update from your Apple dealer.)

- Some specialized software program(s)—a word processor, spreadsheet, or graphics program.

- A printer, or access to one. (You don't need a printer to learn how to use the Mac, but you'll need one to get any productive work done.)

You can run a Mac with a little less in the way of hardware—1 megabyte of RAM and two floppy disk drives instead of a hard drive—but you won't be able to do more than minimal work, and you won't be able to run System 7.

Just how much memory you really need, how large a hard drive, what kind of printer, and whether you need a color system—these all depend on the kind of work you'll be doing. But you can *start* with the essentials listed here, no matter what it is that you need in the long run. All these issues (floppy versus hard drive, printers, memory) are covered in detail elsewhere in the book. This chapter takes you on a tour of basic operations and concepts and leaves the details for later.

Off and Running

Actually, the title of this section should be "On and Running," because that's what your Mac should be doing.

We'll assume that your Mac is set up and ready to go. There's not that much to it, especially for one of the compact models, and the manuals that come with the machine are very clear.

To turn on the Mac:

➡ *If you have an external hard drive, turn it on first.*

➡ *Press the* startup key *on the keyboard.*

The startup key looks like this:

Some keyboards have the startup key in the upper-right corner; some have it in a more centered position along the top. The startup key doesn't work on some older Macintosh models—in fact, older keyboards don't even have startup keys; in either case, turn on the machine by using the power switch on its back.

While the Mac has a lot of built-in intelligence, it doesn't have enough information in it to get very far in the startup sequence. It needs the rest of its *operating system* from a file called (cleverly enough) *System,* which is stored in the *System Folder* on a disk. The Mac knows enough to look for a disk with the system information on it. This kind of disk is called a *system disk* or a *startup disk*.

System Folder

When you turn on your Mac and it finds the system disk, you'll see a smiling "happy Mac" on the screen. If there's no system disk available, you'll see a picture of a disk with a flashing question mark.

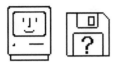

If there's a System disk available, you'll see the "happy Mac" on the screen; otherwise, you'll get a disk with a flashing question mark.

The hard drive you're using should have a System Folder with all the correct system information in it. If you have a hard drive but you're not getting the happy Mac, double check the instructions that came with the computer—and/or the drive, if it's an external one. The drive should be *initialized* and a System should be *installed* on it. (These procedures are covered later in this book, in Chapter 9.)

If you're starting with a floppy disk, the flashing question mark is your signal to feed the Mac a startup disk. (A disk is inserted label side up, metal shutter first.) If you insert a disk without a System at this point, the Mac spits it out and flashes an X in the disk on the screen.

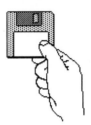

Insert a floppy disk label side up, metal shutter first.

If the floppy disk you're starting with isn't a System disk, you'll see this icon on the screen.

Okay, did you get everything turned on and started? If you did, the first thing you'll see is the famous Mac *Desktop*, with a picture of a disk and a trash can on the screen.

A DESKTOP TOUR

Basics

The basic design of the Mac is a visual one: You use pictures, called *icons*, instead of words, and you use the mouse to manipulate the pictures instead of using the keyboard to type in a command. Instead of typing the equivalent of "Erase the file named 'Monday's Memo' from the disk in the first drive," you can just use the mouse to drag the icon of that memo right into icon of the Trash can.

There are, of course, operations that are more easily executed with words than by manipulating pictures. For those kinds of commands, the Mac provides *menus*, lists of commands that you can choose with the mouse or sometimes activate from the keyboard. The names of the available menus are always across the top of the screen, in the *menu bar.* For instance, when there's something in the Trash can and you want it permanently erased, you don't have to manipulate the Trash can and dump it onto some semblance of a garbage truck to be hauled to the nearest electronic land fill. Instead, you choose the Empty Trash command from one of the menus.

The Desktop

When you start the Mac, you'll see its *Desktop*, the place where you manipulate the information on your disks. The Desktop (see Figure 1-1) is also known as the *Finder*, since that's the name of the program that actually gives you the Desktop.

There's a disk icon in the upper right and the Trash icon in the lower right. The disk icon in the illustration is for a hard drive; if you start up with a floppy, you'll see a different icon in that position. Across the top of the screen is the *menu bar* with the names of the menus that are

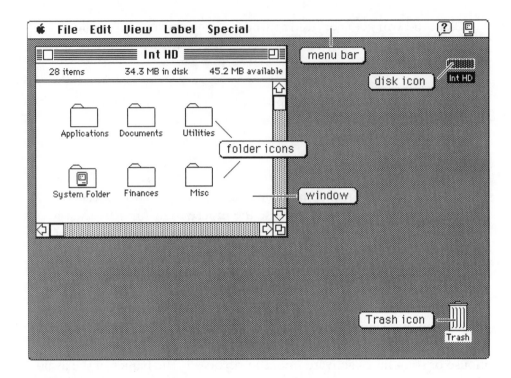

Figure 1-1. The basic Desktop

available on the Desktop. At the right of the menu bar are two small icons that are actually menu "names."

Icons on the Desktop (with the exception of the disk and Trash icons) represent the contents of a disk, and they usually appear in white areas on the Desktop called *windows*. When you start the Mac, you may or may not have windows open on your Desktop—it all depends on how the Desktop was left the last time the disk was used.

The Mouse

There are two basic ways to interact with the computer—the mouse and the keyboard. Most operations other than text entry can be performed with the mouse, although sometimes using "keyboard equivalents" of mouse operations is easier and even faster than using the mouse itself. But the majority of Desktop operations are performed with the mouse.

When you move the mouse around on your desk, its *cursor* moves around on the screen. As you use the mouse for different operations, different cursors appear. The standard one is the *arrow*, or *pointer*. You use the pointer to, well, point to things. The other basic cursors are the *I-beam*, or *text* cursor, which appears when you're working with text, and the *wristwatch*, which shows up when the Mac is busy doing something and you have to wait for it.

Basic cursors

SELECTING

When you point to an icon and *click* the mouse button (press it down and release it immediately), you've *selected* the icon.

You don't have to keep the entire arrow within the icon you're selecting; it's the tip of the arrow that counts. (If the tip of the arrow is outside the icon even though the rest of it is inside, the click won't work.)

➡ *Point to the Trash icon and click the mouse button.*

It's the tip of the arrow that counts. The first two positions will select the Trash; the last one won't.

The Trash icon turns black—it's *highlighted*—to show that it's selected.

Clicking on an icon selects it, turning it black.

There are two ways to deselect something on the Desktop. The first is to select something else:

➡ *Click on the disk icon.*

The disk is selected and turns black; the Trash icon returns to its normal state, since it's now deselected.

The second way to deselect something is to, in effect, click on "nothing":

➡ *Click anywhere on the gray pattern of the Desktop.*

The disk icon is deselected and turns white again (see Figure 1-2).

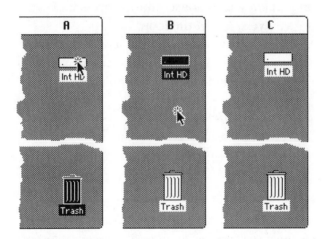

Figure 1-2. Clicking on the disk icon deselects the Trash (A to B); clicking on the bare Desktop deselects an icon without selecting another (B to C).

DRAGGING

You can move things around on the Desktop by *dragging* them with the mouse.

➡ *Point to the disk icon and press the mouse button. (Pressing, as opposed to* clicking, *is pushing the mouse button down and keeping it down.) Then move the mouse.*

When you drag something on the Desktop, an outline of the icon goes wherever you move the mouse. When you release the mouse button, the icon jumps to its new position (see Figure 1-3).

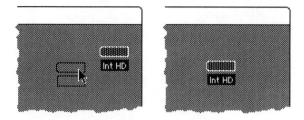

Figure 1-3. Dragging an icon

Windows

A Macintosh *window* shows you the contents of something. On the Desktop, windows show you what's in a disk, what's in folders on that disk, and what's in the Trash waiting to be erased.

To get a window, you *open* an icon. One of the ways to open an icon on the Desktop is by *double-clicking:*

➡ *Point to the disk icon and click the mouse button twice in rapid succession.*

The *disk window* opens, showing the contents of the disk. The disk icon turns dark gray—this indicates that not only is it selected, but it's also opened. (If your disk icon was already opened when you started up, double-clicking won't do any harm.)

The contents of a window on the Desktop can be displayed in several ways. If your windows don't look like those in Figure 1-4, you should choose the By Icon command from the View menu. (And you might have to jump ahead to the section on Menus if you're not sure how to do that.)

Your window won't match the one pictured here, but the basics are the same. Some of the icons in your window are almost certainly *folders*. You can put icons inside different folders—and you can even put folders inside other folders as you organize your information to suit the way you work.

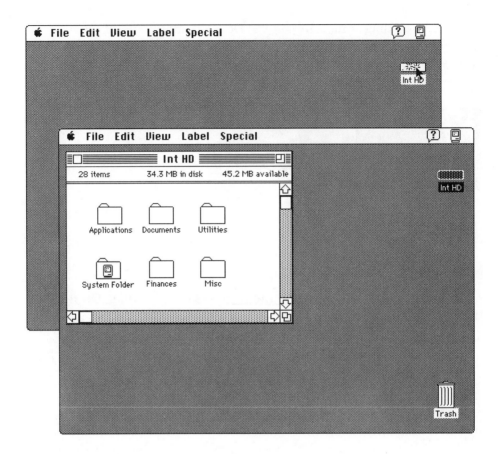

Figure 1-4. Double-clicking on a disk icon opens its window.

Folders can be opened the same way disks can.

➥ *Point to the folder labeled System Folder—it has a special miniature Mac on it—and double-click on it. (If you can't see the System Folder, you'll have to read ahead about how to resize the window or scroll its contents so that you can find the System Folder.)*

Another window opens, this time showing the contents of the System Folder (see Figure 1-5).

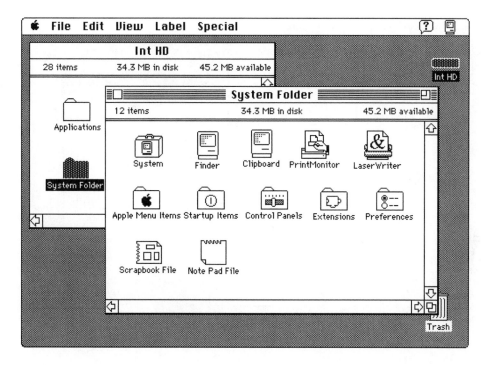

Figure 1-5. Double-clicking on the System Folder icon opens the System Folder window and activates it—the disk window no longer has stripes in its title bar.

Only one window can be *active* at a time. You'll notice that with two windows opened, only one has stripes along the top where the name of the window is—that's the active one. When windows overlap on the screen, the active one is always on top. The System Folder window is active right now because you just opened it.

You can activate a window by clicking in any part of it—as soon as you click, that window comes up to the top.

➡️ *Click in any exposed part of the disk window to activate it (see Figure 1-6). (If your System Folder window is so large that it completely covers the disk window, move the System Folder window by dragging it—grab it anywhere in the striped area along the top.)*

➡️ *Click anywhere in the System Folder window to bring it back on top.*

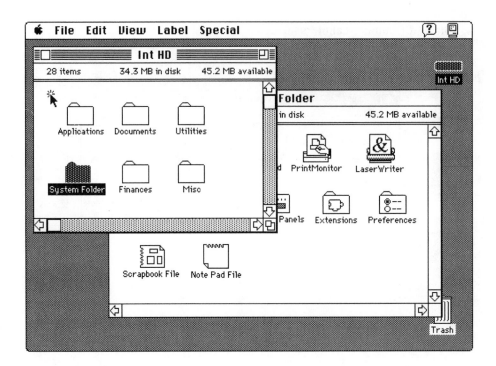

Figure 1-6. Click anywhere in the disk window to activate it and bring it to the top.

HANDLING WINDOWS

Windows on the Desktop are basic Macintosh "document" windows with various controls that let you change their sizes and positions and your view of their contents.

To change the position of a window, you drag the whole window by its *title bar*, the striped area at the top.

➡ *Move the System Folder window around.*

Dragging a window is basically the same as dragging an icon—you'll see an outline of the window following the mouse cursor around (see Figure 1-7), and the window moves to its new position when you release the mouse button (see Figure 1-8).

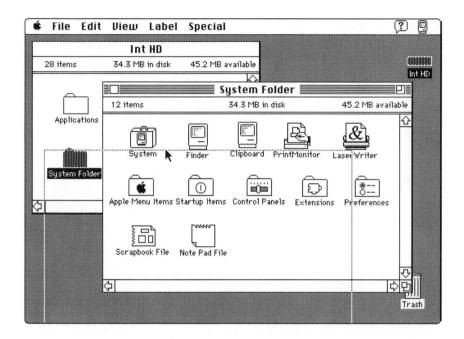

Figure 1-7. When you drag a window, an outline moves with the mouse.

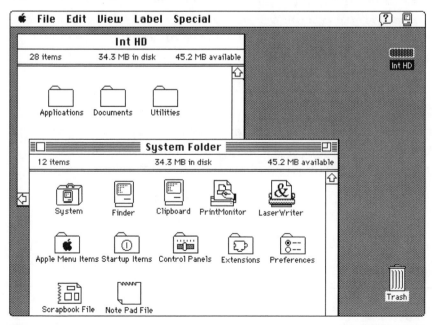

Figure 1-8. When you release the mouse button, the window moves to its new position.

To quickly change the size of a window, you click in the *zoom box*, the nested squares in the upper-right corner. Each click alternates the window between full size and the original size—or the last size you created.

The zoom box

A *full-size window* on the Desktop is one that's just large enough to display all its contents. If it's so full that all the contents can't be displayed, the window fills the screen except for a strip along the right edge so the disk and Trash icons are still visible.

➧ *Click in the zoom box of the System Folder window. (If it doesn't have a zoom box, that's because it's not the active window. Click anywhere in the window to activate it, then click in the zoom box.) Click in the zoom box again to zoom the window back down to its original size.*

To change the size or shape of a window to specific proportions, drag the *size box* that is in the window's lower-right corner. As with other dragging operations, you'll see a dotted outline as you move the mouse and as soon as you let go of the button, the window changes to the new size.

The size box

➡ *Change the shape of the System Folder window so that it is long and narrow; then try short and wide (see Figures 1-9 and 1-10). (If the bottom of the System Folder window is off the screen, as in the last illustration, move it back so that you can get at the size box.)*

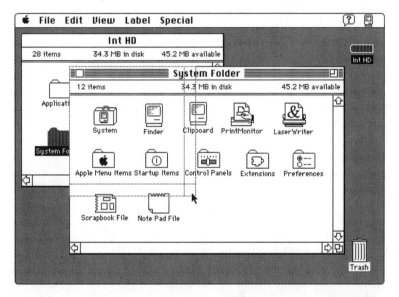

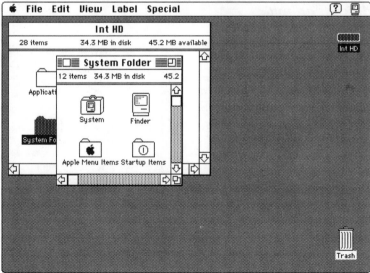

Figures 1-9 and 1-10. Using the size box to resize a window

SCROLLING WINDOWS

When a window is sized so that all of its contents are visible, the *scroll bars* along its right and bottom edges are empty, or white. When some of the window's contents are hidden from view, the scroll bar turns gray. Sometimes the horizontal bar will be white and the vertical one gray (or vice versa), indicating that the unseen items are hidden in only one direction.

⟼ *Resize the System Folder window again—with the zoom box and with the size box—noting when the scroll bars are gray and when they're white. Make the window small enough, finally, so that both the vertical and the horizontal bars are gray.*

When the entire contents of the window aren't displayed at one time, you can use the *scroll controls* to change the view. Clicking in the appropriate *scroll arrow* moves the contents up, down, left, or right, a little at a time (see Figure 1-11). Clicking in the gray area of the *scroll bar* moves the contents in larger increments (see Figure 1-12).

⟼ *Click in the scroll controls of the System Folder window to scroll its icons around.*

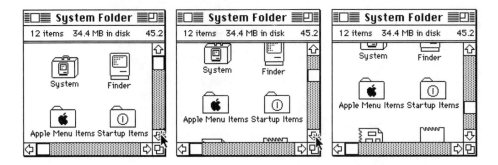

Figure 1-11. Using a scroll arrow moves the contents of a window a little at a time.

Figure 1-12. Clicking in the scroll bar moves the contents of a window in larger increments.

Pressing is another mouse technique to try. You already know that you need to press, not click, the mouse button when you want to drag something. But pressing is also used instead of repeated clicking in the same place.

➡ *Point to one of the scroll arrows and* press *the mouse button. The contents continue scrolling until you release the button.*

The *scroll box* in the scroll bar indicates what part of the overall contents of the window you're looking at. For instance, if one scroll box is at the top of the vertical scroll bar and the other is at the left of the horizontal scroll bar, you're looking at the upper-left corner of the window's contents. When a scroll box is at the center of a scroll bar, you're looking at the center of the window's contents. You can also use the scroll box to view a particular area of your window's contents: Just drag the box to any position along the scroll bar (see Figure 1-13).

➡ *Try the vertical and horizontal scroll boxes.*

Here's a mildly confusing concept for you: It may seem like the scroll controls are moving the *contents* of the window—you saw them move, right?—but they're not. Have you noticed that when you click in the up arrow, the window contents move *down*? That's because despite how everything looks, the scroll controls are moving the *window*, not its

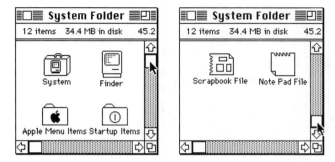

Figure 1-13. Dragging the scroll box displays a different area of the window.

contents. Your window isn't really moving on the screen, but *concep-tually*, it's the window that's moving while the contents remain station-ary. So, a click on the up arrow moves the window up, and its contents, relatively speaking, move down. By the same token, clicking in the left arrow moves the *window* left, and the contents then move to the right (see Figure 1-14). (Some of the Mac's visual interface that works so well in practice sounds confusing when put into words. But try the scroll con-trols and you'll see how intuitive they become, despite the fact that your moving window isn't moving and the contents move in the opposite direction of the arrow that you're using.)

Finally, you can close a window by using the *close box* in the upper-left corner.

➡ *Click in the System Folder window's close box.*

The close box

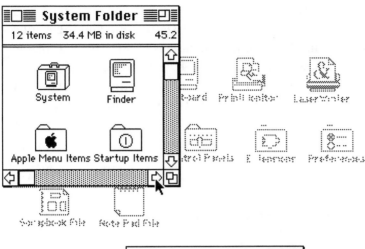

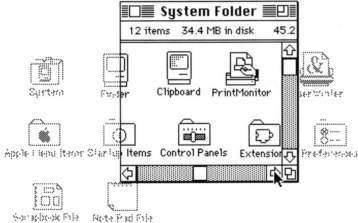

Figure 1-14. Using the right scroll arrow scrolls things toward the left because, conceptually, it's the window that's moving, not its contents.

Menus

The *menu bar* at the top of the screen displays the *menus* available while you're on the Desktop. The first one is the Apple menu, followed by File and Edit. These three menus are almost always available, no matter what you're doing on your Mac, although the commands within them change according to circumstances. The View, Label, and Special menus are specific to the Finder. At the right of the menu bar are two more menus, with icons that serve as "names": the Help menu and the Applications menu. These menus, like Apple, File, and Edit, are always available.

Before you use a command, you usually have to indicate, by selecting, what the command is going to be applied to. In this case, we want to open the Trash to see what's in it, so first you have to select it.

➡ *Click on the Trash can to select it.*

➡ *Point to the File menu and* press *(not click) the mouse button.*

The File menu opens, listing the commands available.

➡ *With the mouse button still down, slide the mouse down to the Open command.*

As you pass over each menu command, it's *highlighted*—the letters reverse to white on black instead of black on white.

➡ *With the mouse pointer on the Open command, release the mouse button (see Figures 1-15 and 1-16).*

The window for the Trash opens, just as if you had double-clicked on the icon. Now try another command:

➡ *Use the mouse to open the File menu again; this time slide down to the Close Window command and release the mouse button there.*

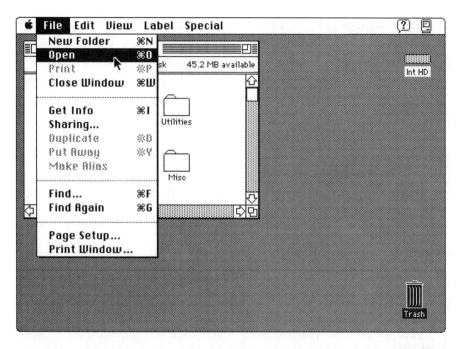

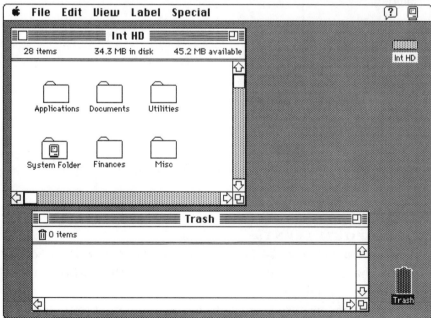

Figures 1-15 and 1-16. Using a menu command to open an icon

The Trash window closes, just as if you had clicked in its close box. In this case, the Close command was applied to the *active* window—the Trash window was active (with the striped title bar) because you had just opened it. If you wanted the Close Window command to apply to a different window, you would have had to select that window before choosing the command.

Sometimes menu commands are *dimmed,* or *gray,* in the menu because you can't use them in a current situation. If you don't have an icon selected, for instance, the Open command is dimmed because there's nothing to open; if there's no window open, the Close Window command is dimmed.

File	
New Folder	⌘N
Open	⌘O
Print	⌘P
Close Window	⌘W
Get Info	⌘I
Sharing...	
Duplicate	⌘D
Put Away	⌘Y
Make Alias	
Find...	⌘F
Find Again	⌘G
Page Setup...	
Print Window...	

Commands are dimmed in a menu when they don't apply to the current situation.

KEYBOARD EQUIVALENTS

Many menu commands have *keyboard equivalents* or *command-key equivalents*. That means you can activate them from the keyboard instead of choosing them from a menu.

Keyboard equivalents are listed right in the menu next to their commands. To use a keyboard command, you hold down the Command key (the one with the "cloverleaf" symbol on it—sometimes there's also an apple outlined on the key) and then press the letter that's shown in the menu. You keep the Command key down while you press the letter, and although letters are always indicated in uppercase in the menu, you don't have to use the Shift key.

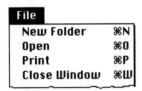

Although Command-key equivalents are shown as uppercase letters, you don't have to use the Shift key when you type them.

Try this:

➡ *Click in the Trash icon to select it.*

➡ *Press Command-O.*

The Trash window should open just as if you had double-clicked on the icon or used the mouse to choose Open from the File menu. Now:

➡ *Press Command-W.*

This closes the window—it's the same as using the mouse to click in the close box or choosing Close from the File menu.

The Help Balloons

Now that you know how to use menus, you can access the Mac's built-in Help function. The Help menu is the "balloon" with the question mark that's at the right of the menu bar. To turn on the help feature, select Show Balloons from the menu.

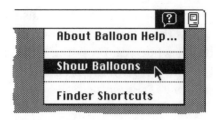

Now, whenever you point to something on the screen (you *don't* have to click on it) a helpful balloon of information appears. Pointing to any icon, for instance, gets you a description of what the icon stands for (see Figure 1-17).

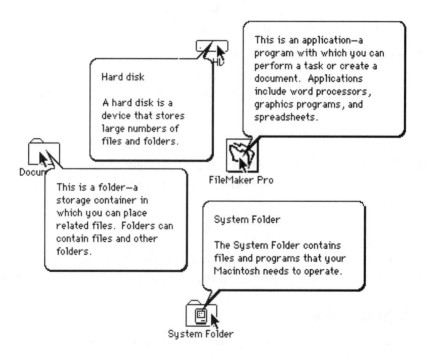

Figure 1-17. Pointing to an icon opens a Help balloon description of that icon.

Sometimes the description will change slightly, depending on the state of the icon. Figure 1-18, for instance, shows the difference between pointing to an empty Trash icon and a full Trash icon.

Figure 1-18. A balloon description can change depending on the state of an icon.

Pointing to various spots on a window provides information about that part of the window—so if you forget what the zoom box does (or what it's called), you can point to it and find out. You can also point to any other section of a window for help. The composite picture in Figure 1-19 shows some of the balloons you get from within windows.

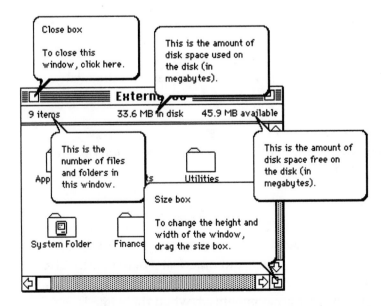

Figure 1-19. You can even get information about parts of a window.

To turn balloon help off, choose the Hide Balloons command from the Help menu. (You'll get a description of the command as you choose it, but that won't interfere with the command itself.)

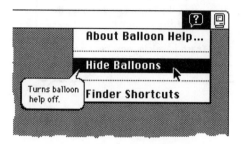

More Desktop Procedures

You've already learned the basics of your Macintosh Desktop. Here are a few more operations you can perform based on what you already know. To get ready:

➡ *If the disk window isn't open, double-click in the disk icon to open it.*

➡ *If the disk window isn't* active, *click anywhere in it to activate it.*

The disk window has to be opened and active so that the next command will work.

CREATING AND NAMING FOLDERS
Folders are used on the Desktop to organize the information on your disks. To create a new folder:

➡ *Choose New Folder from the File menu.*

A new, empty folder appears in the window (see Figure 1-20).
There's a distinction—both visual and practical—between an *icon* being selected and its *name* being selected. When just the icon is selected, the icon and its title are highlighted; when the name is

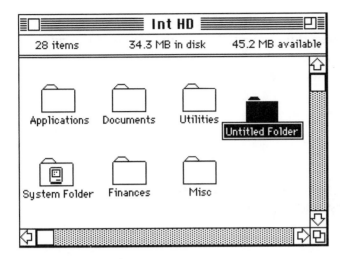

Figure 1-20. A newly created folder is automatically selected and ready for its title to be edited.

selected, everything's still highlighted but the name is surrounded by a frame. If you type something while an icon's selected, nothing happens; if you type when the name is selected, you change the name.

When a folder is created, it and its name (Untitled Folder) are automatically selected. If you've clicked someplace else by mistake and deselected it, you have to click on the folder's *name*, not just the folder itself, in order to edit it.

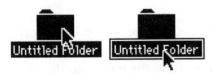

Left, selecting an icon; right, selecting a title

You can change the folder's title to anything you want. With the folder's name selected:

➡ *Type a new name—try First Folder if you can't think of anything more creative.*

Since the entire title was selected before you started typing, the typing you did replaced the selected text—that's one of the rules of Macintosh text entry.

Now make another folder:

➥ *Choose New Folder from the File menu again.*

➥ *Leave the title as Untitled Folder.*

PUTTING ICONS INTO OTHER ICONS

Try putting the first folder inside the second one:

➥ *Drag the First Folder icon until the mouse pointer is on top of the Untitled Folder icon. As usual, the outline of the dragged item moves with the mouse. The* Untitled Folder *icon turns black when you're on top of it. Release the mouse button, and the First Folder disappears and the Untitled Folder turns white again (see Figure 1-21).*

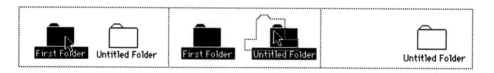

Figure 1-21. Dragging a folder into another folder

That's how you put one icon into another one—whether you're putting files or folders into folders, something into the Trash, or even moving things from one disk to another: Drag the icon into the "target" until the target turns black and then release the mouse button.

Now, take the first folder *out* of the second folder:

➥ *Open Untitled Folder by double-clicking in it.*

You'll see the First Folder inside it.

➡ *Drag the icon of the First Folder out of the Untitled Folder window. Wherever you release the mouse button is where the folder moves to—put it back in the disk window (see Figure 1-22).*

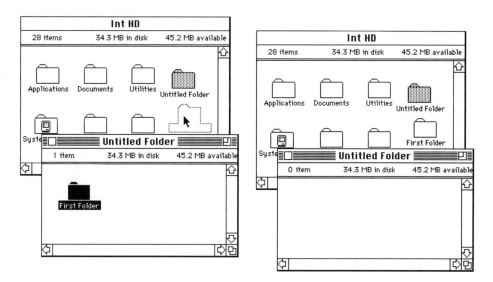

Figure 1-22. Dragging a folder out of another folder

➡ *Close the folder window by clicking in its close box.*

USING THE TRASH

You're finished with the folders, so you can drag them into the Trash. First, select them both:

➡ *Click on one of the folders to select it.*

➡ *Hold down the Shift key and click on the other folder.*

Both folders are now selected. This method of extending an original selection to include something else is called *shift-clicking* (see Figure 1-23). Without the Shift key, clicking on the second folder would have deselected the first.

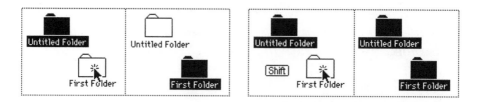

Figure 1-23. Clicking on another folder normally deselects the first, but if the Shift key is held down, the second one is added to the selection.

➡ *Grab either icon with the mouse and drag it to the Trash.*

As shown in Figure 1-24, outlines of both icons will move (unless you clicked on one of the folders after selecting them both—when you start the drag, you have to keep the mouse button down or it's interpreted as a click and, therefore, a new selection).

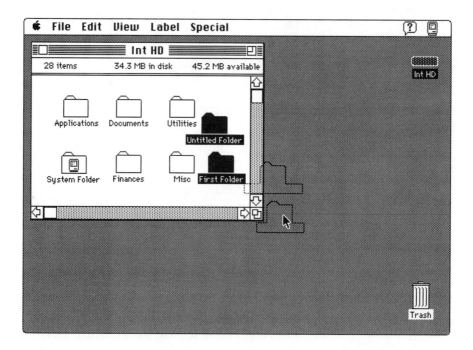

Figure 1-24. Dragging one item in a multiple selection moves all the selected items.

Drag until the mouse pointer is on top of the Trash can; when the can turns black, release the mouse button. The Trash fattens to let you know that something's in there.

Empty and full Trash cans

> ➡ *Double-click on the Trash can to open its window.*

You'll see the two folders that you dragged into the Trash. The Trash serves as a holding area for the files and folders you want erased from the disk. You can put as many items as you want into the Trash, but you can take them right back out again if you change your mind. When you want to erase the files, you use the *Empty Trash* command in the Special menu. But don't empty the Trash yet—we're going to use these folders to demonstrate one more important Macintosh concept.

The Clipboard

The Clipboard concept is central to Macintosh computing; it pioneered the easy transfer of information between documents—even between documents from different applications. With the Clipboard you could put a picture into a word processing document, or you could add to that same document a table that you created in a spreadsheet.

The Clipboard is a temporary storage area. You put material on it by *copying* or *cutting* it from the original source—using the aptly named *Copy* and *Cut* commands in the Edit menu. The Clipboard holds only one item, so copying or cutting something new to it replaces whatever was already there.

Once something's on the Clipboard, you put it someplace new by *pasting* it down—with the Edit menu's *Paste* command.

You can use the titles of the two folders in the Trash to experiment with these commands.

➡ *Click on the name* First Folder *underneath the folder's icon so that it's selected for editing—you'll see the frame around it.*

➡ *Place the mouse cursor anyplace within the word* First *under the icon and double-click. (When the mouse cursor is over the folder's title, it changes from the arrow to the I-beam, or text cursor.)*

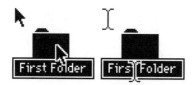

The arrow changes to the text cursor when it's over the folder title.

When you double-click on the word, the entire word is selected— this is a basic Mac text-editing technique (see Figure 1-25).

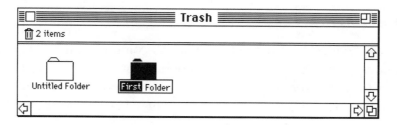

Figure 1-25. Double-clicking on a word selects it.

➡ *Choose* Cut *from the Edit menu.*

The word disappears from the folder title.

➡ *Click on the* Untitled Folder *title to select it.*

➡ *Place the mouse cursor between the words* Untitled *and* Folder *and click.*

When you click the I-beam anywhere within text, you leave behind a blinking vertical line—this is also referred to generally as a cursor, or the blinking cursor, but specifically it's known as the *insertion point*. It shows you the spot you're working on in any text: If you type, the letters appear at the insertion point; if you use the Delete key, the deletion begins at the insertion point. And if you paste something, the pasted material appears there.

➡ *Choose* Paste *from the Edit menu.*

The word *First* is inserted between *Untitled* and *Folder*. If the title really mattered, you'd have to insert a space before or after the pasted word (it depends on where, exactly, you pasted it—before or after the existing space between the two original words).

The Clipboard retains whatever you've placed on it until you cut or copy something new to it (or until you shut off the computer). With the cursor still blinking in the folder's title:

➡ *Choose* Paste *again from the Edit menu.*

Another copy of the word *First* is pasted into the title. Of course, *UntitledFirstFirst Folder* is a pretty strange title, so:

➡ *Choose* Undo *from the Edit menu.*

The folder title reverts to its original title, *Untitled Folder*. Undo cancels the last thing you did. If you had just typed something into the title, that would disappear—and if you had typed *over* something else by selecting the text before you typed, then Undo would restore the original text (see Figure 1-26).

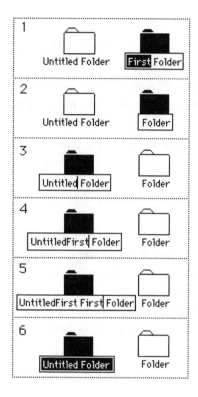

Figure 1-26. 1) Double-click to select a word; 2) Cut; 3) Click to place the insertion point; 4) Paste; 5) Paste again; 6) Undo.

Dialog Boxes

A *dialog box* is a special way to communicate with the computer or with the application you're running. It may have buttons you can push or check, boxes you can type in, lists you can select from, and even its own menus that pop up at the press of the mouse button.

An *alert* is a simple dialog that doesn't provide much in the way of dialog—it just warns you about something and asks if you want to proceed, or it lets you back out. Since you have two items waiting to be emptied from the Trash, you can see an alert dialog (and use your first button):

➡ *Choose* Empty Trash *from the Special menu.*

➡ *A dialog box appears telling you what's in the Trash and asking if you really want to empty it (see Figure 1-27). Click in the OK button.*

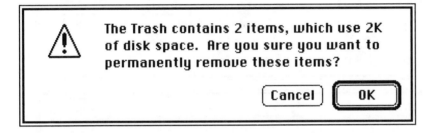

Figure 1-27. This dialog box appears when you choose Empty Trash.

The folders are erased from the disk and the Trash can icon reverts to its slim, empty self.

You can take a look at another dialog box from the Desktop:

➡ *Choose* Print Directory *from the File menu.*

The exact dialog you get depends on which printer you're using, but it will look something like one of Print dialogs shown in Figure 1-28.

This isn't a complicated dialog, as dialogs go, but you get to use another button:

➡ *Click in the Cancel button to put the dialog away.*

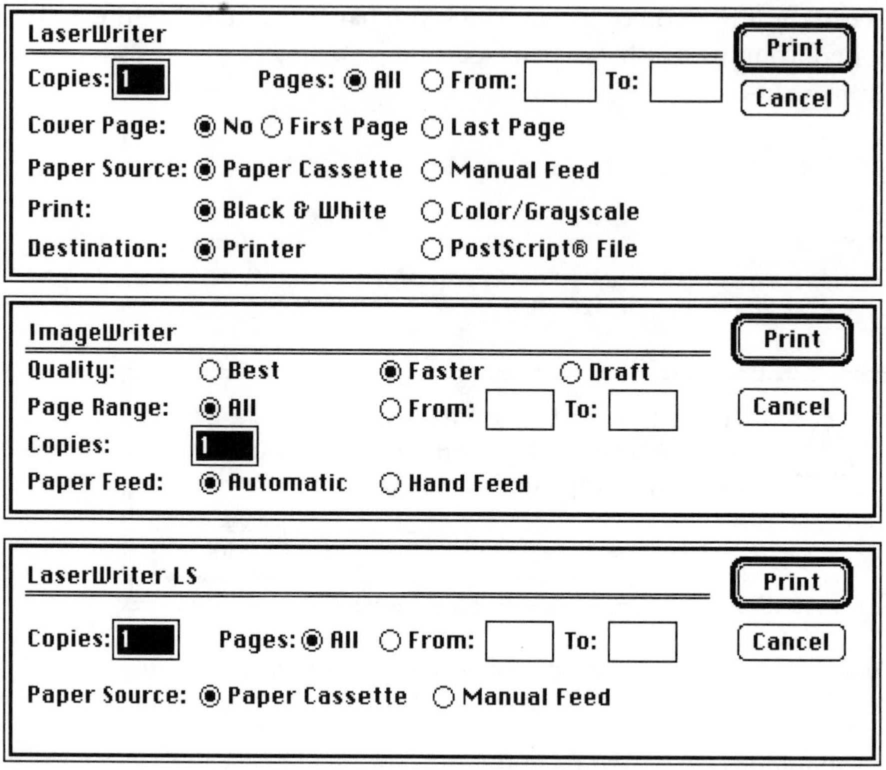

Figure 1-28. Print dialog boxes

Shutting Down

Now, the simplest operation of all—shutting down the computer. Simple, yes, but there's still a right way and a wrong way to do it. Just shutting off the power to the computer is the wrong way. The right way is:

➡ *Choose* Shut Down *from the Special menu.*

This gives the Mac a chance to do last-minute housekeeping before you turn it off. Sometimes what you *think* is done is only done on the

```
Special
  Clean Up Window
  Empty Trash...
  ..............................
  Eject Disk      ⌘E
  Erase Disk...
  ..............................
  Restart
  Shut Down
```

screen, and the information hasn't yet made it to the disk that stores the information for the next time you turn on the Mac. The Shut Down command updates whatever disks you've been working with, ejects any floppy disks you're using, and shuts off the power. (In some models, you have to shut off the power yourself—when the housekeeping's finished, you get a dialog box that tells you it's safe to shut off the Mac.)

SUMMARY

You've learned a little bit about a lot of different things in this chapter: the basics of working on your Desktop and interacting with your Mac using the mouse and through menus and dialog boxes.

Each of the topics encountered in this chapter are more fully explored in their own chapters throughout the rest of the book.

The Thinking Machine

ABOUT THIS CHAPTER

The material in this chapter is pretty generic, in two ways. First, the bulk of it applies to computers in general, not just to the Macintosh. Second, even the information that is Mac-specific is treated in only a general fashion. For instance, you'll find out what RAM is, but for information about how much RAM you need in your Mac and how to divvy it up among various tasks, you'll have to check later chapters.

This chapter is more than just Computer Basics 101 (although it's that, too); it contains information and defines terms that the rest of the book assumes you're familiar with.

HOW MUCH DO YOU NEED TO KNOW?

There are many levels of understanding something. A child knows what makes a car go. A grownup gets in and drives.

Or is this what makes a car go: You turn the key in the ignition, manipulate the gas and brake pedals, and turn the steering wheel. You also follow lots of rules (like which side of the road to drive on and what traffic lights mean), but it's that key and those pedals and the steering wheel that really make it go.

Or is this what makes a car go: the major automotive systems—the engine, ignition, lubrication, fuel, cooling, electrical, and drive systems. You might even be able to make a reasonable guess as to the cause of minor problems and replace some subassemblies when necessary, as well as change the oil and filter, and even a tire.

Or is *this* what makes a car go: the engine that is basically an air pump drawing in air (because of decreased pressure caused by the intake stroke of the four-stroke cycle) to be mixed with fuel vapors that are ignited at the appropriate instant, burning at temperatures greater than 4500° F when the expansion of the air (due to the intense heat) drives a piston down on the power stroke, and the crankshaft that converts the linear motion of the piston into the rotary motion that is ultimately transmitted to the wheels.

So there are lots of levels of understanding how something works. But you don't have to know that all the other automotive systems support the primary engine four-stroke cycle if you want to drive a car—the ignition key does the trick. (For that matter, a child with a cooperative adult doesn't even need to know about the ignition key to get the car to go.)

To operate your Mac, you certainly don't need the level of understanding implied by the complexity of Figure 2-1.

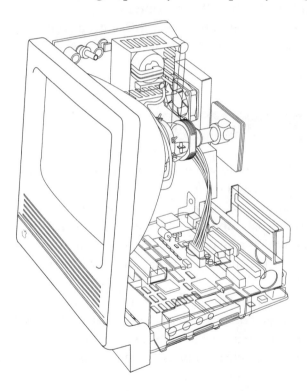

Figure 2-1.   You don't need to know about all this to use your Mac to the fullest.

But merely turning the key and driving away is good only at the beginning, while you're learning about the machine. To get the most out of your computer, you need to know a little bit about what's going on under the hood. Then you'll understand why you're doing what you're doing (most of the time, anyway) and be able to figure out what's going on when things aren't happening quite the way you expect them to (lots of times, anyway). You'll also be able to avoid many problems and troubleshoot the inevitable ones. And, with the basic jargon under your belt, you'll be more likely to understand any solution offered by a book you've looked something up in or an expert to whom you've turned for help.

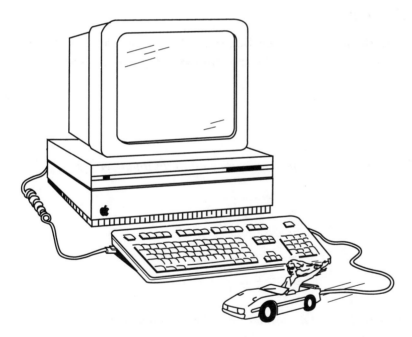

Figure 2-2. Just hopping in and driving away is good only at the beginning.

THE INFORMATION PROCESSOR

Basics

A computer can do a lot of things, but every activity boils down to one concept: the manipulation of information. You put information (data) in, the computer does something, you get information back—and you can store the data along the way. Everything in or attached to the computer is involved in one or more of these four basic computing functions: *input*, *output*, *processing*, and *storage*.

Input and Output

Your main input devices are the keyboard and the mouse, and your main output devices are the screen and the printer (see Figures 2-3 and 2-4).

Figure 2-3. The keyboard and the mouse are your main input devices.

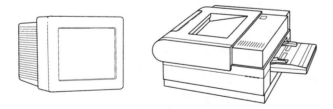

Figure 2-4. The monitor and the printer are your main output devices.

There are other ways to get information in and out of your computer: Sound goes in through a microphone and out through a speaker; text and graphics can be entered into the computer from printed material through the use of *scanners*; and information comes in from and goes out to other computers through a network connection or a *modem*, the device that connects a computer to a telephone line.

Storage

Most computer information committed to long-term storage is stored on *magnetic media,* disks and platters that can take a magnetic charge. Since computers work with units of information that are simply zeroes or ones, and each tiny particle on a disk can be charged either positively or negatively, using magnetic media is a handy way to store computer information.

Floppy disks and hard drives are the most common storage devices, but there are others, too, like tape systems for backing up important work, and CD-ROM drives for holding vast amounts of data in a very small space.

Processing

The interface may be the Mac's heart and soul, but its brain is its *central processing unit,* or *CPU.* This is where the most important work is done. Whether it's as simple as figuring out which key you've pressed on the keyboard and displaying it on the screen, or as complex as solving a formula that takes into account thousands of spreadsheet entries spread across several separate files, the CPU manipulates and transforms the information.

The CPU is also referred to as the *processor, processing chip,* or simply, the *chip* (because it's made from a slice, or chip, of silicon). There are other kinds of chips in the computer, too, but "chip" by itself usually means the processor. Processor chips are generally referred to by the numbers assigned by their manufacturers. Macs use Motorola processors from the 68000 series—the higher the number (it usually increases by tens), the more advanced the chip's capabilities.

The term *microcomputer* comes not from your desktop computer's size in relation to its big mainframe cousins, but because its CPU is a single component, or *microprocessor.* (The CPUs in large computers are made of many components.)

RAM AND ROM

Basics

Memory chips store information electronically, as opposed to the magnetic storage used on disks. A memory chip has thousands (even millions) of microscopic electronic switches that can be in either an on or off position.

Memory chips have thousands of switches in on and off positions.

In some cases, the switches are permanently set in their positions. This is *ROM*, or *read-only memory*: It can't be changed, but the computer can "read" it—can get information from it—at any time.

In other memory chips, the switches are set and reset as you operate the computer. They remain in position only as long as they're being fed electricity, so when you shut off the computer, the information stored on these chips is lost. This is *RAM*, or *random-access memory*. The computer can jump directly to any spot (called an *address*) in RAM to retrieve data stored there without having to wade through everything in front of it.

ROM is also accessible at random spots, so that's not the difference between the two. The real difference is that ROM is permanent information "hard-wired" into the computer, and RAM is changeable and *temporary.*

MEASURING INFORMATION

Basics

When we discuss a computer's capacity for handling information, the basic unit of measurement is a *bit*. A bit is the smallest piece of information you can deal with, and it can represent one of only two things. It doesn't matter much what those two things might be: on-off, yes-no, black-white, zero-one.

The word *bit* comes from *binary digit*. In the binary numbering system, there are only two digits, and since the computer uses electrical switches that can be either on or off at any given time, a binary approach is the logical one for computers.

Binary Numbering

Our decimal numbering system uses ten digits, zero through nine, and relies on a digit's *position* in a number to define what it actually stands for. As you move a place to the left in a series of digits, the number that place represents increases, with each position representing a power of 10. As shown in Figure 2-5, the first position (counting from the *right*) stands for ones; the second place stands for tens, the third is for hundreds, and so on. Putting the digit 5 in the third place makes it represent 5 hundreds, or 500—the zeroes act as place holders.

10^4	10^3	10^2	10^1	10^0
(10,000)	(1,000)	(100)	(10)	(1)

Figure 2-5. Place values in decimal numbering

The binary number system uses only two digits: zero and one. Just as in the decimal system, the position of a digit defines its value. The place values for binary numbers increase by powers of 2 instead of 10. As Figure 2-6 shows, that means the first place (again, counting from the *right*) stands for ones, the second position stands for twos, the third place is for fours, and so on. Putting the digit 1 in the third place makes

Figure 2-6. *Place values in binary numbering*

its value 4; a 1 in the fourth position stands for the number 8. As in decimal numbering, you use zeroes as place holders, so 100 binary equals 4, while 1000 binary is 8. (Since there are only the two digits in binary numbering, you get long strings of numbers very quickly.)

"121" is equal to one hundred twenty-one in decimal because (reading from the *right*), the first digit shows how many ones there are, the second shows how many tens, and the third, how many hundreds. As shown at the top of Figure 2-7, 1 hundred, 2 tens, and 1 one equals 121.

In binary, however, 1111001 represents one hundred twenty-one. Reading from the right, as shown at the bottom of Figure 2-7, that string of binary digits represents 1 one, no twos or fours, 1 eight, 1 sixteen, 1 thirty-two, and 1 sixty-four. Added together, the total value of 1111001 binary is 121 decimal.

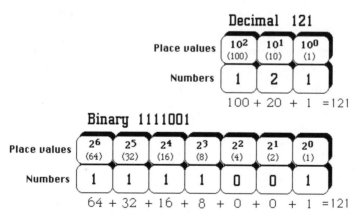

Figure 2-7. *The decimal and the binary computations of one hundred twenty-one*

If you look at some of the larger "round" numbers in binary, listed below, you'll see some of the "magic" series of computer numbers. So if you ever wondered why the first three Macs were released with 128,

512, and 1024 kilobytes of memory instead of some other sequence after the original 128, or why current memory chips are available in 256 and 1024 kilobyte sizes, now you know it has to do with the binary system of numbering that computers know and love.

Binary			Decimal
10000000	(2^7)	=	128
100000000	(2^8)	=	256
1000000000	(2^9)	=	512
10000000000	(2^{10})	=	1024

Bits, Bytes, and Beyond

A bit is such a tiny unit that we deal with the larger ones based on it. Eight bits make a *byte*. Early microcomputers actually had their miniscule memories measured in bits and bytes, but a *kilobyte* is, practically speaking, the lowest common unit of measurement for today's personal computers.

A kilobyte (abbreviated as simply K) is 1024 bytes. *Kilo* normally means 1000, but in the binary world of computers, 1024 is the nearest "round" number to a thousand.

The original Mac had 128K, and the next had 512K, with the Ks referring to the amount of memory in the machines. The Mac Plus weighed in with a hefty (for its time) 1024K. Current Mac models start with 2048K, but most are easily upgraded to 4096K, 5120K, or 8192K.

Since these numbers get pretty unwieldy, we need the next unit of measurement for convenience. (Just think what would happen if you had to use feet as a unit of measurement instead of miles. It's not so bad if you're referring to a building lot that's 50-by-100 feet, but do you think you could run a four-minute 5280 feet? Is your nearest user group a distance of 105,600 feet from home?)

The next unit of measurement is a *megabyte*, referred to as a *meg* and abbreviated as M, Mbyte, or MB. It's made up of 1024K, or 1,048,576 bytes (more than a billion bits). In round numbers, that's a thousand kilobytes, or a million bytes. The amount of RAM in your Mac, and the capacity of a hard drive, are referred to in megabytes.

Here's a roundup:

8 bits	= 1 byte
1024 bytes	= 1 kilobyte
1024 kilobytes	= 1 megabyte

NECESSARY JARGON

Basics

Rather than stick these terms at the back of the book in a glossary of some sort, they're right up front where you're more likely to read them. Some (like "software" and "application" and "document") are absolutely necessary for you to know; others are convenient (*very* convenient) for you to know.

Hardware and Software

The *hardware* of the computer is its electronic and mechanical components, the parts that you can pick up and move around. By itself, hardware doesn't do anything; *software* is the key to getting your vehicle moving. Software is what you can't touch, the *programs,* or sets of instructions, that control the hardware and tell it what to do.

Most programs are stored on the disks that the computer accesses, but some of the computer's basic instructions are permanently stored in its hardware, in ROM. This type of software/hardware hybrid is sometimes called *firmware*.

The information in ROM and additional information read in from a disk make up the computer's *operating system*—the basis from which you can interact with the computer and run other programs for productive work, or for fun and games.

When a computer is designed to do more than one thing at a time— for example, to let you type while it's working on recalculating a gargantuan spreadsheet or to let you draw one picture while another's being processed for printing—it's said to be *multitasking*.

A *bug* is a design flaw, usually in a software program, but it's far from unheard of in hardware. Bugs can be minor and merely annoying or they can be major and *crash, hang,* or *bomb* your program or your entire system. Crashing renders your computer temporarily useless—the screen may go blank, the mouse cursor may freeze, or input from the keyboard may be ignored. Many times you have to *reboot*—start up the computer all over again—to get back to work.

Inside the Computer

Besides the main processing chip, many computers have a *coprocessor* that's a whiz in some specialized area—mathematical computations or graphics handling, for instance. In the Mac world, it's usually a *math coprocessor* we're referring to. When things get complicated, the main chip forwards the problem to the coprocessor, which takes care of the problem and sends the answer back.

Which processor is in a computer, and whether or not there are coprocessors, affect the speed of computer operations. But every computer marches to the beat of its own drummer, which is a quartz crystal that beats millions of times each second in response to an electric current. The beats control things like how often the screen is refreshed and when the CPU checks what's going on at the keyboard or with the mouse. *Hertz* is a measurement of cycles per second; *megahertz* is a million cycles per second. A Mac running at 8 MHz is ticking away at 8 million cycles per second. This is referred to as its *clock rate* or *clock speed*.

Another factor that affects the computer's speed is the size of the *bus* (path) that it uses to transfer data. Macs based on the 68000 chip move 16 bits at a time on the bus; the data buses in 68020- and 68030-based machines handle twice that—32 bits at a time. The size of the data bus is what's being referred to in the description of a computer as *16 bit* or *32 bit*.

The memory chips that go in a Mac are in units called *SIMMs* (pronounced as a single word), for *single in-line memory modules.*

Slots are the places you put *cards* or *boards*—special or additional computing power that you can snap into your computer so it can handle something not in its main design. Running a large monitor, for instance, is not always a built-in proposition; with some models—you need a *video board* in your computer so that you can connect your monitor to it.

Outside the Computer

Peripherals are the hardware devices that you attach to your computer; the keyboard, the mouse, and the printer are all peripherals. You plug them into *ports* on the computer. (Apple, in keeping with its friendly computers-can-speak-English approach, uses the term *connectors.*)

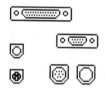

Some of the connector shapes on the back of your Mac

Serial and *parallel* ports are the two major types, and their names describe how information is transferred across their cables and through the connectors. A serial port handles a stream of bits, one at a time. A parallel port is more like a multilane highway: each byte is divided up into its 8 bits of information and they travel in parallel, leaving one place and arriving at another at the same time. (Obviously, parallel portage is a lot faster.)

SCSI (pronounced "scuzzy") stands for *small computer serial interface*, and it's a standard connection in the computer industry, although Apple implements it in a slightly nonstandard way. Most hard drives and other storage devices (like CD-ROM drives) are SCSI devices. Apple also has its own special standard connection called *ADB,* for Apple Desktop Bus. It's the round connector used for the keyboard and the mouse.

When two or more computers are connected, you have a *network*—even if they're just connected to the same printer. Exchanging files between computers on a network is called *file sharing;* sometimes it's done through a *file server,* which is an intermediary, central computer.

Macintosh Terminology

The Mac's approach to popular computing was so innovative in so many ways that it introduced a host of new terms to the computing lexicon. First, and probably foremost, there's its *graphical interface* that uses little pictures called *icons* to represent information; you work with the icons on the *Desktop,* the main screen that lets you manipulate the information on your disks.

While *file* is still the general term that refers to any discrete collection of information on a disk, the Mac uses the term *application* for any program that lets you create something, and *document* for the thing that you create. While on other computers you *run* a *program,* on a Mac you *launch* an *application.*

The Mac also introduced *desk accessories,* little utility programs that you can run at any time no matter what else you are doing: You don't have to quit out of a word processor if you just need the Calculator for a minute, or stop using your spreadsheet if you want to jot something down in the Note Pad. And when you want to move information from one place to another, you can just *cut* or *copy* it to the *Clipboard,* where it stays so you can *paste* it down someplace else.

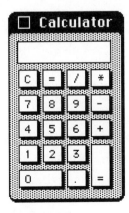

The Calculator—the quintessential desk accessory

SUMMARY

This chapter introduced dozens of general computer terms and concepts that you'll be familiar with in no time. The next chapter takes you back to terms and operations that are strictly Macintosh.

System Basics

Interface Basics

THE CLIPBOARD

SUMMARY

ABOUT THIS CHAPTER

The famous Mac interface has many components, and each component has many facets. A button on the screen, for instance, is a basic way to communicate with the Mac—but there are three kinds of buttons, and each is used to indicate a different kind of information.

The Macintosh interface is more than just what's on the screen, though. The mouse and special keys on the keyboard are just as important, as are concepts like the Clipboard and the Undo command.

THE MOUSE

Basics

When you roll the mouse around on your desk, the *mouse cursor* on the screen moves accordingly. By moving the mouse and clicking its button, you can interact with the Macintosh—give commands, draw pictures, and move things on the screen. Everything you do with the mouse is based on four basic operations: point, click, press, and drag.

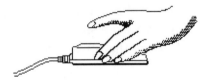

The mouse

Try using a *mouse pad*—a small, inexpensive rubbery pad that is available at any computer store—under your mouse for good traction. (It also reserves rolling space on your desk.)

If you're using a mousepad and come to its edge (or if you're at the end of your comfortable reach or the empty space on your desk), just pick up the mouse and put it back down in the center or at the other end of your "rolling area." Since the mouse cursor on the screen moves in response to the rolling of the ball at the bottom of the mouse, nothing moves until you put the mouse back down—and, when you do, the movement continues from the spot where you left the cursor.

Cursors and Hot Spots

The appearance of the mouse cursor changes depending on what program you're in and what you're doing.

There are three basic mouse cursors. The *arrow*, or *pointer*, is available when you're using menus or manipulating windows or other objects on the screen. The *text cursor*, or *I-beam*, appears whenever the cursor is over text. The *wristwatch* shows up when the Mac's busy processing something and it indicates that you're not allowed to do anything (sometimes the hands on the wristwatch spin around while you're waiting).

Basic cursors

On every cursor—and there's a plethora of cursors in various Mac applications—there's a *hot spot*, the one point that really counts. When you're using the arrow, whatever the very tip of the arrow is pointing to is what gets selected or dragged. The entire arrow doesn't have to be within the area you're selecting—but if all *except* the tip is inside, you won't be selecting what you want.

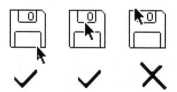

The tip of the arrow is what counts.

Finding a cursor's hot spot is usually so intuitive that you don't have to think about it—you just use it and things generally happen the way you expect. The center of a cross-hair cursor, the tip of a lasso, the point of a pencil, and the leading edge of pouring paint are all examples of cursor hot spots.

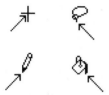

Cursor "hot spots" vary but are usually predictable.

Although "cursor" generally refers to the mouse cursor, there's another kind of cursor, too: the blinking vertical line that indicates where you're working in text. This special indicator is the *insertion point*, but it is also often referred to as a cursor.

Point, Click, and Double-Click

Pointing with the mouse is simply moving it so that the cursor on the screen is touching something.

Clicking the mouse is briefly pressing its button and then immediately releasing it. A click of the mouse is used to *select* something on the screen, to place an *insertion point* in text so that you know where you're typing, or to "push" a *button*. (All the italicized words are covered in detail in later sections.)

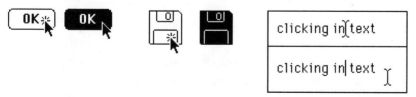

Clicking in a button, on an icon, and in text

The most-often used variation of the click is the *double-click*—two clicks in rapid succession. A double-click often "opens" something—a disk or folder on the Desktop or a document in a list. A double-click is also used in text to select a whole word rather than having to drag across the word. Some programs use triple-clicks and even quadruple-clicks to signify something special.

Press and Drag

A *press* of the mouse button is just what it sounds like—-you hold the button down instead of releasing it immediately. In some situations, you press the button without moving the mouse to get some continued action. A press in a window's scroll arrow, for instance, keeps the window's contents scrolling. But a press of the mouse button is most often used in conjunction with moving the mouse—an operation called *dragging*.

Dragging is sometimes done with the mouse cursor to describe a line or shape. When you're on the Desktop, you drag the pointer to draw a rectangle for selecting icons (see Figure 3-1).

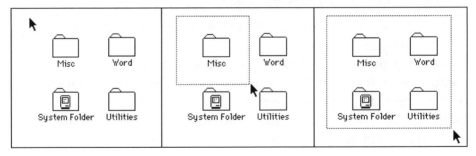

Figure 3-1. Dragging a rectangle on the Desktop

When you're in a graphics program, you drag the cursor—it's usually shaped like a drawing tool—to define a line or shape.

Dragging a graphics tool

When you drag the text cursor, you select the text that you're dragging across.

Dragging across text selects it

Dragging across text selects it

Often, though, you'll be dragging an item—not just the cursor. To drag something, you grab it by pressing the mouse button when the pointer's on the item, drag it (or its outline), and then let go of the button when the object is in the desired position. On the Desktop, you drag icons from one place to another. In many graphics programs, you drag elements around in the window to place them where you want them.

Dragging an icon

Also See . . .

▪ The speed at which you need to double-click the mouse button for it to be interpreted as a double-click instead of two single clicks and the mouse's tracking speed (how fast the cursor moves across the screen in response to rolling the mouse) are both settings that you can control. See Chapter 11.

THE KEYBOARD

Basics

Because the Mac, even when used for word processing, is so much more than a typewriter, its keyboard goes beyond the standard alphanumeric keys that you'll find on typewriters.

There are several different keyboards available for the Mac—there are even keyboards from companies other than Apple. They all have certain keys in common, although some offer more special-function keys and put certain keys in different positions on the keyboard.

Figure 3-2 shows Apple's Extended Keyboard.

esc		F1	F2	F3	F4		F5	F6	F7	F8		F9	F10	F11	F12		F13	F14	F15		◁

The key layout for an extended keyboard.

Figure 3-2.   The key layout for an extended keyboard.

Modifier Keys

All Mac keyboards have three *modifier* keys, and some have a fourth. A modifier key is one that doesn't do anything by itself, but it modifies the basic function of whatever key you use with it.

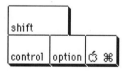

The modifier keys

The *Shift* key changes the character you're typing from the keyboard, just as it does on a regular typewriter.

The *Option* key acts as a second Shift key, letting you access further characters from each key on the keyboard.

The *Command* key (the one with the cloverleaf symbol, and sometimes also an apple outline on it) is used to give commands from the keyboard instead of from menus.

The *Control* key isn't available on all keyboards, so it has yet to have a very specific function in the Mac world. It usually serves as an additional Command key.

The four modifier keys are often used in combination. For instance, Shift-P will type an uppercase P, Option-P will type the pi symbol (π), and Shift-Option-P gives the uppercase pi (Π).

Cursor Control Keys

There are two types of *cursor control* keys that control the location of the insertion point in text. (They don't control the mouse cursor.)

The arrow keys appear on all but the earliest Mac keyboards, although they're in different locations on different keyboards. The arrows are used to move the text insertion point one letter at a time horizontally, or one line at a time vertically.

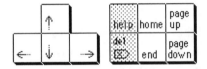

Cursor control keys

The Home, End, Page Up, and Page Down keys are available on extended keyboards. Their functions vary slightly from one application to the next. Home and End, for instance, may move the cursor to the top or bottom of the current screen of text, or to the beginning or end of the document. Page Up and Page Down might move the cursor forward and backward by a "page"—that's a screenful of text—or by what would be a printed page of the document.

The Numeric Keypad

Extended keyboards have numeric keypads that make number entry more convenient. Standard mathematical operators are on the pad, too (the asterisk is for multiplication and the slash is for division), as is a period that can be used for decimals.

The Clear key in the numeric pad is used with mathematical programs like spreadsheets and desk accessories like the Calculator to clear the last numeric entry you made. In many cases, the key with the equal sign and the Enter key perform the same function. The Enter key is also used instead of the Return key for many Macintosh operations.

clear	=	\	✳
7	8	9	−
4	5	6	+
1	2	3	
0		·	enter

The numeric keypad

The Clear key usually has a second label on it: *Num lock,* or "numeric lock." In programs that enable the keypad to function in two ways—sometimes as a cursor control pad, sometimes for number input—the Clear key toggles the keypad between those two states. When you're in numeric lock, you can type numbers. (Extended keyboards have a light labeled "num lock," but few Macintosh programs actually use it.)

Function Keys

There are fifteen *function keys* along the top of an extended keyboard. These keys perform various functions in different programs but are most often used when you build your own *macros* and have to assign them to a key. (A macro is a series of commands executed by a single key press. Apple's MacroMaker program is covered later in this book.)

Almost all programs recognize F1 through F4 as Undo, Cut, Copy, and Paste commands (they're labeled that way right on the keyboard), so you can use the function keys instead of selecting those commands from the Edit menu.

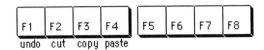

The first four function keys are "hard-wired" to Edit menu commands.

Special-Purpose Keys

The *Delete* key (labeled *Backspace* on older keyboards) is available on every keyboard. It's used to move the blinking text cursor backward one character at a time, erasing a character at a time. It's also used to erase selected material (text or graphics) in a document.

The *Forward Delete* key (on extended keyboards) deletes the character in front of the blinking text cursor, and also sometimes— depending on the program you're in—erases selected material.

The standard Delete and Forward Delete keys

The *Esc* (escape) key on larger keyboards works in most applications as a Cancel command.

The Escape key

Some applications use the *Help* key (on extended keyboards) to switch you into a "help mode" where you can get information about the program. If you're working in an application that doesn't, in effect, acknowledge the existence of the Help key, you sometimes get a printed character when you press the Help key.

Not all applications make use of the Help key.

And, finally, we come to the key you'll use before all the others—the *Startup* key. Most Macs use this key—just press it and the computer is turned on.

The Startup key

Also See . . .

- Chapter 6 explains how to use the Option key to access special characters from the keyboard.

- The different types of keyboards (and their pros and cons) are covered in Chapter 12.

MENUS

Basics

Using *menus* is one of the basic ways you communicate with your Mac. No matter what application you're in, there's usually a *menu bar* along the top of your screen that has *menu titles* in it. Sometimes *menu icons* are used instead of titles.

When you point to a title with the mouse cursor and press the mouse button, the menu opens, listing the available *commands* (see Figure 3-3). Related commands are usually grouped together in a menu, separated by dotted lines.

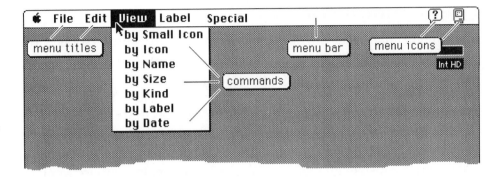

Figure 3-3. A menu opens when you press on its title.

As you slide the mouse down through the menu, each command the mouse cursor touches is highlighted as you pass over it. When you get to the command you want, you choose it by releasing the mouse button.

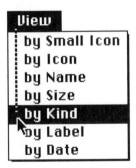

Slide the pointer to the command you want.

You'll also find menus in other places besides the menu bar: There are *submenus* in some of the main menus; there are *popup* menus in dialog boxes, and some programs even pop up menus on the screen wherever your mouse happens to be. Whatever the kind of menu, though, the basic operations are the same.

Types of Menu Commands

Some menu commands are direct orders and are executed as soon as you choose them. *Quit*, for instance (available as the last item in almost every application's File menu), lets you leave the program you're in. Direct commands have no special marks before or after them in the menu.

Commands in the menu followed by an ellipsis (these three periods . . .) are less direct. When you choose one of these, you get a *dialog box*—a window that asks for or gives information. The *Print* command, for instance, opens a dialog box that lets you choose from various printing options before you give the real print command (see Figure 3-4).

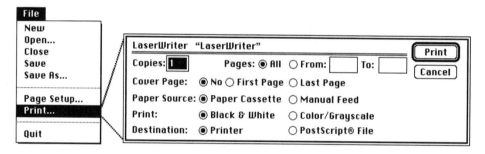

Figure 3-4. Commands followed by an ellipsis will open a dialog box.

Other menu items are not so much commands as they are options that you can activate and deactivate—these are sometimes called *toggles*. When an option is activated, it has a checkmark in front of it. Selecting the item once activates it; selecting it again deactivates it, removing the checkmark.

A list of text styles, for instance, might include Bold, Italic, and Underline—you can choose any or all of them and then turn them "off" if you change your mind. (Some toggle commands change their names instead of getting checkmarks. A command like *Show Ruler*, common in word processors, usually changes to *Hide Ruler* once you've used it— once you show the Ruler, you can't show it again, you can only hide it.)

Checkmarks indicate activated toggle commands.

Another type of menu item, a *submenu,* is not a command at all; it's a name for another menu that's attached to the main menu. Submenus are covered in a later section.

Dimmed Commands

When a menu command is *dimmed*—shown in gray—you can't select it. Commands are dimmed whenever they don't make sense in your current situation: You couldn't, for instance, Save, Close, or Print a document if you don't have one open.

```
┌─────────────────────┐
│ File                │
├─────────────────────┤
│ New                 │
│ Open...             │
│ Close               │
│ Save                │
│ Save As...          │
│ ................... │
│ Page Setup...       │
│ Print...            │
│ ................... │
│ Quit                │
└─────────────────────┘
```

Commands are dimmed when they can't be used.

Scrolling Menus

Sometimes a menu has too many items in it to show on the screen at one time. (This usually happens with only two menus—the Apple menu at the far left of the screen, and the Font menu when you're working with a system that has many fonts installed.)

When a menu has additional items that aren't displayed, you'll see a black arrow at its bottom. When you slide the mouse pointer down to the arrow, the menu starts scrolling upward and an arrow appears at the top of the menu to show that there now are more choices up in that direction. You don't have to catch the item you need as it scrolls by— once the menu is scrolled, you can slide the mouse up and down inside it to reach the item you need. Black arrows at the top or bottom of the menu indicate whether there are any items in those directions (see Figure 3-5).

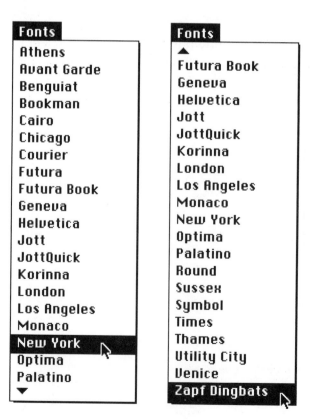

Figure 3-5. Using a scrolling menu

Submenus

When an item in a menu has a black arrow to its right, that means it has a submenu attached. Pausing on the submenu's name makes the submenu pop out. All you have to do is slide the mouse cursor from the main menu into the submenu and select the item you want.

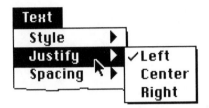

Pausing on a submenu title pops out the submenu.

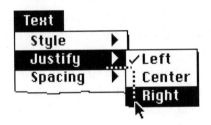

Choosing from a submenu

Sometimes the menu pops out to the left of the main menu, despite the fact that the arrow points to the right—it all depends on how much room you have on the screen.

This menu-within-a-menu construction—and it's not limited to only two levels—is formally known as *hierarchical menus*.

Keyboard Equivalents

Many menu commands have *keyboard equivalents* that let you give the command without using the menu. Basic keyboard equivalents are listed right in the menu. Most use the Command key and a character key from the keyboard. Command-P, for instance, is the usual keyboard equivalent for the Print command. Figure 3-6 shows the standard keyboard equivalents for the commands in the File menu.

```
┌─────────────┐
│ File        │
├─────────────┤
│ New...    ⌘N │
│ Open...   ⌘O │
│ Close       │
├·············┤
│ Save      ⌘S │
├·············┤
│ Print...  ⌘P │
├·············┤
│ Quit      ⌘Q │
└─────────────┘
```

Figure 3-6.   Keyboard equivalents are listed right in the menu.

To use a keyboard equivalent, you press the Command key and, while holding it down, you press the second key. Although letters listed in the menu are uppercase, *don't* use the Shift key; they're in uppercase because that's how they appear on the keyboard.

Some keyboard equivalents use more than just the Command key as the modifier for the character key. So, while Command-P may stand for Print, Command-Shift-P might stand for Paragraph, and Command-Option-P for Print All.

Each modifier key gets its own symbol in the menu—Figure 3-7 shows what they look like in some of the possible combinations.

```
┌──────────────────────────────────────┐
│ Modifier Keys                         │
├──────────────────────────────────────┤
│ Command-Shift Key              ⌘⇧ K   │
│ Command-Option Key             ⌘⌥ K   │
│ Control-Command Key            ^⌘ K   │
├······································┤
│ Command-Shift-Option Key      ⌘⇧⌥ K   │
│ Control-Command-Option Key    ^⌘⌥K    │
└──────────────────────────────────────┘
```

Figure 3-7.   Every modifier key has its own menu symbol.

Some nonprinting keys on the keyboard can be used with a modifier (for a sequence like Command-Spacebar or Command-Shift-Enter), but they need symbols to be represented in the menu. You wouldn't, for example, be able to see a space character that the spacebar "prints," nor is there any character printed when you use Tab or Enter. Figure 3-8 shows the special character keys and their symbols.

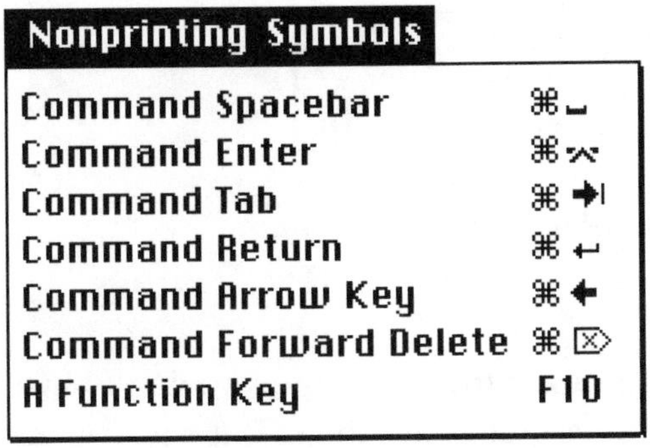

Nonprinting Symbols	
Command Spacebar	⌘ ␣
Command Enter	⌘ ⌤
Command Tab	⌘ ⇥
Command Return	⌘ ↵
Command Arrow Key	⌘ ←
Command Forward Delete	⌘ ⌦
A Function Key	F10

Figure 3-8.   Non-printing keys have special symbols for menus.

Popup Menus

Popup menus appear chiefly in dialog boxes, although you may find them in some other types of windows in some programs. A popup menu is usually indicated by a rectangle with a drop shadow.

To use a popup menu, you just press anywhere within the rectangle and the menu opens. Depending on where the menu is and what it's for, the menu may pop down from the spot you're pressing on (as shown in Figure 3-9), or open to the right or left with commands above and below the menu title itself (Figure 3-10). You'll see popup menus in Open and Save dialog boxes all the time—you use them to move up and down through the folders on your disk.

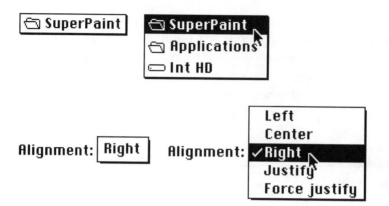

Alignment: Right   Alignment:

Figures 3-9 and 3-10.   Two of the several kinds of popup menus

Quickies

▪ If you change your mind about choosing from a menu, you don't have to slide the mouse all the way up to the menu title to get out—just slide it off the menu onto the screen and let go of the mouse button.

▪ When you choose from a submenu, you don't have to slide horizontally from the command in the main menu into the submenu and then down to the command you want. You can move diagonally from the main menu into the submenu; if you move quickly enough, the submenu won't disappear.

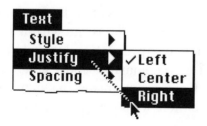

You can move diagonally into a submenu.

▪ The speed at which a scrolling menu scrolls depends on where you hold the mouse cursor. Pointing to the tip of the arrow at the edge of the menu scrolls the menu faster than if you point to the "back" of the menu's arrow.

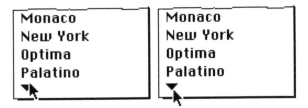

Pointing to the back of the menu's arrow (left) scrolls the menu more slowly than if you point to its tip (right).

■ Many applications (including the Desktop) have menu commands that change if you hold down Shift or Option while you open the menu. (Close, for instance, might change to Close All.)

Also See . . .

■ When you release the mouse button when selecting a menu command, the command usually blinks in acknowledgment before the menu disappears. The blinking is something you can configure yourself for your Mac—one, two, or no blinks. See Chapter 11.

WINDOWS

Basics

Theoretically, a window lets you look into something—so you can see what's in a document, a folder, or a disk. More practically, a window is a white area on the Mac screen that you work in. You can type, draw, or move items in a window; you can move the window itself and change its size and position on the screen. And, because you can have more than one window open at a time, you can quickly move from one task to another, easily transferring information as you go.

The most common type of Macintosh window is the *document window*, where you work on what you create in an application, or where you work with your files on the Desktop. *Dialog boxes* and *floating windows*, each covered later, are other types of windows.

Some desk accessories *have* windows (that can be obvious, as when a desk accessory has a document-type window, or one that looks like a dialog box), but sometimes a desk accessory *is* a window, as is the case with the Calculator, shown in Figure 3-11.

Figure 3-11. The Calculator is a window, too.

No matter how many windows you have open, there's only one *active* window at time. The window you're working in is the active one; when its a document window, its title bar is striped. A white title bar indicates an *inactive* window. If there's any overlap of windows on the screen, the active one is always on top. Any commands you use, and any actions you take, apply to the active window or its contents.

Figure 3-12 shows two Desktop windows. The System Folder window is active—its title bar is striped and it's on top of the disk window, which has a white title bar.

If you're running a color or grayscale system, windows and icons have a slightly different, more three-dimensional look, as shown in Figure 3-13.

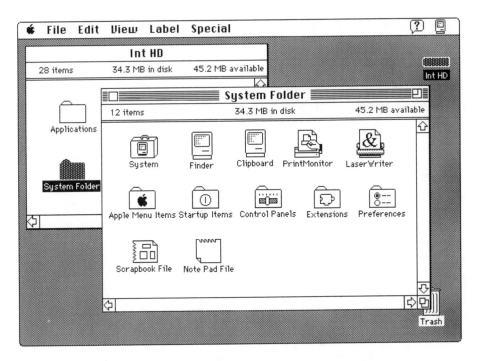

Figure 3-12. The active window is the one on top—and if it's a document window like the ones in this picture, it will have a striped title bar.

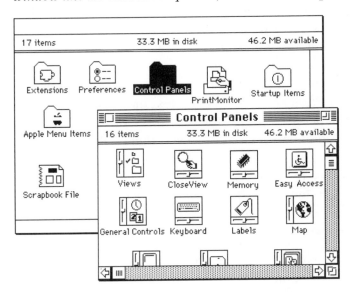

Figure 3-13. Color or grayscale windows and icons have more visual depth than black-and-white ones.

Anatomy of a Window

There are several types of Macintosh windows, but the most common is the document window. Document windows have many elements, several of which are echoed in other types of windows. Use the elements of a window (shown in Figure 3-14) in the following ways:

▪ Move a window by dragging its *title bar*. If the title bar is striped, then the window is the active window.

▪ Change the size of a window by dragging the *size box*.

▪ Click the *zoom box* to quickly change the size and position of a window. The zoom box toggles you between a full-size window and the window size and position you create yourself. "Full-size," though, is a description that's constantly redefined by whatever application you're in. On the Desktop, full-size always leaves a strip along the right edge of the screen so that you can always see the Trash can and disk icons, and it's never larger than is necessary to display all the window's contents. Some applications also leave the right edge free; some fill the screen completely with a zoomed-out window; and some applications consider a full-size window to be no larger than the actual size of the document.

▪ Use the window's *scroll controls* to see something that's not currently in view. You can click in any of the *scroll arrows* to move the window's contents a little bit; holding the mouse button down (*pressing* on the arrow) continues the scrolling. You can also click in the gray area of the *scroll bar* to move the contents in larger increments. In text documents, for instance, a click in a scroll arrow moves the text up or down one line; a click in the scroll bar itself moves the text a "windowful." If the scroll bar is white instead of gray, that means everything's already displayed in the window. The *scroll box* always reflects your current position in a document—if the scroll box is near the top of the scroll bar, you're near the beginning of the document. You can drag the scroll box to quickly move to a certain area of the document. (There's a step-by-step how-to on using scroll controls in Chapter 1.)

▪ Close a window by clicking in its *close box*. (You can also use the Close command from the File menu.)

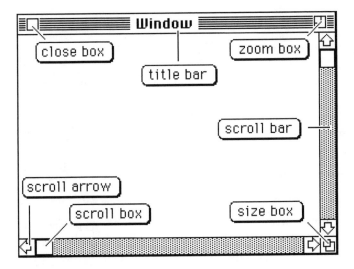

Figure 3-14.   The basic document window

Floating Windows

Here's the exception to the rule that the active window is always on top of all other open windows. *Floating windows*, also variously referred to as *palettes* or even *windoids*, stay at the top of the pile—even on top of the active document window. True to their name, floating windows "float" on top of all the other windows on the screen so that you can always get at their contents. Applications that use floating windows generally use them as "toolboxes" so that you can easily reach tools and functions without going to menus or to a specific spot on the screen. You can work in your document window without the window coming on top of the tool palette and obscuring it. Apple's HyperCard, and popular programs such as SuperPaint and PageMaker, use floating palettes (see Figure 3-15).

Aside from the fact that they float on top of standard windows, floating windows behave much like regular windows. They have title bars that you use to drag them around on the screen (although sometimes they're checked instead of striped, sometimes the bar is on the side instead of at the top, and sometimes there's no title in the bar, as in Figure 3-15), and most have close boxes.

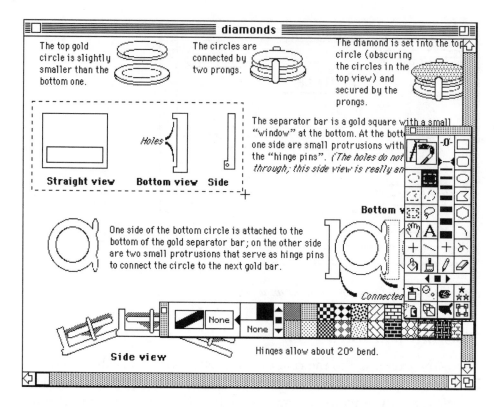

Figure 3-15. You can work in a document window (there's a selection being made here) while floating tool palettes stay on top of it. This picture shows two floating palettes on top of the document window.

Handling Multiple Windows

Not only is it common to have more than one window open at a time, it's an absolute cinch to have your screen cluttered with them. Most applications let you open more than one document at a time, each in its own window, and you can have several applications open at the same time. But it's always easy to tell which one is the active window, and it's just as easy to activate a different one.

The basic way you activate a window is by clicking in any part of it. Figures 3-16 and 3-17 show a Desktop where the active window is PageMaker. Clicking in any part of the Int HD window in the background brings it to the front.

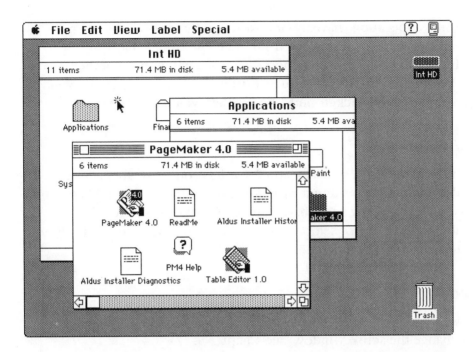

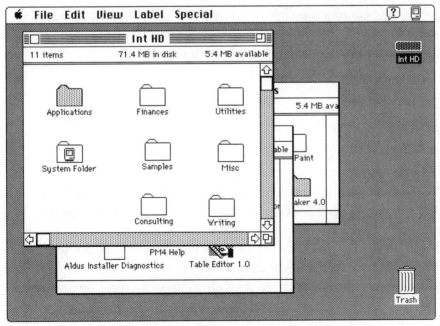

Figures 3-16 and 3-17. Click in a window to activate it.

Some applications have a Window menu that lists all the open documents; selecting the name from the menu brings that window to the front. But clicking in an exposed part of a window—whether it's one that belongs to the program you're working in or to another one you've left running in the background—brings that window to the front.

Quickies

▪ The Desktop has a special feature that lets you move an inactive window without activating it by holding down the Command key while you drag the window's title bar; many applications also provide this capability, although it's seldom documented—so go ahead and try it no matter what you're working in.

Also See . . .

▪ The Desktop provides special menus right within its windows that let you change the active window. See Chapter 5.

▪ The Application menu provides a way to switch from one window to another when the windows belong to different applications—and it lets you control window clutter, too. See Chapter 8.

BUTTONS

Basics

One of the easiest ways to interact with the Mac is by clicking in the buttons that appear on the screen. There are three types of buttons: push buttons, radio buttons, and checkboxes. Each type of button is used in slightly different circumstances and has its own special features.

As with menu commands, if a button is dimmed, or gray, it's not available in your current situation, and clicking on it won't do anything.

Active   ○ Active   ☐ Active
Dimmed   ○ Dimmed   ☐ Dimmed

Buttons, like menu commands, can be dimmed.

Push Buttons

Push buttons work in much the same way most menu commands do—something happens when you click in one. (A button that says "OK" doesn't sound much like a command, but something does happen when you click in it—usually a dialog box goes away and you can get on with your work.)

Cancel   OK   Open

The basic push button

When a push button is highlighted by a heavy line around it, it's called the *default* button—it's the one that the Mac assumes you want to use unless you tell it otherwise. Instead of reaching for the mouse (assuming it's not in your hand), you can just press Return or Enter on the keyboard and it's the same as clicking on the default button.

OK

A default button has a frame around it.

Sometimes a push button will have a command followed by an ellipsis, just as some menu commands do, and it means the same thing: A dialog box will open if you push the button.

Save As...

An ellipsis means using the button will open a dialog box.

Radio Buttons

When you click on a radio button, a bullet appears in the circle to show that it's selected. Radio buttons are used in lists of mutually exclusive choices. When you choose a radio button in a list, whichever one that used to be selected is deselected—you don't have to worry about turning one button off when you turn another one on.

In the example shown in Figure 3-18, clicking on Veal Marsala deselects the Fettucine entree because you can have only one from the list.

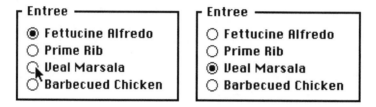

Figure 3-18.   Choosing a radio button in a list of mutually exclusive choices automatically deselects the previous choice.

Checkboxes

When you click in a checkbox, an X appears in it to show that it's selected. Clicking in it again turns the X off, deselecting the button.

Checkboxes are used in lists of items that are not mutually exclusive. While a radio button list might be used to list a variety of fonts, only one of which you could use at a time, checkboxes might be used to list styles because you could select both *bold* and *italic* from the list.

In the example shown in Figure 3-19, you could choose any or all of the items to construct a banana split.

```
┌ Banana Split ──────────────────────────────┐
│  ☐ Chocolate ice cream    ☐ Nuts            │
│  ☒ Vanilla ice cream      ☒ Cherries        │
│  ☒ Strawberry ice cream   ☒ Fudge sauce     │
│  ☒ Whipped cream          ☐ Butterscotch sauce │
└────────────────────────────────────────────┘
```

Figure 3-19.   Checkboxes are used for selecting items that are not mutually exclusive.

Quickies

▪ When you're using a push button, it's pretty easy to see where you can click—anywhere in the framed area of the button. But you don't have to click directly in the circle of a radio button or the square of a checkbox—clicking anywhere on the title of the button works just as well.

☐ **Butterscotch sauce**

Clicking anywhere within the gray rectangle will click the checkbox.

▪ When there's a Cancel button on the screen, you can usually use the keyboard equivalent of Command-period instead of clicking in the button. In many cases, the Esc key also serves as an alternative to clicking in a Cancel button.

DIALOG BOXES

Basics

A *dialog box* is a special type of window that asks you for certain information. Sometimes the information is simply an acknowledgment that you've read the notice in the box; sometimes you need to type a file name in it or choose options from an almost bewildering array of buttons, lists, and popup menus (see Figures 3-20, 3-21, and 3-22).

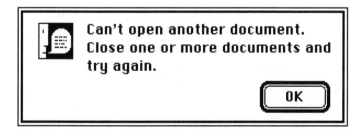

Figure 3-20. A simple dialog box

```
┌─────────────────────────────────────────────────────────────────┐
│ ImageWriter _____    ╭───────╮         │
│                                                  │ Print │         │
│ Quality:      ○ Best      ⦿ Faster   ○ Draft    ╰───────╯         │
│ Page Range:   ⦿ All       ○ From: [   ] To: [   ] ┌────────┐       │
│ Copies:       ▓1▓                                 │ Cancel │       │
│ Paper Feed:   ⦿ Automatic ○ Hand Feed             └────────┘       │
└─────────────────────────────────────────────────────────────────┘
```

Figure 3-21.   A typical dialog box

```
┌═══════════════════ Character ═══════════════════┐
│ Font:            Size:        ╭─────────╮        │
│ ┌──────────────┐┌─┐ ┌──┐┌─┐   │   OK    │        │
│ │ Benguiat     ││⇩│ │12││⇩│   ╰─────────╯        │
│ └──────────────┘└─┘ └──┘└─┘   ┌─────────┐        │
│ Underline:       Color:       │ Cancel  │        │
│ ┌────────────┐┌─┐┌─────────┐┌─┐└─────────┘        │
│ │ None       ││⇩││ Black   ││⇩│┌─────────┐        │
│ └────────────┘└─┘└─────────┘└─┘│ Apply   │        │
│ ┌Style──────┐ ┌Position────────────┐              │
│ │ ☐ Bold    │ │ ⦿ Normal     By:   │              │
│ │ ☐ Italic  │ │ ○ Superscript ┌───┐│              │
│ │ ☐ Outline │ │ ○ Subscript   └───┘│              │
│ │ ☐ Shadow  │ └────────────────────┘              │
│ │ ☐ Strikethru┌Spacing─────────────┐              │
│ │ ☐ Small Caps│ ⦿ Normal     By:   │              │
│ │ ☐ All Caps │ │ ○ Condensed  ┌───┐│              │
│ │ ☐ Hidden  │ │ ○ Expanded   └───┘│              │
│ └───────────┘ └────────────────────┘              │
└──────────────────────────────────────────────────┘
```

Figure 3-22.   A busy dialog box

What differentiates most dialog boxes from other Mac windows is that they are *modal*: You can't do anything else until you've dealt with the dialog box. Most dialogs don't even have title bars, so you can't even move them around on the screen. This is unlike the majority of Mac operations, where you're never stuck in a specific mode—for example, in most operations you can close the document you're working on, or quit the application you're working in, at any point in a work session.

Dialog Box Components

A complicated dialog box can ask you for all sorts of information and provide all sorts of ways for you to enter that information. Here are some of the things you're likely to run into in dialog boxes.

BUTTONS

Any or all of the three types of buttons can show up in a dialog box. One of the buttons in a dialog is usually highlighted as the default button and you can use Return or Enter to "click" it.

A default button has an extra border.

LISTS

Some dialog boxes have scrolling lists of choices; for example, documents on a disk or available fonts. In any case, you can scroll through the list with the scroll controls and then click on your choice.

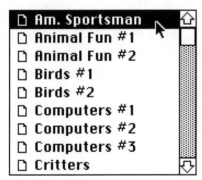

Selecting from a list

TEXT BOXES

A *text box*, also sometimes called a *text field*, is a box in which you can type something—the name of a document, for instance. Sometimes a text box is already filled with a suggested response, or sometimes it can be filled quickly by choosing something from a popup menu.

In the standard LaserWriter Print dialog shown in Figure 3-23, for example, the suggested number of copies is 1; if you want to specify a range of pages to be printed, you'd click the From button and type the page numbers in the From and To boxes.

```
┌─────────────────────────────────────────────────────────────┐
│ LaserWriter  "LaserWriter" _____  ( Print )│
│ Copies:[1]          Pages: ◉ All  ○ From:[    ] To:[    ]      │
│                                                     (Cancel)  │
│ Cover Page:   ◉ No ○ First Page ○ Last Page                   │
│ Paper Source: ◉ Paper Cassette  ○ Manual Feed                 │
│ Print:          ◉ Black & White  ○ Color/Grayscale            │
│ Destination:    ◉ Printer        ○ PostScript® File           │
└─────────────────────────────────────────────────────────────┘
```

Figure 3-23.   A LaserWriter dialog box has three text fields.

The text in a text field can be edited with normal Mac editing techniques—click anywhere in the text and then backspace or type, double-click to select an entire word, and so on. (You'll find the details on text editing in Chapter 6.)

When you have more than one text box in a dialog, you click in the one you want to use. You can also move from one to the next by using the Tab key; using Shift-Tab moves you to the previous text box. When you move to a text field this way, the contents are automatically selected (like the Copies box in the last illustration). Since typing something replaces a selection, you don't have to erase the contents of a text box before typing in the new information.

POPUP MENUS

Menus within dialog boxes offer a quick way to choose from among many options. A popup menu has its name—or the current choice— showing in a rectangle with a drop shadow. Sometimes the presence of a menu is also indicated by an arrow. Pressing the mouse button while you're in the rectangle or on the arrow displays the entire menu. In Figure 3-24, the Underline menu is opened displaying its selections.

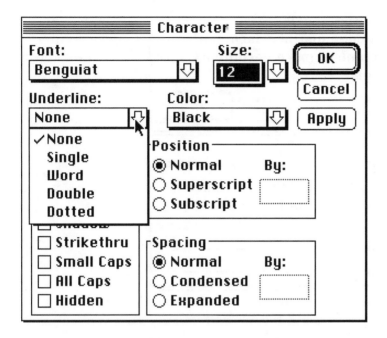

Figure 3-24. A popup menu in a dialog box. This one has arrows to click on, but most popups just have drop shadows.

Alerts

The most simple type of dialog is an alert box. You get a message (usually accompanied by a beep) and an OK button to acknowledge that you read the message, as shown in Figure 3-25. Or, as shown in Figure 3-26, you get a choice between OK (or some description of the operation you're about to perform) and Cancel, in case you want to back out of a procedure after reading the message.

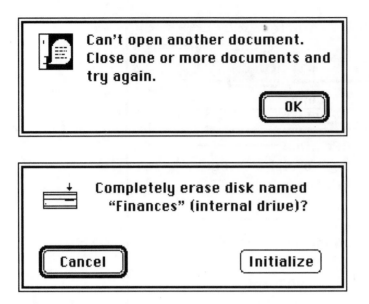

Figures 3-25 and 3-26. Sample alert boxes

Quickies

▪ The highlighted button—the one with the heavy border around it—is the default button and using the Return or Enter key is the same as clicking in the button.

▪ When a dialog box has only a single button, pressing Return or Enter usually activates it even if it's not highlighted as the default.

▪ Command-period and the Esc key each usually work as alternatives to clicking the Cancel button in a dialog box.

▪ If a dialog box has no buttons at all, but instead has a close box, Command-period or the Esc key often work to close it.

▪ The up and down arrow keys often work in scrolling lists to select the next or previous item in the list.

▪ Many applications have their own additional shortcuts in dialog boxes so that you can control everything from the keyboard—sometimes pressing the first letter of a button name "clicks" the button.

Also See . . .

- The most common dialog boxes are the ones that you use to save a new document or to open an existing one. (Details and shortcuts for the Save and Open dialogs are in Chapter 7.)

THE UNDO COMMAND

Basics

The Undo command, available as the first command in the Edit menu, is your escape mechanism when you've made a mistake or changed your mind about some editing operation. If, for instance, you've just applied Bold formatting to some selected text and then decide you don't like it bold, you can just undo your action and the Bold formatting is removed. More important, in instances where you've accidentally erased a selection by hitting the Delete key, you can undo that and your material reappears.

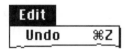

The Undo command is always in the Edit menu.

The Undo command is basically limited to *editing* actions: You can undo formatting you've applied, or recover deleted or typed-over text, or even "unpaint" a picture you've just poured a pattern into, but you can't undo something like saving a document, since that's not an editing operation.

Aside from understanding just which actions are "undo-able," you have to remember that the Undo command applies to the *last* thing you did. So, if you erase some text by mistake and then apply bold formatting to a word, Undo takes off the bold but doesn't recover the text.

Undo and Redo

Since you can undo your last action, what happens if your last action was the Undo command? You get to undo your undo, and return to the original situation. In some applications, the Undo command changes to Redo when you use it. Sometimes the Undo command itself is a little more descriptive, like *Undo Typing*, or *Undo Formatting*, and the Redo command is similarly explained.

THE CLIPBOARD

Basics

The Clipboard is a unique Macintosh concept—you use it to transfer text and graphics from one place to another. You put something on the Clipboard by *cutting* it or *copying* it from its original source; you transfer the contents of the Clipboard to the new place by *pasting* it there. The "new place" can be elsewhere in the same document, a different document for the same application, or even a document in a different application. The Clipboard can hold only one item at a time—but that one item can sometimes be as large as an entire document.

Although menus change from one application to the next, the Edit menu is a standard, and Cut, Copy, and Paste are standard commands that you'll find no matter what program you're working in.

Edit	
Undo	⌘Z
Cut	⌘X
Copy	⌘C
Paste	⌘U

Cut, Copy, and Paste are standard Edit menu commands.

While the Clipboard is a handy concept, it doesn't actually *exist*—it's not, for instance, a desk accessory that you can pull out from under the Apple menu. The material that you put *on* the Clipboard, however, does exist—in the computer's memory (RAM). That means that when you shut off the computer, the contents of the Clipboard disappear. But it also means that as you move from one program to another, the contents of the Clipboard remain intact. It's one of the easiest ways of transferring information from one application to another.

Cut, Copy, and Paste

To use the Clipboard, you:

1. Select something in your document. (Basic selection techniques for text and graphics are covered in Chapter 6.)
2. Use the Cut or Copy command in the Edit menu.
3. Move to where you want to put the Clipboard material— elsewhere in the same document, to a different document, or even to a document for a different application.
4. Use the Paste command in the Edit menu.

Using the Cut command removes the selected material from the source document; using Copy leaves the original intact (see Figure 3-27). (The Clear command that's in most Edit menus removes selected material from the document but doesn't place it on the Clipboard.)

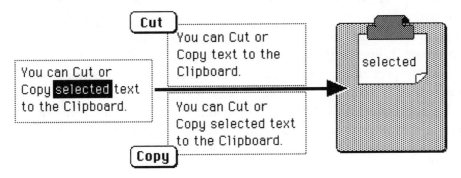

Figure 3-27.   The Cut and Copy commands both place selected material on the Clipboard, but Cut removes that material from the original source.

Just where or how the pasted material appears depends on what kind of program you're using. In a text program, the pasted material appears wherever the insertion point is located. In a graphics program, a pasted item normally appears in the middle of the screen, sort of floating on top of everything else—it stays selected so you can move it around before it's pasted down to become part of the document. In almost every kind of application, choosing Paste when there's an active selection in the document replaces the selection with the Clipboard material.

Pasting doesn't take the item off the Clipboard and put it into a document—pasting puts a *copy* of the item on the Clipboard into the document. The difference is more than semantics—it means that you can keep pasting the same thing over and over into different places without having to go back and copy the original again. The only way you can remove something from the Clipboard (short of turning the computer off) is to Cut or Copy something else; the new material replaces the old on the Clipboard.

What Goes on the Clipboard?

If you're working in a word processor, you can copy paragraphs of formatted text and paste them anywhere in the document—and all the paragraph and character formatting goes with it. Try pasting that same material into a bare-bones text program—the Note Pad desk accessory, for instance—and all you'll get is plain text.

When you're working with the Clipboard within a program, all the information on the Clipboard is interpreted correctly by that same program when you paste it back down again. As you move from program to program, however, the application receiving the information can't always interpret all the information on the Clipboard, so it extracts what it can—usually plain text and simple graphics.

So, although the Clipboard can hold almost any kind of information you put on it, the place you paste that information determines how much of the original information is preserved.

Quickies

▪ Some applications have a Show Clipboard command in the Edit menu or in a Windows or Help menu. When there is a Clipboard window available, it's "view-only": You can see what's stored on the Clipboard, but you can't alter it.

▪ When you use the Undo command after placing something on the Clipboard with Cut or Copy, Undo removes that material from the Clipboard, restoring the previous item.

▪ Each application interprets the contents of the Clipboard when you use the Paste command so that it can get as much information as possible from the Clipboard. When you switch from one program to another, the translation occurs each time you move into an application. If you have information on the Clipboard that you don't need to paste into the application you're moving to, "flush" the Clipboard before you make the switch—you'll get to your destination faster. Flush the current contents of the Clipboard by copying something extremely simple—like a single letter—to it.

▪ When you cut or copy a lot of information to the Clipboard (say, more than 400K of material), there might not be enough room in memory to keep track of it. When that happens, the information is temporarily stored on your disk instead. This happens "invisibly"—you don't have to open a file from the disk to get the information; all you have to do is use the Paste command as usual. However, if you're working on a system without a hard drive, or with a very full one, and you try to put a lot of information onto the Clipboard, it is possible to get an "Out of memory" message.

▪ The keyboard equivalents for Undo, Cut, Copy, and Paste are Command-Z, -X, -C, and -V, respectively: the first four letters on the bottom row of the keyboard, right next to the Command key. If you have an extended keyboard, you can use function keys F1 through F4, respectively, for the four commands.

Also See . . .

- The Publish and Subscribe commands are another way to exchange information between documents and programs. See Chapter 8.

- Chapter 6 describes selection techniques for text and graphics.

SUMMARY

This chapter rounded up all the details of the Mac interface. Now that you're familiar with the details, in the next few chapters you'll find how they're put to use on the Desktop and in applications.

CHAPTER 4

The Desktop and Its Icons

ABOUT THIS CHAPTER

The Macintosh Desktop is so rich in features that it gets two chapters. This one covers the Desktop itself and what you can do with all the icons you'll find there.

THE DESKTOP

Basics

The Desktop is the place you start when you turn on your Mac. It's brought to you by a program called *Finder,* and you'll often hear the Desktop itself referred to as the Finder—the terms are generally interchangeable.

On the Desktop, you manipulate disks and the files on them by using the *icons* (pictures) that represent them (see Figure 4-1). You can move things from one place to another on the same disk, copy things from one disk to another, and organize your work inside as many folders as you like. You can erase files from a disk, and you can even erase entire disks.

Desktop windows let you look inside the icons of disks, folders, and the Trash. You can view the contents of a window as icons that you can move around freely, or you can view a window's contents in list form (see Figure 4-2).

A Finder Menu Tour

When experienced Mac users are exploring a new program, most will get acquainted with it by dragging the mouse along the menu bar, making each menu pop down for a moment. Here's the paper version of that browsing technique. (This is just an overview of the menus; a roundup and short description of each command appears at the end of Chapter 5, and complete details for each command appear with related topics throughout the book.)

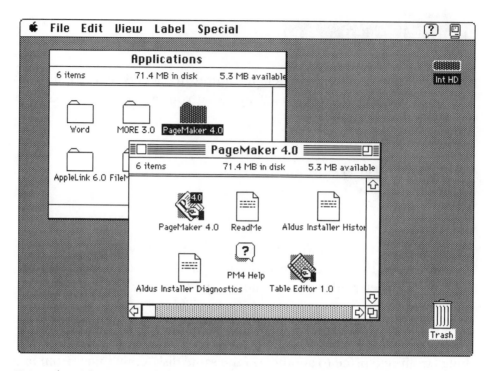

Figure 4-1. The *Desktop has many types of icons—disks, the Trash, folders, and files—and windows that let you see what's in some of the icons.*

The Apple menu is always available to you, no matter what program you're in. The "About" command at its top changes depending on what program you're in, but the rest of its contents remain constant as you move from one application to another. Since you can configure the Apple menu to suit your work habits, it won't look exactly like the one in Figure 4-3, but it will probably start out about the same way.

The File and Edit menus are also available in every program. Some commands in each are standard (like Open and Close in File or Cut, Copy, and Paste in Edit), but each program also adds its own special commands to those menus. Although it's hard to think of the Finder as "just" a program, since the Desktop seems such an integral part of the Mac, it *is* a program and so has its own special File and Edit commands, as shown in Figure 4-4.

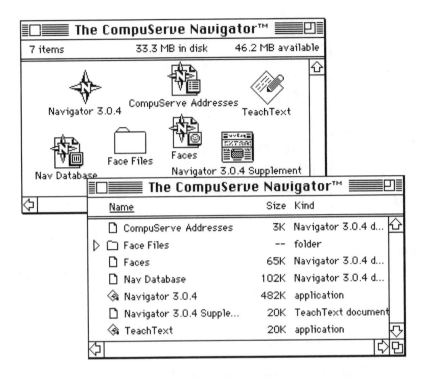

Figure 4-2. The same window in an icon view and a list view

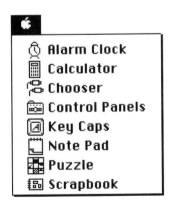

Figure 4-3. The Apple menu

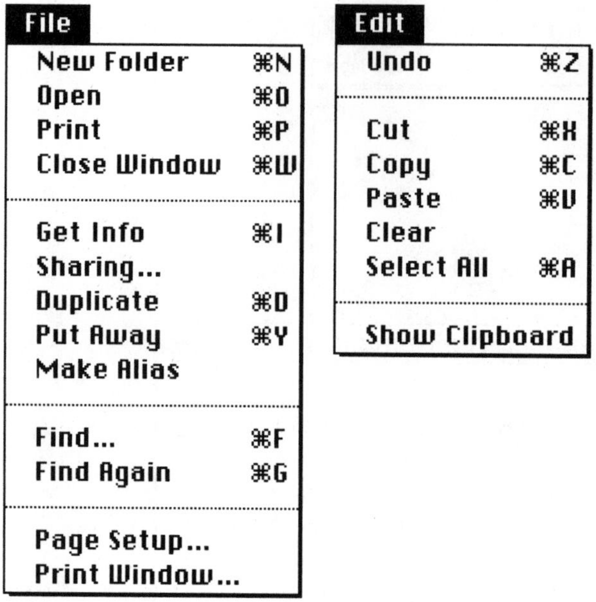

```
┌─────────────────────────┐        ┌─────────────────────────┐
│ File                    │        │ Edit                    │
├─────────────────────────┤        ├─────────────────────────┤
│   New Folder       ⌘N   │        │   Undo             ⌘Z   │
│   Open             ⌘O   │        ├ ─ ─ ─ ─ ─ ─ ─ ─ ─ ─ ─ ─ ┤
│   Print            ⌘P   │        │   Cut              ⌘H   │
│   Close Window     ⌘W   │        │   Copy             ⌘C   │
├ ─ ─ ─ ─ ─ ─ ─ ─ ─ ─ ─ ─ ┤        │   Paste            ⌘U   │
│   Get Info         ⌘I   │        │   Clear                 │
│   Sharing...            │        │   Select All       ⌘A   │
│   Duplicate        ⌘D   │        ├ ─ ─ ─ ─ ─ ─ ─ ─ ─ ─ ─ ─ ┤
│   Put Away         ⌘Y   │        │   Show Clipboard        │
│   Make Alias            │        └─────────────────────────┘
├ ─ ─ ─ ─ ─ ─ ─ ─ ─ ─ ─ ─ ┤
│   Find...          ⌘F   │
│   Find Again       ⌘G   │
├ ─ ─ ─ ─ ─ ─ ─ ─ ─ ─ ─ ─ ┤
│   Page Setup...         │
│   Print Window...       │
└─────────────────────────┘
```

Figure 4-4.   The File and Edit menus

The View, Label, and Special menus are specific to the Finder. The choices available in the View menu depend on how you've defined your window views. Figure 4-5 shows all the possibilities.

```
┌─────────────────────┐
│ View                │
├─────────────────────┤
│   by Small Icon     │
│   by Icon           │
│   by Name           │
│   by Size           │
│   by Kind           │
│   by Label          │
│   by Date           │
│   by Version        │
│   by Comments       │
└─────────────────────┘
```

Figure 4-5.   The View menu

The Label menu is completely configurable; you can change the names of the eight available labels—and, if you're working in color, you can change the color blocks assigned to each label (see Figure 4-6).

```
┌─────────────┐
│ Label       │
├─────────────┤
│ ✓None       │
│·············│
│             │
│ Essential   │
│ Hot         │
│ In Progress │
│ Cool        │
│ Personal    │
│ Project 1   │
│ Project 2   │
└─────────────┘
```

Figure 4-6.   The Label menu

While you can't change any of the commands in the Special menu, the Clean Up command changes itself according to the situation. Figure 4-7 shows the menu with its basic Clean Up Window command available.

```
┌──────────────────────┐
│ Special              │
├──────────────────────┤
│ Clean Up Window      │
│ Empty Trash...       │
│······················│
│ Eject Disk      ⌘E   │
│ Erase Disk...        │
│······················│
│ Restart              │
│ Shut Down            │
└──────────────────────┘
```

Figure 4-7.   The Special menu

At the far right of the menu bar are two menus represented by small icons; like the Apple menu, they're always available. The question mark in the balloon is the Help menu (see Figure 4-8). Its last command is *Finder Shortcuts,* but that will vary depending on the application you're in when you open it.

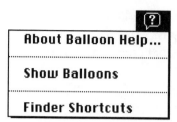

Figure 4-8. The Help menu

The last icon is for the Application menu. When you're on the Desktop, the icon is a miniature Macintosh, but the icon changes to show what program you're in—it's always a miniature of the current application's icon. The bottom section of the menu changes to list any and all programs that are running. Figure 4-9 shows what it looks like when there's nothing running except the Finder.

Figure 4-9. The Application menu

Shutting Down and Restarting

Use the Shut Down command in the Special menu at the end of a work session. If you simply switch off the power to the computer, some final "housekeeping" might not be done and what you think has been saved to a disk might not have been. When you use Shut Down, the Mac not only has the opportunity to update any changes you made to the disk, but it also cycles around through any still-open programs and checks that all their documents have been saved (see Figure 4-10).

Figure 4-10.   Using the Shut Down Command

On some Macintosh models, Shut Down actually shuts off the computer; on others, you'll get an alert after all the housekeeping has been finished, telling you that you can turn off the power to the Mac.

The Restart command, for when you want to start fresh immediately without having to shut the power off and then on again, is also in the Special menu. You'll need the Restart command when you've installed utility programs that run only when the Mac first starts, or if you've assigned another device as the startup disk and want to switch to that system (see Figure 4-11).

Figure 4-11.   The Restart command

Also See . . .

▪ Chapter 11 explains how to change the background pattern and color of your Desktop.

▪ The Finder is a program that needs a certain amount of memory allocated to it. Chapter 11.

▪ Changing window views is covered in Chapter 5 and in Chapter 11.

▪ Configuring the Apple menu is discussed in Chapter 9.

▪ Chapter 5 provides a brief description of each command in the Finder's menus.

ICONS

Basics

The kinds of icons you'll see on your Desktop are:

▪ *disk icons*, and icons for other "volumes" of information that are treated like disks, such as file servers and CD ROM drives.

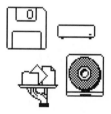

▪ *file icons* for applications, documents, and other programs and files on your disk.

- *folder icons* for organizing your file icons.

- the *Trash* icon.

- *aliases*, which are "clones" of icons that let you put something in more than one place at time.

Report alias

The procedures in this section—like moving, selecting, and renaming—are things that you can do to any type of icon. Procedures that are specific to one kind of icon—like locking a file, erasing a disk, or copying folders—are covered in their own sections.

The Trash and disk icons stay out "loose" on the Desktop, but other icons are usually inside windows. (You can leave other icons out loose, too, but in no time your Desktop will look as cluttered as your real desk top.) Icons out on the Desktop are always standard, full-size icons. Inside windows, though, you can view them in miniature or even as tiny generic icons in front of a list of file names. Most of the illustrations in this section show full-size icons, but whatever you can do to a full-size icon you can also do to its smaller versions.

Top: a full-size icon; middle: its miniature version; bottom: the generic application icon used in list views.

Selecting Icons

To select a single icon, you click on it. A selected icon is *highlighted*—its black and white parts are basically reversed (see Figure 4-12). To deselect it, you click to select something else or you click on "nothing"—an empty spot in a window or on the Desktop (see Figure 4-13).

Figure 4-12.   Clicking on an icon selects *it, turning it black.*

A selected icon on a color or grayscale Desktop basically retains its colors (if any) and is filled with a light color, or gray, to show that it's selected; the name is still highlighted to white on black.

SELECTING AND CHANGING ICON NAMES
When you click on an icon (even the little ones in list views), the *file* is selected but its *name* is not.

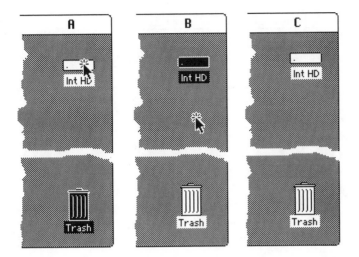

Figure 4-13. Clicking on another icon deselects a selected one (A to B); clicking on the bare Desktop deselects an icon without selecting another (B to C).

To select an icon's name in order to change it, you have to click directly on the name—either as you select the icon, or afterward. A frame around the icon's name shows that it's selected. (In a color system, the name also changes from the inverted white on black to black text against a specific highlight color.)

If you can't select an icon's name by clicking on it, that means the file is locked to keep it from being changed (see Figure 4-14).

Selecting an icon's name or its title in an icon view

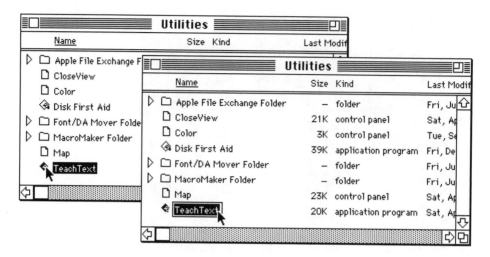

Figure 4-14. Selecting an icon's name or its title in a list view

Once the icon's name is selected, you can edit it by working within the frame. When you put the mouse cursor over a selected name, it changes from the arrow to the text cursor.

The arrow changes to the text cursor when it's over an icon's name.

Basic text-editing techniques (described in detail in Chapter 6) work within the frame. You can type to replace any selected text, click to place the insertion point, type or delete from the insertion point, drag to select a portion of text, double-click to select a whole word, and even use the left and right arrow keys to move the insertion point.

Edit an icon's name inside the frame.

You can't have two icons with the same name in the same window—even if they're different kinds of icons, like a document and a folder. If you try to rename an icon and the name's already taken, you'll get a dialog box informing you of the problem (see Figure 4-15).

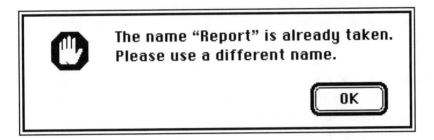

Figure 4-15. You can't have two icons with the same name in the same window.

You can, however, have an icon with the same name as a folder inside that folder (see Figure 4-16).

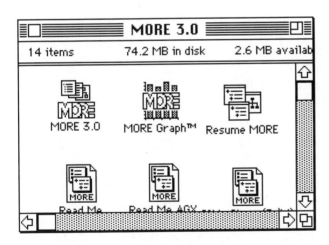

Figure 4-16. One of the icons in this folder has the same name as the folder itself.

KEYBOARD SELECTION TECHNIQUES

There are three ways to select an icon from the keyboard: by typing its name, by using the arrow keys, or by using the Tab key.

When you want to select an icon in the active window by name, you have to type only as many characters as are necessary to uniquely identify it; if nothing matches what you type, the next nearest alphabetic equivalent is selected.

Use any of the arrow keys to select the next item in a specific direction. You can use only the up and down arrow keys in a list view, but all four work in the icon views. (If nothing at all is selected, you can still use an arrow key: You wind up with an icon from one of the corners in an icon view, or at the top or bottom in a list view.)

Finally, you can use the Tab key. No matter how you have your icons or list arranged, Tab selects the next item *alphabetically*. Shift-Tab selects items in reverse alphabetical order.

In the window in Figure 4-17, with the General Controls icon selected, here's what using various keys would select:

left arrow:	Map
right arrow:	Color
down arrow:	Startup Disk
up arrow:	Memory
Tab:	Keyboard (next alphabetical)
Shift-Tab:	File Sharing Monitor (previous alphabetical)
M:	Map (nearest alphabetic equivalent to letter typed)
Mo:	Monitors (nearest alphabetic equivalent to letters typed)

SELECTING MULTIPLE ICONS

You can select a group of icons all at once by catching them within a rectangle you draw with the mouse. Start by pointing to a spot that would be one corner of the rectangle and press the mouse button, then drag the mouse to the diagonally opposite corner. As you drag, you'll see a gray rectangle being drawn. If you're dragging a rectangle around some icons and get to the edge of the window, the window will scroll so that you can keep dragging. Any icon that is even partially within the rectangle is selected (see Figures 4-18 and 4-19).

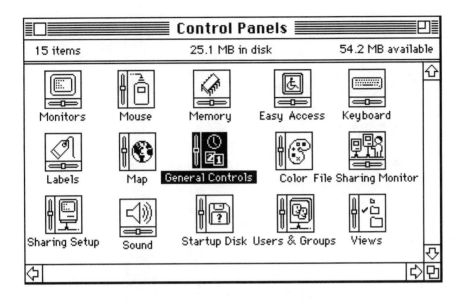

Figure 4-17. You can select icons by using the keyboard.

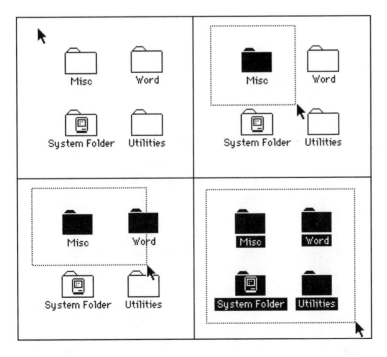

Figure 4-18. Dragging a rectangle to select a group of icons

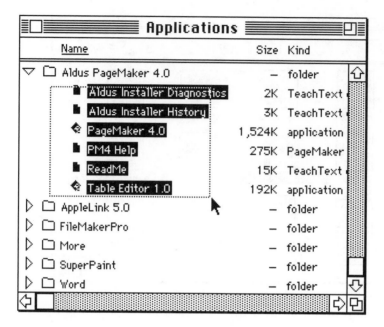

Figure 4-19. Dragging a rectangle in a list view

When you want to select multiple icons that aren't grouped together, use the Shift-click method: Click on the first icon, hold down the Shift Key, and click on any other icons you also want selected (see Figures 4-20 and 4-21). (Without the Shift key held down, clicking on another icon deselects the first one.)

Shift-clicking also deselects an icon from a group: If you Shift-click on an icon that's already selected, it's removed from the selection.

Finally, when you want to select *all* the icons in a window, use the Select All command in the Edit menu.

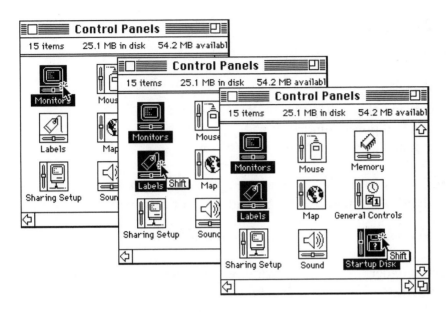

Figure 4-20.   Select icons that aren't next to each other by clicking on the first one and Shift-clicking on the others.

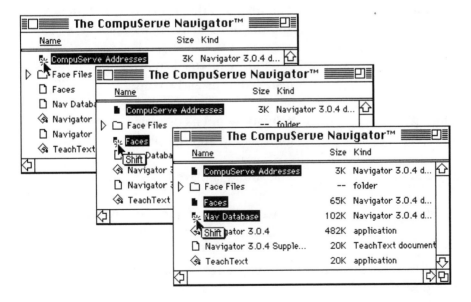

Figure 4-21.   Shift-clicking in a list view

Opening Icons

To open an icon, you can:

▪ Double-click on it.
▪ Select it and choose Open from the File menu.
▪ Select it and press Command-O.
▪ Select it and press Command-down arrow.

Most icons on the Desktop can be opened, but just what "open" means depends on what the icon stands for. For example:

When you open...	*This is what happens:*
...a disk, a folder, or the Trash	A window opens showing you what's inside.
...an application or system utility	The program launches.
...a document	The program that created it launches and the document opens inside it.
...the System file	A window opens displaying the installed fonts and sounds.
...a font file	A window opens displaying font information and samples.
...a sound file	The sound is played.
...a system extension	A dialog opens that either provides and/or asks for information.

Figures 4-22 through 4-24 show the results of opening some of the Desktop icons.

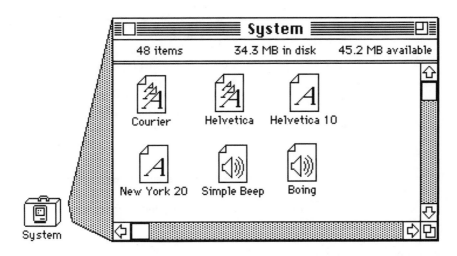

Figure 4-22. Double-clicking on the System file opens its window, showing the fonts and sounds inside it.

Figure 4-23. Double-clicking on the Helvetica font icon displays samples of the font.

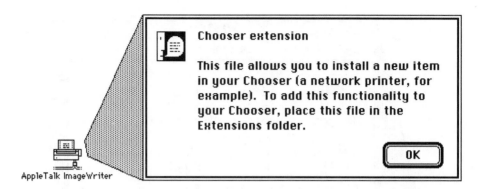

Figure 4-24. Double-clicking on a Chooser extension gives information about it.

ICON APPEARANCES

There are visual clues to let you know whether an icon is currently selected, or opened, or both. Selected icons basically reverse their black and white parts—since most icons are outline drawings, this makes most selected icons turn black. Opened icons are gray, and if an icon is both selected and open, it's dark gray.

Moving Icons

To move an icon, you drag it with the mouse. As you drag, only an outline of the icon moves; when you release the mouse button, the icon itself moves to the new position (see Figure 4-25).

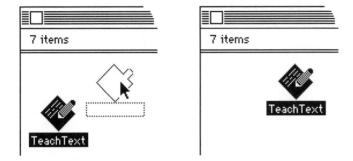

Figure 4-25. Dragging an icon

When you want to drag an icon that's in a list view—to drag it out of the window, for example—grab it by the tiny icon in front of the name (see Figure 4-26).

Name	Size	Kind
The CompuServe Navigator™		
🗋 CompuServe Addresses	3K	Navigator 3.0.4 d...
▷ 🗀 Face Files	--	folder
▪ Faces	65K	Navigator 3.0.4 d...
🗋 Nav Database	102K	Navigator 3.0.4 d...
◈ Navigator 3.0.4	482K	application
🗋 Navigator 3.0.4 Supple...	20K	TeachText document
◈ TeachText	20K	application

Figure 4-26. Dragging an icon in a list view

MOVING ICONS INTO OTHER ICONS

Some icons can contain other icons. You can drag icons into:

- a disk icon
- a folder icon
- the Trash icon
- the System file icon
- an application icon

There are some logical restraints as to just which icons can go into other icons. For example, only system "resources" like fonts and sounds can be dragged into the System file, only documents that can be opened by an application can be dragged into its icon, and a disk icon can't be dragged into a folder icon.

To put one icon into another, you drag the first one until the mouse pointer touches the second one. You'll know you're there when the "destination" icon turns black (see Figures 4-27 and 4-28).

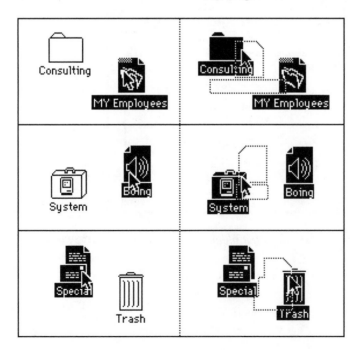

Figure 4-27.   Putting a file into a folder, into the System file, and into the Trash

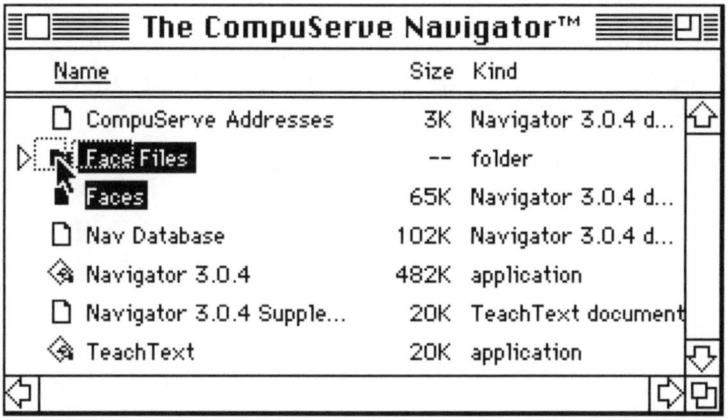

Figure 4-28. Putting an icon into another icon in a list view

Another way to put an icon into another icon is to move it into the destination's *window*, if it's open (although even if the window's open, you can still drag one icon into the other if that's more convenient).

Assigning Labels

An icon has many automatically assigned attributes. It has a *kind* attribute, for instance: It's a folder, an application, or a document. It has a name and the dates that it was created and last modified. You can use these attributes (and others) to sort the items in a Desktop window and as criteria when you're searching for a misplaced file with the Find command.

But what's not automatically available is an attribute that you might call "project." You may be working on a report that ultimately will be a single file of information, but while you're working on it, it's one or more word processing files, some spreadsheets, and several pictures created in different graphics programs. No matter which standard attributes you use to find these files, you won't get them all in one grouping.

The Label menu on the Desktop lets you assign one of eight labels to any file. (You can change the labels in the menu to something meaningful for your work by using the Labels control panel described in Chapter 11.)

To assign a label, simply select the icon(s) and then choose the label from the menu. If you're working with a color or grayscale system, a color is also assigned to each label—you'll see the color in the menu, and the icon gets assigned that color along with the label.

An icon's label appears in list views if you've defined your windows to include labels (see Figure 4-29); if you're in an icon view, you can't see what label's been assigned unless you have a color system (although you can select an icon and then open the label menu to see which label is checked).

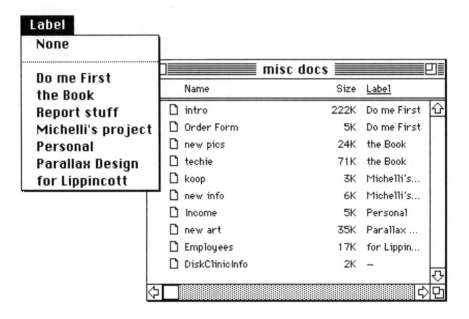

Figure 4-29.   When a list view is sorted by label, the order matches the order in the menu.

To change an icon's label, select the icon and choose the new label from the menu. To remove the label, select the icon and choose None from the Label menu.

The Get Info Window

You can get information about any kind of icon—an application, a document, a system file, a folder, a disk, or the Trash. Just what information you get depends on the icon. To get an icon's information, select it and choose Get Info from the File menu (see Figure 4-30).

The information that's common to most icons is:

- what *Kind* of icon it is—a document, application, system file, folder, or disk.

- the *Size* of the file, in bytes and in K or in M.

- *Where* the file is—in what folders and on what disk.

- when the file was *Created* and when it was last *Modified*.

- a *Comments* box for you to type comments about the file.

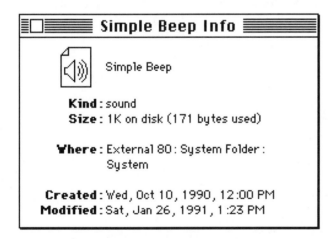

Figure 4-30. A System file for a sound has all the basic information categories available except for a Comments area.

In addition, each type of icon has some special information in its Info window. (Special Info window procedures, like locking files, allocating memory, and designating Stationery pads, are covered in other places in the book; the list here is an overview of the differences in Info windows.)

■ An application's Info window (the one for HyperCard is shown in Figure 4-31) shows its version number and the suggested and currently allocated memory partition. It has a Locked checkbox.

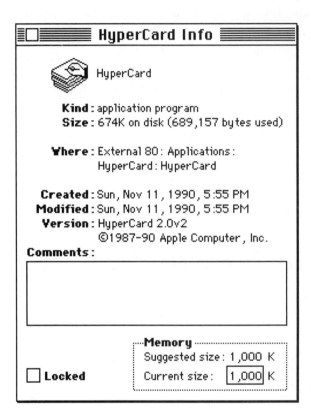

Figure 4-31.   An application Info window

■ A document's Info window specifies its parent application in the Kind information. It has both Locked and Stationery checkboxes (see Figure 4-32).

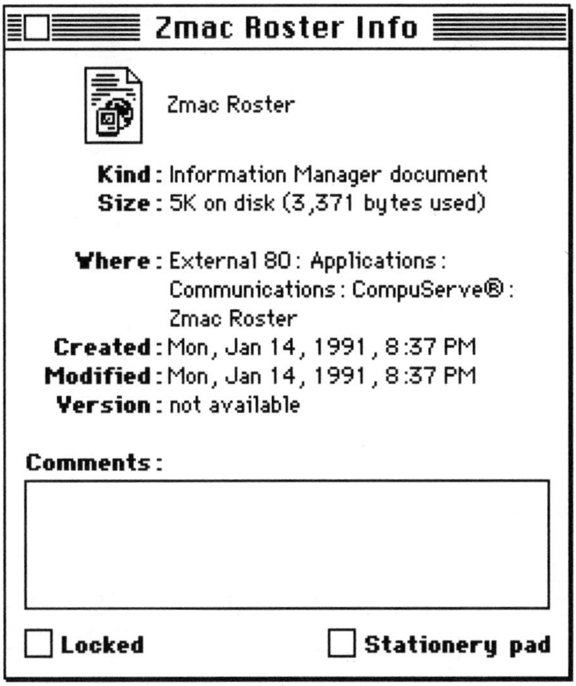

Figure 4-32. A document Info window

- A disk's Info window uses the Size information to report on its capacity and the number of files already stored on it. A hard drive's Info window also identifies its SCSI ID number if it has one (see Figure 4-33). (The creation date reported for a disk is the date that you initialized it, not the date it rolled off the assembly line.)

- A folder's Info window uses the Size information to report how much is stored inside the folder, that is, both the number of items and their total size. The number of items is calculated differently from the way it's reported in the folder's Desktop window. A folder inside a Desktop window is counted as a single item; in the Info window, all the items inside nested folders are counted. Figure 4-34 shows a folder's Get Info window reporting 39 items inside it, while the Desktop window for the same folder shows that only two items are in it.

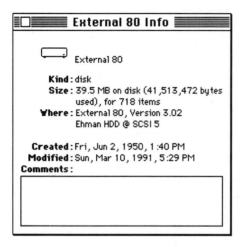

Figure 4-33.   A hard disk's Info window

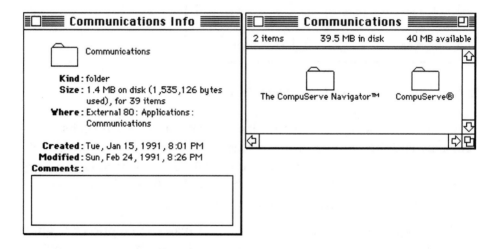

Figure 4-34.   The number of items in a folder is calculated differently for the Info window and the Desktop window.

■ The Info window for the Trash reports its *Contents* (instead of size) and provides a checkbox to turn its alert box on and off (see Figure 4-35).

Figure 4-35.　*The Trash Info window*

Quickies

■ If an icon is already selected but its name isn't, you can press Return or Enter to select the name. This method is particularly handy if you've selected the icon with a keyboard option and don't want to reach for the mouse. Pressing Return or Enter after editing the name deselects the name, but leaves the icon itself selected.

■ When there's an editing frame around an icon's name, the Select All command in the File menu selects the entire name instead of all the icons in the window.

■ The Shift key works to extend a selection even when you're not clicking on the additional icons but dragging a rectangle instead. It doesn't matter whether you selected the original icon(s) by clicking or by dragging; holding Shift down and dragging a rectangle around a group of icons adds them to the initial selection.

▪ If you want to select all the icons in a window except for one or two, it's usually faster to use the Select All command and then Shift-click or Shift-drag to deselect the ones you *don't* want.

▪ Another way to get information about any icon that's in a window is to switch the window into a list view. Most of the information in the Get Info window is also available in list views.

Also See . . .

▪ Chapter 5 explains how to edit an icon.

▪ If you're working in color or grayscale, you can alter the highlight color that's used on file names. See Chapter 11.

▪ Chapter 11 describes how to change the labels listed in the Label menu; Chapter 5 shows how to use labels as criteria for sorting and searching for icons.

▪ The special items in the Info window are covered in several places: locking files and the Trash can warning are discussed later in this chapter, memory allocations for applications are discussed in Chapter 13, and stationery pads are covered in Chapter 7.

FILES AND FOLDERS

Basics

File is a generic term that refers to a collection of information on your disk. A file can be a program—like an application, a utility program, or a desk accessory—or it can be a document that was created by an application or is used by a utility or a system file. In this section, *file* basically refers to any icon that is *not* a folder, disk, or the Trash.

Folders are special icons that don't represent information on your disk; instead they represent imaginary divisions on the disk that let you organize your files.

Locking Files

One thing that you can do to a file icon that you can't do to other types of icons is *lock* it.

There are two reasons for locking a file. When a file is locked, it can't be erased from the disk by mistake. Although you can put it in the Trash, you'll be warned about the locked file when you try to empty the Trash. (There are more details about this in the "Using the Trash" section that appears at the end of this chapter.) It's a good idea to lock all your applications so that you can't trash them by mistake.

The other reason to lock a file applies only to documents. A locked document can't be edited or altered in any way from within an application. You can open it, view it, and print it, but you can't change it. Locked files are often used to serve as templates because you can open them, save them under a different name, and edit the newly named document without making any inadvertent changes to the original.

To lock a file, select it and choose Get Info from the File menu. In the Get Info window, click the Locked checkbox (see Figure 4-36). (Of course, to *unlock* a file, you click in the box to uncheck it.)

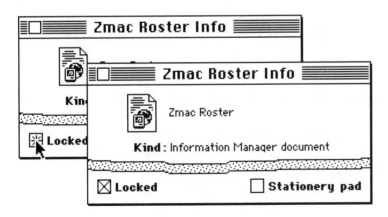

Figure 4-36. Click in the checkbox to lock a file.

There are two ways to tell if a file is locked without having to open its Info window. If an icon's name can't be selected by clicking on it (that is, if you can't get the edit frame to appear), the file's locked—because you can't change anything about a locked file, even its name. Or check for a small lock icon for the file name in a list view (see Figure 4-37). (The icon is usually so far to the right in the columns of information that it's easier to click on the name to see if you can select it.)

≣□	ReuisedArt F-R	□≣

25 items	39.5 MB in disk	40 MB available

	Name	Size	Kind	Last Modified	
	Farm Ways/gg	18K	SuperPaint document	Fri, Aug 18, 1990, 8:40 PM	🔒
	Fast Food Stuff/gg	15K	SuperPaint document	Sat, Sep 2, 1990, 1:30 PM	🔒
	Fruit1/gg	29K	SuperPaint document	Thu, Sep 7, 1990, 9:57 PM	🔒
	Fruit2/gg	33K	SuperPaint document	Sun, Sep 17, 1990, 8:43 PM	
	Fruit3/gg	17K	SuperPaint document	Sun, Sep 17, 1990, 9:02 PM	
	Gluttons/gg	24K	SuperPaint document	Mon, Sep 25, 1990, 8:41 PM	
	Hot Drinks/gg	26K	SuperPaint document	Mon, Sep 25, 1990, 9:03 PM	
	Ice Cream/gg	26K	SuperPaint document	Tue, Sep 26, 1990, 10:20 PM	
	Icon+/gg	24K	SuperPaint document	Mon, Oct 2, 1990, 8:12 PM	

Figure 4-37.   Locked files get a padlock icon in the far right column in list views.

Creating and Using Folders

Desktop folders are much like their real-world counterparts—you use them to organize your information. You can put files, and other folders, inside a folder icon to keep things in logical groups (the logic, of course, is entirely your own).

To create a folder, choose the New Folder command from the File menu. The new folder appears in the active Finder window. The folder that appears has its name already selected and ready for editing. You don't have to click on it, you can just type its new name (see Figure 4-38).

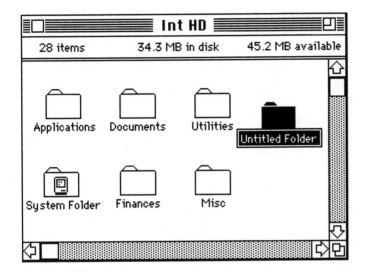

Figure 4-38.   The New Folder command creates a new folder in the active window.

ORGANIZING YOUR DISKS

The way you organize your disk is very personal. There's no "best" way, since everyone works a little differently. It is a good idea, though, to work with nested folders so that you can keep surface clutter to a minimum. You might want to put each application and all its support files in a folder, and keep all those folders in one main Application folder. Having a folder hold documents based on their subject matter is usually a more convenient approach than keeping them grouped by the application that created them (for example, putting all the word processor documents together, all the graphics together).

One of the earlier drawbacks to deeply nested folders (a folder within a folder within a folder within a folder...) is no longer a concern under System 7. Opening a series of folders to get at an application or document that was used often was time-consuming and annoying; now those items can be installed in the Apple menu for easy launching so that you don't have to access their icons on the Desktop.

Moving Files and Folders

When you move files or folders on a disk into another folder, you're only changing the location of the icons you're dragging: There aren't any copies made for the new location.

When you move an icon into a folder that already contains an icon by that name, you'll see the dialog box shown in Figure 4-39. You can cancel the move, or click OK and have the existing icon replaced by the one you're moving.

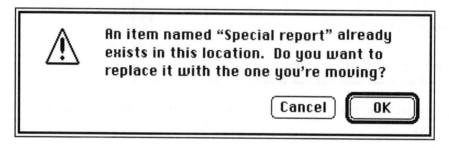

Figure 4-39.   Two icons with the same name can't be in the same place.

When you're moving a folder into another folder (or disk) that has one with the same name, you have to be very careful before agreeing to replace one with the other. The Mac doesn't check the *contents* of the folders for unique or duplicate files, it only checks the folder names. If you agree to the replacement, the folder you're moving, and all its contents, replaces the existing one and all *its* contents.

Copying Files and Folders

When you want to copy a file or folder to another disk, you drag its icon into the disk icon. If the disk is open, you can drag the icon directly into a folder or window instead of into the disk icon. This procedure doesn't move the *original* icon to the other disk (the way moving an icon from one folder to another on the same disk would merely change its location); instead, it puts a *copy* of the icon onto the disk.

During the copying process, there's a Copy dialog box on the screen. The first message it flashes is "Preparing Copy" as it checks the main level of the destination disk for any file with the same name as the one you're copying. Depending on your Mac model, this message may flash so briefly that you won't even notice it.

If the Mac finds a file of the same name in the location you're copying to, you'll be asked if you want to replace the existing file. You can cancel the copying or go ahead and replace the existing file. (You can have a file of the same name inside a folder on the destination disk without running into this problem.)

If there's no file by the same name in the way, or if you agree to replace the existing file, you'll see the other two messages in the Copy dialog. One message is "reading" and the other is "writing," as the Mac alternates between reading information from one disk and writing it to the other. When the file or files being copied are small enough for the Finder's memory to handle, all the reading is done in one sweep and the writing is done in another.

While the reading and writing are in progress, you'll get messages as to how many files still need to be copied (if you're doing more than one at a time or if you're copying a folder), and a progress bar fills up to show how much of the current operation is completed (see Figure 4-40). You can click in the Stop button at any time to cancel the procedure.

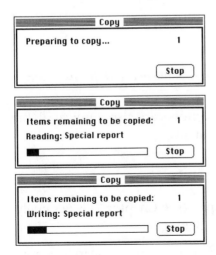

Figure 4-40. The three Copy dialog messages

BACKGROUND COPYING

File copying can be done in the background while you continue working on whatever it is that you want to do.

Set up the copy as usual—drag icons from one folder or disk to another, or drag a disk from one disk to another—and while the Copy dialog is on the screen, you can continue to work on the Mac in any application (except the Finder).

Your work will be a little slower than normal while the Mac splits its attention between you and the background copying, but if you're doing a lot of copying, it might be worth the slowdown.

Duplicating Files and Folders

To make a copy of an existing icon, select it and choose Duplicate from the File menu. You'll see the same Copy dialog you see when you're copying things to another disk.

The duplicate is an exact copy of the original in every way except its name: *copy* is appended to the name. If you duplicate the copy, its title will have *copy 2* after it, and so on.

Duplicating a file or folder makes a copy that's identical except for its name.

When you duplicate a folder, all its contents are also duplicated, but the names of the contents aren't altered at all.

Quickies

▪ Defining a document as a Stationery pad (see Chapter 7) is generally easier than turning it into a template by locking it.

▪ *Locked* and *Not locked* are criteria that you can use in searching for files on your disk with the Find command.

- When you move an icon from one folder to another on the same disk, you can move a *copy* instead of the original: Hold down the Option key as you drag the icon to its new location. This puts a copy in the destination folder and leaves the original behind.

- Every icon has a *path name* that starts with the name of the disk it's on and ends with the icon's name. Folder names appear between them, with colons separating all the names. This is a typical path name: *IntHd:System Folder:Apple Menu Items:Calculator.* (That's why you can't use colons in an icon's name.)

DISKS

Basics

The icon of the *startup disk* always appears in the upper-right corner of the Desktop. What it looks like depends on what you use as a startup disk—a floppy disk or a hard drive. Hard drive icons vary from one manufacturer to another, so there can be a variety of icons representing hard drives on your Desktop.

Each disk that's inserted during a work session gets its own icon on the Desktop; they line up neatly down the right side of the screen.

Any information storage device that the Mac is connected to gets its own icon on the Desktop. If you're connected to a network with a central file server that you can access, it gets an icon on your Desktop; a CD-ROM gets an icon; hard drives that are *partitioned* into segments get an icon for each partition that you mount. The general term for these storage devices is *volume,* and when a volume has an icon on the Desktop, it's considered *mounted.*

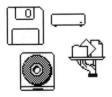

Floppy disks, hard drives, file servers, and CD-ROMs are all volumes that get icons on the Desktop.

The window that opens when you double-click a disk or other volume is the *main* or *disk window;* it's also referred to as the *root level* of the disk.

Ejecting Disks

When you want to temporarily eject a floppy disk disk from a drive, you can use any of these methods:

- Select the disk and choose Eject Disk from the Special menu.

- Press Command-Shift-1 to eject a disk in the internal drive; Command-Shift-2 works for an external drive or for a second internal drive.

- If you're in an Open or Save dialog box, click the Eject button when the disk is selected.

These are temporary procedures because the disk icon is still on the Desktop even though the disk is no longer in the drive. The icon that's left, though, is sort of a "ghost"—a dimmed version of its inserted self, both in selected and unselected forms.

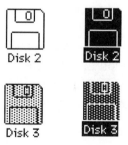

Top: unselected and selected disk icons for a disk in a drive; bottom: the "ghost" versions of an ejected disk.

The icons for opened disks are the same for inserted or ejected disks; in that case, your visual clues come from the contents of the windows—there are "ghosts" in the ejected disk's windows (see Figure 4-41).

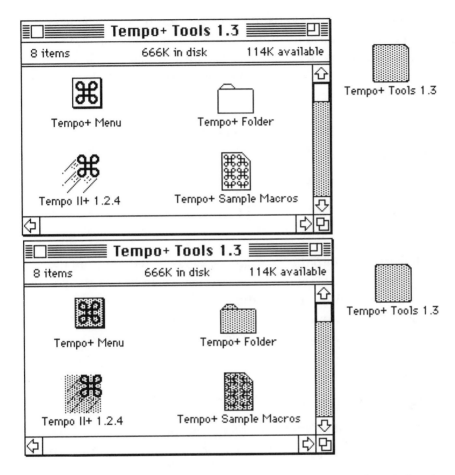

Figure 4-41. Although the opened disk icons are the same, the window icons for an ejected disk (at bottom) are dimmed.

WORKING WITH GHOSTS

The main reason for only temporarily ejecting a disk is that it takes much less time for the Mac to read through a disk's contents again if you want to reinsert it (about 2 seconds, as opposed to 5 to 15 seconds to read through a newly inserted disk). So if you're going to be using the same disk again a little later in a work session, let its ghost hang around. Another reason to leave the ghosts is if you have only one floppy drive and you need to work with two floppy disks, perhaps for copying files between them.

When you manipulate a ghost disk on the Desktop, sometimes you'll be asked to insert the disk; if you try to open one of its folders, for instance, the Finder will need to check the disk. If there's a disk already in the drive, it will be ejected automatically for you (but *its* ghost stays on the Desktop).

AVOIDING AND EJECTING GHOSTS

When you want to eject a disk without leaving its ghost on the Desktop, you can:

- Select it and choose Put Away from the File menu.
- Drag it into the Trash.

Dragging the disk into the Trash *doesn't* erase anything from the disk—it erases the disk from the Finder's memory. In fact, when you use the Put Away command, you'll see the disk icon move to the Trash before it disappears from the Desktop.

You can get rid of a disk ghost by dragging it to the Trash or using the Put Away command.

Copying Disks

When you want to make a copy of a disk, you can always select all its contents and drag them to another disk, but you can also work with the disk icon itself.

To copy one floppy to another, drag one disk icon into the other. (You can work with ghost icons if necessary.) You'll get a dialog that checks if you really want to replace the contents of one with the other (see Figure 4-42).

If you're using a single floppy drive, you'll be asked to insert the disks as necessary during the copy procedure.

When you want to copy a floppy disk onto a hard drive, drag its icon onto the drive icon. (You can't, of course, do this the other way around—the hard drive can't be copied to the floppy.) This won't replace the contents of the hard drive with that of the floppy; instead, it creates a folder on the hard drive named for the floppy disk and places all its files inside.

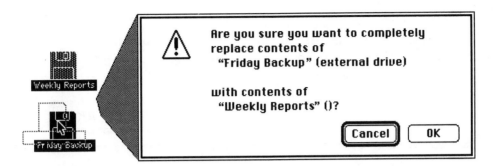

Figure 4-42. This alert checks with you before going ahead with a disk-to-disk copy; there's no drive listed for the second disk because it's not currently in a drive.

Erasing Disks

The best way to erase a disk is to select it and choose Erase Disk from the Special menu. This erases *all* the information from the disk, including any invisible files that were used by programs or the system. Reformatting the disk also checks that there aren't any bad spots on it.

Simply dragging all a disk's files to the Trash is faster, but it not only leaves invisible files, it also leaves the information on the disk in a format that's recoverable with the right software tools (good for a rescue, but bad for security), and it doesn't check the integrity of the disk media.

Quickies

▪ You can use keyboard selection techniques on disk icons if there are no windows open or if you first activate the Desktop itself. To activate the Desktop, press Command-Shift-up arrow. Typing a name or using the Tab or arrow keys then selects disk icons instead of the icons in windows.

▪ If you get a dialog asking you to insert a disk and you can't find it, or if you change your mind about wanting to use it, you can press Command-period to cancel the insert request (even though there's no Cancel button in the dialog). Figure 4-43 shows the dialog that appeared after canceling the Insert request when a folder on a ghost disk was double-clicked.

Figure 4-43. An alert like this may appear after canceling a request to insert a disk.

■ When you can't eject a ghost disk, it's because one of the files on it is currently in use by the system or some application.

Also See . . .

■ Operations involving disks that aren't necessarily Desktop procedures (like locking them and initializing them for use) are covered in Chapter 14.

USING THE TRASH

Basics

When you want to erase something from a disk, you drag its icon into the Trash can. The Trash icon plumps up to show there's something inside.

Empty and full Trash cans

The items in the Trash are still on the disk; they're not actually erased until you use the Empty Trash command from the Special menu. When you do, you'll get the dialog box shown in Figure 4-44. Clicking OK erases the items from the disk. Clicking Cancel doesn't erase them, but it does leave them in the Trash.

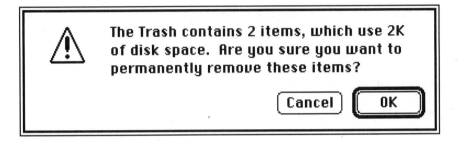

Figure 4-44. The Trash warning dialog

You can remove an item from the Trash simply by opening the Trash icon and dragging the item out of the Trash's window. Or you can select the item and choose Put Away from the File menu and the item zips back into whatever folder it came from.

Avoiding the Trash Warning

The warning that appears when you use the Empty Trash command can be temporarily bypassed or turned off completely.

To turn off the warning permanently (at least until you want to turn it back on again), select the Trash icon, choose Get Info from the File menu, and uncheck the *Warn before emptying* button (see Figure 4-45).

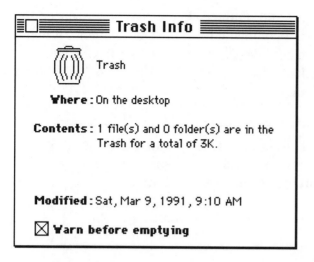

Figure 4-45.   You can turn the Trash warning on and off through its Info window.

To bypass the warning, hold down the Option key when you open the Special menu. The command itself changes; it loses the ellipsis that indicates a dialog box is going to open.

Holding down the Option key lets you bypass the Trash's warning dialog.

If you've turned off the warning in the Info window, holding down the Option key when opening the Special menu temporarily turns it back *on*.

Locked Items

Locked items can't be mistakenly erased from the disk. When you've put a locked file into the Trash and then use the Empty Trash command, you'll get a dialog informing you that the locked items can't be deleted (see Figure 4-46). (You can go ahead and delete the other items.)

Some items in the Trash cannot be deleted because they are locked. Do you want to delete the other items?

Stop   Continue

Figure 4-46. You can't erase locked files.

If you want to erase a locked file, you have to unlock it: Open its Info window and uncheck the Locked box.

Quickies

■ In previous Mac systems, the Trash emptied automatically if you launched an application or shut down. That's no longer true; the Trash doesn't get emptied until you specifically empty it with the command in the Special menu (except as noted in the next Quickie...).

■ If you drag something to the Trash from a floppy disk and then eject the disk, the file will be erased before the ejection—without the warning dialog about emptying the Trash. Only the items from the disk being ejected are erased. Anything else in the Trash stays there.

SUMMARY

This chapter covered all the things that you can do with icons on the Desktop—from the basics of selecting and moving icons to locking them, accessing their Info windows, and deleting them from the disk. It also covered more specific icon operations like copying and erasing disks, assigning labels, and creating folders.

More Desktop Procedures

ABOUT THIS CHAPTER

The last chapter introduced you to the basics of working on the Desktop. In this chapter, you'll learn about Desktop windows, and you'll learn even more things you can do with icons. You'll also find out how to search disks for lost files and use the Mac's Help feature. And, at the end, there's a roundup of all the commands in the Finder's menus.

DESKTOP WINDOWS

Basics

Desktop windows let you see what's on a disk, in a folder, and in the Trash. They are basically document windows that you can manipulate as described in Chapter 3, but they also have many special properties all their own.

The commands in the Finder's View menu let you view the contents of a window as standard or small icons that you can move around freely, or as a list sorted by any of several criteria. Which list views are available in the menu depends on what you've defined for the windows through the Views control panel (covered in Chapter 11). The menu can be as brief as the short one shown in Figure 5-1, or it can include any or all of the commands shown in the longer version.

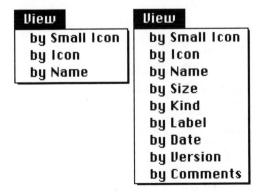

Figure 5-1. The View menu can have as few as three commands, as many as nine, or any number in between.

Each Desktop window has a special header immediately beneath the title bar that shows how many items are in the window, how much information is on the disk, and how much disk space is left. As shown in Figure 5-2, in list views, the header can also identify the columns of information.

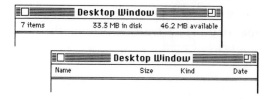

Figure 5-2.   Headers in Desktop windows give information about window and disk contents.

This chapter shows the default settings for windows in its illustrations, but you can define many of their components with the Views control panel. You can alter things like what kind of header appears in the window, what size icons are used in list views, and what font and type size are used for file names; Figure 5-3 shows some of the possibilities.

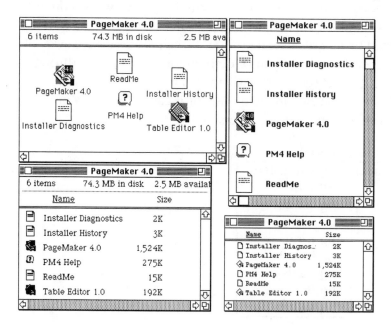

Figure 5-3.   Four very different looks for the same window

Icon Views

The By Icon and By Small Icon commands in the View menu give you the views shown in Figure 5-4. In either icon view, you can drag the icons around to any spot in the window.

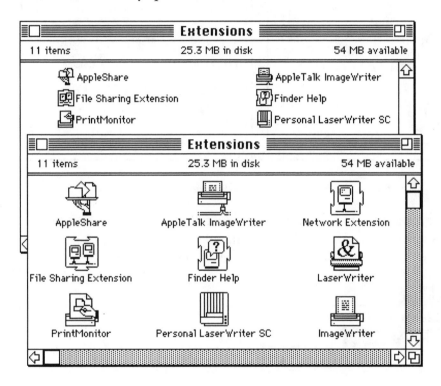

Figure 5-4. The same window in standard and small icon views

THE CLEAN UP COMMAND

The Clean Up Window command in the Special menu aligns all the icons in the active window to invisible grid points (see Figure 5-5).

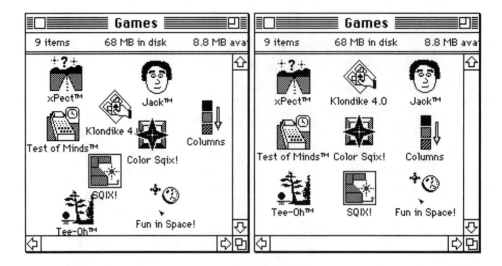

Figure 5-5. Before and after the Clean Up command

If you want to straighten up only selected items in a window, hold Shift as you open the menu: The command changes to Clean Up Selection and only the selected items are moved to the grid.

The Shift key changes the Clean Up Window command.

If you want to align the icons to the grid and sort them at the same time, hold down the Option key as you open the menu. The Clean Up command refers to the last list view that you used in that window, for example, Clean Up by Name, or Clean Up by Kind. The icons will be straightened out and sorted at the same time.

The Option key changes the Clean Up Window command.

List Views

When the contents of a window are viewed as a list, the columns of information are always in the same order—the file name, with its icon, is always first—but the files are sorted according to the view that's chosen. A standard list view shows generic icons for applications, documents, and folders.

The current sorting order is always checked in the View menu, but you can also tell just by looking in the window—the column name that's underlined is the one that the icons are sorted by (see Figure 5-6).

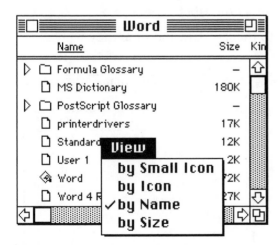

Figure 5-6. The current sort criteria is checked in the menu and underlined in the window's header. A standard list view, like this one, shows generic icons for documents, folders, and applications.

There are seven possible sorting criteria:

▪ *By Name* lists the items alphabetically according to their names (see Figure 5-7). Whether a letter is uppercase or lowercase is not significant, and numbers and most special symbols come before letters. (There's a complete list of the Mac's alphabetizing sequence in Appendix D.) If you want certain files to be listed before others in Desktop windows, or even in the Open dialogs for when you're working in an application, you can alter their names to force them to the top of the list.

▪ *By Size* lists the items according to their sizes, with the largest one on top (see Figure 5-7). If the sizes of folders aren't showing (that's another option you can set in the Views control panel), they'll be listed after all the files with known sizes.

▪ *By Kind* lists items alphabetically by their kinds. Applications are identified as just "application," but documents might be identified as "document" or as a document from a specific application, such as "FileMaker document," "MacWrite Pro document," and so on.

▪ *By Label* lists items according to the labels you've assigned—not alphabetically, but in the order that the labels appear in the Label menu. Items with no labels are listed after all the labeled ones.

▪ *By Date* lists items according to the last date and time they were *modified* (not created).

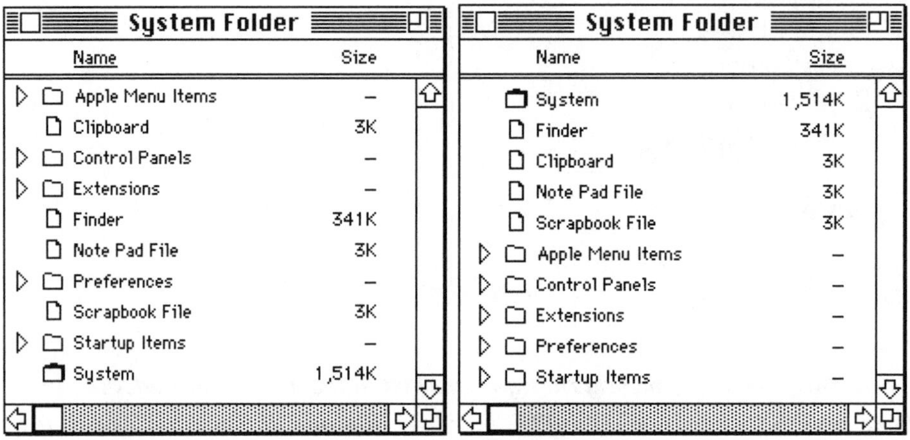

System Folder			**System Folder**	
Name	Size		Name	Size
▷ ☐ Apple Menu Items	–		☐ System	1,514K
☐ Clipboard	3K		☐ Finder	341K
▷ ☐ Control Panels	–		☐ Clipboard	3K
▷ ☐ Extensions	–		☐ Note Pad File	3K
☐ Finder	341K		☐ Scrapbook File	3K
☐ Note Pad File	3K		▷ ☐ Apple Menu Items	–
▷ ☐ Preferences	–		▷ ☐ Control Panels	–
☐ Scrapbook File	3K		▷ ☐ Extensions	–
▷ ☐ Startup Items	–		▷ ☐ Preferences	–
☐ System	1,514K		▷ ☐ Startup Items	–

Figure 5-7. The same window sorted by name and by size

- *By Version* lists items according to their version numbers. All applications, and some documents, have version numbers.

- *By Comments* lists items alphabetically according to the comments entered in their Get Info windows.

Hierarchical Lists

When you're using one of the list views, you can list not only the main contents of the window, but also the contents of any folder in that window.

To expand the outline of a folder's contents, click on the arrow that's in front of the folder. When a folder is expanded, its arrow points downward and all its contents are listed beneath it in an indented column (see Figure 5-8).

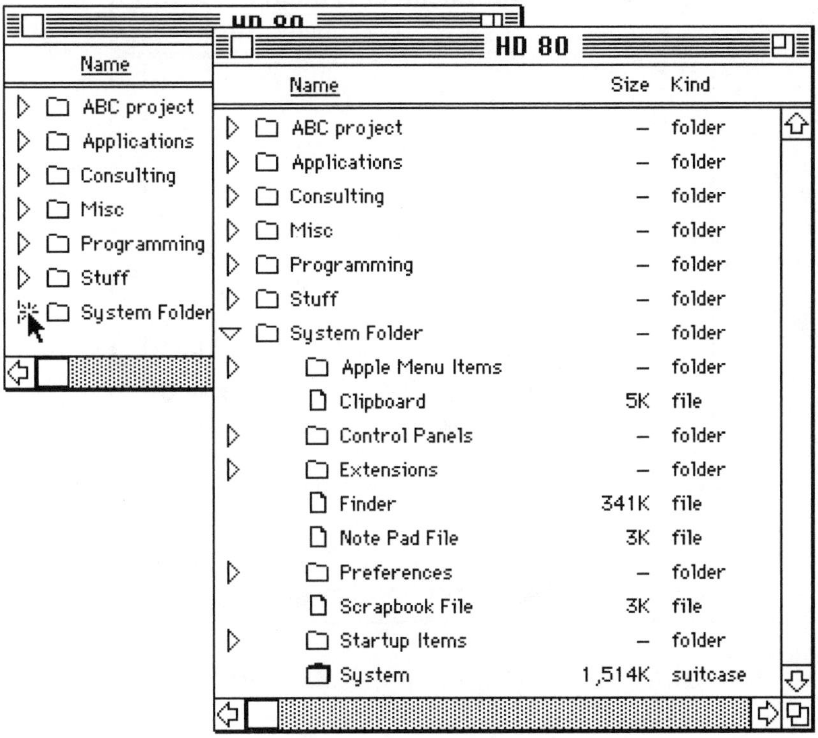

Figure 5-8. Click on a folder's arrow to expand it.

Once the contents of a folder are listed, you can also expand any
folders within that folder by clicking on their arrows. Or, if you want to
expand a folder to all its levels (opening every folder in it, and every
folder in *those* folders, and so on), hold down the Option key while
you click on the arrow. Compare the single-level expansion of the
System Folder shown in Figure 5-8 to the multilevel expansion shown
in Figure 5-9 from an Option-click on the same arrow.

Clicking on the arrow of an expanded folder collapses its outline.
The level of expansion you used inside it (which folders were open) is
"remembered" for the next time you expand it. If you want all the levels
within an expanded folder to be collapsed, hold down Option as you
click on the arrow to collapse the folder; the next time you open it you'll
see only one level in the outline.

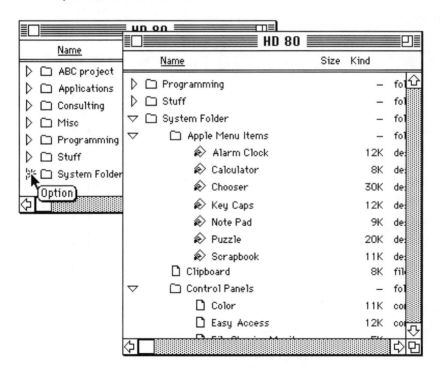

Figure 5-9. Option-click on a folder's arrow to expand all its levels.

Keyboard expand and collapse commands work on any selected folder in a list view. If you're working from the keyboard, you have probably selected the folders from the keyboard—unless you Shift-clicked or dragged to select more than one. The key combinations for expanding and collapsing are:

- Command-right arrow expands a selected folder to one level—the equivalent of clicking on its arrow.

- Command-left arrow collapses a selected folder—the equivalent of clicking on its arrow.

- Command-Option-right arrow expands a selected folder—the equivalent of Option-clicking on its arrow.

- Command-Option-left arrow collapses the selected folder as well as all the folders inside it—the equivalent of Option-clicking on its arrow.

The Path Menu

The title of a folder window serves as a popup menu that describes the "path" of the folder—which folder it's in, and which folder that one's in, and so on, all the way back to the disk. To get the menu, hold down the Command key while you press on the title of an active window (see Figure 5-10). (You have to be on the title itself—not just anywhere on the window's title bar.)

Selecting any window in the menu activates it, opening it if necessary.

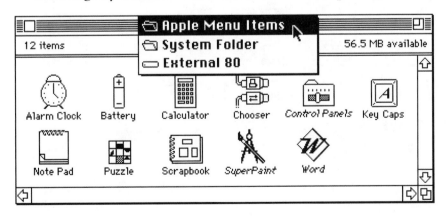

Figure 5-10. Holding down the Command key while pressing on the title of a folder's window shows the folder's path.

Keyboard Window Controls

You can open, close, and activate windows from the keyboard when you're traveling along a path of nested folders. (In these, as in many Desktop operations, the terms "window" and "folder" are synonymous.)

The basic keyboard Open command is Command-down arrow, which opens a selected folder. Adding the Option key to the combination not only opens the selected folder, but also closes the window that it's in. Figures 5-11 and 5-12 show what happens when you open the selected Apple Menu Items folder with each of these key combinations.

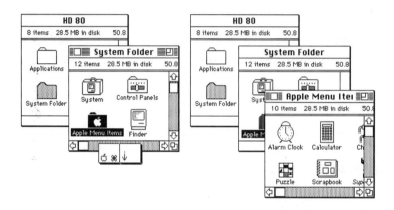

Figure 5-11.   Pressing Command-down arrow opens a selected folder.

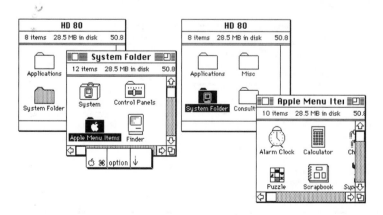

Figure 5-12.   Pressing Command-Option-down arrow opens a selected folder and closes the window that it's in.

To move back up through the folders, you use similar key sequences. Command-up arrow returns you to the "parent" of the current window, activating and bringing it to the top and opening it if necessary. Adding the Option key closes the current window as you move to its parent. Figures 5-13 and 5-14 show how the System Folder window (the "parent" of the Apple Menu Items folder) is activated with each of these key combinations.

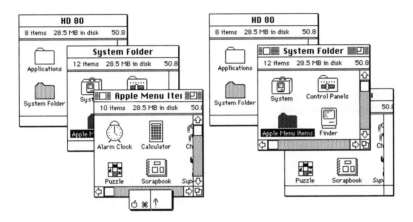

Figure 5-13. Pressing Command-up arrow activates the "parent" of the current window.

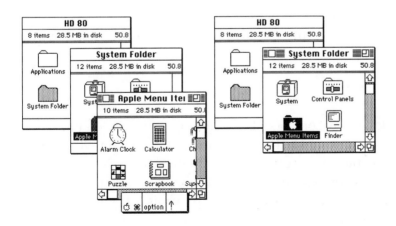

Figure 5-14. Pressing Command-Option-up arrow closes the current window and activates its "parent."

Printing Desktop Windows

The Print Window command in the File menu lets you print the contents of the active Desktop window.

When you choose the command, you'll get a Print dialog box asking how many copies you want, which pages to print, and for other general printing information. (Printing options and dialog boxes are covered in Chapter 16.) When you click the Print button in the dialog, the window is printed.

The settings for the window—view, font, size, and so on—are used in the printout. No matter how much is showing in the window, though, the entire contents of the window will be printed. Each page gets a header that matches the window's header and a page number on the bottom.

Quickies

▪ If you hold down the Command key while you move an icon in a window (in either icon view), the icon snaps to a grid point when you release the mouse button. If you've turned on the Always Snap to Grid option in the Views control panel so that this happens automatically, holding Command when you move an icon prevents it from snapping to the grid when you release it.

- The Desktop itself also has an invisible grid on it. If there are no windows open, or if the Desktop has been activated with Command-Shift-up arrow, the Clean Up command in the Special menu reads Clean Up Desktop and it will align all the Desktop icons to the grid.

- A quick way to sort items in a list view is to click on the column name in the window's header (see Figure 5-15).

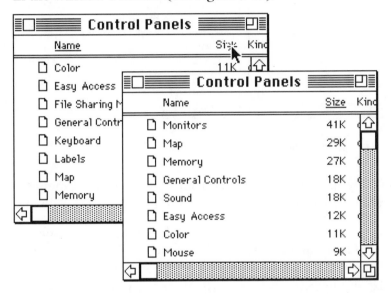

Figure 5-15. Click on a column name to sort items in a list view.

- When you're using a hierarchical window view, the sort criteria affects all the levels in the window. In Figure 5-16, the items in the PageMaker folder at the left are alphabetical, but on the right, they're arranged by size.

- You can move an inactive Desktop window without activating it if you hold down the Command key while you drag its title bar.

- When you hold down the Option key, the Close Window command in the File menu changes to Close All, and it closes all the Desktop windows at once. Adding Option to the menu's keyboard shortcut (Command-Option-W instead of Command-W) also closes all the windows.

- Clicking in any Desktop window's close box while holding down the Option key closes all the Desktop windows.

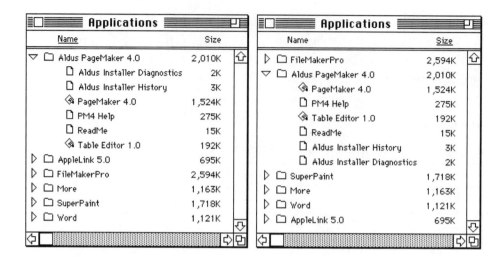

Figure 5-16.   Sorting affects all levels in an expanded outline.

▪ Holding down Option while you select from a window's path menu closes the current window as it opens the selected one.

▪ When you click in a Desktop window's zoom box to open it to full size, it opens only far enough to display all its contents. If there are more things in the window than can be displayed on the screen, the window zooms to the size of the screen—less a strip along the right so that disk and Trash icons are still available. You can force the window to a full-screen size regardless of its contents if you hold Option while you click in its zoom box.

▪ If you're printing a window view that has too many columns to fit across a standard piece of paper, two pages will be printed—one for the right half of the window and one for the left half. You can use the Page Setup command in the File menu to get the page to print sideways on the paper.

Also See . . .

▪ The Views control panel is covered in detail in Chapter 11.

▪ Chapter 16 explains Page Setup and Print dialogs in detail.

CUSTOMIZING ICONS

Basics

Many Desktop icons can be customized to better represent their purpose. If you use icon views, or if you use large icons in your list views, detailed icons—especially for folders—are easier to deal with (see Figure 5-17).

Figure 5-17. Folder icon possibilities

To see if an icon is editable, open its Info window and click on the picture of the icon. If a frame appears around the icon, you can alter it (see Figure 5-18).

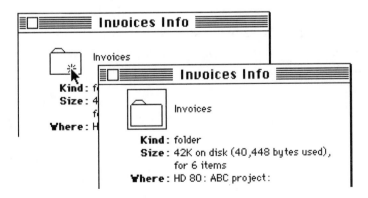

Figure 5-18. Click on the icon in the Info window; if a frame appears, you can edit it.

Editing an Icon

There are no built-in editing tools for icons. Instead, you can edit the icon or create a new one in a paint-type program like MacPaint, SuperPaint, or HyperCard.

If you want to start with the current icon as the basis for a new one, select it in the Info window and choose Copy from the File menu; you can then paste it into your graphics program.

Alter the icon (or create a new one) and copy it to the Clipboard. Return to the Info window, select the icon, and choose Paste from the Edit menu. The new icon is pasted into the Info window and the change is immediately applied to the original icon (see Figure 5-19).

Invoices Info

Invoices

Kind : folder
Size : 42K on disk (40,448 bytes used), for 6 items
Where : HD 80 : ABC project :

Figure 5-19. The new icon pasted into the Info window

Quickies

▪ The maximum size of an icon is 32 by 32 screen dots; if you copy something larger to the Clipboard, it will be scaled to fit into the icon frame in the Info window.

ALIASES

Basics

Sometimes you'll wish that one of your icons could be in more than one place at the same time. You might want a document to be in both its normal descriptive folder, like "Quarterly Reports," as well as in a special folder that holds priority projects. You can't just duplicate the file, because then when you work on one copy, the other wouldn't reflect the changes. Or, you might want a control panel device both in the Control Panels folder and in the Apple Menu Items folder so that it will be listed in the Apple menu.

With the File menu's Make Alias command, you can have it both ways: You can create an *alias* of any file, not just a copy of the file itself, but a copy of its *icon* that you can put anywhere and treat as if it were the original. An alias is a very small document; it takes up only about 2K on the disk because it serves as a pointer to the original icon.

Creating and Using Aliases

To make an alias of a file, select it on the Desktop and choose Make Alias from the File menu. The icon that appears will look identical to the original, but its name (the original with *alias* tacked on the end) will be in italics (see Figure 5-20).

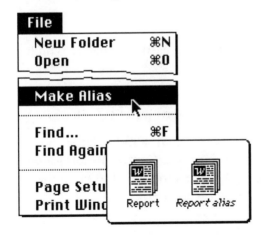

Figure 5-20. When you create an alias, the icon is identical except that its name is in italics.

You can rename the alias—take off the "alias" so that it's the same as the original, or change the name entirely—and you can make as many aliases of the original file as you want, so it can be in many places at once. An alias doesn't even have to be on the same disk as the original.

When you rename an alias, change its location, or erase it from the disk, the original is not affected. But since the alias is a pointer to the original file, when you double-click on the alias to open it, it's the original that's actually opened.

If you erase the original file and try to open the alias, you'll get the dialog shown in Figure 5-21.

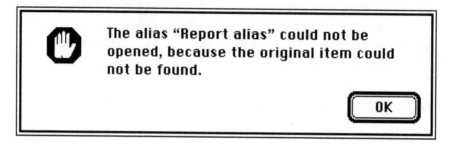

Figure 5-21.   If the original file has been erased, you'll get a dialog like this if you try to open the alias.

You'll use aliases most often for

■ a document that you want to be able to open easily no matter which of several folders you might be in.

■ applications that you want both in their own folders and in the Apple Menu Items folder—and possibly even in the Startup Items folder as well.

■ items that need to be in more than one of the System Folder's folders—control panels that you want in both the Control Panels folder and the Apple Menu Items folder, or extensions that need to be in the Extensions folder and the Apple Menu Items folder.

Aliasing a Folder

When you make an alias of a folder, you can use it as a shortcut to that folder: Anything you put into the alias actually moves into the original folder.

You might assume that if you open a folder alias, it would display what's in the original, but that's not exactly what happens. When you double-click on an alias folder, the original folder opens no matter where it is.

Quickies

- If you try to open an alias and the original is on a disk that's not currently on the Desktop, you'll get a dialog asking you to insert that disk.

- If you want to find the original file for an alias, select the alias and choose the Get Info command. Click in the Find Original button and the original will be found and selected in its window (see Figure 5-22).

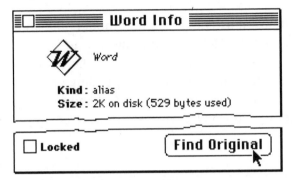

Figure 5-22. Use the Find Original button in an alias's Info window to find the original file.

Also See . . .

- Chapter 9 talks about aliases and the folders in the System Folder.

USING THE HELP MENU

Basics

The Help menu—the balloon with the question mark in it at the right of the menu bar—is a systemwide feature, not just a Desktop menu. But unless an application is "aware" that it's running under System 7, it won't be able to use the Help feature, even though the menu stays available. But you can be sure that it works on the Desktop, and you can try it with any other program that you have.

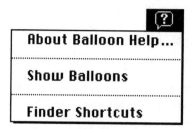

The menu has only three items in it. The first is the About command, which gives you information about the Help system. The second command—it alternates between Show Balloons and Hide Balloons—toggles the Help on and off. The third menu changes depending on the program you're running—on the Desktop, the command is Finder Shortcuts, and it opens a window that lists Desktop shortcuts (see Figure 5-23).

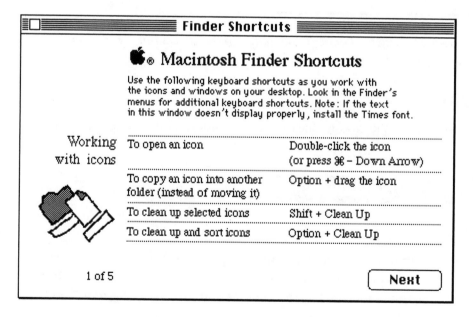

Figure 5-23. There are five pages of Finder Shortcuts available.

Using Help Balloons

To use Help, choose Show Balloons from the menu. Once Help is turned on, point to anything on the screen to get information about it—you don't even have to click the mouse button. You can get general information about an icon or specific information about the function of any part of a window or menu (see Figure 5-24).

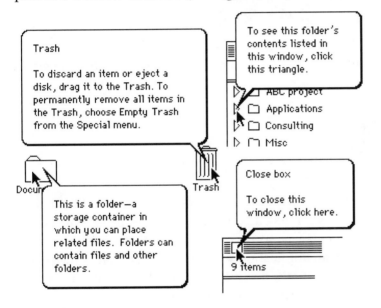

Figure 5-24. Point to anything on the screen to get information about it.

You can continue working while you're in Help mode—opening a folder, for instance, to get help on something that's inside it. You can get information about a menu command by pointing to it in the menu, but you can actually execute the command if you release the mouse button as you would normally.

Turn off the Help feature by choosing Hide Balloons from the menu (see Figure 5-25).

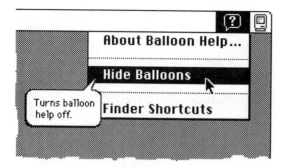

Figure 5-25.   You can choose menu commands even while the Help Balloons are turned on.

FINDING THINGS

Basics

The System 7 Finder finally lives up to its name, with Find and Find Again commands available in its File menu. And, since the Desktop is always just a mouse click away, you can use the Find command even if you're in the middle of an application when you realize that you've lost something. (Anyone who thinks it's impossible to "lose" a file on a disk hasn't been working with hard drives long enough.)

File	
New Folder	⌘N
Open	⌘O
Print	⌘P
Close Window	⌘W
Get Info	⌘I
Sharing...	
Duplicate	⌘D
Put Away	⌘Y
Make Alias	
Find...	**⌘F**
Find Again	**⌘G**
Page Setup...	
Print Window...	

You can use the Find command on a very basic level, or use its More Choices option to be very specific about what you're looking for and where.

The Basic Find Command

When you choose the Find command, you get the dialog shown in Figure 5-26. Type the file name you're looking for and click the Find button. The Mac searches all available disks for anything that matches what you typed. Capitalization is ignored, and the search is done for even partial matches—so searching for *Man* also finds *man, manual,* and even *command.*

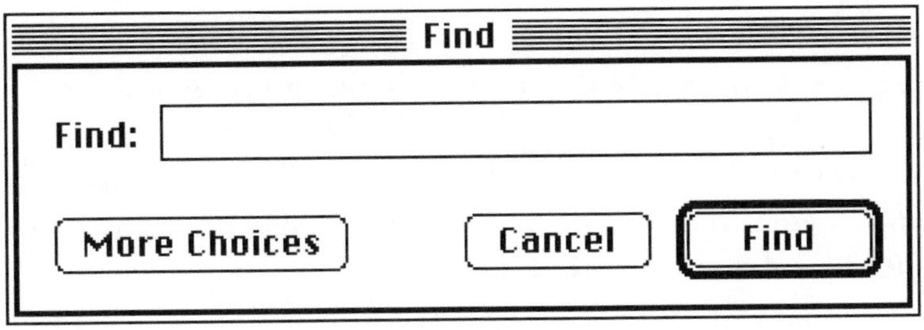

Figure 5-26. The basic Find dialog box

Once all the possible matches are found, the dialog box closes and the first match is displayed—its window is opened and the found file is selected in it. If it's not the one you want, use the Find Again command in the File menu to see the next match. The window with the first match closes, and the next one opens. If the Mac beeps when you use Find Again, that means you've seen all the matches.

The Full Find Command

When you want to be more specific in your search, click the More Choices button; the full Find dialog, shown in Figure 5-27, appears.

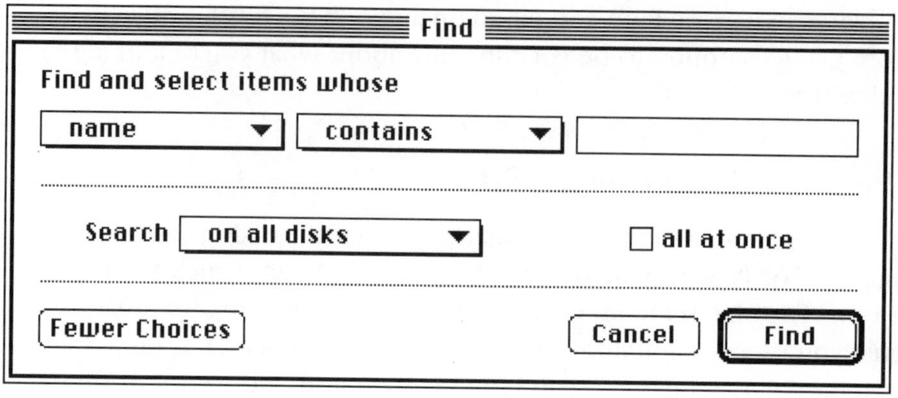

Figure 5-27.   The full Find dialog box

In this dialog box, you specify the *what, where,* and *how* of your search: what you're looking for (a file whose name contains a certain word, a document created before a specific date, and so on); where you're looking (on a certain disk or in a certain folder); and how you want the matches found—one at a time or all at once.

SPECIFYING THE "WHAT"

The top area of the Find dialog lets you specify what you're looking for. In most cases you have three items (two popup menus and a text box) that you use to construct a description like *name begins with "record"* or *modified date is after 6/2/91.*

The first item in the description comes from the popup menu at the left of the dialog box (see Figure 5-28).

How you construct the rest of the description depends on what you choose in the first menu, but most of the time there's a second popup with *comparison operators* (for example, *is, is not, is greater than,* and *is before*) and a text box to enter the text or number you're looking for.

Figure 5-28.   Begin the description of what you're looking for by choosing from the first menu.

Name

When you search for an item by name, the second popup provides six choices: *contains, starts with, ends with, is, is not,* and *doesn't contain.* (see Figure 5-29).

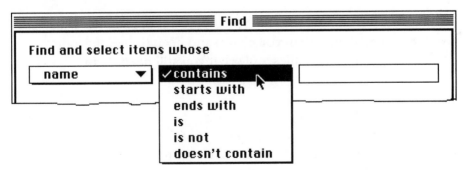

Figure 5-29.   The comparison operators for a search by name

By selecting one of these operators and typing in the text box to the right, you can find almost anything if you remember even only part of its name.

So, if you've compiled a quarterly report and can't remember what you titled it—*Quarterly Report, Quarterly Earnings, First Quarter Sales*—you can use the *contains* operator, type in "quarter," and find any of them. Using the *is* operator finds only exact matches, so typing in "quarter" would find only a file with that as its entire name. (As with the smaller Find dialog, capitalization doesn't matter.)

Size

When you search for an item by size, you can choose one of two operators—*is less than* or *is greater than*. The text field is labeled "K" (for the file's size, in kilobytes) and you type a number in it (see Figure 5-30).

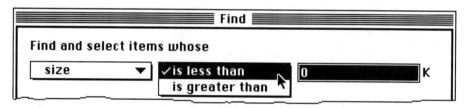

Figure 5-30. The comparison operators for a search by size

You might search by size if you're running out of room on your hard drive (it happens sooner than you think) and need to free up some space—look for the largest files and see if you still need them.

Kind

When you search for a file by its kind, you get two operators: *contains* and *doesn't contain*. You can type the kind of file you're looking for ("MacWrite document" or "file"), or you can enter one of the five standard kinds of files from the popup menu that appears when you press on the arrow next to the text box (see Figure 5-31).

Since the basic operator is *contains,* if you search for "document," you'll get both generic documents and items tagged *Word document, MacPaint document,* and so on.

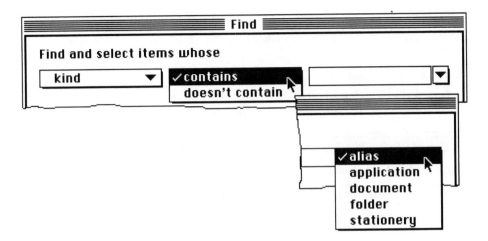

Figure 5-31. When you search by Kind, you can type in the kind of file you're looking for or choose one of the five common ones from the menu.

Label

When you search for a file by its label, you get two operators: *is* and *is not*. You also get a third popup menu that lists the available labels—they're the ones currently in the Label menu, including None (see Figure 5-32).

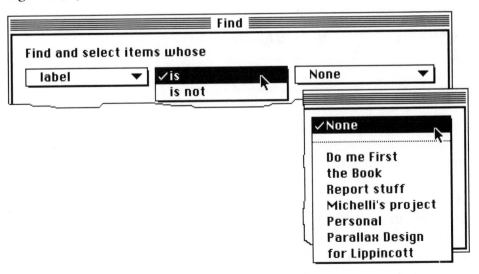

Figure 5-32. When you search by Label, the third popup reflects the current contents of the Label menu.

This is a great way to gather files together at the end of a project (if you've been labeling them) in order to remove them from the disk.

Date Created and Date Modified

When you search by a file's created or modified date, you can use any of four operators: *is*, *is before*, *is after*, and *is not* (see Figure 5-33).

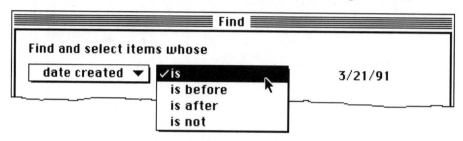

Figure 5-33. There are four operators available for searching by Date Modified or Date Created.

When you're entering a date, you don't type it in a text box. Instead, you alter the current date by clicking on the month, day, or year and then using the up and down arrow controls to change the number (see Figure 5-34).

Figure 5-34. Use the arrows to change the numbers in the date.

Searching for files by date is a good way to find the files that you've created or modified since the last time you made backup copies of important documents.

Version

Every program has a version number; some special documents that come with applications also have version numbers assigned to them. The operators you can choose from when searching by version number are the same as for dates: *is*, *is before*, *is after*, and *is not* (see Figure 5-35).

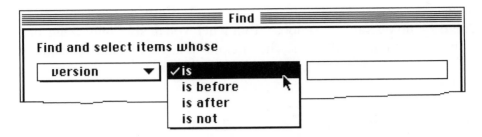

Figure 5-35. Searching by Version supplies you with the same operators as searching by Date.

You type the version number you're looking for in the text box. The Find dialog understands decimal version numbers—so, for instance, you can search for items prior to version 3.02. You can also type in the double decimals (like 1.2.3) that some applications use. (Special files that come with an application might have some other information as the "version" number—a copyright notice, for instance. The version number information that's displayed in a file's Get Info window is what's used for the version search.)

Comments
You have two operators to choose from when you want to search for a file based on the comments entered in its Get Info window: *contain* and *do not contain* (see Figure 5-36).

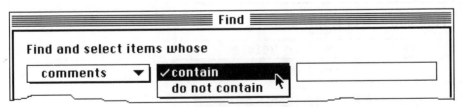

Figure 5-36. You can look for a file based on what you entered (or didn't enter) in its Get Info comments box.

Lock

There are no operators to choose from when you're searching using an icon's locked/unlocked status. The operator is always *is,* and you can choose either *locked* or *unlocked* from the popup menu at the right (see Figure 5-37).

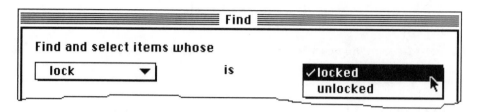

Figure 5-37. You can search for locked or unlocked files.

SPECIFYING THE "WHERE"

The popup menu labeled Search lets you specify where the search should be made. From its three sections, you can choose to search all the mounted disks, any one of the mounted disks, or inside the currently active window or among the selected items (which could be one or more selected folders or a group of files chosen by the previous Find operation). (See Figure 5-38.)

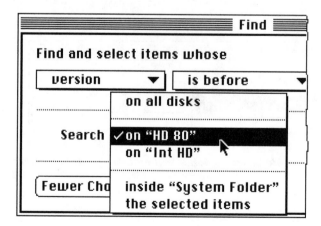

Figure 5-38. Use the Search menu to specify where to look for the files.

SPECIFYING THE "HOW"

Although the Find command always searches the entire area you specified in the Search menu before it shows you anything, you do have a choice as to how the found files are displayed—one at a time or all at once. To control the display, check or uncheck the All at Once button in the dialog.

☒ **all at once**

THE SEARCH PROCESS

When you have all your search criteria set, click in the Find button. The Mac looks for all the files that match what you're looking for.

If you're searching by name, the search is incredibly fast because the Finder keeps track of file names in a special way. If you're searching by some other criteria, you'll see a dialog on the screen reporting the progress of the search; a ball spins around in it to indicate that the search is ongoing. You can click in the Stop button at any time (see Figure 5-39).

Items found on "Int HD":   22

Stop

Figure 5-39.   The ball in this dialog spins as the search proceeds.

Unless you checked the All at Once button, the search process is the same as when you use the smaller Find dialog: A window opens to display the first match, and you use the Find Again command to see subsequent matches.

If you checked the All at Once button, a window opens that shows a list view of the search area—the folder, disk, or windows for each disk—with the matches selected. The list is expanded so that all levels in which items were found are shown. Figure 5-40 shows the results of a search for all items less than 12K in size inside the System Folder.

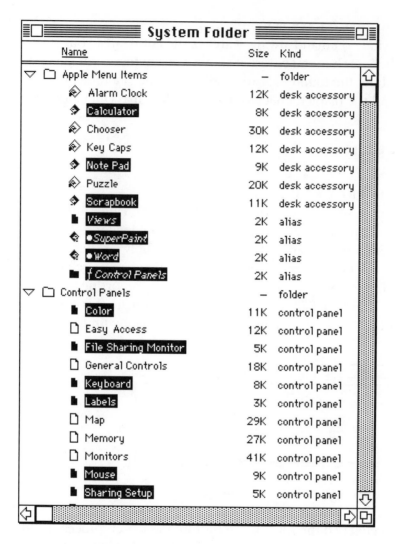

Figure 5-40.   The results of an All at Once search

Since opening and expanding a list for a window can take a little while, you'll probably get another dialog box, like the one shown in Figure 5-41, while the window's being prepared.

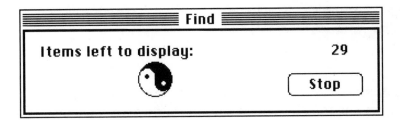

Figure 5-41. This dialog appears when a fully expanded window is being prepared.

NARROWING THE SEARCH

You can use the Find command to find files that match two sets of criteria—all the MacWrite documents that were modified after a specific date, for instance.

To do this kind of search, do a Find on one set of criteria—all the MacWrite documents. Then, while those documents are still selected, do a second Find, for the modified date, and specify *in the selected items* as the "where" of the search. Only the previously found files are checked, and the ones that are selected at the end of the Find process are those that satisfy both sets of criteria.

Quickies

▪ When you do an All at Once search on an entire disk, or on any folders with lots of subfolders, you'll wind up with a fully expanded list view of all the folders. When you're finished viewing the found files, here's the easiest way to collapse everything in the window down to manageable proportions: press Command-A to select everything in the folder and then press Command-Option-left arrow to collapse all the folders.

FINDER COMMANDS ROUNDUP

Basics

This section gives a brief description of each of the commands you'll find in Desktop menus, and it notes in parentheses where you'll find more details about each one.

The Apple Menu

The Apple menu is available from every program. The first command changes to the name of the current application; some applications also add a second command that lets you use a help feature.

About This Macintosh opens a window that gives information about your Mac and how its memory is being utilized (Chapter 13). If you hold down the Option key, the command changes to **About the Finder** and the dialog that opens displays Apple's copyright notice for the Finder program. There's no close box or cancel button in the dialog, but it goes away if you click in it. Don't click in it too soon, though—wait and see what happens.

The File Menu

Although the File menu is one that you'll find in every program, most of the commands in the Finder's version are unique to the Desktop.

```
┌─────────────────────────────┐
│ File                        │
├─────────────────────────────┤
│   New Folder        ⌘N      │
│   Open              ⌘O      │
│   Print             ⌘P      │
│   Close Window      ⌘W      │
│·····························│
│   Get Info          ⌘I      │
│   Sharing...                │
│   Duplicate         ⌘D      │
│   Put Away          ⌘Y      │
│   Make Alias                │
│·····························│
│   Find...           ⌘F      │
│   Find Again        ⌘G      │
│·····························│
│   Page Setup...             │
│   Print Window...           │
└─────────────────────────────┘
```

New Folder creates a new, untitled folder in the active window (Chapter 4).

Open opens the selected icon. Double-clicking on an icon is the same as selecting it and using the Open command (Chapter 4).

Print opens the parent application for the selected document icon and then opens the document and prints it (Chapter 16).

Close Window closes the active window; it's the same as clicking in a window's close box. If you hold down the Option key while opening the menu, the command is Close All and it closes all the Desktop windows (Chapters 3 and 5).

Get Info opens the Info window for a selected icon (Chapter 4).

Sharing is used to set access levels for shared files on a network (Chapter 11).

Duplicate makes a copy of a selected file or folder (Chapter 4).

Put Away moves a selected icon that's in the Trash or on the Desktop back into its folder. If a disk icon is selected, Put Away ejects the disk and removes its icon from the desktop (Chapter 4).

Make Alias creates an alias of the selected file or folder (Chapter 5).

Find opens the Find dialog (Chapter 5).

Find Again finds the next file that matches the last search criteria that you used (Chapter 5).

Page Setup opens a dialog box that lets you set certain options for printing (Chapter X).

Print Window prints the contents of the active Desktop window (Chapter 5).

The Edit Menu

The commands in the Finder's Edit menu are ones common to almost all Edit menus. On the Desktop the Undo, Cut, Copy, Paste, and Clear commands affect the *name* of a selected icon, not the icon itself.

Edit	
Undo	⌘Z
Cut	⌘X
Copy	⌘C
Paste	⌘U
Clear	
Select All	⌘A
Show Clipboard	

Undo reverses your last editing action on an icon's name (Chapter 3).

Cut removes selected text from an icon's name and places it on the Clipboard (Chapters 3, 4, and 5).

Copy places selected text in an icon's name on the Clipboard without removing it. If an icon is selected in a Get Info window, Copy copies the selected icon to the Clipboard (Chapters 3, 4, and 5).

Paste inserts whatever's on the Clipboard into an icon's name at the insertion point; if the entire name is selected, the Clipboard material replaces the selection. If the Get Info window is open, Paste replaces the selected icon with the contents of the Clipboard (Chapters 3, 4, and 5).

Clear deletes selected text in an icon's name without placing it on the Clipboard (Chapter 6).

Select All selects all the items in the active window, or all the items on the Desktop if the Desktop is activated. If an icon's name is being edited, Select All selects the entire name (Chapter 4).

Show Clipboard opens a window that displays the current contents of the Clipboard. You can move the window around and resize it, but you can't do anything to the contents (Chapter 3).

The Label Menu

The choices in the Label menu vary according to how you've defined them with the Labels control panel. (All commands are covered in this chapter.)

```
Label
✓None
.................
  Essential
  Hot
  In Progress
  Cool
  Personal
  Project 1
  Project 2
```

None removes the label from a selected icon.
[Label name] applies the label to a selected icon.

The View Menu

The choices in the View menu vary according to the way you've defined your Desktop windows with the Views control panel. There are always at least three items in it (By Small Icon, By Icon, and By Name), but there can be as many as nine. (All commands are covered in this chapter.)

```
View
  by Small Icon
  by Icon
  by Name
  by Size
  by Kind
  by Label
  by Date
  by Version
  by Comments
```

By Small Icon changes the window view to small icons.

By Icon changes the window view to standard icons.

By Name changes the window to a list view and sorts the items alphabetically by name.

By Size changes the window to a list view and sorts the items by size, with the largest first. If folders aren't set to display their sizes, they are sorted last.

By Kind changes the window to a list view and sorts the items alphabetically by kind (application, folder, document, and so on).

By Label changes the window to a list view and sorts the items by their labels according to the label order in the menu. Items without labels are sorted last.

By Date changes the window to a list view and sorts the items by their modified dates, with the most recent first.

By Version changes the window to a list view and sorts the items according to their version numbers. Items with no version numbers are sorted last.

By Comments changes the window to a list view and sorts the items alphabetically by the comments in the Get Info window.

The Special Menu

The Special menu gives you control over windows, the Trash, disks, and
the Mac itself.

```
┌─────────────────────────┐
│ Special                 │
│  Clean Up Window        │
│  Empty Trash...         │
│ ....................... │
│  Eject Disk       ⌘E    │
│  Erase Disk...          │
│ ....................... │
│  Restart                │
│  Shut Down              │
└─────────────────────────┘
```

Clean Up Window aligns icons in the active window to invisible
grid points. With the Shift key held down, the command is Clean Up
Selection and aligns only selected icons to the grid. With the Option key
held down, the command is Clean Up by (Criteria) with the criteria
being whatever was last used for sorting in a list view in that window. If
the Desktop is active, the command is Clean Up Desktop and loose
Desktop icons align to the grid (Chapter 5).

Empty Trash erases the files in the Trash from a disk. With the
Option key held down, the warning dialog that normally appears before
the Trash is emptied is bypassed. If you have the Trash set for no warning dialog, Option temporarily turns the dialog back on (Chapter 4).

Eject Disk ejects the selected disk, leaving its image on the Desktop
(Chapter 4).

Erase Disk erases the selected disk (Chapters 4 and 14).

Restart restarts the computer without your having to first shut off
the power (Chapter 4).

Shut Down actually turns off the computer on some models after
ejecting any disks that are in drives. On other models, Shut Down does
the final housekeeping for disks in use, ejects floppies, then tells you to
shut the power off (Chapter 4).

The Help Menu

The Help menu is a systemwide menu; its last command changes according to the application you're in. (All commands are covered in this chapter.)

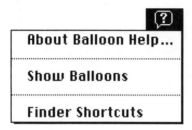

About Balloon Help opens a dialog box with instructions for using the Balloon Help feature.

Show Balloons turns on the Help feature. The command then changes to Hide Balloons so you can turn it off.

Finder Shortcuts opens a window filled with several pages of tips about working on the Desktop.

The Application Menu

The Application menu is a systemwide menu that lets you navigate among opened applications and control window clutter on the screen. The bottom section of the menu lists all open applications. (All commands are covered in Chapter 8.)

Hide Finder hides all the Finder windows from view. This command changes to reflect the current application (Hide Word, Hide MacWrite, Hide SuperPaint, and so on).

Hide Others hides all the windows except for the Finder's (or whatever the current application happens to be).

Show All displays all the windows for all opened applications.

[Application list] lists all the opened applications, with the current one checked.

SUMMARY

Between this chapter and the last, you've learned everything you need to know about the Desktop and how to manage your disks and files. Now it's time to leave the Desktop: The three chapters in the next section will show you the basics of working with applications.

PART III

Working on the Mac

Text and Graphics on the Mac

ABOUT THIS CHAPTER

Almost everything you do with your Macintosh will involve either text (and that includes numbers) or graphics, or both. No matter what program you're working with, the basics of handling text and graphics are standard.

You'll find that the standard interface components covered in Chapters 3 through 5, along with the text- and graphics-handling basics presented in this chapter, will get you going in almost any program on the Mac.

WORKING WITH TEXT

Basics

The basic rule of text handling on the Mac is: *Everything happens at the insertion point.*

The insertion point is the blinking vertical line that appears at the beginning of an empty text document, or anywhere in text that's being edited. It's also sometimes referred to simply as the *cursor*; you'll seldom confuse it with references to the mouse cursor, however, since the contexts are usually very clear.

As you type, letters appear at the insertion point. If you use the Delete key, the insertion point moves backward, erasing text as it goes. If you paste something into a text document, the material is pasted at the insertion point.

```
T|
Ty|
Typ|
Typi|
Typin|
Typing|
```

Letters appear at the insertion point when you type.

```
Delete|
Delet|
Dele|
Del|
De|
D|
```

Using the Delete key erases the letter to the left of the insertion point.

```
Paste|in.
Paste this in.
```

Pasted material appears at the insertion point.

If you want to practice basic text entry and editing techniques but don't have a word processing application, you can use the TeachText application that came on your system disks, or even the Note Pad desk accessory.

Controlling the Insertion Point

Since everything happens at the insertion point, controlling its position lets you edit any part of the text you're working with.

Positioning the insertion point is as simple as clicking the mouse. When you move the mouse cursor within a text area, the cursor changes to the *text*, or *I-beam*, cursor. Put the I-beam where you want to edit the text, and click: The insertion point moves to that spot (see Figure 6-1).

```
┌─────────────────────────────┐
│ clicking in text            │
├─────────────────────────────┤
│ clicking in| text   I       │
└─────────────────────────────┘
```

Figure 6-1. The mouse cursor changes to the I-beam cursor when it's within text; clicking the mouse button leaves the insertion point at the clicked spot.

The insertion point can be placed only within existing text. You can't, for instance, click halfway down a blank window to begin typing. Instead, you have to "type" your way to that spot by pressing Return to move the insertion point there.

Small movements of the insertion point are easier to control by using the arrow keys on the keyboard. The left and right arrows move the insertion point one character backward or forward; the up and down arrows move the insertion point up to the last or down to the next line of text.

The Home, End, Page Up, and Page Down keys on extended keyboards also control the insertion point, although their specific actions depend on the application you're in (see Figure 6-2). Many applications also have special keyboard sequences that move the insertion point by handy increments like words, sentences, or paragraphs.

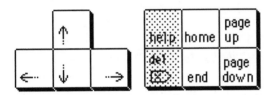

Figure 6-2. You can control the position of the insertion point from the keyboard.

Entering and Editing Text

Entering text is pretty much straightforward typing, *except that* when you reach the end of a line, you don't press the Return key to move down to the next line. The insertion point automatically moves to the next line—if you're in the middle of a word, the entire word is shifted down to the next line. This feature is called *text wrap* (see Figure 6-3).

As on an electric typewriter, you can hold a key down and it will be repeatedly typed.

When you want to start a new paragraph (which is simply moving down to the beginning of the next line before reaching the end of the current one), *that's* when you press Return.

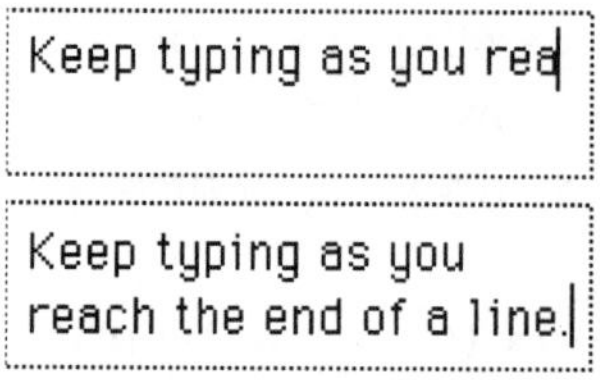

Keep typing as you rea|

Keep typing as you
reach the end of a line.|

Figure 6-3. With text wrap, *you're automatically moved down to the next line* *without pressing Return.*

For simple editing, place the insertion point where you want to change something and then type from there.

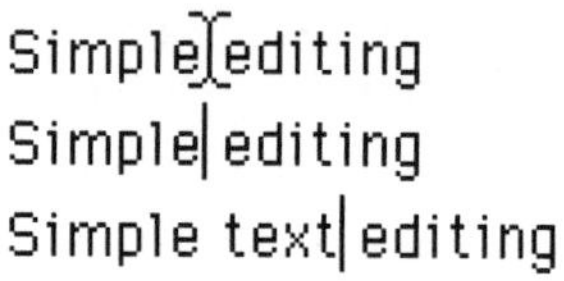

Simple editing
Simple| editing
Simple text| editing

Add text by clicking to place the insertion point and then typing.

You can delete text using the Delete key, which moves the insertion point backward, erasing letters as it goes. Extended keyboards also have a Forward Delete key, which erases letters in front of the insertion point (if the application supports Forward Delete). (See Figure 6-4.)

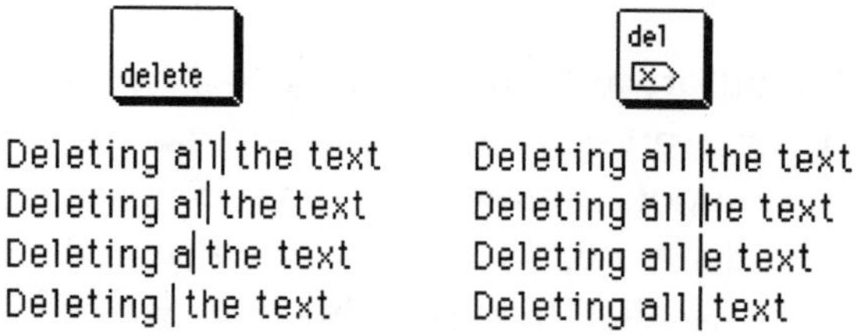

delete	del ⊠▷
Deleting all| the text	Deleting all |the text
Deleting al| the text	Deleting all |he text
Deleting a| the text	Deleting all |e text
Deleting |the text	Deleting all |text

Figure 6-4. The Delete key deletes text behind the cursor; the Forward Delete key *deletes text in front of it.*

SELECTING TEXT

Large editing procedures are done on *selected* text. Although various programs may have their own additional selection techniques, the basics of text selection are the same throughout Mac programs. There are three standard ways to select text: by dragging, double-clicking, or Shift-clicking.

Selected text (like selected icons on the Desktop) is always *highlighted*. On black-and-white systems, highlighted text appears white against black; on color systems, the text remains black and the highlight is in color.

The basic way to select text is to drag across it with the mouse. All the text from the beginning of the drag to the end is highlighted to show that it's selected (see Figure 6-5).

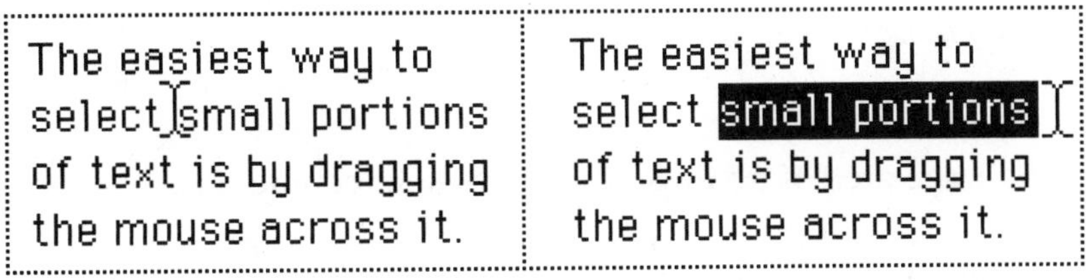

| The easiest way to select small portions of text is by dragging the mouse across it. | The easiest way to select small portions of text is by dragging the mouse across it. |

Figure 6-5. Dragging the mouse's text cursor from before the word small *to after the word* portions *results in all the text in between those points being selected.*

When you drag to select text, you don't have to drag along the path of the text; that is, if you want to select the middle of a paragraph, as shown in Figure 6-6, you don't have to drag to the end of the line and then to the beginning of the next—you simply drag straight from the starting point to the finish. (You can drag backward through the text, too.)

To select a single word, you double-click on it. In some applications, this also selects the trailing space, while in others only the word itself is selected (see Figure 6-7).

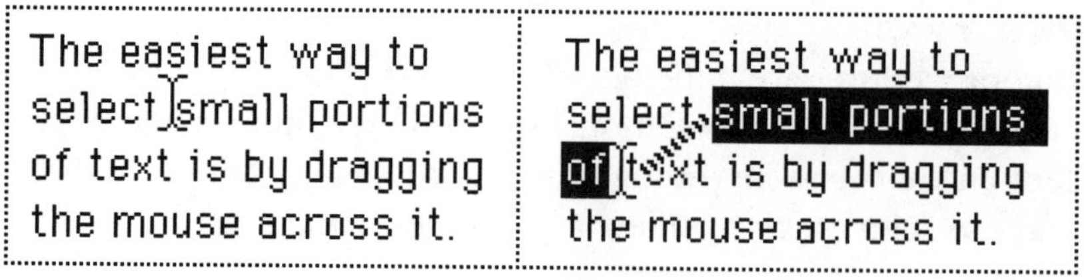

The easiest way to select small portions of text is by dragging the mouse across it.

The easiest way to select small portions of text is by dragging the mouse across it.

Figure 6-6. You don't have to drag along the path of the text to select it.

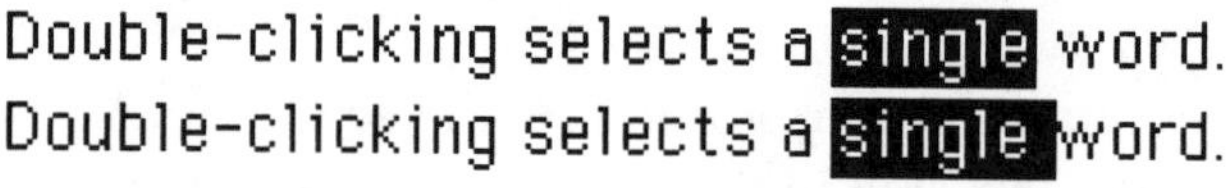

Double-clicking selects a single word.
Double-clicking selects a single word.

Figure 6-7. Double-clicking on text always selects a whole word, but in some applications it selects only the word (top) and in others the selection includes the trailing space (bottom).

To select a large area of text, use the Shift-click technique:

1. Place the insertion point at one end of the section you want to select by clicking.
2. Move to the other end of the section—even if you have to scroll the window to get there.
3. Hold down the Shift key and click again.

Everything between the original click (where the insertion point is) to the Shift-click spot is selected, as shown in Figure 6-8.

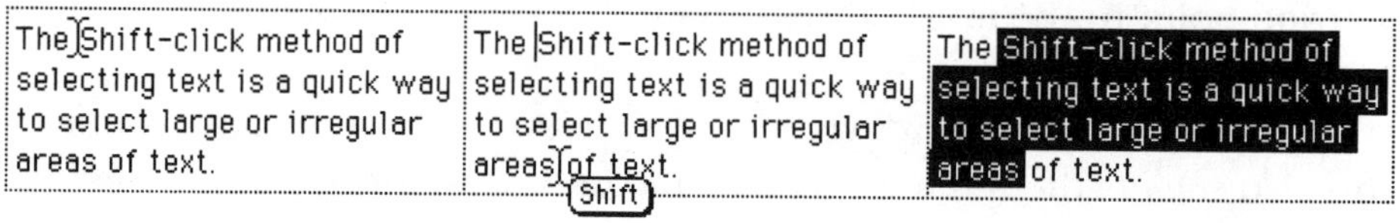

The Shift-click method of selecting text is a quick way to select large or irregular areas of text.

The Shift-click method of selecting text is a quick way to select large or irregular areas of text.
[Shift]

The Shift-click method of selecting text is a quick way to select large or irregular areas of text.

Figure 6-8. Shift-clicking to select text

CHANGING A SELECTION

Shift-clicking is not only a way to make a selection, it's also a way to change a selection. Just as you can Shift-click on the Desktop to add or remove an icon from a selection, you can Shift-click in text to extend or shorten the selection no matter what method was used for the initial selection.

All you have to do is hold down the Shift key and click where you want the selection to end. If you Shift-click beyond the original selection, it's extended to that point; if you Shift-click within the selection, it's shortened to that point (see Figure 6-9).

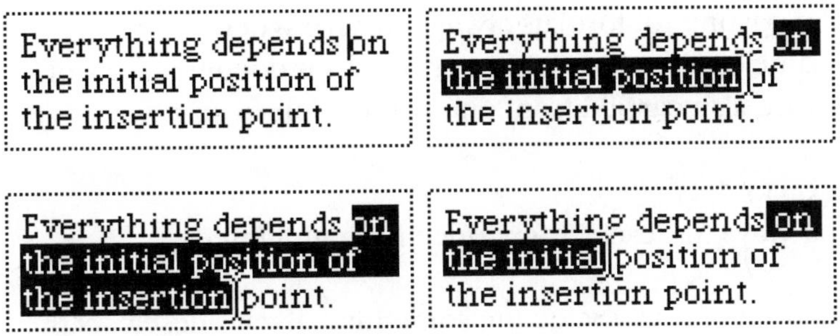

Figure 6-9. Top: the original position of the insertion point and a Shift-click selection. Bottom left: a Shift-click to extend the selection; Bottom right: a Shift-click to shorten the same selection.

WORKING WITH SELECTIONS

Once you have an area of text selected, whatever would normally happen at the insertion point affects the entire selection instead:

- Typing replaces the selection with whatever you're typing.

- The Paste command replaces the selection with the current contents of the Clipboard.

- The Cut or Copy command from the Edit menu places the selection on the Clipboard.

- The Delete key deletes the selection without placing it on the Clipboard.

- The Clear command (if the application provides one in the Edit menu) also erases the selection without placing it on the Clipboard.

- Character formats (fonts, styles, and sizes as described later in this chapter) are applied to the entire selection.

When there's text on the Clipboard from a Cut or Copy command, pasting places it into the document at the insertion point (or over the current selection), moving all the text after the insertion point to make room for the pasted text. Whether or not any formats (like bold text) survive the copy-paste procedure depends on where you copied from and where you're pasting to; formats always survive when you're working in the same application (within or between documents), and many times they are also carried from one application to another.

DESELECTING TEXT

There are several ways to deselect text once it's highlighted:

- Select another area of text. (Selecting something always deselects the previous selection, whether you're in text or on the Desktop.)

- Click anywhere in the text to deselect the selection and position the insertion point at the same time.

- Use the left or right arrow key. This usually deselects the selection and places the insertion point at the beginning of the selected area (if you use the left arrow) or the end of the selected area (if you use the right arrow), although some applications don't follow this convention. Some applications let you use the up and down arrows to deselect text, while others ignore those keys when there's an active selection.

- If you have an extended keyboard and the application you're using supports the Home, End, Page Up, and Page Down keys, using one of those keys usually deselects the selected text and places the insertion point at the beginning or end of the page or document.

WHERE TEXT EDITING WORKS

The basic Mac text editing techniques—typing, deleting, using the arrow keys, and dragging, double-clicking, and Shift-clicking for selections—work almost anywhere you can type. So, while it's no surprise that these techniques work in a word processor, you'll find that they also work in desk accessories like the Note Pad, on the Desktop when you're editing file names, and even in dialogs that have text boxes.

Applying Character Formats

Character formats are the characteristics you assign to text in a Macintosh document: the font, size, and style of the letters. Some applications have menus for each of these options. Many have a separate Font menu and combine sizes and styles into another menu that goes by various names. Other applications combine all three formatting options in one menu, or scatter some of them in other menus, or even have all of the formatting combined into one dialog box.

FONTS

Fonts are basically typefaces, the design of the characters you're typing. The fonts listed in a Font menu are the ones that are installed in your system. Figure 6-10 shows the basic fonts that come with your Mac, but there are thousands of different fonts available.

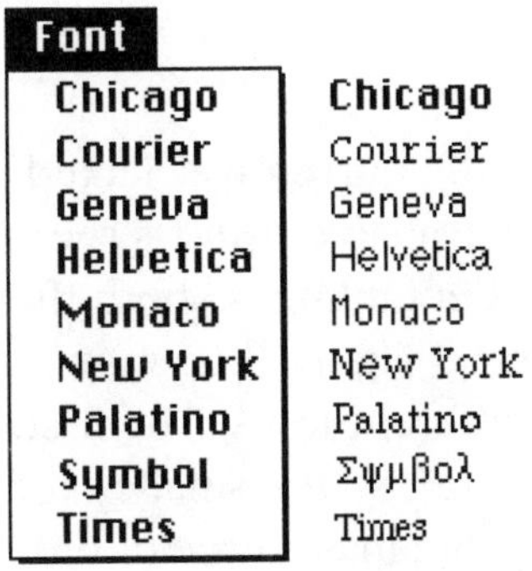

Font	
Chicago	Chicago
Courier	Courier
Geneva	Geneva
Helvetica	Helvetica
Monaco	Monaco
New York	New York
Palatino	Palatino
Symbol	Σψμβολ
Times	Times

Figure 6-10.   A standard font menu and font samples

SIZES

The sizes used for text are *point* sizes. Each point is ¹⁄₇₂ of an inch, not coincidentally the size of a single dot on the Mac screen. The sizes that appear in a Size menu depend on the application you're using. Some give a limited list of font sizes, some are more thorough, and some even have an *Other* command so you can specify a size that's not listed in the menu (see Figure 6-11).

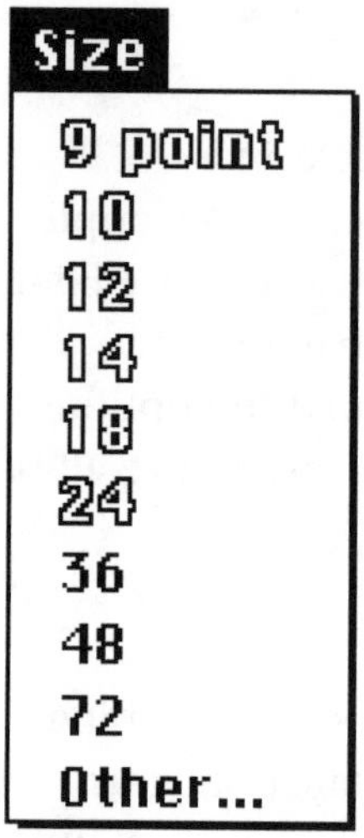

Size

9 point
10
12
14
18
24
36
48
72
Other...

Figure 6-11. Different applications provide different lists of point sizes in the menu.

When a size is outlined in a menu, that means the currently selected font is available in that size. Using a size that's not available distorts the font on the screen, but it may print out correctly, depending on both the type of font and the kind of printer that you're using. Figure 6-12 shows 10-point, 12-point, and 24-point samples of two different fonts. The first, Monaco, is available in only 9-point and 12-point sizes, so the smaller and larger samples are both distorted; New York, available in all three of the sample sizes, is not distorted in any of the samples.

Size

9 point
10
12
14
18
24

Monaco   New York

Monaco   New York

Monaco   New York

Size

9 point
10
12
14
18
24

Figure 6-12.   The look of the Size menu changes depending on the font you've chosen, and the look of the font at different sizes depends on what's available.

STYLES

The standard styles used in Style menus are Bold, Italic, Underline, Outline, and Shadow; the commands themselves usually appear in those styles in the menu. Each of these styles is a toggle command, so if Bold is already selected and you select it again, the Bold is turned off. You can tell which styles are currently in use by seeing which are checked in the menu. The styles are not mutually exclusive, so you can turn them on in any combination: ***bold italic***, *italic underline*, and so on (see Figure 6-13).

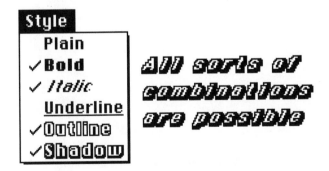

Style

Plain
✓ **Bold**
✓ *Italic*
Underline
✓ Outline
✓ Shadow

Figure 6-13.   Styles currently in use are checked in the menu.

The only style command that is not a toggle is one that removes all the styles from text. It goes by various names in different programs, but the most common names are Plain, Plain Text, and Normal Text. Choosing one of these commands removes formatting from text and unchecks all the other styles in the menu.

APPLYING THE FORMATS

You can apply character formats to text in one of two ways: before you type, or afterward. If you want to apply formats before you type, choose the font, size, and style you want from the appropriate menus and then start (or continue) typing. Everything you type from that point on has the new characteristics (see Figure 6-14).

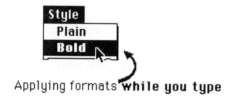

Applying formats while you type

Figure 6-14.   Selecting a format applies it to everything you type afterward.

If you're a good typist and there are keyboard commands for style options, it's usually easier to type the style changes as you go along, especially when you're applying them to only a single word or phrase (see Figure 6-15).

Using keyboard formatting

Figure 6-15.   Typing formatting commands is sometimes easier than using the menu.

To apply formats after the text is entered, go back and select the text you want changed and then choose the font, size, or style from the menu; the formatting is applied to only the selected text (see Figure 6-16).

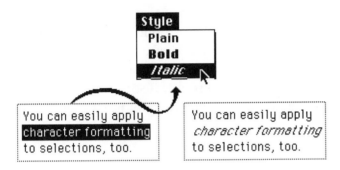

Figure 6-16. Formats are applied to selections.

Paragraph Formats

Just as you can apply special formats to characters in text, you can also apply overall formatting to paragraphs of text. Most word processors consider a paragraph selected if the insertion point or any selection is within the paragraph.

The way you actually apply the formats depends on the application, but basic paragraph formats consist of the following:

▪ *Margins* for a paragraph are almost always measured from the right and left *page margins*, which are set separately. You might have a 1-inch margin all around the page; if you have a 1-inch left margin for a paragraph, the text actually starts 2 inches from the edge of the page. Figure 6-17 shows a page with four paragraphs; the dotted line is the paper margin set at 1 inch. The second and third paragraphs (the first paragraph is the title at the top) have margins flush with the paper margins: The paragraph margins are zero. The last paragraph has a left margin of 1½ inches, so it starts 2½ inches from the edge of the paper. The right margin of the last paragraph is also 2½ inches from the edge of the page, but it's measured from the *left page margin*, so it's considered to be set at 6 inches.

■ *Alignment,* or *justification,* is how the lines of text align with the left and right paragraph margins. Text can be left or right justified, centered, or fully justified. In the sample page shown in Figure 6-17, the top paragraph is centered; the middle two are left-aligned, which leaves their right edges jagged; and the final paragraph is fully justified, with the text lining up along both the left and right paragraph margins.

Figure 6-17.   Paragraph formats

■ *First line indent* is a defined property of a paragraph so that a new paragraph is automatically indented without your pressing the Tab key. The first lines of the middle paragraphs in Figure 6-17 have half-inch indents; the last paragraph has no indent for the first line.

■ *Line spacing* is the space between the lines in a paragraph. Most applications give you a choice of at least single, double, and space-and-a-half line spacing. The actual size of the space between the lines depends on the size of the text you're using. In Figure 6-17, the second paragraph is double-spaced and all the others are single-spaced.

- *Paragraph spacing*, available in many word processors, adds extra space before and/or after each paragraph without your having to type extra Returns.

- *Tab stops* are the places the cursor moves to when you use the Tab key. Many applications provide up to four kinds of tabs: left (standard), right, center, and decimal. In Figure 6-18, the dotted lines show where the tab stops were set for each column of numbers.

14.2	14.2	14.2	14.2
273.5	273.5	273.5	273.5
45.71	45.71	45.71	45.71
7.956	7.956	7.956	7.956

Figure 6-18.   Left, right, centered, and decimal tab alignments

Typing Special Characters

A regular typewriter gives you two characters for each key: Holding down the Shift key lets you access the second set of characters, the uppercase alphabet and various symbols.

The Mac, of course, is much better than a typewriter, so it gives you access to two more character sets. You get to these characters by using the Option key, and the Shift and Option keys together.

The exact characters you get with Option and Shift-Option can vary from one font to the next, but the basic characters and arrangements are pretty standardized.

The four character sets are shown in Figures 6-19 through 6-22.

You can view all the characters available for any font by using the Key Caps desk accessory that comes with your System (see Chapter 10).

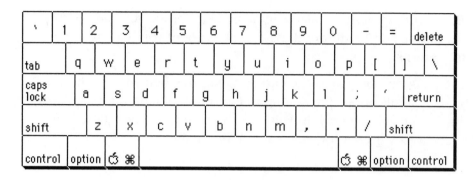

Figure 6-19. The unshifted character set

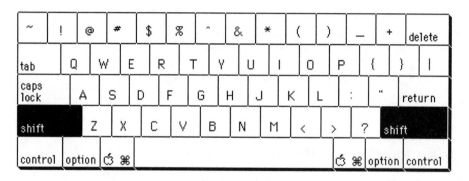

Figure 6-20. The shifted character set

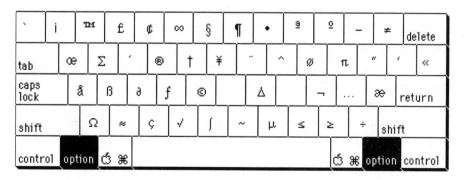

Figure 6-21. The Option character set

Figure 6-22. The Shift-Option character set

USING ACCENT MARKS

The Option and Shift-Option character sets include some accented letters, like ç and å. But standard accent marks are also available as separate characters so that you can place them over any letters you wish. Putting the accents and the letters together is easy, but the method is far from obvious.

If you type Option-e, nothing appears on the screen, although according to the keyboard charts, you should get an acute accent mark (´). The reason nothing happens is that the accent mark is meant to go over a letter; when you actually type the letter, both the accent and the letter appear. When you type Option-e, you get nothing, but if you follow it by another e, you'll get é.

The following accents, produced by the key combinations noted, need a letter typed before they'll appear on your screen. (If you want the accent itself, just type a space instead of a letter.)

Acute accent	Option-e	´	(é)
Grave accent	Option-`	`	(è)
Circumflex	Option-i	^	(ô)
Umlaut	Option-u	¨	(ü)
Tilde	Option-n	~	(ñ)

Quickies

▪ The Caps Lock key on the Mac differs from a typewriter's shift lock in that Caps Lock affects only the alphabet characters—punctuation marks and numbers are still entered as unshifted characters (so you get 4 instead of $) when you use their keys.

▪ The Shift key alters a text selection even if you drag instead of click.

▪ Using Shift to change a text selection extends (or shortens) a selection in the unit of the original selection. So, if you double-click to select a whole word and then click or drag with the Shift key held down, the selection will always include whole words. If you're in an application that lets you select sentences or paragraphs as a unit, Shift-clicking selects entire sentences or paragraphs afterward.

▪ When you have a text selection that's a combination of styles or sizes, nothing will be checked in the menus as the current style or size. But if you're working in an application that gives you a dialog box with checkboxes in it to represent styles and your selection has more than one style, the checkboxes involved will be filled with gray. Clicking on a gray checkbox changes it from gray to checked to unchecked and to gray again; in this way you can apply the style to the entire selection, take it off from the entire selection, or return the selection to its mixed state. In Figure 6-23, starting with the selection at the top, both checkboxes are gray; altering them to on or off gives the results shown.

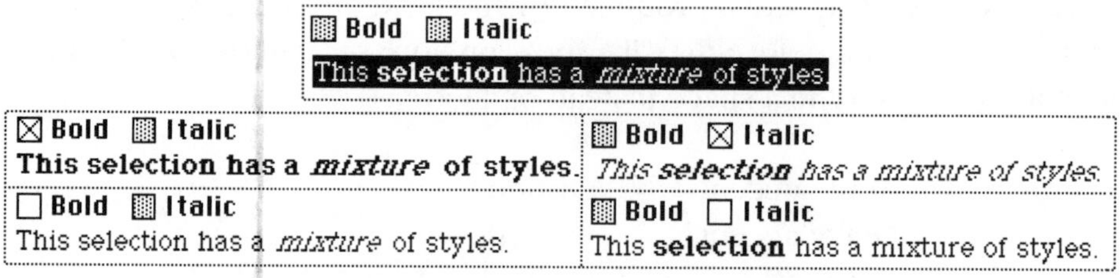

Figure 6-23. Checkboxes are usually on or off, but a gray state can indicate that a description applies to some parts of the selection and not others.

Also See...

- The speed at which the insertion point blinks, how long a delay there is from the initial press of a key until the character is repeated, and how fast repeated characters are typed are all settings that you can control. See Chapter 11.

- Chapter 11 discusses setting the highlight color.

- Print distortion, fonts, and printers are covered in Chapters 15 and 16.

- Chapter 9 explains how to install fonts in your System file.

WORKING WITH GRAPHICS

Basics

There are two basic types of graphics used on the map: *bit-mapped* and *object-oriented*.

Bit-mapped graphics use individual dots to create images. If you make a circle, the Mac sees it only as a series of dots that have no special relationship to each other. If you make a square that overlaps the circle, that's just some more dots—the graphics program doesn't see two distinct shapes. If you try to separate the two images, as in Figure 6-24, you'll find that the "obscured" portions of a shape don't even exist.

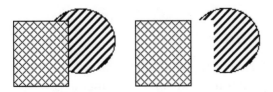

Figure 6-24. Bit-mapped images don't exist as independent shapes.

In Macintosh graphics, this dot-by-dot approach is referred to as *painting,* because the original bit-mapped graphics program for the Mac was named MacPaint. Standard bit-mapped graphics on the Mac are 72 dots per inch, the resolution of the screen.

Object-oriented graphics treat items as discreet objects. If you make a circle, and then an overlapping square, they each retain their individual identities. If you move an object, you'll find that the objects beneath it are intact; you can even change the relative positioning of the objects, bringing to the front one that was behind (see Figure 6-25). You can change certain properties of an object (its line thickness, or fill pattern, or overall proportions, for instance) easily and quickly.

Figure 6-25. Object-oriented graphics exist as independent shapes.

In Macintosh graphics, this kind of art is called *drawing,* because (you guessed it) the first object-oriented graphics program for the Mac was named MacDraw. Standard Mac drawing programs use the collection of graphic-generating routines called *QuickDraw* that is built into the Mac's ROM.

Creating Bit-Mapped Graphics

Although there are several popular painting programs for the Mac, they have many standard features in common. (You can experiment with the painting tools in the HyperCard program that came with your Mac.)

Most painting programs have a palette of tools to select from. You click on the tool, your mouse cursor changes to the tool shape, and you drag the mouse in the document window to make your pictures (see Figure 6-26).

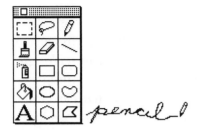

Figure 6-26. *HyperCard's painting tools, and dragging the Pencil to make a picture*

Tools such as shape-makers (oval, rectangle, and so on) and paint brushes and buckets use patterns as the "paint" on black-and-white systems, and a combination of patterns and colors on color systems. Figure 6-27 shows a circle filled with checkered "paint" that was selected from a palette of patterns. Because the patterns in painted objects become part of the overall bit-mapped paint image, you can't change them except by painting over them or erasing all of their dots.

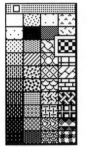

Figure 6-27. *The pattern selected in the palette is the one used when you paint a shape.*

Selecting Bit-Mapped Graphics

There are two standard ways to select bit-mapped graphics within a painting program. The first is to use a tool called the *selection rectangle*. Dragging a rectangle around any part of a picture selects everything within the rectangle—even the seemingly "empty" space that's around the image but within the rectangle (see Figure 6-28). A selection is indicated by the moving dashed lines surrounding the selection. (Because they're like the lights flashing in sequence on a movie marquee, this is sometimes called the *selection marquee*.)

Figure 6-28.   Dragging a selection rectangle

When you move the rectangle selection, or copy it to the Clipboard and paste it somewhere else, the white area is part of the image and will obscure anything behind it if it's placed over another bit-mapped image (see Figure 6-29).

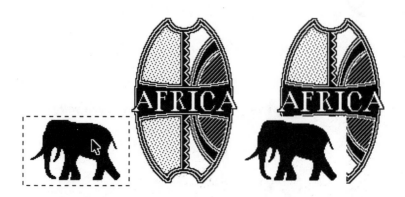

Figure 6-29.   Moving a rectangle selection ruins part of the background image.

The second standard bit-mapped selection technique is to use a tool called the *lasso*. When you encircle an image with the lasso and release the mouse button, a line is drawn back to the starting spot and then tightens up around the picture, excluding any white space outside the image. The lassoed image usually has dashed lines moving around its perimeter (see Figure 6-30) and doesn't obscure the bit-mapped image behind it (see Figure 6-31).

Figure 6-30. When you let go of the mouse button, the lasso line is drawn to the original spot (bottom, center) and then tightens up around the image.

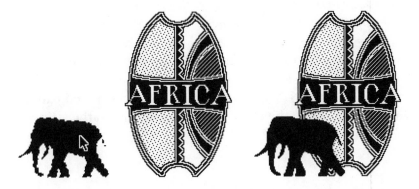

Figure 6-31. Moving a lassoed selection doesn't affect the background image.

Creating Object-Oriented Graphics

Object-oriented drawing programs also provide a palette of tools for you to work with, although they are always fewer in number than painting tools. Figure 6-32, for instance, shows the painting tool palette and the drawing tool palette from SuperPaint, a program that provides both painting and drawing capabilities. (HyperCard doesn't have draw capabilities.)

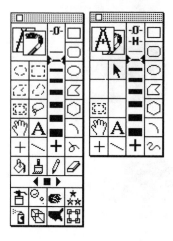

Figure 6-32.   SuperPaint's tool palettes: There are many more paint tools (left) than draw tools (right).

But what basic object-oriented graphics may lack in variety, they make up for in ease of editing and higher-quality printed output.

Since draw objects are defined as objects with certain attributes, such as a 2-pixel-wide frame and a checkered fill, you can redefine the properties without having to alter the image dot by dot. If, for instance, you make a checkered circle in a draw program (like the one shown for the paint program in Figure 6-27), you can change the checkered pattern to stripes simply by selecting the circle and then clicking on the stripe pattern in the palette.

Even if you change the size of an object, it retains its other definitions. Figure 6-33 shows checkered circles in paint and draw figures. They're indistinguishable at their original sizes but when you shrink or enlarge them, the bit-mapped image is distorted while the object image retains its definitions for line width and fill pattern.

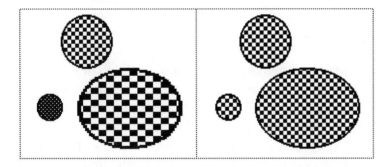

Figure 6-33.   A paint image distorts when you shrink or enlarge it (left); a draw object retains its attributes when you change its size (right).

Selecting Object-Oriented Graphics

Selecting an object in a drawing program is much like selecting an icon on the Desktop: You click on it.

Instead of inverting like a selected icon, however, the selected draw object gets "handles"—little boxes on the outer corners of the rectangular area that surrounds the object. The handles are used to change the size and shape of the object as well as to indicate that it's selected (see Figure 6-34).

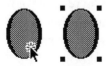

Figure 6-34.   Clicking on an object selects it, and its "handles" appear.

Selecting multiple objects is also like selecting icons: You can Shift-click to select them, or you can use the mouse pointer to drag a rectangle around the ones you want.

PostScript Graphics

PostScript is a special "page description" language from Adobe, Inc., that is used by many laser printers to describe the text and graphics to be printed on a page.

While basic drawing programs use the drawing routines stored in the Mac's ROM to describe the objects to be printed, some graphics programs (Adobe's Illustrator and Aldus's Freehand are the most popular) send PostScript descriptions to the printer instead. Because of this, PostScript graphics can take advantage of the high resolution of whatever printer you're using and the images can contain perfectly smooth curves and very fine lines. (Most of the pictures in Chapter 2 are PostScript images.) You can work with a PostScript-output graphics program on any Mac, but the figures won't print correctly unless you use a printer that understands PostScript.

These programs still take an object-oriented approach onscreen, however: Items that you draw are discrete objects that can be easily selected, manipulated, and redefined.

Pasting Graphics

What you can do to a selected image depends on what type of graphic it is and what program you're using. But, as everywhere else on the Mac, a selected item can always be cut or copied to the Clipboard.

When you paste an image into a graphics document, what happens to it still depends on what kind of image it is and where you're pasting it.

If you paste a bit-mapped image into a drawing program, it becomes a *bit-mapped object* and can be selected by just clicking on it (instead of using a selection rectangle or lasso). A selected bit-mapped object gets handles like a regular object, which you can use to change its proportions (usually distorting it in the process), but you can't change its patterns the way you can with a standard object. Pasting a draw object into a paint program changes it into a bit-mapped image.

Pasting a paint or draw image into a PostScript graphics program doesn't turn the image into a PostScript image, however; if the program accepts the image at all, it will probably let you use it only as a template for tracing the *real* PostScript image. PostScript graphics are not usually copied to the Clipboard when you use the Copy command, and pasting an image that you created in a PostScript graphics program into something that can't handle PostScript often leaves you with a bit-mapped image of the original.

Combining Text and Graphics

Because you can copy text or graphics to the Clipboard, you can usually combine text and graphics in the same document even if the application you're working in doesn't let you create both text and graphics.

When you paste graphics into a text program, the picture is handled as a single object no matter how it started out—as a bit-mapped image, an object, or a group of objects. Most word processors will let you scale the graphic, or crop it, but no other adjustments are usually available.

The graphic that you paste appears at the insertion point. Many programs simply insert the graphic as if it were a very large text character and make it part of the current paragraph; other applications insist on separating graphics from text paragraphs (see Figure 6-35).

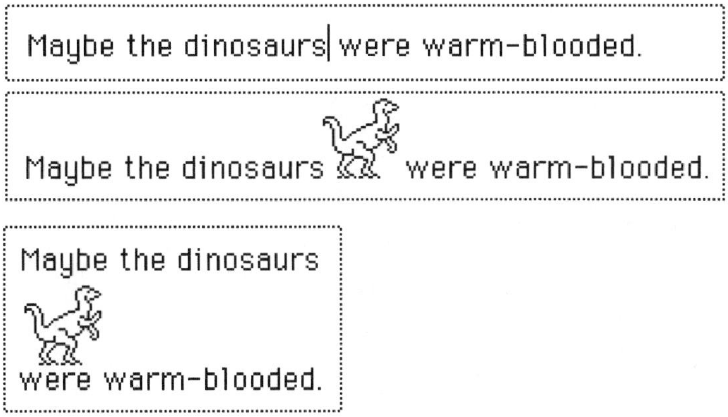

Figure 6-35. With the insertion point as shown at the top, some text applications will insert a pasted graphic within the line (middle), while others separate text from graphics (bottom).

Text is not usually pasted into a graphics program, although most graphics programs will accept it. In a drawing program, text is usually handled inside an object called a *text block,* and you can edit the text in the block as if you were using a mini word processor (see Figure 6-36).

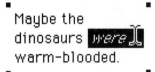

Figure 6-36.   A block of text in a draw program can be edited.

If you paste text into a paint program, though, the letters become just a series of dots that you can alter only by changing the dots—they're no longer letters. Figure 6-37 shows bit-mapped text being erased.

Figure 6-37.   Text in a bit-mapped program becomes part of the bitmap.

Graphics Formats

When you begin to import or exchange graphics files between programs (instead of using the Clipboard), you'll find that there are some standard graphics formats used by many programs.

Each program has its own "native" format—a MacDraw program creates MacDraw files, for instance—but many also give you the option to save in one of the generic graphics formats:

- *Paint* or *PNTG* is the standard MacPaint-type graphics format. It's black and white, 72 dots per inch, and fits on a standard 8½ -by-11 page.

- *PICT* (for picture) is a standard Mac file format that contains all of the instructions the Mac needs to redraw the picture. PICT images can be bit-mapped images, objects, or a combination of the two. PICT files can even store color and grayscale images.

- *TIFF* stands for *tagged image file format* and was originally intended as an exchange standard between different kinds of computers. TIFF files are bit-mapped images, but they can be of any size and resolution, and they can be black and white, color, or grayscale. Image scanners that read photographs and other pictures into the Mac usually store the images as TIFF files.

- *EPS* is *encapsulated PostScript*. An EPS file contains PostScript information for the printer combined ("encapsulated") with information for the Mac's screen display.

CLIP ART

The Mac is such a graphics-oriented machine that soon after it was introduced it inspired the electronic equivalent of the graphics industry's clip art collections—pictures that you can cut out and use in your own documents. Although there's clip art available in most graphics formats, the bulk of it is available as Paint or EPS.

Bit-mapped clip art is generally more textural than EPS, since so many patterns can be used and dot-by-dot control is available. Figure 6-38, and the African shield, elephant, and dinosaurs shown in this chapter are from a bit-mapped clip art package from Dubl-Click Software. EPS graphics generate high-quality, smooth-lined images that are preferred by most graphics professionals. Figure 6-39 is a sampling of EPS clip art from 3G Graphics.

Figure 6-38.   Bit-mapped clip art

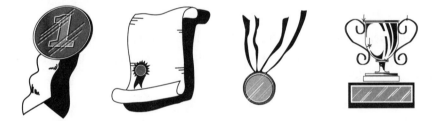

Figure 6-39.   EPS clip art

Screen Pictures

The Mac has a built-in camera (of sorts) that allows you to take a picture of your screen at any time—a *screen shot*.

Pressing Command-Shift-3 creates a PICT format file on your Desktop that contains a picture of the Mac screen, including the menu bar. You can't take the picture if the mouse button is held down (which means that you can't get a picture of a menu while it's open).

The document that's created is titled *Picture 1,* and subsequent screen shots are numbered sequentially. Since it's a PICT file, you can open the document in any program that lets you use PICT files.

Picture 1

The picture files are TeachText documents, so you can also open them in TeachText, Apple's bare-bones word processor that comes with your system. Although you can't alter the image in TeachText, you can select any part of it by dragging a rectangle with the mouse cursor and then copy the selection to the Clipboard. Once you have it on the Clipboard, you can paste it into a graphics program to manipulate.

Also See . . .

- The issue of graphics and printing resolution is covered in Chapter 16.

SUMMARY

Although each Macintosh application has its own special features and ways to handle text and graphics, the basics presented in this chapter provide the core routines for almost every program. And, now that you have these basics covered, the next two chapters introduce you to handling the applications themselves and the documents that they create.

CHAPTER 7

Applications and Documents

ABOUT THIS CHAPTER

The basics of using an application (opening and closing it) and handling documents within it (opening, closing, and saving them) are generally the same no matter which programs you're using. And once you know the basics, you can get up and running in almost any Mac program with very little effort.

APPLICATIONS

Basics

Programs on the Macintosh that let you create or do things are called *applications;* the files that they create are called *documents*. A word processor is an application; the memo, or the Great American Novel, that you write with it is a document.

As explained in Chapter 2, *file* is the general term used to refer to a discrete collection of information on a disk. Both applications and documents are files, although the word is more often used to refer to a document. *Program* is a term used interchangeably with *application.*

Since you usually access a document through the application that created it, there's a common misperception among beginners that a document is part of the program, somehow stored within the application itself. But the documents you create are saved as completely independent files on your disk.

On the Desktop, an application's icon and the icons of the documents it creates are usually related visually; some samples are shown in Figure 7-1.

Figure 7-1. Most document icons are visually related to their application icons.

Installing Applications on a Hard Drive

While some applications are single files of reasonably small size, others can be quite large and even include all sorts of support files (like dictionaries for word processors) that go along with the application. When you buy a program to use on your Mac, you get anywhere from one to a half-dozen floppy disks holding the information you need. An application and its support files have to be copied to your hard drive so that you can use them from there.

Many multidisk programs come with their own "installer" programs. You insert one floppy into the drive, double-click on the Installer icon that's on that disk, and then follow the onscreen instructions for inserting the other disks. There's always an installer for a program that's larger than 800K; since it won't fit on a standard disk, it has to be split among two or more disks, and the installer program puts the pieces back together on your drive. The instruction manual that comes with each program will indicate whether or not there are special installation procedures for you to follow.

When there's no special installation program, you manually copy the application and any of its support files by dragging them from the floppy disk to your hard drive. You should avoid dragging the System Folder that might be on the application's floppy disk over to your hard drive.

This is the basic procedure you should follow:

1. Create a folder on your hard drive for the application and its support files. (Most applications want their support files in the same folder as the application; some want them in the System Folder. You'll have to check the instructions that come with the application itself.)

2. Insert the floppy with the application on it, and open the disk so that you can see the contents.

3. Select the items you need from the floppy's window and drag them to the folder on your hard drive (see Figure 7-2).

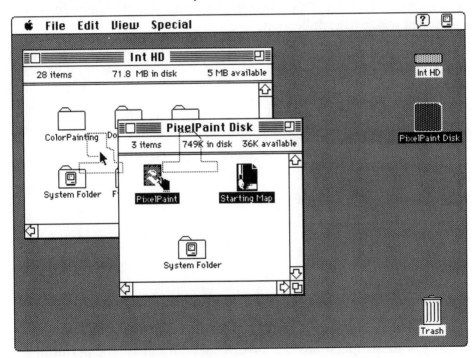

Figure 7-2.   Drag only the files you need from the master disk to the hard drive.

Although dragging the floppy disk icon itself automatically creates a folder on your hard drive and copies the disk's contents into it, this procedure also often causes a serious problem—that's how an extra System Folder can sneak onto your hard drive, leading to unexplained system crashes.

Opening and Closing Applications

To use an application, you *start* it, *run* it, *open* it, or *launch* it—the terms are interchangeable. There are lots of ways you can open an application:

▪ Double-click on the application icon on the Desktop.

▪ Select the application icon on the Desktop and choose Open from the File menu.

▪ Double-click on the icon of any document that belongs to the application you want to open. This opens the application and then opens that document inside the application.

▪ Drag the icon of a document into the icon of an application, as shown in Figure 7-3.

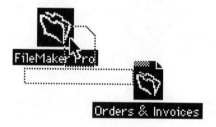

Figure 7-3. You can open an application by dragging a document icon into the application icon.

▪ Choose the application from the Apple menu if you've installed it there.

Any of these operations that involve an icon can also be performed with the alias of the icon.

Closing, or *quitting*, an application is very straightforward: choose Quit from the File menu.

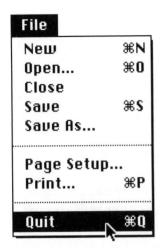

If you use the Quit command and you haven't saved the work you've done in the application, you'll get a dialog box asking you if you want to save the document.

Quickies

▪ You can set any application or document to open automatically when the computer starts up by placing it, or its alias, into the Startup Items folder in the System Folder.

Also See . . .

▪ Chapter 9 explains how to use the Startup Items folder and how to install items in the Apple menu.

▪ Sometimes when you try to open an application, you'll get a dialog that tells you there's not enough memory to open it. Chapter 13 deals with memory issues.

HANDLING DOCUMENTS

Basics

Working with documents in a Mac application is much like real paper-work. If you're going to type a letter in the nonelectronic world, for instance, you put a piece of paper in the typewriter, type on it, take it out of the typewriter, and perhaps file it away in a folder in a file cabinet—you can always take it out later to look at it or add to it.

Disks are like file cabinets—they hold all your work, and even store it in folders. In fact, the analogy is so apt that the commands you use to manipulate documents are in a menu named *File*.

While each application has its own File menu with its own special commands, most include certain standard commands as the core of the File menu (see Figure 7-4). In the first section of the menu, you'll find the commands that let you handle documents and the "file cabinet" that's your disk. The New command gives you your blank piece of paper; Open lets you take out a document that you've worked on before. Close removes the document from the screen, while Save and Save As let you specify the name of the document and where you want it filed away.

Figure 7-4. The core commands of the File menu

Creating a Document

Most applications start with an empty window—a blank document. (When you're working in an application, *document* is just about synonymous with *window*.) If there isn't a window to work in, or if you've used the original one and want to start a new one, use New from the application's File menu.

The window that opens when you choose New, or when you start an application, is named *Untitled* and it remains that way until you save the document to the disk and give it a name.

Some applications—databases in particular, but some others as well—force you to name a new document before you get a window to work in.

Handling Multiple Documents

Most applications let you open more than one document at a time—which means that you'll have more than one window open for that application. The basic rules of window handling as described in Chapter 3 apply to multiple windows within an application: The active window, with its striped title bar, is always on top, and clicking in an exposed part of an inactive window activates it, as shown in Figures 7-5 and 7-6.

Many applications provide a Window menu that lists all the opened documents; choosing one from the menu brings it to the top of the pile.

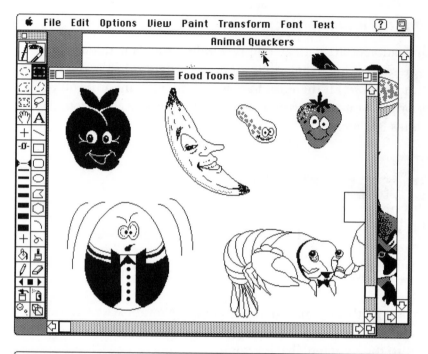

Figures 7-5 and 7-6. Clicking in any exposed part of a background window activates the window.

Saving, Closing, and Opening Documents

As long as you're working on a document, everything you do in it is contained in RAM—the portion of memory that's cleared when you shut off the computer. In order to have all your work available at a later time, you have to put the document onto the disk, with the Save command.

File	
New	⌘N
Open...	⌘O
Close	
Save	⌘S
Save As...	

The Save dialog that appears (it's covered in detail in the next section, Directory Dialogs) lets you name your document and decide where to save it—on what disk and in what folder.

Once you've named your document and saved it, you can keep working on it, adding to or editing what you've done so far. But all those changes are stored only in memory and you have to specifically save them to the disk if you want to keep them. Using the Save command again doesn't open the dialog box—it just automatically saves the changes to the original document.

USING SAVE AS

When you want to save your document—edited or not—under a different name, or in a different place, use Save As.

File	
New	⌘N
Open...	⌘O
Close	
Save	⌘S
Save As...	

This opens the same dialog box that the Save command initially uses—but it very conveniently includes the current name of the document. You can save the document under the same name in another location, or you can make a minor change in the name to reflect the changes you made in the document. If, for instance, your original document is *Picture-Version1*, you can just change the final character to name the edited version *Picture-Version2*.

Using Save As creates a new document on the disk—the version you saved before remains where (and how) it was.

DOCUMENT NAMES

You can name your document anything you want, using up to 31 characters (counting spaces) in the name.

The only character you can't use in a file's name is the colon (:). The colon is used by the Mac when it keeps track of a file's *pathname*—the name of the file and all the folders that it's in and the disk that it's on. So, you may think your file's name is *Monday's Memo*, but the Mac knows it as *HD40:Business:Memos:Monday's Memo*. If you forget and try to use a colon in a file name, nothing drastic happens. Some applications just replace the colon with a space or a hyphen; others give you an alert telling you that you can't use the colon.

Capital letters don't count when it comes to file names—the Mac sees *MY MEMO, my memo,* and *My Memo* as the same name.

DUPLICATE NAMES

You don't have to worry about wiping out an existing document if you inadvertently use the same name again. When you try to save a document into a folder that already contains a document with that name, you'll get an alert that looks something like Figure 7-7.

If you truly want to save over the existing document, you can click *Replace* and the current document replaces the existing one. Clicking *Cancel* lets you name it something else.

Documents with the same name can peacefully co-exist on your disk as long as they're in separate folders, but a descriptive, unique name for each document makes things less confusing.

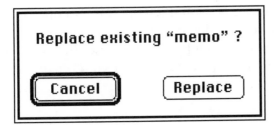

Figure 7-7. The Mac keeps you from replacing a file by mistake.

CLOSING A DOCUMENT

When you've saved a document and you're finished working with it, you close it; this is a simple matter of choosing Close from the File menu or clicking in the window's close box.

If you haven't saved the document at all, or if you haven't saved the most recent changes to it, you'll get an alert, like the one shown in Figure 7-8, that gives you a chance to save it before the window closes.

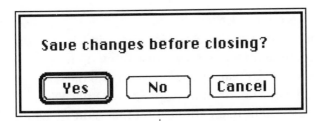

Figure 7-8. You'll get a dialog like this if you try to close a document without saving it first.

This basic "save changes" dialog gives you three options. *Yes* opens the Save dialog if you've never saved the document, or it simply saves the changes to the original if you've saved it before. *No* closes the document without saving it or the most recent changes to it. *Cancel* closes the alert dialog and cancels the Close command so that you can go back to the document.

OPENING A DOCUMENT
The Open command lets you open a document that was previously saved to the disk.

The Open dialog (covered in detail in the next section, Directory Dialogs) that appears in response to the Open command lets you find the file you want to open.

When a document is opened inside an application, the file on the disk isn't affected—a *copy* of the document is placed into memory and the original file isn't altered until you use the Save command to save the changes you make.

OPENING "FOREIGN" DOCUMENTS
Some applications can open documents created in other, similar applications. Sometimes the compatible documents will just show up in the application's Open dialog, although usually the program will have a special command like Open Any File, or Import, or Show Other Files.

If you want to open a document in an application that didn't create it and you can't see the document in the Open dialog, you can try this Desktop procedure: Drag the icon of the document into the icon of the application. If the file is compatible enough with the application, it will open.

Quickies

▪ There are some applications—like Apple's HyperCard, and many databases—that save your information automatically without your having to use a Save command.

▪ When a document name is too long to fit in a dialog box list, the letters in the name are compressed so more of the title can squeeze in. If that doesn't work, a partial title is used, followed by an ellipsis (trailing dots). So if you're going to use long, similar titles, make sure there's some differentiation at the beginning of the name, not just at the end. Figure 7-9 shows a list of documents that are in a folder. The first title appears in normal type, but the second one is in a condensed style to fit in the list. The titles of the following items, despite the condensed type, can't be completely displayed, and there's no way to tell which file is which chapter.

Figure 7-9. Even with condensed type, some titles can't be fully displayed.

▪ Although documents are generally stored in memory until you save them to the disk, sometimes there's not enough memory—especially for a large document. Most applications create temporary disk files while you're working to store the document information that doesn't fit in RAM. The original file, though, is not altered until you specifically change it, and the temporary files are erased by the application when you quit. If you move to the Desktop, however, you may see icons in the application's folder or the System Folder labeled "temp" or something similar; don't throw them away as long as the application is still running.

▪ Many applications give you the choice of saving a document in a special format that's more likely to be understood by other programs. There are several generic graphics formats, as described in Chapter 6, but there's also a very standard text format. A *text file* can be opened by almost any program—a word processor, a database, or a spreadsheet, for instance. The imported text loses its character and paragraph formatting, and numbers lose any formulas embedded in the file, but paragraph breaks and tabs are transferred intact.

▪ Text files are sometimes referred to as *ASCII files*. ASCII stands for *American Standard Code for Information Interchange,* and it's a system that assigns a number code to every keyboard character (including nonprinting ones like Tab and Return) so that files can be easily exchanged between programs, and even between different computer systems. There's an ASCII code chart in Appendix C.

DIRECTORY DIALOGS

Basics

Directory Dialog Box is Apple's official name for the dialog boxes that appear when you use the Open or Save commands. In this book, and in most places, you'll find them referred to more familiarly as the Open and Save dialog boxes.

The buttons and menus inside the dialogs let you navigate among mounted disks and through the folders on them.

The Save Dialog

The Save dialog box (shown in Figure 7-10) appears in response to the initial use of the Save command and any time you use Save As. It lets you name the document and show where—on what disk and in what folder—you want it saved.

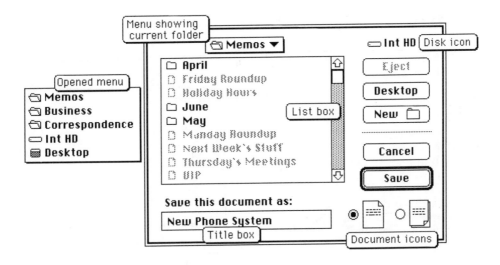

Figure 7-10. A standard Save dialog box

The current folder is shown in the drop-down menu. When you open the menu (shown at the left of Figure 7-10), it shows the path (all the folders) from the current one all the way up to the disk, and it also lets you get at the Desktop level of your work—the list of disks (and other storage devices) that are actually on your Desktop. The list box displays the files and folders that are in the current folder. Files are listed in gray, since you can't save a document into another document. There's a text box below the list for you to type the name of the document, and there are several buttons to control what's going on.

Both the list box and the text box can be affected by things you do from the keyboard; which box is affected depends on which one is active. When the text box is active, its contents are selected or there's a blinking insertion point in it, as shown at the left of Figure 7-11. If the list box is active, it has an extra frame around it, as shown at the right of Figure 7-11. Whenever the list box is active, the Save button turns into an Open button because you'll be opening a disk or a folder in the list.

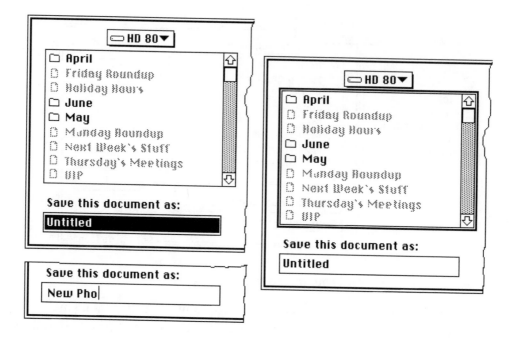

Figure 7-11. An active text box has either its contents selected or a blinking insertion point (left); an active list box has an extra frame around it (right).

When the dialog first opens, the text box is active. You can activate either box by clicking in it or by using the Tab key to alternately activate each box.

The general order of tasks for saving a document is:

1. Name the document.
2. Choose a disk.
3. Find the folder you want, or create a new one.
4. Click the Save button.

NAMING THE DOCUMENT

To name the document, type the name in the text box. Standard text editing techniques (like double-clicking to select a word and using the left and right arrow keys to move the insertion point left and right) work in the text box.

The icons to the right of the text box let you save the file as a standard document or as a stationery pad (this is covered in the next section, Stationery.)

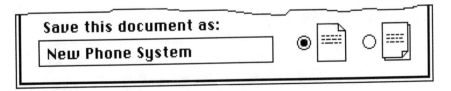

The text box and document icons

CHOOSING A DISK

To choose a disk, click the Desktop button or choose the Desktop level from the drop-down menu; the menu then displays *Desktop* as its title. The list box will show everything that's on the Desktop: disks, any loose documents that aren't in windows, and the Trash can (dimmed, since you can't save anything into it or open anything from it).

The list in an Open dialog is always alphabetical—except when it's showing the Desktop level, where there are two alphabetical groupings. All available disks are listed first, in alphabetical order; then comes an alphabetical list of the loose items on the Desktop. (In Figure 7-12, the file *Daily To-Do* comes after the disk *Int HD* because of this grouping.) The Trash can is listed after both groups.

The fastest way to open a disk is to double-click on it in the list. You can also open a disk by clicking on it and then clicking the Open button or pressing Return.

If a floppy disk is in the drive and you want to remove it to insert another, select the disk in the list and click the Eject button. The button will be dimmed if you've selected something (like a hard drive) that can't be ejected.

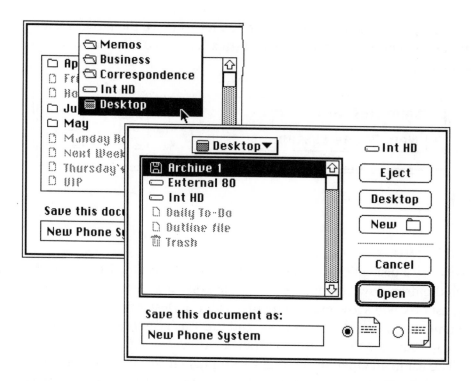

*Figure 7-12. Move to the Desktop level with the menu or the Desktop button,
then choose a disk from the list. The Save button has changed to an Open button
because the list box is active.*

CHOOSING A FOLDER

Using the menu, the list, or both, you can move to any folder on a disk.
You can always tell what disk you're working with because it's identified
by the disk icon in the upper-right corner of the dialog.

To move to a folder that's inside the current one (shown in Figure
7-13), you open it the way you open a disk in the Desktop list: Select it
and use the Open button, or just double-click on it.

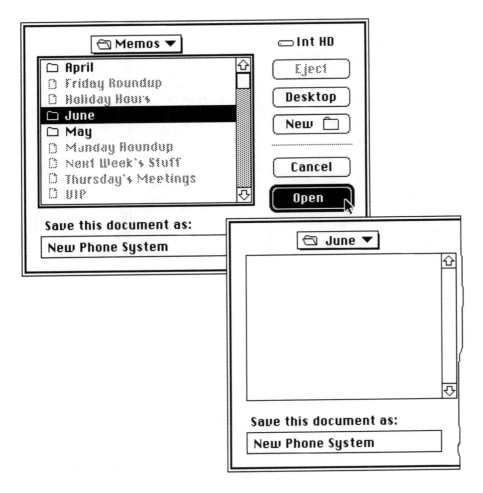

Figure 7-13. Moving to a folder in the list

To go to a folder that's *above* the one you're in, use the drop-down menu, as shown in Figure 7-14. If you want to save the document in one of the folders listed, just choose it from the menu.

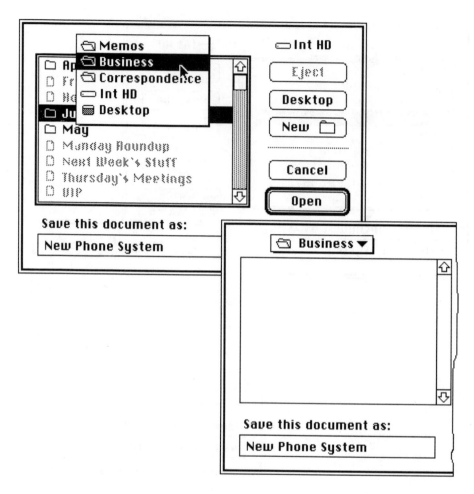

Figure 7-14. Moving to a folder in the menu

If you want to save the document into a folder that isn't in the current path, go up as far as necessary using the menu, then choose the folder you need from the list. This procedure combines the two previous operations; sometimes it's a little cumbersome, but it can't be avoided.

Say, for example, that your folder structure on the Desktop is like the one shown in Figure 7-15. If you start out in the Memos folder and want to save something into the Letters folder, you have to move up to the Business folder first (using the menu in the dialog), and then back down into the Letters folder (using the list). In fact, if you've created a new memo right after starting an application, you're going to start out in the Applications folder, then move up to the disk itself, then move down through the Correspondence and Business folders to find the Memo folder.

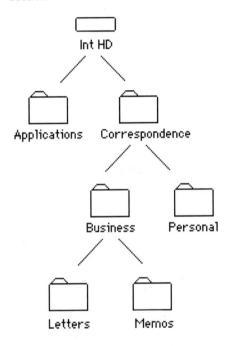

Figure 7-15.   A Desktop folder structure

CREATING A NEW FOLDER

To create a new folder, use the New Folder button. You'll get the dialog box shown in Figure 7-16, in which you can name the new folder. This new folder goes into the current folder, and it's opened so you can save the document into it.

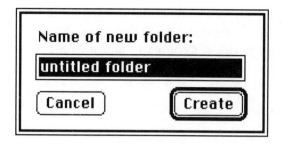

Figure 7-16.   The New Folder dialog box

SAVING THE DOCUMENT

When you're finally in the folder you want, click the Save button to actually save the document. If the default button is Open instead of Save, that means the list box is still activated. Click in, or Tab to, the text box and then click the Save button or press Return.

If you change your mind about saving the document, you can click the Cancel button to close the dialog box.

The Open Dialog

When you use the Open command in an application's menu, the Open dialog, shown in Figure 7-17, appears.

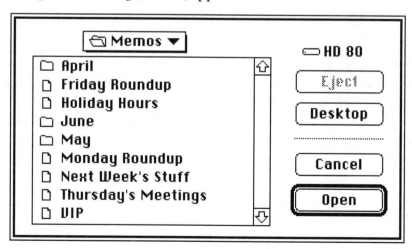

Figure 7-17.   The standard Open dialog

As you can see, it's similar to the Save dialog, although there's no place to type a file name and you can't create a new folder. But you use the list box, menu, and buttons to navigate through disks and folders in the same way. (Since the list box is the only box, it's always active and doesn't need a frame to indicate its state.)

When you find the document you want, open it the same way you open disks and folders in the list: Double-click on it, or select it and click the Open button or press Return.

While the Save dialog shows you everything that's in the current folder, with unavailable items dimmed, the Open dialog lists only the things you can actually open: disks and folders, and documents for the current application. Documents that the application can't open aren't listed, even if they're in the current folder.

Quickies

▪ You can move up one folder in the path without using the menu: Press Command-up arrow or click on the disk icon.

▪ Use the up and down arrow keys to select any active (not dimmed) item in the list.

▪ Use the tilde (~) key to select the last item in the list.

▪ When the list box is active, you can type letters to select an item in it. (As in naming files, capital letters don't count so you don't need the Shift key). If you type enough letters to uniquely identify any item, that's what's selected. If you type letters that don't match a file name, the next nearest alphabetic equivalent is selected. In the list shown in Figure 7-18, typing *m* selects the folder *May*, but typing *mo* selects the file *Monday Roundup*. Typing *o* selects *Project X*, since that's the file that is alphabetically next after *o*.

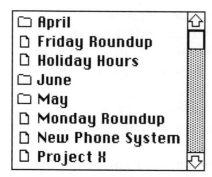

Figure 7-18.   You can select items in a list by typing.

▪ You can use keyboard commands for many of the buttons in the Open and Save dialogs: Return or Enter for the Open/Save button; Command-period or Esc for Cancel; Command-N for the New Folder button; and Command-D for the Desktop button.

▪ The Open and Save dialogs illustrated in this chapter are the standard ones. Many applications expand the capabilities of the dialogs with their own extra buttons and menus.

STATIONERY

Basics

The concept of *stationery* documents is based on the real-world procedure of tearing a piece of paper from a pad of printed stationery: Each piece is blank except for preprinted items like a letterhead or checklist or other fill-in-the-blank features.

A Macintosh stationery document is a one that you can use as a template for other documents. You save it with certain items already in it, like a letterhead at the top of the page, or a blank page formatted for the text and paragraph styles you want to use.

Applications won't "know" about the Stationery capabilities of System 7 unless they've been rewritten to take advantage of it. If you can't create stationery from the application's Save dialog, though, you can force the issue from the Desktop.

Creating Stationery

When an application is up-to-date, it will have document icons with buttons in its Save dialog (see Figure 7-19). The one at the left (it looks like a single page) is for normal documents; the one at the right (it looks like a pad of paper) is for stationery.

Figure 7-19. Left: the Normal icon; right: the Stationery icon

You prepare stationery the same way you create a regular document. When you want to turn a document into stationery, all you have to do is click the Stationery button before you save it.

When you close a document that you've saved as stationery, you'll get the standard "Do you want to save changes before closing?" dialog because, as far as the Mac is concerned, you haven't really saved the document just because you made a stationery pad out of it.

SUBSTITUTE STATIONERY

If the application you're using doesn't yet support the stationery concept, there won't be any Normal/Stationery icons available in the Save dialog. Here's how you create stationery for those applications:

1. Save the document as usual, then go to the Desktop and find the document's icon.
2. Select the icon and choose Get Info from the File menu.
3. At the bottom of the Info window, you'll see the button you need—click the *Stationery pad* checkbox.

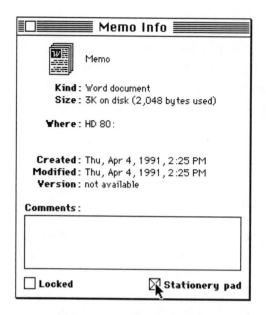

Figure 7-20. Creating stationery from an Info window

Using Stationery

"Real" stationery documents (the ones created from within a Save dialog) have their own special icons in Open dialogs and on the Desktop, as shown in Figure 7-21.

Figure 7-21. Left: standard and stationery icons in a list; right: standard and stationery icons on the Desktop

When you open a Stationery document, it opens as an untitled, and unsaved, document in the application. You add the material that you want, then save the document as usual; since it started out as untitled, you have to give it a new name—and the original stationery document remains unchanged.

ALTERING STATIONERY

If you want to change the Stationery document itself, open it, make the changes, and then save it as Stationery using the same name as before. You'll be asked if you want to replace the existing file, and you should click *Yes*.

USING SUBSTITUTE STATIONERY

Stationery created through a Get Info window may or may not have special icons in lists and on the Desktop, depending on the application that originally created it.

When you open substitute stationery, what happens depends on the application. Some applications refuse to deal with stationery at all; when you open a stationery document in one of these unfriendly programs, the Mac system intervenes briefly with the dialog shown in Figure 7-22, telling you that you're opening a document that you defined as a Stationery pad. But, since the application doesn't know anything about stationery, once the document actually opens, it's just the original document and saving any changes will affect the original "stationery." If you want to keep the original document as a template, use the Save As command as soon as the document opens, saving it under a different name; then, all the changes you make will be saved to that file instead of to the original.

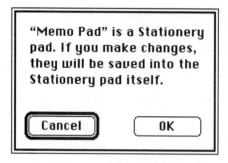

Figure 7-22. The Mac interrupts with this message when you open substitute stationery in an application that doesn't know what to do with it.

Some applications understand a little more about the Stationery concept because they had some similar capability before it was built into the Mac's system. In those cases, when you open the stationery document, you might see a dialog like the one shown in Figure 7-23, asking you to name the new document before the window opens. This keeps the stationery document from having any changes made to it.

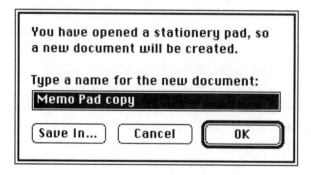

Figure 7-23. Some applications ask you to name a new document so the stationery template won't be changed.

Quickies

■ To prevent accidentally changing a document that you've defined as stationery on the Desktop when the application doesn't know anything about stationery, check the Locked button in the document's Get Info window.

SUMMARY

Now you know all the basics of working within an application; opening, closing, and saving documents; and creating Stationery. The next chapter shows you how to deal with more than one application at a time.

CHAPTER 8

Working with Multiple Applications

ABOUT THIS CHAPTER

You can have more than one program at a time running on the Mac. The first half of this chapter shows you how to handle multiple applications and the window clutter they cause. The second half explores a special way to share information between programs whether they're both running or not.

USING MULTIPLE APPLICATIONS

Basics

You don't have to do anything special to run two or more applications at the same time on your Mac; just launch them one at a time using any of the techniques covered in the last chapter.

Just how many programs you can have going at once depends on how much memory your Mac has, since each application needs its own chunk of memory to "live" in. On a machine with 2M of RAM, you'll be able to run only one major program, since the Mac's system and the Desktop need their pieces of memory, too.

When you're running multiple applications, only one is *active* at any time: Its windows are on top of all the others, and its menus are in the menu bar. The Application menu at the far right of the menu bar displays a miniature icon of the current application.

In Figure 8-1, there are two major programs and a desk accessory open. The active application is Microsoft Word—its document window is on top, and its menu and icon are in the menu bar. There's a SuperPaint window showing beneath it, and the inactive Calculator is to the right. Beneath it all is the Desktop, with the disk icon, the Trash, and part of one of its windows showing.

The Application menu at the right of the menu bar—its "title" is a mini icon of the active application—lets you control two things: which application you're in, and which windows show on the screen. Figure 8-2 shows what the Application menu for Figure 8-1 would look like: There are four programs running (counting the Calculator and the Finder), and Word is checked because it's the active one.

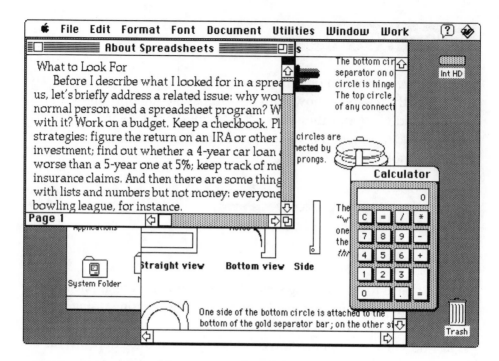

Figure 8-1. Although several programs are running on this screen, Word is the active one: Its window is on top, and it "owns" the menu bar.

Figure 8-2. The Application menu

Moving Between Applications

There are four ways you can move from one application to another:

- Choose the destination program from the Application menu.

- Click on any exposed part of a window that belongs to the application you want to go to. If you want to go to the Desktop, you can also click on any "loose" icon—such as a disk or the Trash—or you can click directly on the Desktop itself—the gray (or colored) background.

- Double-click on the application's icon on the Desktop. Although it will be gray because it's already open, double-clicking on it activates the application.

- Hide the windows of the current application to move back to the application you used last.

Figure 8-3 shows what happens if, starting with the setup in Figure 8-1, you move to the SuperPaint program. The SuperPaint document window comes to the front, its menus appear on the menu bar, and its

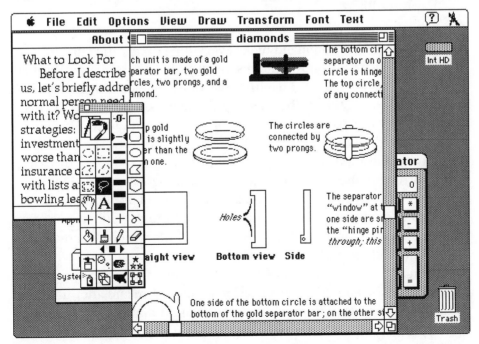

Figure 8-3. Activating another program brings its windows to the top and changes the menu bar.

icon is at the top of the Application menu. (If there had been more than one document window open in SuperPaint when it was last used, they would all come in front of the other windows on the screen.) The figure shows a special case: One of SuperPaint's floating tool palettes, in use when SuperPaint was last used, also appears when SuperPaint is activated again. Unlike regular document windows, a floating window hides itself unless its application is the active one.

Controlling Windows

The Application menu provides an easy way to control window clutter when you're running multiple applications. You can hide the windows for everything except the current application, or you can hide the current application.

The Hide Others command hides everything *except* the current application. Figure 8-4 shows the results of Hide Others if SuperPaint is active, as it was in Figure 8-3. (In the case of the Finder, only its *windows* are hidden—you'll still see the Desktop in the background, and the disk and Trash icons, as well as any loose icons that weren't in windows.)

The Hide Application command hides all the windows belonging to the active application. The actual command changes to reflect the name of the current application—Hide Word, Hide SuperPaint, Hide Finder, and so on. When you use this command, the current application is hidden, and the last application you used is activated. Figure 8-5 shows what happens if, starting at Figure 8-3, with all the windows showing, you use the Hide SuperPaint command.

When an application is hidden, its icon is dimmed in the Application menu. Figure 8-6 shows the Application menu before and after using the Hide Others command from within SuperPaint. A dimmed application can still be chosen from the menu; as soon as it's activated, its windows are displayed.

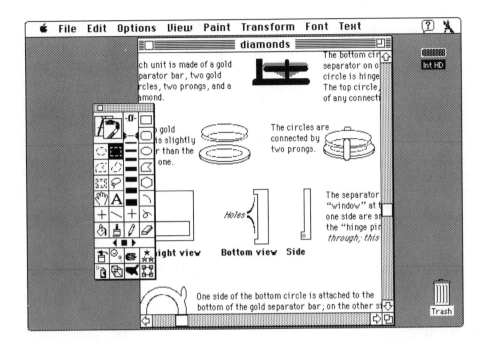

Figure 8-4. The result of the Hide Others command

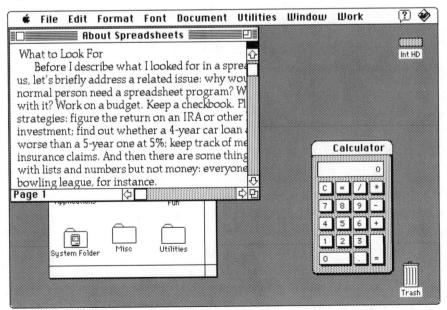

Figure 8-5. The result of the Hide Application command

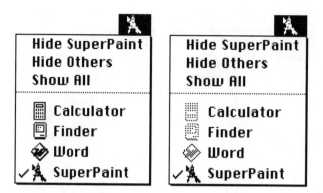

Figure 8-6. A dimmed icon in the Applications menu means that the program's windows are hidden.

Finally, the Show All command displays all the windows for all opened applications again.

Quickies

▪ You don't have to launch one application at a time. You can select multiple icons on the Desktop (any combination of documents and applications) and then choose Open from the File menu, or double-click on any one of the selected icons, to open them all.

▪ You don't have to stick with the just-this-one or everything-but-this-one window hiding options. If, for instance, you want to see only two applications of the five you have open, you can hide all but one and then move to the other one that you want activated; alternatively, you can switch, in turn, to each of the applications whose windows you want hidden and use the Hide Application command.

▪ To hide the current program's windows as you move to another application, hold down the Option key while you select the destination program from the Application menu.

Also See . . .

▪ Chapter 13 explains how available memory is allocated to the applications you want to use.

PUBLISH AND SUBSCRIBE

Basics

The Clipboard transfers information from one document to another, and
some applications can import documents created in other applications,
but the most elegant method of sharing information between documents
is the Publish and Subscribe feature. With it, you can create links between
documents—even if they belong to different applications—so that when
you change the material in one document, the changes appear in
the other.

Although Publish and Subscribe are system-level Macintosh features,
applications need the ability to access them. You'll know if the application you're using has this ability by checking for Publish and Subscribe
commands. Most programs will have four related commands (two of
them change depending on circumstances) in the Edit menu, as shown
in Figure 8-7.

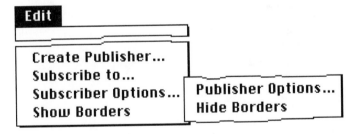

Figure 8-7. The four basic Publish and Subscribe commands

Terminology

When there's part of a document that you want to use in other documents, you *publish* it. The material that you're sharing is the *publisher*.
(Neither the application nor the document itself is the publisher—the
term refers specifically to the material within the document that you've
selected to publish.)

When you want to access a published item, you *subscribe* to it. An item in a document that comes from a publisher is a *subscriber*. (Again, it's not the document or its application that's the subscriber—the item itself is the subscriber.)

For example, an image in a graphics document full of pictures can be the publisher; the same image in the letterhead of a word processor document would be the subscriber. A single document can have more than one publisher; it can have more than one subscriber; it can even have both publishers and subscribers. And, there can be many subscribers to a single publisher: A logo, for instance, might be used in every letter and memo that you write.

The *edition* is the actual link between the publisher and the subscriber; it's a separate file that the Mac creates whenever you create a publisher. Changes in the publisher are sent to the edition, and subscribers check their editions to see if any changes have been made.

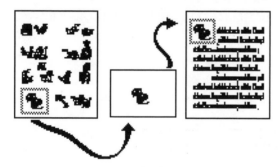

Figure 8-8. A publisher in one document (left, framed in gray) sends information to the edition file (center) which, in turn, sends information to the subscriber in another document (right, framed in gray).

Creating Publishers and Subscribers

CREATING A PUBLISHER

To create a publisher, you start by selecting something in a document that you want to share with other documents (you can even select the whole document). Figure 8-9 shows a chart selected inside a spreadsheet program (note the "handles" at its corners).

	A	B	C	D	E	F	G	H	I	J	K
1	Week	1	2	3	4	5	6	7	8	9	10
2	Pledges	90	160	195							
3	Donations		75	85							
4											
5											
6											
7											
8											
9											
10											
11											
12											
13											
14											
15											
16											
17											

Figure 8-9. A chart selected in a spreadsheet program, ready to be published

Next, you choose the Create Publisher command from the application's Edit menu. You'll get a dialog box like the one shown in Figure 8-10; it shows a miniature of the item you're publishing and asks you to name it and save it someplace on your disk. (All the buttons, and the menu, work the same way as in a standard Save dialog.)

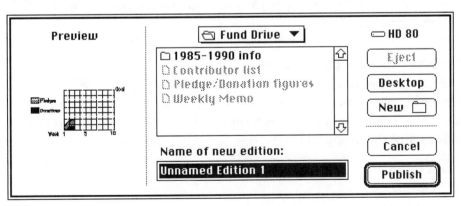

Figure 8-10.   The Publish dialog

When you click the Publish button, your selection becomes an official publisher and an edition file is created on the disk.

To identify publishers in a document, use the Show Borders command from the Edit menu. As shown in Figure 8-11, a publisher is framed by a gray border. If you don't want to see the borders, use the Hide Borders command.

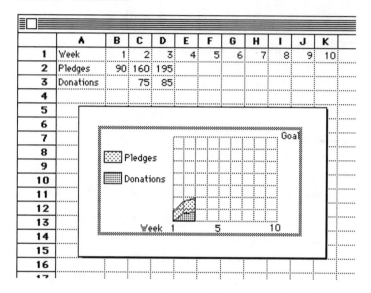

Figure 8-11. Publishers are framed in gray borders when you use the Show Borders command.

CREATING A SUBSCRIBER

To create a subscriber, you open the document where you want the subscriber to be and use the Subscribe To command. Figure 8-12 shows the dialog that opens. When you click on an edition in the list, it's previewed at the left of the dialog. If it's the one you want, click the Subscribe button.

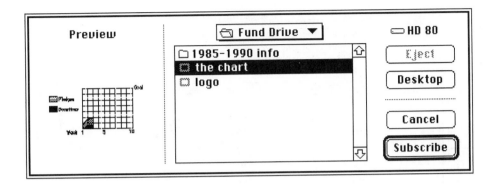

Figure 8-12.   The Subscribe dialog

A subscriber is inserted into your document the same way Clipboard material would be. So, if you're in a word processor, the subscriber appears at the insertion point; in a graphics program, it appears as an object that can be moved around. Figure 8-13 shows the chart published from the spreadsheet program when it's subscribed to by a word processing program. The very same image that is a publisher in one document is now a subscriber in another.

Figure 8-13.   The subscriber placed in a word processor document

As the fund raiser referred to in all these illustrations progresses, new weekly numbers would be entered into the spreadsheet, which changes the chart. Since the chart is a publisher, its edition is updated. The subscriber in the word processor, in turn, is updated by the edition. When you open the Weekly Memo document that contains the subscriber, the chart is changed to reflect the latest entries in the spreadsheet (see Figure 8-14).

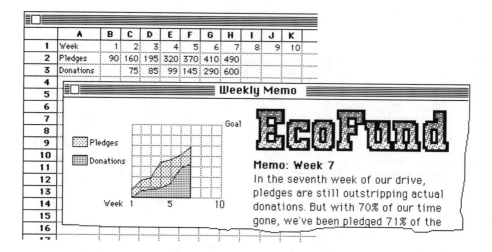

Figure 8-14.   The subscriber image in the word processor file is updated to match the information in the publisher.

You can use the Show Borders command to see subscribers, too. Subscribers are framed in a darker border than the one used for publishers, as shown in Figure 8-15.

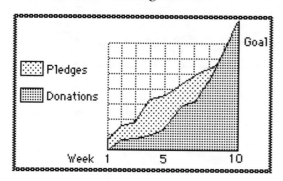

Figure 8-15.   Subscribers have darker borders than publishers.

HANDLING SUBSCRIBERS

Once a subscriber is in a document, you can't usually edit it directly, but you can still treat it as you would any other object in that program:

- Text or graphics subscribers can be selected for copying, cutting, or deleting.

- A text subscriber in a graphics or page layout program can have its frame resized to hide or display all its contents (see Figure 8-16).

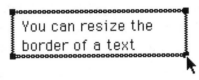

Figure 8-16. Resizing the border of a text subscriber hides some of the text inside.

- A graphics subscriber in a graphics or page layout program can have its frame resized to change the size of its contents. Most word processors also handle graphics (and therefore graphics subscribers) in such a way that you can resize them in the document. (Note that the resized graphic in Figure 8-17 is the relatively low-resolution screen representation of the image; depending on the type of graphic and the kind of printer you're using, the reduced image can print as clearly as the larger version.)

Figure 8-17. Resizing the border of a graphics subscriber alters the size of the graphic.

THE EDITION FILE

An edition file is created when you publish something; it consists of the published material only—not the entire document that it came from. The edition serves as the link between the publisher in the original document and the subscriber in another document.

Each application makes its own identifiable edition icon, which you can always change, as described in Chapter 5.

If you double-click on an edition icon on the Desktop (see Figure 8-18), a special window opens, showing the edition's contents. Clicking on the Open Publisher button in the Edition window opens the document (and the application) that created the edition, if they are available.

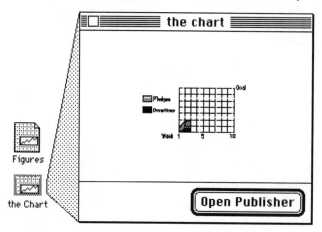

Figure 8-18.   At left, an application's normal document icon (top) and its edition icon (bottom). When you double-click on the edition, you get the Edition window.

Publisher and Subscriber Links

The links between the publisher and the edition, and the edition and the subscriber, can be updated automatically or manually. The links can also be broken at any time. These options are controlled through the Publisher Options and Subscriber Options dialog boxes.

UPDATING THE LINKS

To set the updating option for a publisher, select the publisher in its original document, then choose Publisher Options from the Edit menu. The Publisher Options dialog shown in Figure 8-19 opens. The two updating options are listed under "Send Editions." If you click the On Save button, the edition will be updated every time you save the document that contains the publisher. If you click the Manually button, the edition will be updated only when you say so—when you click the Send Edition Now button.

The menu in the Publisher Options dialog box is not a functional one. It pops open to show the edition's path so you can see where it's stored, but you can't select anything from it.

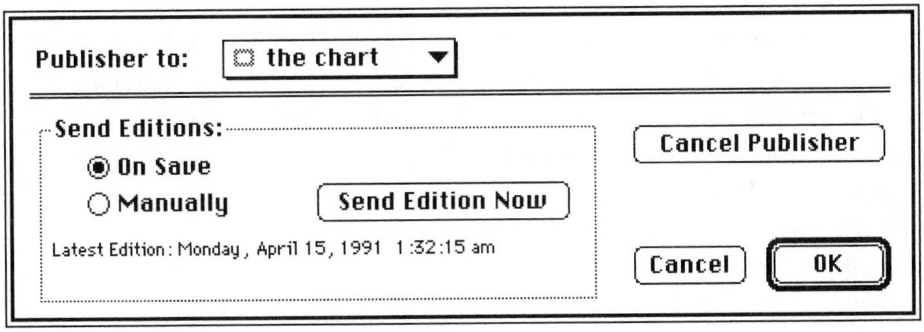

```
┌─────────────────────────────────────────────────────────────┐
│                                                             │
│   Publisher to:   [☐ the chart      ▼]                      │
│  ─────────────────────────────────────────────────────────  │
│   ┌Send Editions:┄┄┄┄┄┄┄┄┄┄┄┄┄┄┄┄┄┄┄┄┄┐  ┌──────────────────┐│
│   ┆   ◉ On Save                       ┆  │ Cancel Publisher ││
│   ┆   ○ Manually    [ Send Edition Now ]                     │
│   ┆  Latest Edition: Monday, April 15, 1991  1:32:15 am      │
│   ┆                                    ┆  [ Cancel ] [ OK ] ││
│   └┄┄┄┄┄┄┄┄┄┄┄┄┄┄┄┄┄┄┄┄┄┄┄┄┄┄┄┄┄┄┄┄┄┄┄┘                    │
└─────────────────────────────────────────────────────────────┘
```

Figure 8-19. The Publisher Options dialog

From the subscriber end of things, you have basically the same choices. Select the subscriber in the document and choose Subscriber Options from the Edit menu. Use the Automatically button if you want the subscriber updated each time the edition is updated. Click the Manually button if you want to control the timing of the updates; use the Get Edition Now button when you want to update the subscriber.

The Subscriber Options dialog box (shown in Figure 8-20) also has an Open Publisher button. When you click that button, the document that contains the subscriber's publisher opens in its application so that you can edit it.

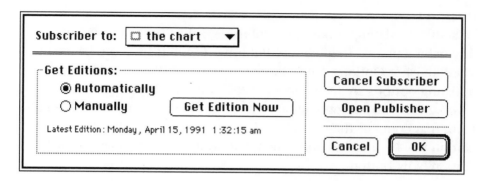

Figure 8-20.   The Subscriber Options dialog

CANCELING THE LINKS

Once you've created publishers and subscribers (and the editions that bridge the two), the material is not irrevocably linked. You can cancel the link between the publisher and the edition, the one between the subscriber and the edition, or both.

To cancel the links, select the publisher or the subscriber and open the Options dialog. Click the Cancel Publisher (or Cancel Subscriber) button.

If the publisher document has never been saved, canceling the link to the edition means that the edition file will be erased from the disk when you close the document. Otherwise, canceling links has no effect on the material in the publisher, the subscriber, or the edition. Both the publisher and the subscriber items remain in their documents. The edition still exists as a separate file on the disk, even if the links to both the publisher and the subscriber are canceled.

Editing Publishers

When you edit a publisher and update its edition, how those changes are handled in subscribers depends on whether the publisher is text or graphics, and what kind of application the subscriber is in. (Some applications will make up their own rules and exceptions, but the following information is the general standard.)

EDITING A GRAPHICS PUBLISHER

There are four basic things that affect a graphics publisher: editing the material within the publisher's border, repositioning the border, adding material that's only partially within the border, and changing the size or shape of the border.

When you change material inside the frame, the changes are reflected in the subscriber. Repositioning the frame is just another way of changing the material inside the frame: The new frame's contents show up in the subscriber. Figure 8-21 shows an original publisher and its two edited versions, and the results for the subscriber. The original version is at the top; in the middle, the pattern of the oval has been changed; at the bottom, the border has been moved. In both edited pictures, the subscriber frame still reflects exactly what's inside the publisher frame.

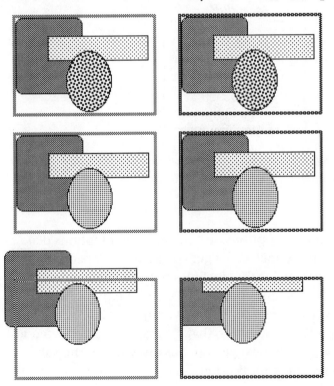

Figure 8-21. Editing a publisher (left) and the subscriber results (right)

If you edit a graphics publisher in a bit-mapped graphics program, whatever's inside the frame goes to the edition. When you edit a publisher in an object-oriented graphics program, you have the option of including whatever's inside the publisher frame, or only objects that are *completely* inside the frame. Figure 8-22 shows the difference between these two options; at the left is the edited publisher with a triangle only partially within the border, and at the right are the results of the two publishing options.

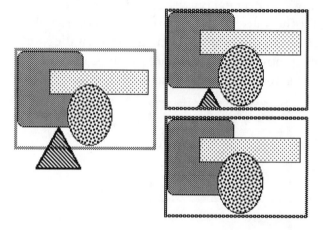

Figure 8-22. A graphics publisher (left) can publish everything inside the frame (top right), or it can include only objects that are completely inside the frame (bottom right).

To choose between these options, use the Publisher Options dialog box. In many graphics programs, you'll get an extended version of the dialog (as shown in Figure 8-23) that includes buttons that control these options. The Clip button includes partial objects in the publisher; the Snap button excludes any object not totally within the frame.

If you resize the publisher's border, that change, too, is reflected in the subscriber, but the type of change depends on whether the subscriber is in a text or graphics application.

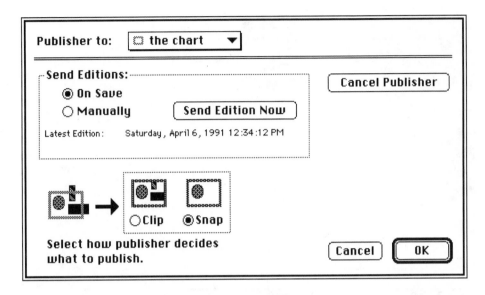

Figure 8-23.   Some graphics programs have extended Publisher Options dialogs.

In a text application, the subscriber's frame size changes along with the change in the publisher's border size. As the border size changes, text in the subscriber's document is shifted around to accommodate it.

In an application where the size of the subscriber border can be set independently (in graphics programs, page layout programs, and many word processors), the subscriber's frame size doesn't change to match the new size of the publisher's border. Instead, the new publisher material is scaled up or down to fit inside the subscriber's border. Figure 8-24 shows the results of changing the size of a graphics publisher's border.

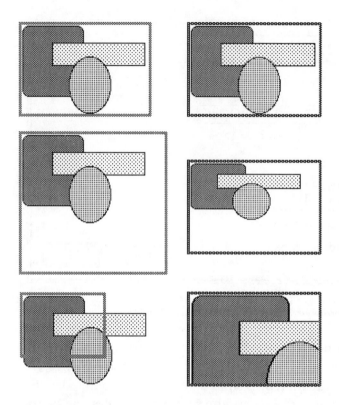

Figure 8-24. When you change a graphics publisher's border (left), the subscriber in a graphics program scales the contents to fit inside its current border (right).

EDITING A TEXT PUBLISHER

When you edit a text publisher, the publisher's border expands or contracts to surround the edited material, as shown in Figure 8-25. The effect this has on a subscriber depends on whether the subscriber is in a text or graphics application.

In a text application, the subscriber expands or contracts as the publisher changes, shifting the main text of the document as necessary; this is shown in Figure 8-26.

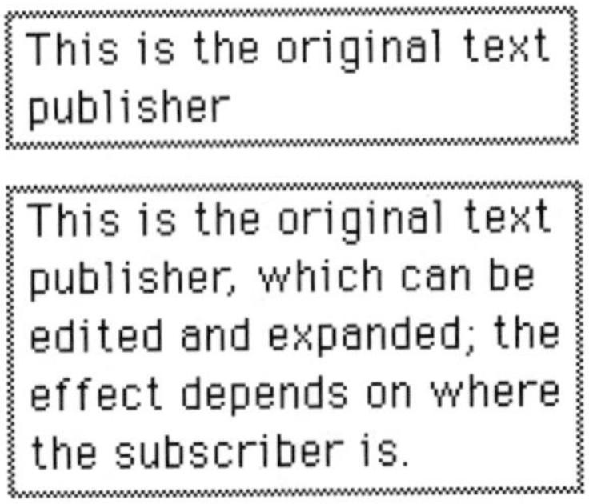

```
┌┄┄┄┄┄┄┄┄┄┄┄┄┄┄┄┄┄┄┄┄┄┐
┆This is the original text┆
┆publisher                ┆
└┄┄┄┄┄┄┄┄┄┄┄┄┄┄┄┄┄┄┄┄┄┘

┌┄┄┄┄┄┄┄┄┄┄┄┄┄┄┄┄┄┄┄┄┄┐
┆This is the original text┆
┆publisher, which can be  ┆
┆edited and expanded; the ┆
┆effect depends on where  ┆
┆the subscriber is.       ┆
└┄┄┄┄┄┄┄┄┄┄┄┄┄┄┄┄┄┄┄┄┄┘
```

Figure 8-25.   The border of a text publisher expands or contracts as you edit the enclosed material.

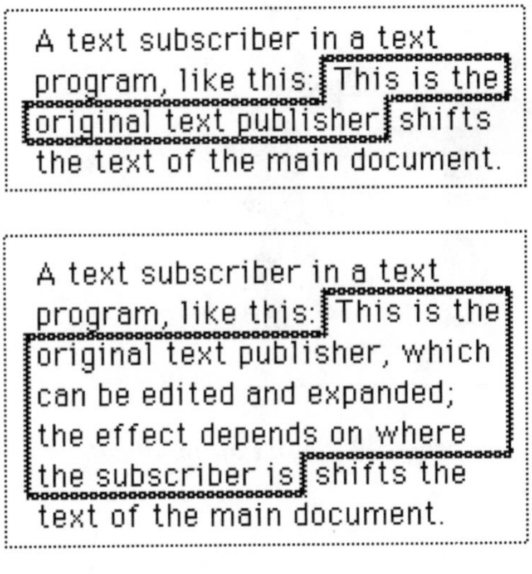

```
┌┄┄┄┄┄┄┄┄┄┄┄┄┄┄┄┄┄┄┄┄┄┄┄┐
┆ A text subscriber in a text      ┆
┆ program, like this:▛This is the▜┆
┆▙original text publisher▟shifts   ┆
┆ the text of the main document.   ┆
└┄┄┄┄┄┄┄┄┄┄┄┄┄┄┄┄┄┄┄┄┄┄┄┘

┌┄┄┄┄┄┄┄┄┄┄┄┄┄┄┄┄┄┄┄┄┄┄┄┐
┆ A text subscriber in a text       ┆
┆ program, like this:▛This is the ▜┆
┆▙original text publisher, which   ▟┆
┆ can be edited and expanded;       ┆
┆ the effect depends on where       ┆
┆ the subscriber is▛shifts the     ┆
┆ text of the main document.        ┆
└┄┄┄┄┄┄┄┄┄┄┄┄┄┄┄┄┄┄┄┄┄┄┄┘
```

Figure 8-26.   In text applications, a text subscriber expands or contracts along with the publisher.

Since graphics applications (and programs that do page layout) usually deal with text inside a special text box, changes to a text publisher don't usually change the size of the subscriber's border. Instead, you'll get as much text as can fit in the current border; if you resize the border, you'll see the rest of the text. Figure 8-27 shows an edited text subscriber in a graphics application.

Figure 8-27.   A text subscriber in a graphics program doesn't automatically expand to include the publisher's changes.

Quickies

▪ Different applications provide different levels of Publish and Subscribe options; some will even let you edit a subscriber directly within its frame.

▪ Since a subscriber is part of the document where it resides, you can give the file to other people without worrying about the fact that they have no access to the edition.

▪ You can move an edition from one folder to another on the same disk and the publisher and subscriber will both still be able to find it.

▪ If an edition is deleted or otherwise unavailable (on an unmounted disk, for example), the subscriber can't be updated, but it's still a part of the document. If you open the Subscriber Options dialog, you'll find the edition name and its last known path dimmed in the menu, as shown in Figure 8-28.

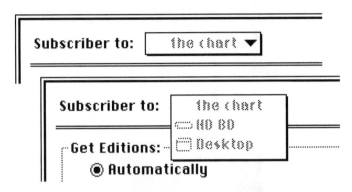

Figure 8-28. The subscriber and its path are dimmed in the menu if they can't be found.

▪ In most graphics programs, you can double-click on the border of a publisher or subscriber to open the Options dialog box.

▪ In many programs, option-double-clicking on a subscriber opens the publisher, if it is available.

▪ If you need multiple subscribers from a single edition, you can make them quickly by subscribing to the edition from within one document and then copying the subscriber to the Clipboard and pasting it into the other documents.

SUMMARY

In the last five chapters, you learned how to work on the Desktop, in applications, *with* applications, and even *between* applications. Now it's time to learn more about the Mac's operating system and its system software, and that's just what the next three chapters cover.

System Software

CHAPTER 9

The System Folder

ABOUT THIS CHAPTER

The System Folder is an integral part of the Mac's operating system; the programs and files inside it work almost invisibly behind the scenes to make using the Mac not only productive, but also a pleasure.

Yet, for all the complexity of operation the Mac provides, taking care of its system files is simplicity itself.

THE SYSTEM FILE

Basics

The System file that's in the System Folder works along with information stored in the Mac's ROM to provide an operating system for the Mac. Other items in your System Folder also add to the Mac's functionality. All the programs and support files that Apple provides to run the Mac come under the umbrella term *system software*.

The System file contains not only operating system information, but also *resources* like fonts and sounds. These resources are available to all the programs you run on the Mac. An application, for instance, checks the font resources in the System so it can build its Font menu. You can't get at the System file's operating system instructions, but you can add and delete its resources.

The System file looks like a suitcase. You can open it the way you open any other icon: Double-click on it. When it opens, you'll see the resources that are inside (see Figure 9-1).

You'll find the words *system, System, system file,* and *System file* throughout this book, and in other places, too. The capitalization (or lack thereof) isn't capricious. Without a capital letter, *system* can refer to:

■ The version of the system software you're using ("What system are you running?").

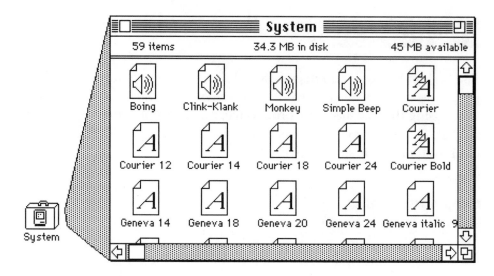

Figure 9-1. Double-click on the System file icon to see the resources inside.

▪ The environment you've created by adding or deleting items like fonts, sounds, and system extensions ("What's your system like?").

▪ Your hardware setup—a Mac LC with a 40M internal drive and a LaserWriter II NT, for example ("What Mac system do you have?").

Capitalized, *System* means the System file in your System Folder, or, with a number (System 7), it refers to a version of the system software. *System file*, capitalized, refers to the System file in the System Folder; without the capital, *system file* refers to any file inside the System Folder.

System Version Numbers

The Mac's system files, like other programs, have numbers that identify their versions. A major change in a program is reflected in the main number—System 6 to System 7, for example. Version numbers start out with no decimals or with a zero in the decimal place (7.0) and minor enhancements increase the decimal number: 7.1, 7.2, and so on. Very minor updates to software (usually to fix bugs) are often assigned a second decimal number, like this: 7.0.1, 7.0.2, and so on.

There are two ways to check what system you're running: Choose About This Macintosh from the Finder's Apple menu, or select the System file and then choose Get Info from the File menu. Both dialogs (shown in Figure 9-2) identify the system version number.

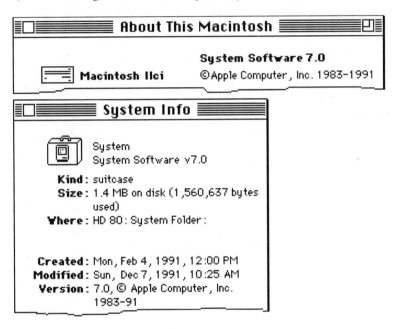

Figure 9-2. The Finder's About command and the System file's Info window both identify the System that's running.

System Installation

The Mac needs a *startup disk* to get going—a disk with system software on it. Macs with internal hard drives, and even many with external drives, come with system software already installed. But if you have a drive that has no System on it, or if you're updating to the most recently released system software, you use Apple's Installer program to do it.

Installer

The Installer is on the first disk of the set for Apple's system software. You start the computer with that disk in the drive so it will be used as the startup disk, and then you double-click on the Installer icon to start the program. From there, all you have to do is follow the onscreen instructions. (The main screen is shown in Figure 9-3.) The only decision you have to make is whether to use the Easy Install or the Customize option.

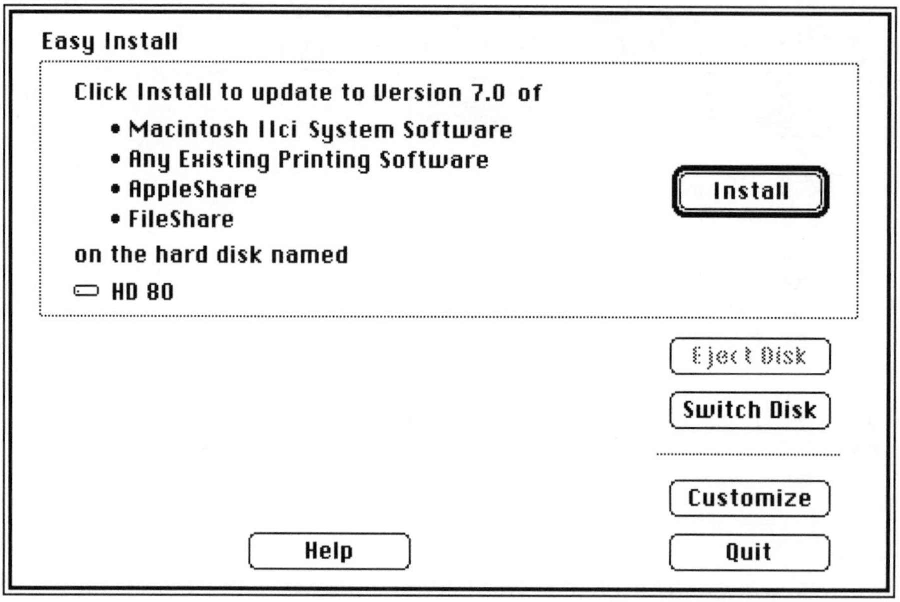

```
┌─────────────────────────────────────────────────────────┐
│  Easy Install                                           │
│  ┌ ─ ─ ─ ─ ─ ─ ─ ─ ─ ─ ─ ─ ─ ─ ─ ─ ─ ─ ─ ─ ─ ─ ┐       │
│   Click Install to update to Version 7.0 of            │
│      • Macintosh IIci System Software                   │
│      • Any Existing Printing Software         ┌────────┐│
│      • AppleShare                             │ Install ││
│      • FileShare                              └────────┘│
│   on the hard disk named                                │
│      ⬭ HD 80                                            │
│  └ ─ ─ ─ ─ ─ ─ ─ ─ ─ ─ ─ ─ ─ ─ ─ ─ ─ ─ ─ ─ ─ ─ ┘       │
│                                              ┌──────────┐│
│                                              │Eject Disk││
│                                              └──────────┘│
│                                              ┌──────────┐│
│                                              │Switch Disk││
│                                              └──────────┘│
│                                                          │
│                                              ┌──────────┐│
│                                              │Customize ││
│                          ┌──────────┐        └──────────┘│
│                          │  Help    │        ┌──────────┐│
│                          └──────────┘        │  Quit    ││
│                                              └──────────┘│
└─────────────────────────────────────────────────────────┘
```

Figure 9-3. The Installer's main screen

Easy Install configures a system for the Mac model that you're using to run the Installer. It installs the correct System file for that model, printer software to replace what's currently on the drive, and the basic networking software.

Use the Easy Install option if:

▪ You're installing the System on an internal hard drive, or on an external hard drive that will be used only with the computer model from which you're running the Installer program, *and*

- The drive you're installing on already has printer software on it for the printer you'll be using. (Easy Install updates only *existing* printer drivers.)

CUSTOMIZING INSTALLATIONS

Different Mac models need different System files, even when the version number is identical. Because earlier Macs have less information in their ROMs, they need more information inside the System file to "fill in the blanks" so that users will have the same basic functionality in their systems no matter which Mac model they're using. Various models also need different support files in the System Folder: You don't need color devices on a black-and-white system, for example. So, if you install system software for a specific machine on an external drive, you might not be able to use that drive as a startup if it's connected to a different model.

The three areas in which you can customize your system are: the basic system software, printer drivers, and networking software.

Figure 9-4 is an enhanced version of the Customize dialog box. The actual dialog has a small list box that scrolls to display five distinct areas, with many items listed within some of those areas. The areas are:

A. Software for any Mac and for all printers. (These will prepare a disk for use with any hardware setup.)

B. Software for each Apple printer. (Although there are only two shown in Figure 9-4, all Apple printers are listed in the dialog.)

C. Special networking software.

D. System software for each Mac model. (There are only two shown in the figure; however, all models are listed in the dialog.)

E. Minimal system software for any Mac model, or for an individual model. (There are only three shown in the figure; however, all models are listed in the dialog.)

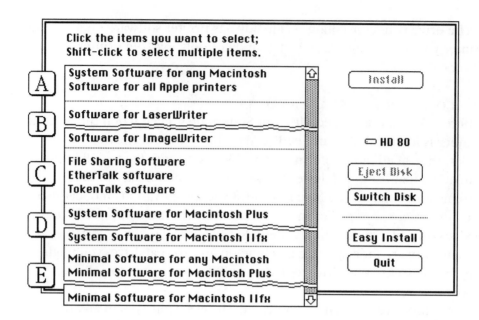

Figure 9-4.   The Customize dialog present a very long scrolling list of options in five categories.

Choose your system software from section A, D, or E:

- Install a system "for any Macintosh" (A) if the drive you're installing it on might be used with more than one Mac model. (Maybe you'll be bringing the drive between work and home.)

- Install a system for a specific Macintosh (D) if you're installing it on a drive that's going to be used exclusively with a model other than the one that's doing the installation.

- Install a minimal system for any Mac or for a specific Mac model (E) to create a floppy startup disk. (You can use this as an emergency startup if something's wrong with your hard drive. System 7 doesn't run from a floppy except in a very minimal way, and then very slowly.)

In addition to selecting your system software, you have to choose your printer software: either for all Apple printers (A) or for the specific printer(s) you'll be working with (B). Shift-clicking on the printer choice(s) will keep the system software choice from being deselected.

If you need networking software installed, select the type from special networking software (C). The File Sharing Software choice will allow you to share files with any other Mac that's on the same network as you are—in this case, a network can be as simple as two Macs hooked up to the same printer.

When you've made your selections, click the Install button and feed in the floppy disks when you're prompted to do so. When that's finished, click the Quit button.

Installing and Removing Resources

The two basic types of resources you'll be handling are fonts and sounds. There are two kinds of font resources, each with its own icon; sound resources also have a special icon.

Courier Courier 12 Simple Beep

A TrueType font icon (left); a screen font icon (middle); and a sound icon (right)

To install a font or sound, drag it into the System file icon or its window. To remove a font or sound from the System file, open the System file and drag the icon out of the window.

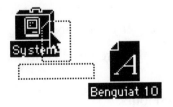

Installing a font into the System file

Quickies

▪ Make sure that you use the Installer program; don't just drag the System and support files from one disk to another. Besides being assured of the correct system for your machine when you use the Installer, using it preserves the resources you've added to your existing system.

▪ You can get system software updates from your Apple dealer. Minor updates are usually free; they are also available from most user groups.

▪ You don't even have to open the System Folder when you want to install a font or sound. If you drag a system resource into the *closed* System Folder, you'll get a dialog asking if you want the resource placed inside the System file.

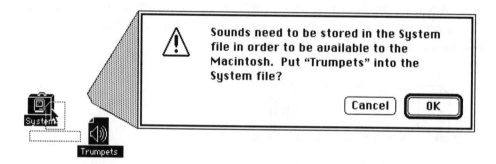

Figure 9-5. Dragging a sound into a closed System Folder

Also See . . .

▪ Chapter 14 explains how to *initialize* a new hard drive to get it ready for use; this must be done before you can install any software on it.

▪ Chapter 11 explains how to use the sounds that are installed in your System.

▪ Chapter 15 discusses TrueType and screen fonts.

THE SYSTEM FOLDER

Basics

The System Folder has a special icon on it so it's easy to pick out in a
crowd (at least until you start editing folder icons). It doesn't really
matter what the folder is named: Any folder that holds the System file
acts as the System Folder and will be "stamped" with the icon.

System Folder

The Folders in the Folder

In prior versions of the Mac System, the System Folder (which was the
only folder with a special icon on it) was cluttered with all sorts of items:
inits (programs that run when you start the Mac), control panel devices,
preference files for various applications, files waiting to be printed by
Print Monitor, downloadable fonts, and more.

   Now the System Folder has special folders inside it to take care of
this clutter, and they have their special icons, too (see Figure 9-6).

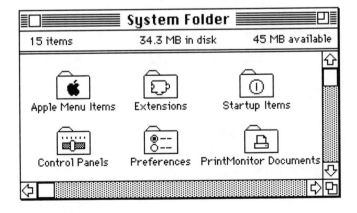

Figure 9-6.   The System Folder's folders

THE APPLE MENU ITEMS FOLDER

Apple Menu Items

To list something in the Apple menu, you simply put it, or its alias, into the Apple Menu Items folder. You don't have to restart the Mac; additions to the folder appear instantly in the menu, neatly alphabetized and identified by miniature icons. Figure 9-7 shows the Apple menu as the Installer creates it and the way it might look after you've customized it.

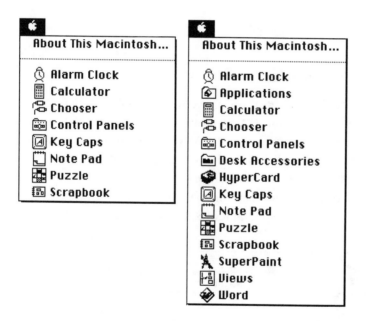

Figure 9-7. The default Apple menu and a customized menu

Selecting an item from the Apple menu opens it, so you have immediate access to desk accessories, control panels, applications, and even the documents that you use often.

You can put an entire folder (or its alias) into the Apple Menu Items folder; in fact, when you install your system, an alias of the Control Panels folder is placed inside the Apple Menu Items folder. When you select a folder from the Apple menu, you're switched to the Desktop (if you weren't already there) and the folder's window opens.

Because you can put single items or folders into the menu, you can set up either instant or a more hierarchical access to the things you need. For example, the applications you use most often can be listed in the menu separately by putting their aliases directly in the Apple Menu Items folder. Applications that you use less often can have their aliases in an Applications folder in the menu. When you want to get to one of those applications, you select the folder from the menu and then double-click on one of the application icons in the window that opens. (This is easier than digging through folder levels on the Desktop.)

THE EXTENSIONS FOLDER

Extensions

System extensions are programs and files that increase the functionality of your Mac. They have to be in the Extensions folder in order to work because that's where the Mac looks for them.

Some types of extensions are:

- Printer "drivers" that act as liaisons between your applications and the printer you're using.

- Drivers that let you access other hardware peripherals, like CD-ROM drives.

- Network configuration software.

- Downloadable fonts for laser printers.

- Files for the Help Balloon feature.

- *Inits* (also known as *startup documents*), programs that run automatically when you start your Mac to add some special feature to the system, like a clock in the menu bar or a utility that automatically saves your work at preset intervals.

Figure 9-8 shows some of the system extensions included with Apple's system software.

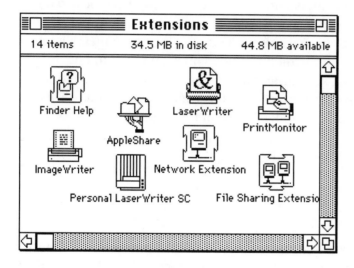

Figure 9-8. System extensions in the Extensions folder

THE STARTUP ITEMS FOLDER

Whatever you place in the Startup Items folder will be opened each time you start up the Mac. (The icon for the folder, by the way, represents the power switch on the back of the modular Macintoshes.)

Prime candidates for this automatic opening are:

- Applications that you use every session.

- Documents that you use every day (like a to-do list that you check first thing in the morning).

- Desk accessories that you use constantly (like the Alarm Clock that you can keep ticking away in the corner of your screen).

Most of the items that you put in this folder will be aliases of the items you want opened, since you won't find this a convenient place to actually store applications or documents.

There's a difference—fine but important—between the init programs that run automatically on startup (they go in the Extensions folder) and programs and documents that you want opened automatically on startup (they go in the Startup Items folder).

THE CONTROL PANELS FOLDER

Control Panels

Control panels are utilities that let you configure certain system settings, like the Desktop pattern, the Label menu, the look of Desktop windows, how the mouse and keyboard work, and even what sound the Mac uses as an alert warning.

Control panels don't have to be in this folder to work, but keeping them together for easy access makes so much sense that the Installer program puts an alias of the Control Panels folder into the Apple Menu Items folder (see Figure 9-9).

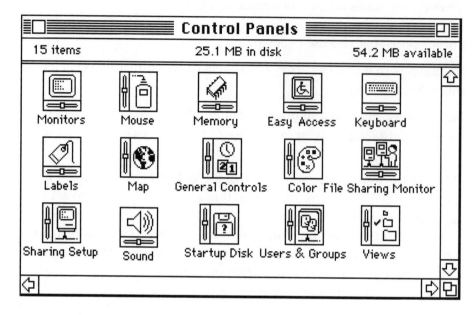

Figure 9-9. The Control Panel folder

THE PREFERENCES FOLDER

Many applications let you configure things like menu commands, how a new window appears, and what the defaults are in certain dialog boxes; they store these choices in a *preference*, or *settings,* file.

An application that knows how to behave under System 7 will store these kinds of files inside the Preferences folder instead of loose in the System Folder as was the case in previous systems.

THE PRINTMONITOR DOCUMENTS FOLDER

PrintMonitor Documents

If you use the PrintMonitor for background printing, it creates its own
PrintMonitor Documents folder to hold its files.

Other System Folder Contents

Not everything in your System Folder will be neatly organized into its
subfolders. Here's a list of some of the other things you'll find in the
main level of the System Folder, as displayed in Figure 9-10:

- The Finder application that gives you your Desktop (top row).

- A Clipboard icon that you can double-click to check the current
contents of the Clipboard (third row).

- Special files used by desk accessories; some of these will have special,
easily identifiable icons (like the Scrapbook and the Note Pad in the third
row), while others use generic document icons (like the last item in the
third row).

- Preference and settings files and folders from applications that don't
yet know how to "behave" under System 7 (fourth row).

- Temporary files used by applications that are usually erased when you
quit the application (last row). You'll see them if the application is still
running or if the system crashed before you quit the application.

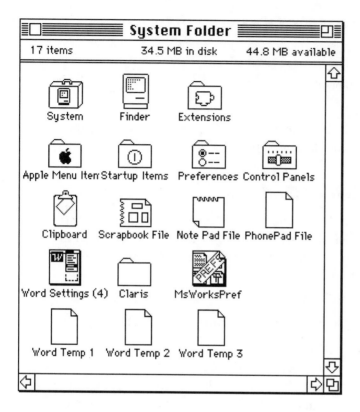

Figure 9-10. The System Folder holds more than just subfolders.

Quickies

▪ Since items are listed in the Apple menu alphabetically, you can rearrange things by renaming the icons in the Apple Menu Items folder. Figure 9-11 shows the before and after of an Apple menu: first with both applications and folders listed together, and then with all the applications grouped together and all the folders grouped together beneath them. This was accomplished by typing a bullet (the Option-8 character) in front of each application name and an Option-F character in front of each folder name.

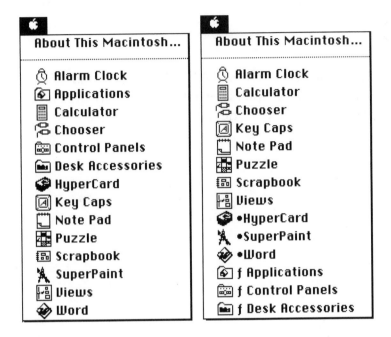

Figure 9-11. Before and after renaming certain items

■ If you're not sure whether a file is a control panel device or an extension (or something else entirely), try dragging the file into the closed System Folder. You'll be notified of where the item belongs if it should go into the Control Panels folder, the Extensions folder, or even the System file itself.

Also See . . .

■ Desk accessories are covered in Chapter 10; control panels are explained in Chapter 11.

■ Chapter 16 explains how to use the Print Monitor.

SUMMARY

Those are the basics of the Mac's System Folder, the magic behind the Mac's operation. The next two chapters detail two special types of files inside the System Folder: desk accessories and control panels.

Desk Accessories

ABOUT THIS CHAPTER

Desk accessories are one of the ways the Mac proves that good things come in small packages. There are hundreds of desk accessory programs available from commercial, and even free, sources; Apple gets you started by providing seven with its system software.

USING DESK ACCESSORIES

Basics

It used to be easy to define *desk accessory* as a little program listed in the Apple menu that you could take out and use even while running another application. Now that the Mac operating system lets you run more than one application at a time and put anything in the Apple menu, the definition is more difficult. Essentially, a desk accessory is a very small program; the quintessential desk accessory is the Calculator.

A desk accessory is familiarly referred to as a DA (the letters are pronounced separately). There are hundreds of DAs available from commercial, and even free, sources, but Apple provides these basics with your system software:

- Alarm Clock
- Calculator
- Chooser
- Key Caps
- Note Pad
- Puzzle
- Scrapbook

You open a desk accessory the way you open any program: Double-click on it. Or if it's listed in the Apple menu, select it to open it. To quit a DA, use its own Quit command or the one in the Mac's File menu; to quit a DA that consists of a single window (like the Calculator), just click in its close box.

DA Files

Some desk accessories don't store any information. The Alarm Clock, for instance—you take it out, you use it, and you put it away. You don't save a document with the Alarm Clock information in it.

Many desk accessories let you create documents just the way applications do, but none of Apple's standard DAs falls into this category.

Then there's the type of desk accessory that lets you store and retrieve information, but you never get to name a document or open it. These DAs (the Note Pad and Scrapbook fall into this category) use a single document that's both opened automatically when you open the desk accessory and saved automatically. It seems like the information is part of the desk accessory itself, but there is, in fact, a separate file on the disk (in the System Folder) that stores the information.

Desk accessories that access their files automatically can work only with a file that has the correct name. If you go to your Desktop and rename the *Scrapbook File* to anything else, the next time you open your Scrapbook, it will be empty.

Old DAs in System 7

In previous systems, desk accessories were stored in the System file itself or collected into files called "suitcases" because of their icons.

To access an "old" desk accessory under System 7, double-click on the suitcase file. The desk accessories inside will be displayed with generic application icons. Drag the desk accessories that you want out of their windows and onto your new system disk.

There's no guarantee that the older DAs will function correctly under System 7, however, since some applications must be updated to work with new system software.

Quickies

▪ Many desk accessories add a menu to the menu bar, but sometimes that's easy to overlook—so don't forget to look.

▪ The Mac's basic File and Edit menus remain in the menu bar when most DAs are running; their commands are usually functional even if the DA has its own menu.

▪ For easy access to desk accessories that you don't want listed separately in the Apple menu because you don't use them *that* often, create a Desk Accessory folder and put it inside the Apple Menu Items folder.

▪ If a DA has a file stored anywhere on the disk, double-clicking on the file opens the DA.

ALARM CLOCK

Basics

The usefulness of the Alarm Clock is often overlooked—perhaps because it's so tiny. You can use it to check the time or date, but also to *set* the time or date for your Mac, as well as to beep an alarm at a preset time.

When you take out the Alarm Clock, its appearance depends on how it looked when it was last put away. It may be a single bar with the time in it, or it may be open to display its controls. You toggle between the time bar and the full version by clicking on the little handle in the right corner. You don't have to drag the handle into position—just a click moves it. Figure 10-1 shows both versions of the Alarm Clock; in the full one, the time, date, and alarm icons are on the bottom and there's an editing area in the middle.

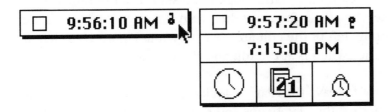

Figure 10-1.   Clicking on the switch in the right corner of the Alarm Clock toggles it between the short and full versions.

Setting the Time and Date

To set the time in the Alarm Clock, open it and click on the time icon in the bottom left; the currently set time appears in the edit area, along with up and down arrows for adjusting the numbers.

To change the time, click on the numbers for the hour, minutes, or seconds; once a number's highlighted, you can change it by typing or by clicking in the arrows. Move to the next group of numbers by clicking or by using the Tab key. To activate the new time, you can click anywhere in the Alarm Clock window (except on the numbers you're editing), press Return or Enter, or even just put the Alarm Clock away (see Figure 10-2).

Figure 10-2. Change the time by selecting the numbers and using the arrows at the right of the edit area.

To change the date, follow the same procedure, but first click on the calendar icon at the bottom of the window.

Setting the Alarm

To set the alarm, click on the alarm clock icon, set the alarm time the same way you set the clock time, and then turn the alarm on by clicking on the switch in the left of the edit area. As shown in Figure 10-3, when the alarm is on, the switch is at the top and the icon shows a ringing alarm clock.

You don't have to leave the Alarm Clock out in order for the alarm to work. When it "rings," the Mac beeps and the apple in the Apple menu flashes alternately with the alarm clock icon until you acknowledge the alarm by opening the Alarm Clock and turning off the switch in the edit area.

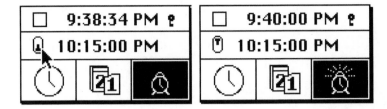

Figure 10-3. When you turn the alarm on, the icon changes.

If the Mac is off at the alarm time, the Apple menu will be flashing when you turn your machine back on.

Quickies

▪ If you leave the Alarm Clock out while you're working in other windows and position it so that it's visible, you'll get a constant readout of the time; the time is updated even when the Alarm Clock is not the active window.

Also See . . .

▪ Chapter 11 explains how to set the Mac's time and date through the General control panel.

CALCULATOR

Basics

To use the Calculator, click on its keys with the mouse, or type in the numbers; you can use the numbers across the top of the keyboard or the ones on the numeric keypad. The asterisk (*) is used for multiplication, and the slash (/) for division. The Clear key on the keyboard is the same as the C key on the Calculator. The Enter key on the keyboard is the same as the Equals (=) key on the keyboard or the Calculator.

Figure 10-4. The Calculator

Copying and Pasting

When you've figured something out on the Calculator, you don't have to type the answer into your document (if that's why you were doing the figuring). Just choose Copy from the ever-present Edit menu, and the Calculator's answer is copied to the Clipboard—you don't have to select it first.

Even more interesting is the Mac's ability to paste a problem into the Calculator from a document. If, for example, you copy *7*5/2* from a document, open the Calculator, and choose Paste from the Edit menu, all the buttons will flash in order as if you had clicked on the numbers, and the answer, 17.5, appears.

CHOOSER

Basics

The Chooser desk accessory lets you select printer options, and, if you're connected to a network, it lets you choose network zones and connect to file servers.

Figure 10-5 shows what the Chooser window looks like when it first opens. The left panel, which is active (note the extra frame around it), shows all the drivers that were installed when you used the Installer.

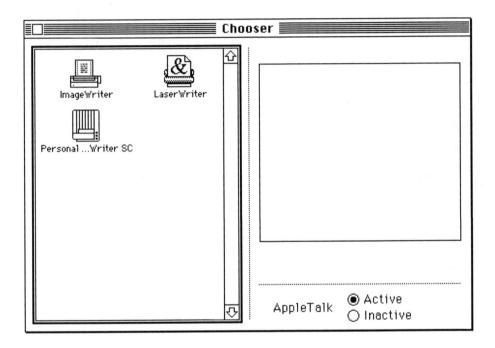

Figure 10-5. The Chooser

Choosing a Printer

When you click on a printer icon in the left panel, the right panel is activated and lists available options. Sometimes the option is a list of available printers of that type, or as shown in Figure 10-6, the sole printer available. Sometimes the options consist of indicating which port the printer is connected to, as shown in Figure 10-7.

Two buttons at the bottom of the Chooser window let you set the AppleTalk status. (AppleTalk is Apple's networking protocol.) If you're on a network, AppleTalk has to be activated; sometimes, however, a

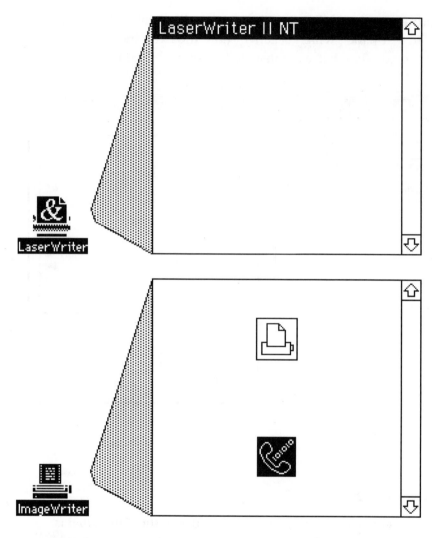

Figures 10-6 and 10-7. Sample printer options in the Chooser

single LaserWriter connected to your computer is a network. Check the manual that came with your printer to see if you need AppleTalk on.

There's no OK button in the Chooser window, but when you put it away by clicking in its close box or choosing Close or Quit from the File menu, any changes you made take effect.

Quickies

▪ When either Chooser panel is activated, you can select an item in it by typing its name (or just enough letters to uniquely identify it) or by using the arrow keys. Use the Tab key to alternately activate each panel.

▪ Even if your printer's connected, it won't show up in the list in the right Chooser panel unless it's turned on and warmed up. If you open the Chooser before the printer's warmed up, you'll have to wait for the printer to appear in the list.

Also See . . .

▪ The Chooser also lets you turn background printing on and off; this is covered in Chapter 16.

KEY CAPS

Basics

Key Caps lets you see what characters are generated by different key combinations. Typing on your keyboard or clicking on a Key Caps key with the mouse puts the character in the Key Caps window.

Pressing Shift or Option, or both, changes the displayed set of characters to the ones you'll get by using those keys. To change the font being displayed in Key Caps, select a font from the Key Caps menu.

Figure 10-8 shows the lowercase character set for the Chicago font and the shifted character set for the Symbol font. The squares and rectangles indicate that there are no characters available on those keys. (In some fonts you'll find a lot of blank keys in Option and Shift-Option combinations.)

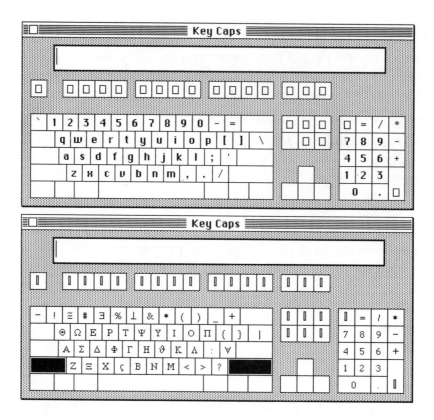

Figure 10-8. · The unshifted Chicago character set (top); the shifted Symbol character set (bottom)

Copying and Pasting

If you paste text into Key Caps, you'll see each letter highlighted individually before the text appears at the top of the window.

While there's no good reason to paste into Key Caps, there is a good reason to copy from it. If you've found just the group of special characters that you need, there's no reason to memorize which keys generated them. Just copy them from the Key Caps window and paste them into your document.

To copy something from Key Caps, first drag across the characters to select them. (This is in contrast to the Calculator, where the displayed numbers don't have to be selected in order to be copied.)

Quickies

- There's no reason to do the following maneuver other than the fact that it can be done and is pretty neat the first time you see it: If you position the window of the program you're using so that you can still see the Key Caps window as you type, you'll see each letter you hit on the keyboard highlighted in Key Caps even while you're working in the other window.

- The special accented characters described in Chapter 6 can be displayed in Key Caps. If you hold down the Option key, the keys that produce the accents are framed in gray, as shown at the top of Figure 10-9. Press the accent you want (while Option is still held down) and then release both keys. Key Caps then displays the keys you can use with the accent by framing them in black, as shown at the bottom of the figure.

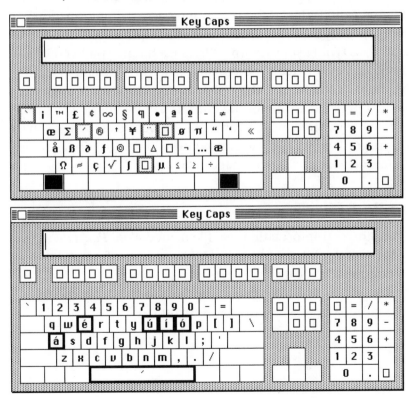

Figure 10-9.   Key Caps displays the special accent characters by framing them in gray and black.

NOTE PAD

Basics

The Note Pad provides eight pages on which you can enter notes. There's not a lot of room on each page and there's no way to change the size or style of the text, but basic text-editing functions (such as double-clicking and dragging to select text, and using arrow keys to move the insertion point) are available.

You can type directly in the Note Pad or paste text into it. The Cut, Copy, and Paste commands work within the Note Pad (so you can move information from one page to another), but they also work between the Note Pad and any application you're using.

You can, for instance, keep your name, address, and telephone number stored in the Note Pad, and then copy and paste that information into a word processor document. Depending on your typing skills, this might be a lot faster than typing your return address each time you need it. The Note Pad is also a handy place to store names and phone numbers.

Flip the pages of the Note Pad by clicking in its lower-left corner. Clicking in the upturned corner of the current page sends you to the next page; clicking in the exposed corner of the next page sends you to the previous page. The pages cycle around, so you can go forward from page 1 to page 8 or backward from page 8 to page 1.

The Note Pad File

The Note Pad stores its information in a file named *Note Pad File* in your System Folder. You don't have to open the file or save information into it; that's all done automatically.

If there's no file named *Note Pad* in the System Folder when you open the Note Pad, a new one is created for you.

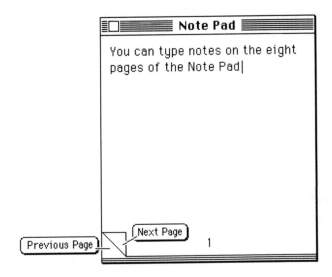

Figure 10-10. Click in the page corners to turn pages in the Note Pad.

Quickies

▪ Although the Note Pad accesses only the one file, you can work with multiple Note Pads by going to the Desktop and renaming the original file. The next time you open the DA, a new *Note Pad File* is created. By renaming files as necessary, you can switch from one file to another.

PUZZLE

Basics

You'll probably recognize the Puzzle desk accessory from your childhood. It provides two sets of tiles to play with (both are shown in Figure 10-11) and you toggle between them by using the Clear command in the Edit menu. Clicking on a tile next to the blank space moves that tile into the space; you can shift two or three tiles at a time if the one you click on is in a horizontal line with the space.

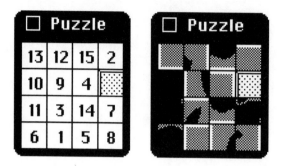

Figure 10-11. Toggle between the two Puzzles with the Clear command.

Making Your Own Puzzle

You can paste any image into the Puzzle; if it's too big to fit, it will be scaled down. The picture is automatically scrambled into pieces when you paste it in, as shown in Figure 10-12.

If you use the Clear command on your own picture, it's erased from the Puzzle; afterward, Clear once again toggles between the two standard Puzzles.

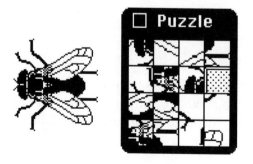

Figure 10-12. You can turn any picture into a puzzle.

SCRAPBOOK

Basics

The Scrapbook stores text and graphics, and even sounds, on an unlimited number of pages. It's a great way to store text and images that you use often, or that you want to transfer from one application to another when you don't need the immediacy of a Clipboard transfer or the active linking of Publish and Subscribe.

The Scrapbook stores and retrieves its information automatically, using a file named *Scrapbook File* stored in the System Folder.

Scrapbook Pages

When you open the Scrapbook, the page that's displayed is the one you were looking at when you last used it. As shown in Figure 10-13, at the bottom, in the left, is a page number and total page count, and at the right is a note as to the type of information stored on that page. The basic types are *PICT* for images, *TEXT* for plain text, and *snd* for sounds.

Figure 10-13. The Scrapbook

The Scrapbook window is a fixed size; if you put in a large picture, you won't see the whole thing. But the whole picture is stored, so when you retrieve it, you'll get the whole thing back.

To turn the pages, use the scroll bar and arrows at the bottom of the Scrapbook.

Cut, Copy, and Paste

To cut or copy the displayed page from the Scrapbook, just choose Cut or Copy from the Edit menu; you don't have to select anything first. (You can use the Clear command to delete a page without putting it on the Clipboard.)

When you're pasting something into the Scrapbook, just choose Paste from the Edit menu; a new page will be created to hold the pasted item. The new page is inserted on top of the page that's showing, so if you want the new page to be something other than page 1, move to a different part of the Scrapbook before pasting.

Scrapbook Contents

You can paste text, graphics, or sound into the Scrapbook.

When you paste text, it appears in 12-point plain Geneva, no matter how it was formatted when you copied it; most of the formats are retained in the Scrapbook even though it doesn't display them. But whether you'll get those formats back when you retrieve text from the Scrapbook depends on where you're pasting the information. If you paste it into a document in the same application from where it originated, you'll get the formats. If you paste it into a document in a *similar* application (such as from one word processor to another), you'll *probably* get the formatting with it.

You can paste bit-mapped or object-oriented images into the Scrapbook; both will be identified as PICT files. The Scrapbook can store color and grayscale PICT images, too.

You can transfer sounds between the Scrapbook and the System file by using the Sound control panel as an intermediary. The control panel lists the sounds in the System; you can select one, cut or copy it, and then paste it into the Scrapbook. Or you can paste a sound from the Scrapbook into the list, which places it into the System file.

A page with a sound on it displays the sound icon and there's a Play Sound button available (which is a good thing—there's no other way to identify what the sound is because you can't name Scrapbook pages). (See Figure 10-14.)

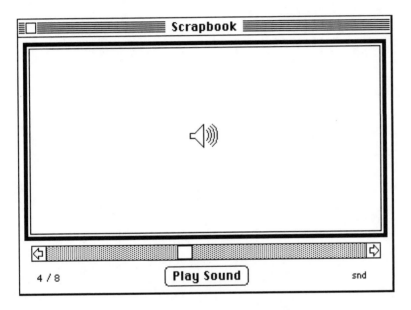

Figure 10-14. A sound can be stored in the Scrapbook.

Quickies

- You can create and manipulate multiple Scrapbook files the same way you can for the Note Pad: Rename the files in the System Folder.

Also See . . .

- The Sound control panel is covered in Chapter 11.

SUMMARY

That's the roundup of Apple's desk accessories. None of them takes long to learn, but all of them (with the possible exception of the Puzzle) can remain useful for a long time; some, like the Chooser, are absolute necessities.

Control Panels

ABOUT THIS CHAPTER

USING CONTROL PANELS

Basics
Quickies

BRIGHTNESS

Basics

CLOSEVIEW

Basics
Magnification Levels
White on Black
Keyboard Options

COLOR

Basics
Setting the Highlight Color
Setting Window Color
Quickies

EASY ACCESS

Basics
Quickies

FILE-SHARING CONTROL PANELS

Basics
The Control Panels

GENERAL CONTROLS

Basics

KEYBOARD

Basics

LABELS

Basics
Label Colors
Quickies

MAP

Basics
Entering Cities
Quickies

MEMORY

Basics
Setting the RAM Cache
Setting the Virtual Memory Size
Also See . . .

MONITORS

Basics
Setting Color Levels
Using Two Monitors
Quickies

MOUSE

Basics
Tracking Speed
Double-Click Speed

SOUND

Basics
Adjusting the Sound and
  the Volume
Recording Sounds
Quickies

STARTUP DISK

Basics

VIEWS

Basics
Setting the Font and the Size
Icon Views
List Views
Quickies

SUMMARY

ABOUT THIS CHAPTER

Previous Macintosh systems provided a Control Panel desk accessory that let you access various *control panel devices* (or *cdevs*) to adjust certain system settings. With System 7 the approach is a little different: Each device is a control panel itself. This chapter covers the control panels that Apple provides with its system software.

USING CONTROL PANELS

Basics

Most control panels let you check and adjust system settings such as how fast you must click the mouse for it to be interpreted as a double-click, what the background of your Desktop looks like, and which disk acts as the startup.

When you install your system software, control panels are placed inside the Control Panels folder, and an alias of the folder is placed in the Apple Menu Items folder so that you can easily get at your control panels.

Control Panels

To use a control panel, open it by double-clicking on its icon, make your choices, and then put it away. Some control panel settings take effect immediately; for others, the changes you make won't take effect until you restart the computer.

The basic control panels included in the system software are:

- Brightness
- CloseView
- Color
- Easy Access

- File Sharing Monitor
- General Controls
- Keyboard
- Labels
- Map
- Memory
- Monitors
- Mouse
- Sharing Setup
- Sound
- Startup Disk
- Users & Groups
- View

What's considered "basic" in the way of control panels depends to some extent on your system setup. The Brightness control panel, for example, is used only with the Mac Classic and portables; other models have dimming controls right on the monitor. The Sound control panel, too, changes depending on your model, since some models let you input sound as well as play it. Sharing Setup, File Sharing Monitor, and Users & Groups are control panels used when you're on a network.

Quickies

- Since there's an alias of the Control Panels folder in the Apple menu, it's easy to open the folder. But that means there's a two-step process every time you want to use a control panel: Open the folder and then double-click on the icon. If there are control panels that you use often, make aliases of them and put them "loose" in the Apple Menu Items folder so they'll be listed in the Apple menu. Then, selecting the control panel from the menu opens it immediately.

BRIGHTNESS

Basics

Most Mac models have dials on their monitors that let you control the screen brightness, but the Classic and the Portable have a Brightness control panel instead.

To adjust the brightness of your screen with the control panel, drag the bar on the brightness control to the left or right (see Figure 11-1).

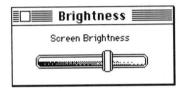

Figure 11-1. Drag the bar to adjust the screen brightness.

CLOSEVIEW

Basics

The CloseView control panel was designed to help visually impaired people use the Mac more comfortably, but it can also be used to magnify things on the screen for precision work in a program that doesn't provide magnification. CloseView can also reverse the standard black-on-white Mac approach to white-on-black.

The CloseView window, shown in Figure 11-2, gives you a master on/off control and separate controls for the magnification level, black-white reversal, and keyboard shortcuts.

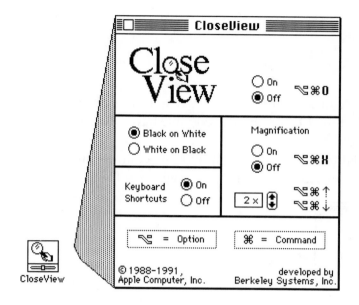

Figure 11-2. The CloseView control panel

Magnification Levels

Once the master control at the top of the window is turned on, a thick black rectangular frame surrounds the mouse cursor as you move it around on the screen (see Figure 11-3). The size of the frame depends on the current magnification-level setting because it shows how much of the screen will be displayed if you turn on the magnification.

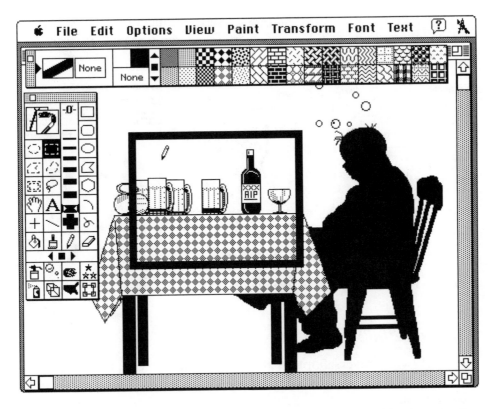

Figure 11-3.   A black frame follows the cursor (the pencil in this picture) when CloseView is turned on.

Use the arrows in the magnification area of the window (as shown in Figure 11-4) to change the magnification level; you can set it anywhere from 2 to 16 times normal.

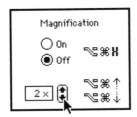

Figure 11-4.   Click on the arrows to change the magnification level.

Figure 11-5 shows the effect of a 2x and a 4x magnification of the CloseView window itself. You can work in a magnified view the same way you work normally on the Mac.

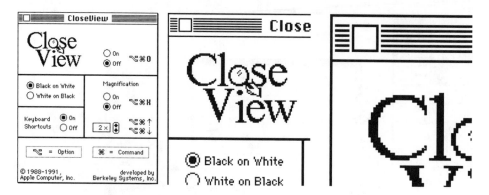

Figure 11-5. Standard, 2x, and 4x magnification

White on Black

The black/white reversal option affects the entire screen, even the menu bar. Figure 11-6 shows part of the CloseView window in its reversed colors.

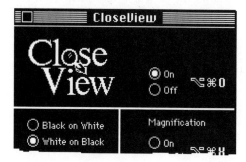

Figure 11-6. A sample of the white-on-black option

Keyboard Options

You can turn the keyboard control of CloseView options on or off. If they're on, you don't have to take out the control panel to activate any of the options that have keyboard equivalents: turning the master switch on and off, turning magnification on and off, and changing the magnification level.

COLOR

Basics

The Color control panel (available only on color and grayscale systems) lets you set the highlight color for text selection and the basic color for "window frames" (see Figure 11-7).

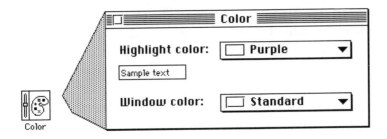

Figure 11-7.   The Color control panel

Setting the Highlight Color

You can select from standard highlight colors by choosing the one you want from the popup menu, as shown in Figure 11-8. Choosing the Other command at the bottom of the menu opens the Color Wheel dialog so that you can create a custom highlight color.

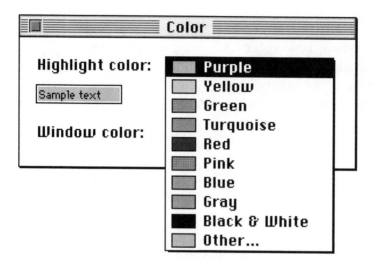

Figure 11-8.   The highlight color menu

USING THE COLOR WHEEL

The Mac's color wheel lets you choose colors from a wide range—over 16 million colors are available when you're working on a full-color monitor.

As shown in Figure 11-9, the block of color in the upper left displays two shades: the currently set highlight color and the new one that you've created. You create the new color by working with the numbers in the six text boxes (you can type them or use the arrows to change them), or by working with the color wheel itself and the scroll bar next to it.

The current color setting is indicated by a small circle in the color wheel; click the cursor (which is a large circle when you're in the color wheel) to move it to a new spot. When you choose a new color by clicking, the numbers in the text boxes change to describe the new color. The only number not affected by clicking in the color wheel is the Brightness setting. You change the brightness of a color by using the scroll bar to the right of the wheel; as the scroll box moves down, more black is added to the color.

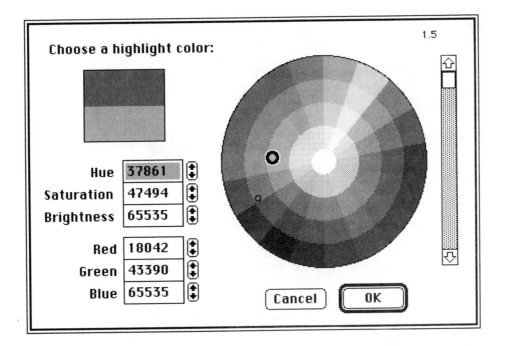

Figure 11-9. The color wheel

Setting Window Color

To change the basic color of window frames on a color or grayscale system, select the color you want from the second popup menu in the Colors window, as shown in Figure 11-10. This changes the window's title bar and scroll controls, but not its contents.

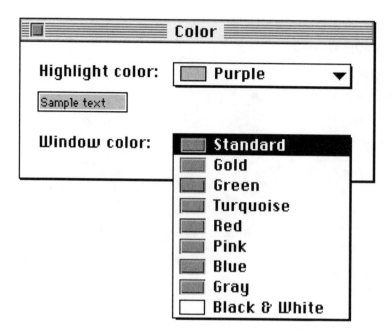

Figure 11-10. Choose a window color from the second menu

Quickies

▪ Selected text doesn't invert when it's highlighted in color, so don't choose a dark highlight color.

▪ On color and grayscale systems, you can still choose Black & White for the window color. This doesn't affect the contents of the window, but it does mean that your screen will redraw more quickly.

EASY ACCESS

Basics

Easy Access is another control panel that was originally designed to help handicapped people use the Mac and wound up having wider applications for all users. Easy Access lets you use the keyboard to control the mouse cursor on the screen, set a delay so a key press won't be recognized right away, and configure the keyboard so you can send a key sequence like Command-Shift-S without having to press more than one key at a time.

The Easy Access window doesn't have to be open for you to turn its features on and off; each has a keyboard sequence that you can use to activate or deactivate it. There's an option for audio feedback (the Use On/Off Audio Feedback button, shown in Figure 11-11) so you can be sure that you've turned the feature on or off. When you turn a feature on, you'll hear a whistle with a rising pitch; when you turn a feature off, the whistle's pitch is going down.

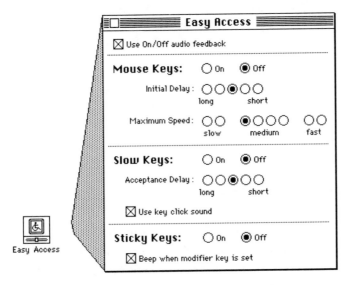

Figure 11-11.   The Easy Access control panel

MOUSE KEYS

Mouse Keys lets you control the mouse cursor by using the keyboard's numeric keypad. You toggle Mouse Keys on and off by clicking the buttons in the Easy Access window or by pressing Command-Shift-Clear.

Once Mouse Keys is turned on, you use the keys in the numeric keypad instead of the mouse. As shown in Figure 11-12, the keys surrounding the 5 key move the cursor in any of eight directions. The 5 key acts as the mouse button for clicks and double-clicks. The zero key locks the mouse button down (so you can drag things and use menus) and the decimal point key unlocks it.

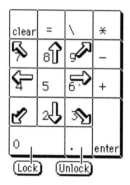

Figure 11-12.   The keypad controls for the mouse cursor

As shown in Figure 11-13, the rest of the buttons in the Mouse Keys area of the window let you set how long a delay there is between the initial key press (which moves the cursor a distance of one pixel on the screen) and the time that the cursor continues to move in the indicated direction. The second set of speed controls are for how fast the cursor will move once it gets going.

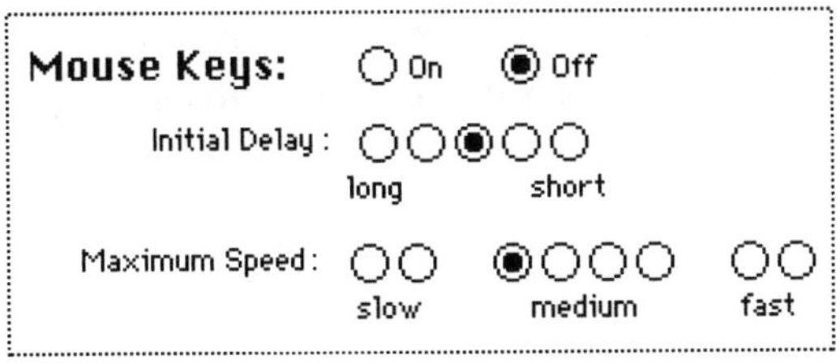

Mouse Keys: ◯ On ⦿ Off

Initial Delay : ◯◯⦿◯◯
long   short

Maximum Speed : ◯◯   ⦿◯◯◯   ◯◯
slow   medium   fast

Figure 11-13. Mouse Keys controls

SLOW KEYS

Slow Keys lets you add a delay to every key press so that accidental presses won't register. Turn Slow Keys on with the buttons (shown in Figure 11-14) or (if you're not in a text window that will interpret the key press as typing) by holding down the Return key. Then set how long or short a delay you want by using the radio buttons. Since sometimes it's hard to tell when a delayed key actually registers, you should always leave the Use Key Click Sound option on.

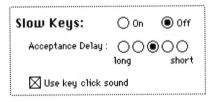

Slow Keys: ◯ On ⦿ Off

Acceptance Delay : ◯◯⦿◯◯
long   short

☒ Use key click sound

Figure 11-14. Slow Keys controls

STICKY KEYS

With Sticky Keys, you can type key combinations like Command-Shift-Option-P by pressing only one key at a time.

Turn Sticky Keys on and off with the buttons in the Easy Access window (see Figure 11-5) or by pressing the Shift key five times. Once Sticky Keys is activated, a single press of any modifier key (Shift, Option, Command, or Control) "sets" the key so that the Mac thinks the key is still being held down when you press the next key. So, you can press

Shift and then P and get an uppercase P. If you follow a modifier key
with another modifier key, they both stay down until an alphanumeric
key is pressed.

Figure 11-15.   Sticky Keys controls

You can lock down a modifier key so that it stays down for more
than one subsequent key press. To lock and unlock a modifier key, press
it twice. For example: You might want to use the keyboard to issue a
Command-S for Save and then a Command-Q for Quit. Lock the
Command key down by pressing it twice, then press S and then Q. The
Mac interprets those actions as a Command-S followed by a Command-Q.

Sticky Keys settings offer both audio and visual feedback. You can
check the Beep When Modifier Key is Set in the window so that when a
modifier key sticks down, you'll hear a beep (which sounds different
from the system beep). But there's also always an indication in the menu
bar what the Sticky Key status is. As shown in Figure 11-16, if Sticky
Keys is on, a bracket appears in the upper-right corner; if a modifier is
set, an arrow points down into the bracket; if the modifier is locked, the
bracket is filled.

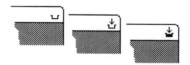

*Figure 11-16.   Sticky Keys is activated (left); a modifier key is set (middle); a
modifier key is locked down (right).*

Quickies

▪ Since just tapping one of the cursor-motion keys moves the cursor by only a single pixel on the screen, you can use Mouse Keys to fine tune the placement of objects in graphics and page layout programs that don't provide that kind of feature themselves.

▪ You can do the equivalent of a Shift-click with Mouse Keys by using Sticky Keys to lock the Shift key while you manipulate the cursor with Mouse Keys.

▪ There are two additional keyboard options for turning off Sticky Keys: Command-period, and pressing any two modifier keys at the same time.

FILE-SHARING CONTROL PANELS

Basics

There are several control panels and one Desktop command that are used for basic file sharing on the Mac. Because this book takes a one-person/one-Macintosh approach, and these are items meant for network procedures, they're covered only briefly here.

The Control Panels

The Sharing Setup control panel, shown in Figure 11-17, lets you name your Macintosh, identify yourself for the network, and enter a password that lets you get at everything on your computer if you're accessing it from elsewhere on the network. It also lets you activate and deactivate the file-sharing and program-linking options that let other people on the network access information in your computer.

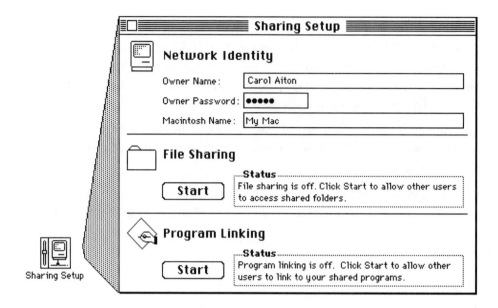

Figure 11-17.   The Sharing Setup dialog

The Users & Groups control panel (Figure 11-18) lets you identify the people allowed to access your computer over the network.

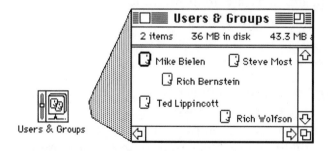

Figure 11-18.   The Users & Groups control panel

You use the Sharing command in the Desktop's File menu (Figure 11-19) to set the *access level* for a file or folder, specifying who's allowed to see it and who's allowed to alter its contents.

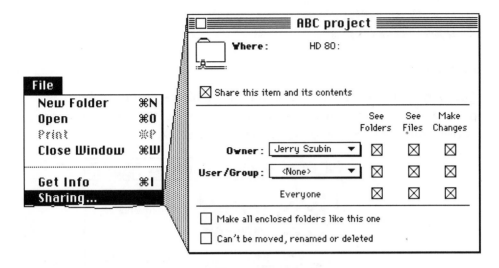

Figure 11-19. The Sharing command and its dialog box

Finally the File Sharing Monitor (Figure 11-20) lets you check what items are currently set to be shared and who's connected to the network.

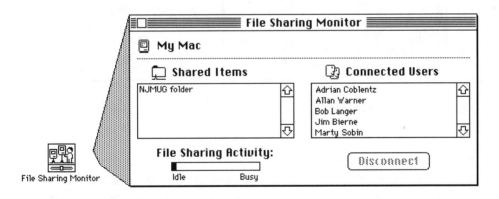

Figure 11-20. The File Sharing Monitor control panel

GENERAL CONTROLS

Basics

The General Controls panel lets you set the basics of the Desktop pattern and color, the insertion point blink speed, the menu blinking option, and the time and date (see Figure 11-21).

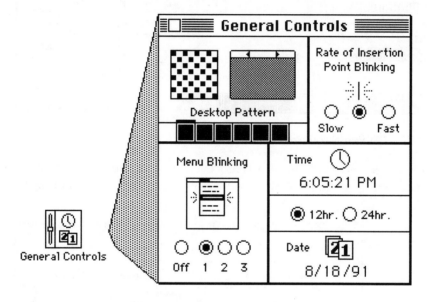

Figure 11-21. The General Controls control panel

DESKTOP PATTERN

There are several preset Desktop patterns to choose from and you can also create your own. To page through the preset patterns, click on the little arrows above the miniature desktop. When you see the one you want, click on the pattern and your Desktop changes instantly (see Figure 11-22).

To edit a pattern, click or drag the mouse cursor inside the magnified pattern to the left of the miniature Desktop; the mouse will draw in the current color.

You can tell which is the current color by the black bar over it (see Figure 11-22). To choose a different color, click in one of the boxes below the patterns. On a black-and-white system, the two end boxes are white and all the others are black. If you're working in color, you can change the color of any box by double-clicking on it; that opens the color wheel, which you can use to set the color of the box. (Using the color wheel is explained earlier in this chapter, under "Color.")

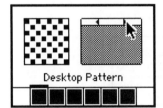 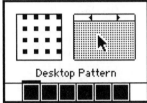 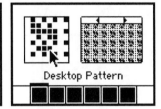

Figure 11-22. Paging through patterns (left); clicking on a pattern to activate it (middle); editing a pattern (right)

INSERTION POINT AND MENU BLINKING

You can choose from three speeds for the blink rate of the insertion point by clicking in one of the three speed buttons. The blink rate is demonstrated above the buttons, as shown in Figure 11-23.

When you select a menu command, it blinks before the menu closes; this feedback helps indicate that the command was indeed selected. You can set the number of blinks to one, two, or three, or you can turn it off completely (see Figure 11-23).

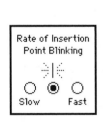 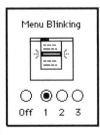

Figure 11-23. The insertion point blinking control (left) and the menu blinking control (right)

SETTING THE TIME AND DATE

Your Mac always knows what time it is and what date it is—as long as you set it to begin with.

To change the time, click on one of the time numbers and then type or use the arrows to change it, as shown in Figure 11-24. You can also choose between a 12-hour clock (marked with AM and PM) and a 24-hour clock (where 1:00 PM is 1300).

The date can be changed in the same way: Click on the number and then type or use the arrows to change it.

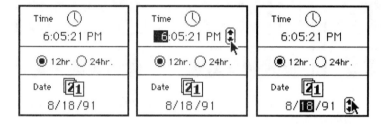

Figure 11-24.   Changing the time and date

KEYBOARD

Basics

The Keyboard control panel lets you set both the repeat rate for keys and the delay from the initial press of the key to when it starts repeating.

You can choose any of five speeds for the repeat rate by clicking in the appropriate button. There are four delay times to choose from and you also have the option of turning the repeat off entirely (see Figure 11-25).

The bottom of the Keyboard control panel lets you select the keyboard layout you're using; the basic system software provides only one choice.

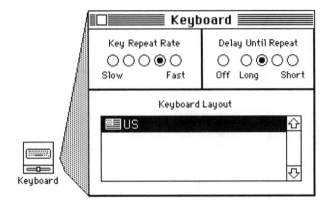

Figure 11-25. The Keyboard control panel

LABELS

Basics

The Labels control panel lets you change the contents of the Label menu. If you're working on a color system, it also lets you change the label colors.

To change the name of a label, simply edit it in the window. The changes are immediately reflected in the Label menu (see Figure 11-26).

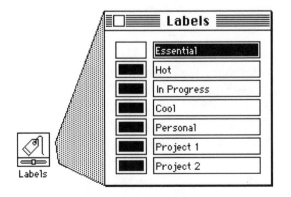

Figure 11-26.   The Labels control panel and the Label menu on a black-and-white system

Label Colors

As Figure 11-26 shows, the Labels window shows color blocks even in a black-and-white system, although the Label menu doesn't. Figure 11-27 shows the window and menu in a color system.

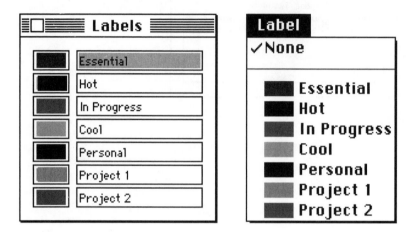

Figure 11-27. The Labels control panel and the Label menu on a color system

If you're working in color, you can double-click on any of the color blocks in the control panel window to open the color wheel and choose a new color for the block. (Using the color wheel is described earlier in this chapter, under "Color.")

Quickies

▪ If you change the name of a label that's been applied to icons, all the labeled icons will change to the new label.

Basics

The Map control panel lets you check the latitude, longitude, and time zone of a selected city. It also lets you check the time difference and the distance between the selected city and a base city (see Figure 11-28).

Map 355

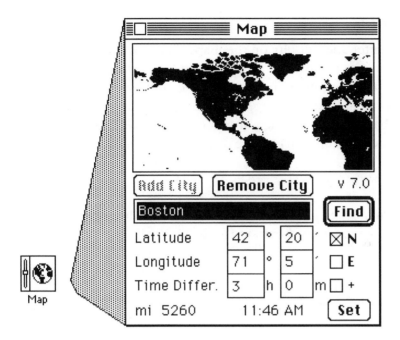

Figure 11-28. The Map control panel

There are only a few cities already in the Map, marked by tiny blinking dots. Click on a dot, or drag around on the Map until you touch one, and its information will be displayed. As you drag to the edge of the picture, it will scroll so you can see more of the map.

Or you can type the name of the city you want in the text box and then click the Find button; if it's not on the map (and it probably won't be), the Mac will beep.

The checkboxes at the right of the window are for latitude, longitude, and time difference. If the N is checked, the measurement is North latitude; unchecked, it's South latitude. If the E is checked, the measurement is East longitude; unchecked, it's West longitude. If the Plus (+) is checked, the time difference is how many hours later it is than the base city; unchecked, the time difference refers to how many hours earlier it is than the base city.

Entering Cities

If you want to enter another city on the map, click in its approximate location and enter its name; then click the Add City button. The latitude, longitude, and time zone are entered automatically, based on the spot where you clicked in the map.

To set the base city from which distance and time difference are measured, locate it (or enter it) on the map and click the Set button.

Quickies

▪ To cycle from miles to kilometers to degrees in the distance measurement, click on it, as shown in Figure 11-29.

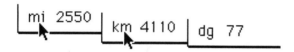

Figure 11-29.   Click on the unit of measurement to change it.

MEMORY

Basics

The Memory control panel lets you set the amount of memory put aside as a disk cache, and how much of your hard drive will be converted to virtual memory.

The theory and practice of both these memory options are detailed in Chapter 13. Briefly, though, a disk cache is a portion of RAM set aside to hold information that's accessed often from the disk. Virtual memory sets aside a portion of your hard drive and treats it as RAM.

All Macs can use the disk cache feature, but only some models can use virtual memory.

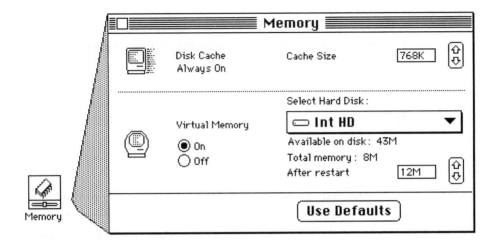

Figure 11-30. The Memory control panel

Setting the RAM Cache

You set the RAM cache size by using the arrows to make the number higher or lower. The number changes in increments of 16, 32, and 64 for the lower numbers and then by increments of 512. The RAM cache is always on, and the lowest amount you can apportion to it is 16K.

The RAM cache you set doesn't take effect until you restart the computer.

Setting the Virtual Memory Size

There are three controls in the Memory window for virtual memory: Turn it on or off with the radio buttons; indicate which drive will be used through the popup menu; and set the amount of virtual memory by using the arrows to raise or lower the number (see Figure 11-30).

The numbers in this area of the window are all labeled *M*, for *megabyte*. The number in the text box that you adjust with the arrow includes the built-in RAM in your machine.

Also See . . .

- Chapter 13 discusses memory considerations and explains more about RAM caches and virtual memory.

MONITORS

Basics

The Monitors control panel lets you set the number of colors your monitor displays; if you have more than one monitor attached to your system, you can use the control panel to let the Mac know the relative positions of the monitors and which one should be considered the main monitor (see Figure 11-31).

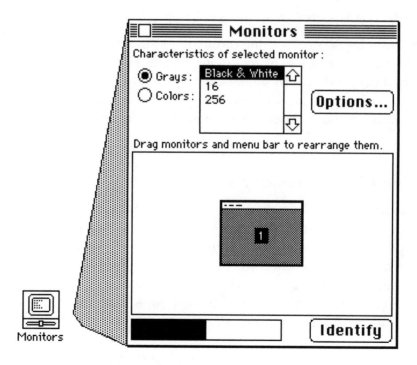

Figure 11-31. The Monitors control panel

Setting Color Levels

You set the colors for your monitor by clicking in the Grays or Colors button and then clicking on Black & White or the number of colors you want displayed. The choices you're able to make will depend on the monitor you're using, but you can always choose something *less* than what your monitor is capable of displaying. For example, you can set a grayscale monitor to display only black and white, or you can have your color monitor work in grayscale or black and white.

The bar at the bottom of the window will display the range of colors you've set for the monitor.

The Options button opens a small dialog that identifies the video card that the current monitor is connected to.

Using Two Monitors

If you have two monitors attached to your computer, the Mac treats them in many ways as one large monitor, letting the mouse (and anything it's dragging) move right from one to the other. But in order for this to work correctly, you have to indicate the relative positions of the monitors.

You show the Mac where the monitors are by dragging the icons in the Monitors control panel to their correct positions. Figure 11-32 shows a standard Apple 13-inch monitor to the lower left of a double-page monitor. If you press the Identify button in the window, you can check which icon stands for which monitor. When you press the button, the icon's number flashes briefly on the monitor it represents.

When you're using multiple monitors, you also get to choose which one has the menu bar: Simply drag the miniature menu bar from one icon to the other.

The number of colors and the relative positioning of multiple monitors is acknowledged immediately, but the menu bar change doesn't take effect until you restart the computer.

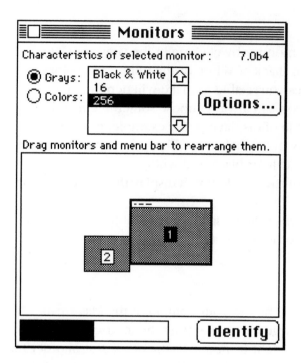

Figure 11-32.   The Monitors control panel shows all the monitors you have attached.

Quickies

▪ Some applications won't let you open their windows to the full size of a larger monitor if you've set the default monitor to be the smaller of the two.

MOUSE

Basics

The Mouse control panel lets you set the tracking speed and the double-click speed for the mouse (see Figure 11-33). Tracking speed is the relationship between how you move the mouse on your desk and how the mouse cursor moves on the screen.

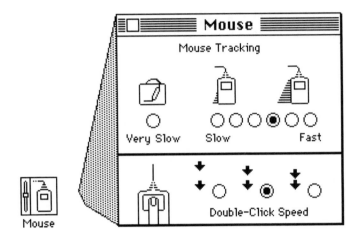

Figure 11-33. The Mouse control panel

Tracking Speed

There are six variable-speed controls in the window for mouse tracking, labeled Slow to Fast. If you use one of these buttons, how *far* the cursor moves on the screen depends on how *fast* you move the mouse. At any setting, if you move the mouse slowly, the cursor movement will match the distance you've moved the mouse. If, however, you move the mouse quickly when you've chosen one of the slower settings, the cursor will move about twice as far as you move the mouse; at faster settings, moving the mouse quickly can move the cursor four or five times the distance the mouse covers.

At the slowest speed (the Very Slow button, for use with graphics tablets), there is no difference between the mouse and the cursor distance: Moving the mouse two inches on your desk moves the cursor two inches on the screen, no matter how quickly or slowly you move the mouse.

As general rules, use Very Slow only if you're using a graphics tablet as an input device, use one of the two slowest settings when you're first learning the Mac, and then use a setting related to the size of your screen—the bigger your screen is, the faster the tracking speed should be.

The new setting for Tracking speed takes effect immediately, so you can test it even before you close the Mouse window.

Double-Click Speed

The second adjustment in the Mouse control panel is for double-click speed—just how fast you have to click the mouse for the clicks to be interpreted as a double-click instead of two single clicks. When you click one of the three speed choices, the button on the mouse in the window flashes at the speed you've chosen.

SOUND

Basics

The Mac's basic beep sound is used as an alert in many different situations. A beep usually accompanies an alert dialog box and is sometimes used instead of a dialog to let you know that you're trying to do something that, under the circumstances, isn't possible. (Clicking anywhere outside a dialog box, for instance, usually results in a beep.)

The alert sound doesn't have to be a beep, though, and the Sound control panel lets you choose from among several sounds, as well as control the overall volume of the Mac's speaker.

And, if your Mac model has sound input capabilities, the Sound control panel lets you record sounds to use as the alert.

Adjusting the Sound and the Volume

The basic Sound control panel is shown in Figure 11-34.

To adjust the Mac's volume, use the Speaker Volume control, sliding the bar to any position from 0 to 7. If you set the volume to zero, there won't be any sound at all; instead, the menu bar flashes whenever the Mac would normally beep.

Figure 11-34. The Sound control panel

To select an alert sound, click on it in the list. The list shows all the sounds installed in the System file (as described in Chapter 9).

Recording Sounds

If your Mac has sound input capability, your Sound control panel will look like the one shown in Figure 11-35. If you click on the microphone icon, the sound controls in the figure will appear. When you click the Record button, you have up to 10 seconds to record your sound; the bar at the bottom of the control dialog shows you how long you've been recording and how long you have left. The Pause button stops the recording temporarily; to resume recording, click Pause again.

The recording stops automatically when the 10 seconds are up; if your sound is over before the 10 seconds, click the Stop button.

You can use the Play button to play back the sound. If you want to save it, click the Save button; you'll be asked to name the sound, and the name will appear in the list with the other sounds.

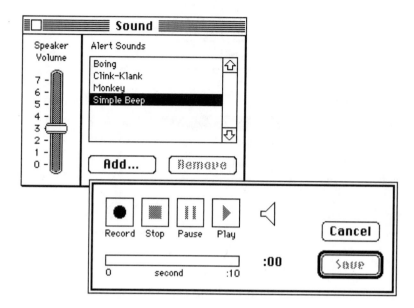

Figure 11-35.   The Sound control panel for sound input systems and the Sound Controls dialog

Quickies

▪ You can use the Cut, Copy, or Clear command on a selected sound in the list. If you use Paste while the Sound control panel is open, a sound on the Clipboard will be pasted into the list.

▪ Sounds can be cut and copied between the Sound control panel and the Scrapbook.

STARTUP DISK

Basics

When you start your Mac, it looks at all the disks available until it finds one with a System on it that can be used as the startup disk. If you have more than one startup disk attached, the Mac uses the first one it finds. There's a specific scanning order the Mac uses for this procedure (it's discussed in Chapter 14), but you can circumvent this natural order of things by using the Startup Disk control panel.

In the panel, you'll see an icon for each of the startup disks currently available; just click on the one you want the Mac to use as the System disk next time you start the computer (see Figure 11-36).

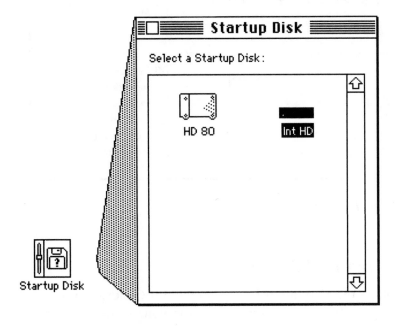

Figure 11-36. The Startup Disk control panel

VIEWS

Basics

The Views control panel lets you define how Desktop windows appear and how their contents are displayed; the settings in the Views control panel also control what's in the Desktop's View menu (see Figure 11-37).

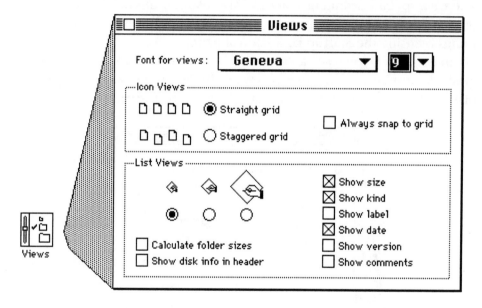

Figure 11-37. The Views control panel

Setting the Font and the Size

The Desktop starts out with icons labeled in 9-point Geneva, but you can change the font and the size to anything that's in your System (and, since it's so easy to install fonts in your System, the possibilities are endless). Figure 11-38 shows some of those possibilities.

Figure 11-38. You can use any font for icon names.

To change the font, select one from the popup menu; you can choose a size by selecting it from the second menu or by typing in the text box (see Figure 11-39).

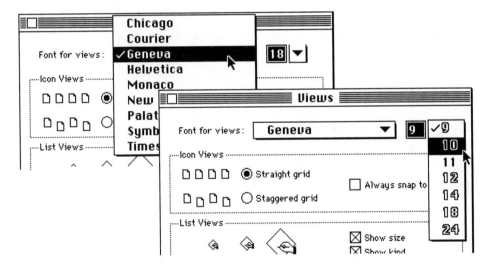

Figure 11-39. Selecting a font and a size from the menus

Font and size changes affect not only icon names in icon views, but all the text in a window, including header information and everything in list views, as shown in Figure 11-40.

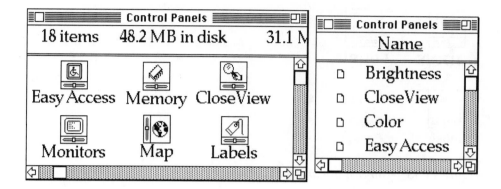

Figure 11-40.   Font and size changes affect icon and list views, and window headers.

Icon Views

The Views control panel provides three controls (as shown in Figure 11-41) for icon views.

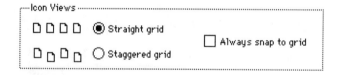

Figure 11-41.   The options for icon views

The invisible grid that the Clean Up commands in the Special menu use can be either a straight or a staggered one; Figure 11-42 shows both. As you can see, a staggered view prevents long icon names from running into each other. (The size of the grid itself changes as you change the font size; when you choose a large font size, the grid points are spaced farther apart to make room for names that take up more space.)

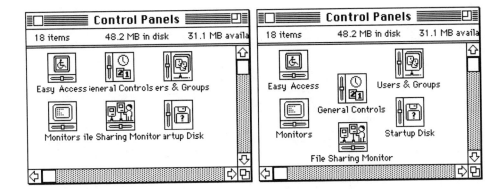

Figure 11-42. The straight grid (left) and the staggered grid (right)

If you use the Always Snap to Grid option, any time you drag an icon in the window it will move to a grid point when it's released.

List Views

There are four main options for list views as shown in Figure 11-43: icon size, displaying folder sizes, including disk information in the window header, and which columns are included in the list.

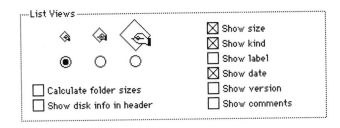

Figure 11-43. The options for list views

Of the three icon size choices, the smallest is the generic icon that identifies a file only as an application, a document, or a folder in a list. Figure 11-44 shows the results of changing the icon size; in the third example, the font was also changed to better match the large icon size.

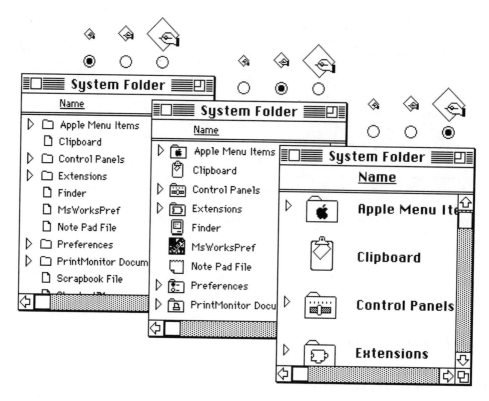

Figure 11-44. Changing icon sizes

As a default, list-view windows don't display the size of folders in the Size column, and they show only column names in the window header. But you can change these defaults with the Calculate Folder Sizes and Show Disk Info in Header options in the Views control panel, as shown in Figure 11-45.

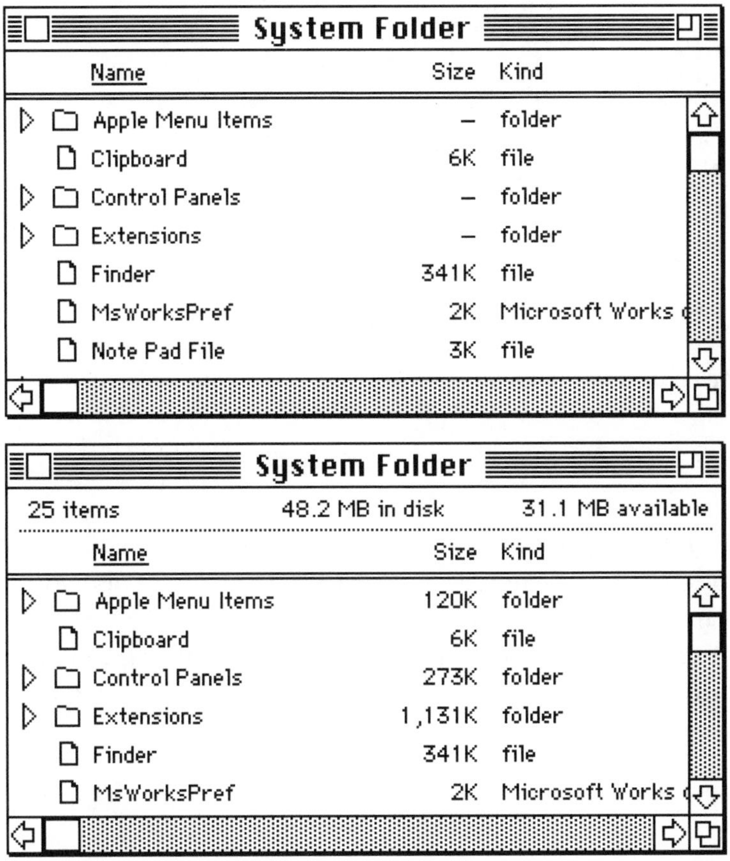

Figure 11-45.   The default list view (top) and both folder sizes and disk information in the header turned on (bottom)

Finally, you can control the columns that are displayed in the window by selecting from the list of checkboxes; the choices also affect what's listed in the View menu, as shown in Figure 11-46. A file's name is always in the window, but you can include or exclude Size, Kind, Label, Date, Version, and Comments by checking or unchecking them in the control panel window.

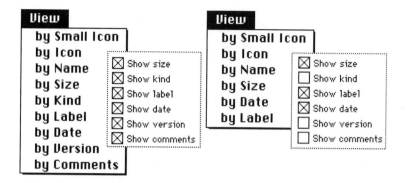

Figure 11-46. The choices in the Views control panel change the View menu.

Quickies

▪ The Command key temporarily reverses the Always Snap to Grid option. If the option is off, holding down the Command key when you drag an icon means it will snap to the grid when you release it. If the option is on, holding down Command keeps the icon from snapping to the grid on release.

SUMMARY

That's the roundup of the control panels that Apple provides; as you purchase additional hardware and software, you'll add to your control panel collection.

In the last three chapters, you've learned a lot about your system software; the next three chapters deal with your system's hardware.

PART V

Macintosh Hardware

CHAPTER 12

Basic Hardware

ABOUT THIS CHAPTER

MACINTOSH MODELS

Basics
Models and Features
Connectors
Quickies
Also See . . .

MONITORS

Basics
How It Works
Size and Resolution
Video RAM and Depth
Quickies
Also See . . .

MOUSE AND KEYBOARD

Basics
Keyboards
The Mouse
Quickies
Also See . . .

THE PROGRAMMER'S SWITCH

Basics
Using the Reset Button
Quickies

SCSI DEVICES

Basics
Terminators
Device Numbers
Quickies

OTHER HARDWARE

Basics
Mouse Alternatives
Scanners
CD-ROM Drives
Modems
Also See . . .

SUMMARY

ABOUT THIS CHAPTER

This chapter takes a general approach to basic Macintosh hardware, dealing with information and issues common to all Macintosh models. (There are so many different models available now that it's beyond the scope of a single book, especially one for beginners, to cover the ins and outs of every model.)

MACINTOSH MODELS

Basics

There are many ways to categorize a Macintosh: by the processor chip that it uses, by its clock speed and sound capabilities, by whether or not it can handle color, and so on. But the two main categories of Macintoshes are the *compact* Macs with built-in screens and the *modular* Macs where the monitor is a separate unit. (There aren't enough models of the Mac Portable for it to be considered a category.)

There are six compact and modular models currently in production (this book was written in mid-1991), but hundreds of thousands of units of previous models are still in use. Many older Mac models can be upgraded to the functionality of the current models using parts available from Apple or from other manufacturers.

Models and Features

You've probably already purchased your Mac and you're using this book to help you get the most out of it, so discussing the pros and cons of each model isn't going to be helpful. Instead, Table 12-1 shows a chart of the current compact and modular Mac models and their main features for a quick comparison.

Table 12-1. Comparing Features of Current Compact and Modular Mac Models

	Classic	SE/30	Mac LC	Mac IIsi	Mac IIci	Mac IIfx
CPU	68000	68030	68020	68030	68030	68030
Co-processor	no	yes	no	optional	yes	yes
Speed	8 MHz	16 MHz	16 MHz	20 MHz	25 MHz	40 MHz
Color ROM	no	yes	yes	yes	yes	yes
Built-in video card	n/a	no	yes	yes	yes	no
Slots	none	1 PDS	1 PDS	1 NuBus or PDS	3 NuBus	6 NuBus, 1 PDS
ROM	512K	256K	512K	512K	512K	512K
Sound input	no	no	yes	yes	no	no

Most of the categories in the chart are generally defined in Chapter 2. Here are some specific comments about the categories as they apply to Macintosh computers:

- *CPU:* Although the CPU is not the only determinant of speed, the higher the CPU chip number, the faster the machine works. There are also some other advantages to having a more advanced chip—System 7's virtual memory feature, for example, won't work without a 68030 chip.

- *Co-processor:* Macs that have co-processors use the Motorola 68882 math co-processor. The fact that it's a math chip doesn't speed up only number-handling programs like spreadsheets—calculating how a complicated graphic should look on the screen also takes intensive number manipulation.

- *Speed:* The clock speeds shown here are approximate. (The Classic, for instance, actually has a speed of 7.8336 MHz.)

- *Color ROM:* The best monitor in the world won't do you any good if your Mac doesn't "speak" color—color routines have to be in the computer's ROM in order for it to talk to a color monitor. All the modular Macs have color capabilities, but the SE/30, despite its built-in black-and-white screen, can also handle a color monitor if you use the right card.

- *Built-in video card:* If a Mac has color capabilities, the color monitor still has to be connected to a special card that goes in the machine. Some models have a video card as an integral part of the machine; for others, you have to use one of the available slots to hold a card that you purchase separately.

- *Slots:* There are two kinds of slots in the compacts and modulars: *NuBus* and *PDS (processor direct slot).* The Mac IIsi is unique in that it has a single slot that can be used with either kind of card. Don't worry too much about the kind of slots you have—if you're adding a card, just make sure it's rated for your Mac model.

- *ROMs:* All current models except the SE/30 have 512K ROM (and it probably won't be long before the SE/30 also comes standard with the larger ROM).

- *Sound Input:* Although with the right equipment from other manufacturers you can input sound to any Mac model, the chart indicates which machines have built-in sound input capability.

Connectors

Most connectors, or *ports,* at the back of the Macintosh are common to all models, although there are some differences. Some models, for instance, have a sound input port as well as an output port; some models have two ports for input devices like the mouse and the keyboard.

The devices you connect to your computer are *peripherals,* and many of them are generally referred to by the kind of cabling and connectors they use: a *SCSI device,* or an *ADB device,* for instance.

You won't have many problems connecting equipment to your Mac; with a few exceptions, cables can't plug into the wrong ports. The sound input and sound output jacks take the same plug, and the printer and modem ports take the same plug, but all are clearly labeled with icons.

APPLE DESKTOP BUS

The *Apple Desktop Bus,* or *ADB,* port is the connector used for the keyboard and/or the mouse. Some models have two ADB ports; since ADB devices can be chained to each other, one ADB port is sufficient for several devices.

The ADB port

VIDEO PORT

If you have built-in video support for an external monitor, the video port will be marked with an icon. If you install a video card, the edge of the card that protrudes through the back of the case has the same connector, but there won't be any icon.

The video port

SCSI PORT

Every Mac model has an SCSI port for connecting peripherals like hard drives; SCSI devices can be connected to each other, so a single SCSI port is all you need. (SCSI devices are described later in this chapter.)

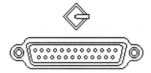

The SCSI port

PRINTER PORT

The printer port is used for connecting most printers, although some printers use the SCSI port. The configuration of the printer port is basically the same as the modem port, so you can plug a printer into the modem port if the printer port is being used as a connection for network cabling.

The printer port

MODEM PORT

The modem port, marked with a telephone icon, is used for connecting a modem to your computer. You can also use the modem port for a printer.

The modem port

SOUND PORTS

All Macs have a sound output port, marked with an icon that represents a speaker with sound coming out of it. Some Macs also have a sound input port, marked with an old-fashioned microphone icon.

The sound input and output ports

FLOPPY DISK DRIVE PORT

The floppy disk drive port is used to connect an external floppy disk drive to the computer.

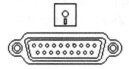

The floppy disk drive port

Quickies

■ The sound output port takes a standard plug that's used on many audio devices. You can connect a set of earphones or a speaker to the port, or even insert a plug to deaden the sound completely.

Also See . . .

■ Chapter 2 explains all the basic hardware terms like *processor* and *ROM*.

■ Chapter 13 discusses RAM and virtual memory.

MONITORS

Basics

Since the SE/30 can accommodate an external monitor, and companies other than Apple provide monitor options even for the Classic, you may find yourself monitor-shopping no matter which Mac model you own.

What you can display on your screen depends on three things: the monitor itself, the video card you use to control the monitor, and the capabilities of the Mac that you're using.

Monitors come in many sizes, but in only three basic varieties: black and white, grayscale, and color. (*Monochrome* is often, mistakenly, used to refer to a black-and-white monitor; it's actually the same as grayscale.)

Each type of monitor can work in a "lesser" mode: a grayscale monitor will work in black and white, and a color monitor can display grayscale or black and white.

A monitor has to be connected to a *video card* or *board* inside your computer. The card contains the video circuitry that drives the monitor, as well as extra RAM (called, predictably enough, *video RAM* or *VRAM*) to handle screen information. The kind of circuitry and the amount of RAM on the card determine what type of monitor it can control.

The Mac Classic is the only current model that can't produce a color display, even given an extra card and monitor; it doesn't have the color information (called Color QuickDraw) in its ROM. Macs with color ROM can produce 16.7 million different colors and 256 shades of gray.

You may already know whether or not you need a color monitor, and if you need one that lets you see an entire page on the screen, but there are more things than that to keep in mind if you're comparison-shopping.

How It Works

Understanding the inner workings of a monitor isn't necessary to your making the best use of it, but it helps to understand the mechanics and the terminology if you're making comparisons when deciding on a new, or additional, monitor.

The back of a black-and-white monitor's screen is coated with white phosphors. A gun inside the monitor shoots a stream of electrons at the screen; wherever the electrons hit, the phosphor glows briefly. The gun shoots in a horizontal line across the screen, starting at the upper-left corner. When it reaches the right edge, it stops firing, moves back to the left, and shoots another stream in a line slightly lower than the previous one. The combination of glowing phosphor dots and the ones that haven't been activated during the gun's pass gives you the white and black dots—*pixels*—on your screen.

Since the phosphor glow fades quickly, the gun has to make all its horizontal passes and move back to the top of the screen to refresh the phosphor with another dose of electrons to keep it glowing in the right spots. If this doesn't happen fast enough, the screen image flickers. How quickly a monitor does this is called the *scan rate* or the *refresh rate.* On a compact's 9-inch screen, the gun shoots 342 lines of 512 pixels each in only a *sixtieth* of a second, so the entire screen is redrawn 60 times each second. Scan rates are measured in *hertz* (cycles per second); the Classic's scan rate is 60.1 Hz.

In a grayscale monitor, the electron gun shoots at varying intensities to provide shades of gray on the screen. (The "gray" of the Desktop on a black-and-white monitor isn't a true gray; it's made by *dithering,* which is alternating black and white dots to fool the eye into seeing gray.)

A color monitor's screen is coated with colored phosphors so that each pixel is made up of a red, a green, and a blue dot. (That's the *RGB* in the phrase *RGB monitor.*) The electron gun (or, in some monitors, one of three electron guns) fires at one or more of the dots, whose combined colors appear as a single colored pixel on the screen.

Size and Resolution

A monitor is normally measured in the same way a TV screen is measured: diagonally. But since rectangular monitors can be of different proportions and in different orientations, and since screens include a nonusable border area around the perimeter, diagonal measurement is only a general guideline. Instead, consider the *orientation, resolution, pixel count,* and *display area* when you look at a screen's "measurement."

The orientation of the screen can be *portrait* (a vertical rectangle) or *landscape* (a horizontal rectangle). Screen sizes and orientations are also referred to in terms of how many 8 1/2-by-11-inch pages can be displayed, that is, whether it is a *full page* or *double-page display.* A full-page display, for instance, is usually about a 15-inch diagonal and has a portrait orientation.

A monitor's *resolution* is how many *dots per inch* (dpi) it displays. A *pixel* is a single dot on the screen. The smaller the pixel, the higher the resolution, as shown in Figure 12-1.

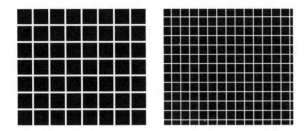

Figure 12-1. These "screens" are the same size, but the one on the right, with smaller pixels, has a higher resolution.

As a screen's resolution changes, it affects how much can be displayed. For instance, Apple's 12-inch color monitor is 64 dpi; the Classic's 9-inch screen is 74 dpi. They each display 512 pixels across their widths, so you don't see any *more* on the 12-inch monitor—you see the same thing *larger*. Figure 12-2 shows two screens that are the same size; the one on the left, however, is a lower resolution and so shows less of the picture, but in a larger format.

Figure 12-2. The screen on the left is a lower resolution than the one on the right, although they're both the same size.

The *pixel count* of a monitor is the total number of pixels it displays. Although the color 12-inch monitor and the Classic's 9-inch screen have the same number of pixels horizontally, the 12-inch monitor displays 384 pixels vertically, as opposed to the 342 vertical pixels of the Classic. The monitor has a pixel count of 196,608, providing 12 percent more than the Classic's 175,104 pixel count.

Finally, a monitor has a border area of up to a half-inch around its perimeter; subtracting the border from the screen size gives you the actual *display area*. Apple has two 12-inch monitors, but their display areas differ by about a quarter of an inch in each direction, for a total difference of more than 3 1/2 square inches.

Table 12-2 shows the specifications for Apple's five monitors and the compacts' screen.

Table 12-2. Monitor Specifications

	Mac Classic and SE/30	*Macintosh 12" Monochrome*	*Macintosh 12" RGB*	*AppleColor Hi Res RGB*	*Apple Macintosh Portrait*	*Apple 2-Page Monochrome*
Type	black & white	gray	color	color	gray	gray
Size	9"	12"	12"	13"	15"	21"
DPI	74	76	64	80	80	77
Pixels	512 x 342	640 x 480	512 x 384	640 x 480	640 x 870	1152 x 870
Display area	7" x 4.75"	8.35" x 6.26"	8.08" x 6.02"	9.3" x 6.9"	8" x 10.87"	15" x 11.3"
Scan rate	60.15 Hz	66.7 Hz	60.15 Hz	66.7 Hz	75 Hz	75 Hz

Video RAM and Depth

Even if you have a monitor that can display color, a card that can control a color monitor, and a computer that can produce color, there's still the issue of how *many* colors (or grays) can be displayed at one time. The Mac can produce more than 16 million different colors, but how many can be displayed at once depends on how much video RAM is available.

In a black-and-white system, each pixel on the screen corresponds to 1 bit in the computer's memory. Because a bit can represent one of two things, there's a perfect correspondence between a single bit in memory and a single dot on the screen that can be either on or off. This is where the phrase *bit-mapped* comes from: every dot on the screen is *mapped* to a bit in memory.

But when you move to color or grayscale, where a single dot on the screen can be one of many different shades, you need more than 1 bit of memory to keep track of a pixel's state. If you provide 2 bits of memory for each pixel, then the computer can keep track of four possible shades for that pixel, because there are four possible combinations of 2 bits of information:

1st bit	*2nd bit*
0	0
0	1
1	0
1	1

So, with two bits of memory per pixel, you can have four (or 2^2) different colors.

A color system is usually referred to as providing 4-bit, 8-bit, or 24-bit color, or *depth*. The number of colors you can get when each screen pixel is allotted those amounts of memory are:

4-bit	(2^4)	16 colors
8-bit	(2^8)	256 colors
24-bit	(2^{24})	16.7 million colors

In each case, the Mac can still produce 16.7 million colors, but the amount of video RAM limits how many of them can be displayed on the screen at one time. (Grayscale monitors are limited to a maximum 256 shades of gray because of the way the shades are produced.)

Since every pixel on the screen takes a certain amount of memory, larger screens need more VRAM. Apple's 4•8 video display card, for instance, is so named because it provides 8-bit color with smaller screens, but only 4-bit color with larger screens because the video RAM has to be divided among more pixels.

Table 12-3 shows the display possibilities for combinations of Apple products: its modular Macs, its five monitors, and its three main cards (the built-in one in some models, the 4•8, and the 8•24). As you can see, the same computer with the same card produces more depth on a smaller monitor than on a larger one—and the built-in card won't work at all with some model/monitor combinations.

Table 12-3. Color and Grayscale Output Capabilities

	Mac LC	Mac IIsi/IIci			Mac IIfx	
	built-in	built-in	4 • 8	8 • 24	4 • 8	8 • 24
12" Monochrome	16 grays	256 grays	256 grays	256 grays	256 grays	256 grays
12" RGB	256 colors	256 colors	256 colors	16.7 million colors	256 colors	16.7 million colors
13" Hi Res RGB	16 colors	256 colors	256 colors	16.7 million colors	256 colors	16.7 million colors
15" Portrait	n/a	16 grays	16 grays	256 grays	16 grays	256 grays
2-Page Monochrome	n/a	n/a	16 grays	256 grays	16 grays	256 grays

Quickies

▪ Most monitors have a special plastic coating to reduce glare. Clean your screen only with nonabrasive cleaners, and don't spray a cleaner directly onto the screen because it could drip down inside the monitor.

▪ While you can leave your computer on for days at a time, leaving a single image on the screen may "burn" the image into the phosphor coating. If you leave the computer on, turn the brightness down on the screen—most monitors have a dial for brightness, and the Classic has a control panel to adjust it. *Screen savers* are programs you can buy that put a moving image on the screen whenever your computer is inactive for more than a few minutes.

▪ The time it takes to display something on the screen is not dependent only on the monitor's scan rate. It takes a lot of calculating to figure out how a complicated graphic, especially in grayscale, color, or a three-dimensional view, should look. You can get specialized cards to speed these computations—one of Apple's video cards, the 8•24GC, has a *graphics accelerator* included on it.

Also See . . .

▪ Because the resolution of the screen doesn't always match the resolution of the printer you're using, you can't always count on having WYSIWYG—*what you see is what you get*. Printer resolution considerations are covered in Chapter 16.

MOUSE AND KEYBOARD

Basics

The mouse and the keyboard are your basic input devices. They're connected to the computer with an ADB (Apple Desktop Bus) connector, and so are considered ADB devices. Most models let you connect the keyboard and mouse to the computer separately, but connecting the mouse through the keyboard is usually more convenient. Since most keyboards have an ADB port on both sides, you can connect the mouse to whichever side will make it more convenient for you to manipulate the mouse.

Keyboards

Apple provides three basic keyboards. One is included with the Mac Classic and is also available as part of the Mac LC package. For other Mac models, you can choose between the basic Apple keyboard and the Apple extended keyboard. (Both of these keyboards also work with the Classic and the LC.)

Figures 12-3 through 12-5 show the layouts of the three keyboards.

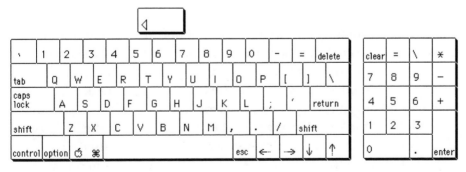

Figure 12-3. The Classic keyboard

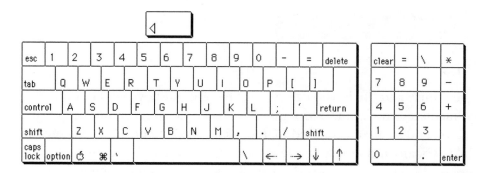

Figure 12-4. The standard keyboard

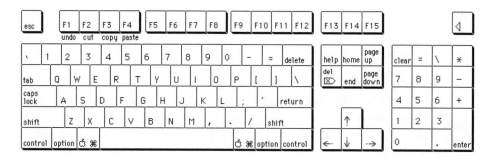

Figure 12-5. The extended keyboard

There are several minor differences from one keyboard to the next, like the shape of the Return key, the placement of the backslash key, and the arrangement of the arrow keys. But the main differences are between the extended keyboard and the others: The extended keyboard has function keys and extra cursor control keys.

Preferences for key placement, and even the "feel" of the keyboard, are very personal decisions, but most people quickly get used to whatever keyboard they're using. If you can afford the room on your desk, though, go for the extended keyboard: The extra keys are very useful not only for cursor control but also as shortcuts for commands in many programs.

The Mouse

Apple has gone through several mouse designs since the Mac was first introduced, with each one a little sleeker and yet sturdier than the last.

While you can operate the mouse on any clean, flat surface, one that's smooth with just a hint of traction is best. *Mouse pads* are available in any computer store; they provide an excellent surface, stake out an area on your desk for rolling the mouse, and keep dirt and lint in the rolling area to a minimum.

With or without a mouse pad, the mouse is bound to collect dirt inside it sooner or later. If you turn the ring that holds in the ball at the bottom of the mouse, the ring comes off and the ball comes out. You can clean the ball with a soft cloth, wipe off the rollers inside the mouse, and then put it back together.

Quickies

▪ Never plug in the keyboard, mouse, or other ADB device while the computer is on. Turn off the computer if you have to connect or reconnect something to the ADB port.

▪ Although ADB devices are designed to be chained together, if you chain more than three, the signal to the computer may weaken enough to make the last devices unusable.

Also See . . .

▪ Chapter 11 explains how to adjust the *mouse-tracking speed*—how the cursor on the screen moves in relation to movements of the mouse.

▪ Chapter 3 discusses the functions of all the special keys on the keyboard.

THE PROGRAMMER'S SWITCH

Basics

The *programmer's switch*, located somewhere on the front or left side of most Mac models, consists of two little plastic push buttons. (The LC doesn't have a programmer's switch.) The *Reset* button, at the left of front-mounted switches and at the back of side-mounted switches, is marked with an arrow. The *Interrupt* button is marked with a circle.

The Reset and Interrupt buttons

Using the Reset Button

Although the programmer's switch was originally meant for programmers to use during the development of programs for the Mac, you'll find the Reset button very useful.

The Reset button resets everything in the computer's memory; using it is like switching the computer off and then on again, clearing RAM. If you run into a "freeze" (that is, if your computer stops working so that you can't even use a Restart command that may be on the screen), you can use the Reset button instead of turning off the power and turning it back on again. Restarting the machine this way is sometimes called a *soft restart,* and it's better than repeatedly turning the machine off and on because there's less electrical stress placed on some of the components.

Since the Reset button erases everything in memory, don't use it unless you have no other choice.

Quickies

▪ The Mac LC has no programmer's switch. The keyboard equivalent of the Restart button is Command-Control-Startup; the keyboard Interrupt is Command-Startup.

- The Interrupt button really is just for programmers. If you press it by mistake, you'll see a dialog box in the center of the screen that's empty except for an arrow. Type a G and press Return; the dialog box will go away, but you may find that the application you were working in will have quit.

SCSI DEVICES

Basics

SCSI, pronounced *scuzzy*, stands for *small computer serial interface.* It's simply a specific type of connection between certain computer devices. All internal and most external hard drives are *SCSI devices:* peripherals like scanners and CD-ROM drives are also SCSI devices.

The Mac has only one SCSI port, so when you have more than one external SCSI device you connect the first one to the computer, the next one to the first device, and so on. This arrangement is called a *chain*, or a *daisy chain*. You can attach up to seven SCSI devices to the computer (but the internal hard drive counts as one of them).

Terminators

SCSI devices have to be *terminated* to keep the signal that's traveling from the computer to the device(s) from echoing back after reaching the end of the line. You do this by using a *terminator,* or *terminating resistor*. Devices with built-in terminators are called *self-terminating*. An external terminator comes with most SCSI devices; it looks like a SCSI cable without the cable—just the connector (see Figure 12-6).

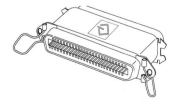

Figure 12-6. A SCSI terminator

A single SCSI device connected to the computer has to be terminated. All internal hard drives are terminated; external hard drives are either self-terminating or need a terminator attached. (Every external SCSI device has two SCSI ports so you can either chain the next device or connect a terminator.)

When you have a SCSI chain, the first and last devices need to be terminated. So, if there are only two devices in the chain (an internal and an external hard drive, for instance), both need to be terminated. If you have more than two devices, the first and last should be terminated, but not the ones in between.

Device Numbers

Every SCSI device gets an ID number, and each device in a chain must have a different number. There are eight ID numbers, 0 through 7, available; the computer itself gets the number 7, and an internal hard drive gets the number 0. (The computer counts as a SCSI device for ID number purposes, although it doesn't count when it comes to termination.)

External SCSI devices usually have some sort of number wheel with which you can set the device number.

Quickies

▪ If you have a SCSI chain, *every device in the chain should be turned on* when you start the computer, even if you don't plan on using them all.

▪ Most SCSI cables are very short, but extensions are available if your setup requires them. However, the total length of cabling on a SCSI chain should never exceed 20 feet.

OTHER HARDWARE

Basics

Because every Mac model provides several ports and most provide slots, you can attach many different peripheral devices to your computer.

Peripherals used for input, output, and storage generally can be classified according to the port they use. A modem, for instance, is a *serial* device; printers can be serial or SCSI devices; many input peripherals are ADB devices.

This section briefly describes some of the most popular peripheral devices.

Mouse Alternatives

Trackballs and graphics tablets are ADB input devices that are often used instead of, or in addition to, the mouse.

Trackballs (essentially, upside-down mice) are a popular alternative to the mouse. Trackball proponents feel that they have finer control over cursor movements when they can manipulate the ball directly. Another advantage of trackballs is that they take up less space on a desk surface.

A *graphics tablet* gives you a special pen to use on a tablet; the pen movements are translated into cursor movements on the screen. Many artists prefer the more traditional feel of a pen for creating graphics on the screen.

Scanners

Scanners are another kind of input device, although they're significantly different from the ADB input devices. Most scanners, because they transfer large amounts of data into the computer, are SCSI devices.

With a scanner, you can take something from paper—a drawing, a photograph, or even text—and put it onto the screen so that you can edit it and/or incorporate it into a document. Some scanners work with only black-and-white pictures, and some handle color. Software that can "read" scanned text and translate it into true, editable text (instead of just a *picture* of the text) is called an *OCR (optical character recognition)* program.

CD-ROM Drives

CD-ROM drives are SCSI devices that use compact discs (just like the ones in stereos) for information storage. A CD can store an enormous amount of data: more than 500 megabytes. The *ROM* in CD-ROM, however, indicates that this is a read-only technology; you can't use it as if it were a giant hard drive, saving your own data onto the disc.

A CD-ROM Desktop icon

But CD-ROMs are still incredibly useful when you need access to large amounts of information that you won't have to alter, like dictionaries and encyclopedias.

Modems

When you want to hook your Macintosh to a telephone so it can communicate with other computers, you use a *modem.* A modem (the name comes from the words *modulate* and *demodulate*) changes the computer's digital signal to an analog signal that can be sent over telephone lines; it also changes the analog signal coming in to a digital signal the computer can understand (see Figure 12-7).

The speed at which a modem sends and receives information is known as its *baud rate.* Early modems worked at 300 and 1200 baud, but the standard ones now are 2400 and 9600 baud.

Figure 12-7. At one end, the modem modulates the computer signal so it can be transmitted over telephone lines; at the other end, a modem demodulates the signal so the other computer can use it.

Also See . . .

- Chapter 14 covers disks and drives in detail.

SUMMARY

That's all the basics of Macintosh components and peripherals. You'll find more information about memory and disk drives in the next two chapters.

Memory

ABOUT THIS CHAPTER

There are different kinds of computer memory, but when the term *memory* is used without a qualifier, it refers to RAM. And that's what this chapter is all about. You'll learn how the Mac's RAM is used and how you can allocate portions of it for specific purposes. You'll also find details about increasing the amount of memory in your computer.

BASIC MEMORY ALLOCATIONS

Basics

The Mac uses its RAM for an incredible amount and variety of work. In some cases, you don't have any say in the matter—the computer just takes what it needs. In others, you can allocate specific amounts of memory for certain operations.

There are two major uses of RAM: for system software and for applications. You can't directly assign a portion of memory for the system software, although you indirectly affect the automatic allocation when you alter the system by adding or removing resources or extensions, or by setting a disk cache. Applications come set for the minimum amount of RAM they need to function, but you can easily assign more to any program in which you're doing memory-intensive work.

Checking Memory Usage

If you're not sure how much memory your Mac has, use the About This Macintosh command from the Desktop's Apple menu.

The window that opens, as shown in Figure 13-1, tells you not only how much memory is in your machine, but also how it's being used and how large a block of memory is still free.

The amount of Total Memory is reported in kilobytes (K); 1 megabyte, or M, equals 1024K. The dialog pictured is for a machine that has 8M (8192K) of memory. The second memory report at the top of the window shows that the *largest unused block* of memory is 1596K; there may be more total memory free, but since RAM is used in blocks, it's the size of the block that counts.

The bottom part of the window alphabetically lists each item that has been assigned a memory *partition*, and how large that partition is. The bar for each item represents the memory partition; the black part of the bar is how much of the partition is currently in use.

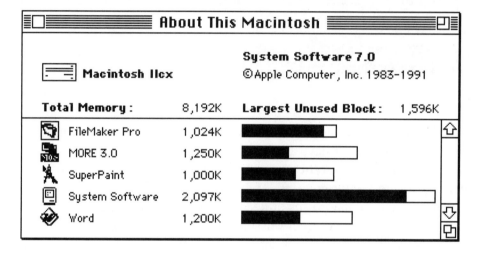

Figure 13-1.   The About This Macintosh dialog shows how memory is being used.

System Software

The amount of RAM initially reserved for the system software varies, based on your general system configuration. RAM-based portions of system software include parts of the operating system and the Finder, certain system extensions that stay in memory, and the disk cache.

The RAM allocation for system software is *dynamic:* It changes as necessary even during a work session, depending on what you're doing. Figure 13-2 shows two views of the About window: one before any applications are launched, and one after two applications and a desk accessory are opened. Notice that although that was the *only* change in the system environment, the allocation for system software jumped from 1985K to 2022K.

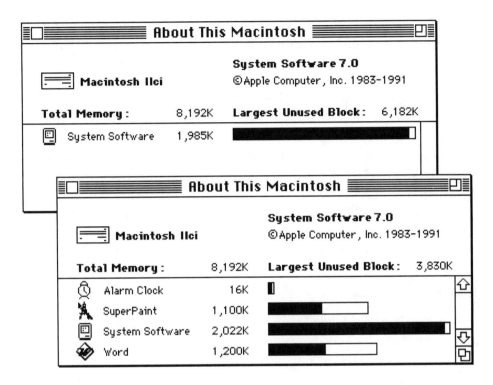

Figure 13-2. *The memory partition for the system software changes as you work.*

Parameter RAM

PRAM (pronounced "pea-ram") stands for *parameter RAM:* a special, small piece of RAM—256 bytes—reserved for storing information about the time, date, and some basic control panel settings. The information stored in PRAM includes:

- time and date settings
- keyboard repeat rate
- insertion point and menu blink rates
- mouse tracking and double-click speed
- volume setting
- modem and printer port settings
- startup disk setting

PRAM is like regular RAM in that it needs constant electrical refreshing to stay "alive," but it lives through the shutdown because it draws its power from the Mac's battery. (Did you ever wonder how the Mac remembers what time it is even though you shut it off?) When you turn on your computer, the information in PRAM is read into regular RAM.

Sometimes the information in PRAM gets corrupted; you may find that time and date settings, or other basic control panel settings, aren't remembered even though you know the battery is still fresh. When that happens, you perform a procedure known as "zapping the PRAM."

To zap the PRAM, restart your system while holding down Command-Option-P-R. The computer will start up, the screen will flash, and then the system restarts. This resets all the PRAM options to their defaults—except for the time, which remains set.

The Disk Cache

Few applications are loaded completely into memory; the core of the program is there for speedy operation, but the other parts stay on the disk until you need them. Since the Mac can retrieve information from RAM much faster than from a disk, getting disk information slows down your work.

You can speed things up by setting aside a portion of RAM to store information that's frequently accessed from the disk. This is called a *disk cache,* or *RAM cache* (pronounced "cash," not "catch").

You don't have to choose which information is stored in the cache—in fact, you *can't* choose, because the Mac does it automatically. When you have a disk cache set up, the Mac watches you work and stores oft-repeated operations in the cache on a "first-in, first-out" basis—that is, storing a new instruction in an already-full cache bumps out the oldest piece of information there.

The Mac always has a disk cache, but you can adjust its size through the Memory control panel (see Figure 13-3). The memory you assign to the cache is added to the RAM allotted to the system software and doesn't take effect until you restart the Mac.

Figure 13-3. Setting the disk cache

Quickies

▪ Strictly speaking, a disk is a kind of memory, too—after all, it stores information for the computer. But we generally differentiate between the electronic-switch memory of RAM and ROM and the magnetic "memory" of disks by referring to the latter as *storage*.

▪ While you can't control what goes in and out of a disk cache, there are utility programs that let you create a *RAM disk,* whose contents you can control. A RAM disk is a portion of RAM that's treated like a disk; but anything that's on the RAM disk is accessed much faster than the items on real disks. (Anything on a RAM disk also disappears when you turn off the computer, so you have to remember to copy its contents to a real disk before you shut down.)

APPLICATION PARTITIONS

Basics

When you start your Mac, it sets aside a certain amount of memory for the system software to use and then assigns a chunk of memory to each application you run on a first-come, first-served basis.

The amount of RAM needed for each application varies; most need a minimum of 1 megabyte of memory to work, but some need more for even minimal functionality. (When you buy a program, the packaging should indicate how much memory is needed.) Many programs that run in a megabyte or less of memory will work more efficiently when there's more memory made available to them.

If you try to launch a program and there's not enough memory left for it, you'll get a dialog box like the one shown in Figure 13-4.

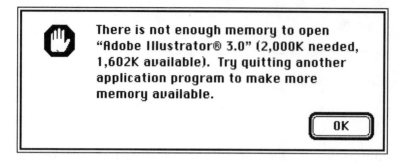

There is not enough memory to open "Adobe Illustrator® 3.0" (2,000K needed, 1,602K available). Try quitting another application program to make more memory available.

OK

Figure 13-4. An "out of memory" dialog box

Some applications keep their documents entirely in RAM while you're working on them; others keep only portions of the document in memory. The memory used for documents is taken out of the application's RAM partition, so if you work with very large documents, or keep several open at once, you may need more memory for an application than the stated minimum. (Text documents, even formatted ones, don't use much memory; graphics documents, especially grayscale or color ones, take large amounts of RAM.)

If you try to open a document and there's not enough memory left, you'll get a dialog box like the one shown in Figure 13-5.

Not enough memory to open the document.

OK

Figure 13-5. Running out of memory within an application

While every application comes set to use a certain amount of memory, you can easily adjust the size of the partition to avoid both of the "out of memory" dialog boxes.

Checking and Changing Partitions

To check how much of a memory partition an application needs, or to change the partition, select the application's icon on the Desktop and choose Get Info from the File menu.

Figure 13-6 shows HyperCard's Get Info window. At the bottom is the *Suggested size* of 1000K and a text box that indicates the *Current size*—also 1000K, in this instance. To change the memory partition for an application, just type the new size in the text box. The next time you run the application, it will get a partition of that size.

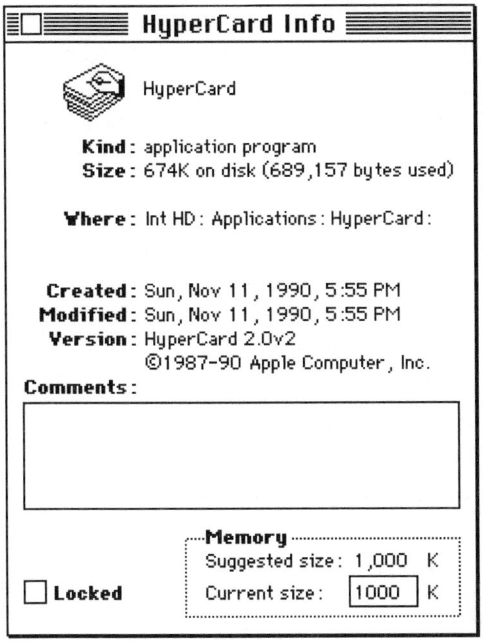

```
┌─────────────────────────────────────────┐
│ ▦□▤▤▤▤ HyperCard Info ▤▤▤▤▤ │
├─────────────────────────────────────────┤
│                                         │
│      ◈  HyperCard                        │
│                                         │
│    Kind : application program            │
│    Size : 674K on disk (689,157 bytes used) │
│                                         │
│   Where : Int HD : Applications : HyperCard : │
│                                         │
│                                         │
│  Created : Sun, Nov 11, 1990, 5:55 PM   │
│  Modified : Sun, Nov 11, 1990, 5:55 PM  │
│   Version : HyperCard 2.0v2             │
│            ©1987-90 Apple Computer, Inc. │
│  Comments :                             │
│  ┌────────────────────────────────┐     │
│  │                                │     │
│  │                                │     │
│  │                                │     │
│  └────────────────────────────────┘     │
│             ┌─Memory──────────────┐     │
│  □ Locked   │ Suggested size : 1,000  K │   │
│             │ Current size : [1000] K │     │
│             └─────────────────────┘     │
└─────────────────────────────────────────┘
```

Figure 13-6. The Info window shows suggested and actual partition sizes.

Deciding how much memory to give a program is really a trial-and-error experience. If you're working in an application and you run out of memory, you'll get a dialog box telling you that an operation can't be performed or a document can't be opened; at that point, you quit and give the application more memory. But how much? Try 200K or 300K at a time until you find what's right.

Figure 13-7, for instance, shows the memory allocation and usage for a program (Version 2.0 of SuperPaint) when it's given its suggested memory size of 700K. The bar at the top shows what the usage is when there are no documents open; the application itself takes about half of the partition, or around 350K. The second bar shows the memory usage with a blank document open. The third bar shows what it's like when a second document is open. As you can see, the allotted memory is used up quickly.

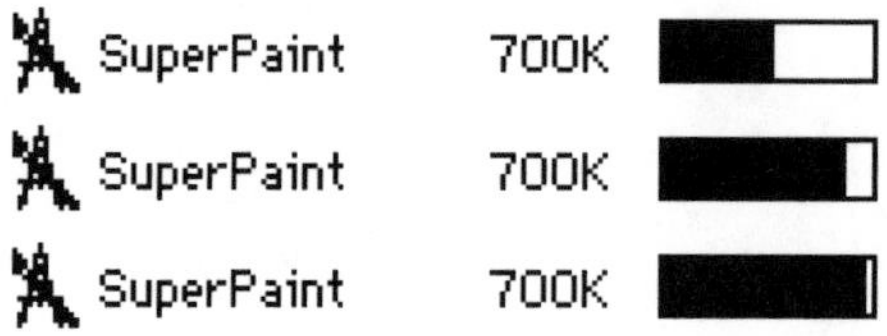

Figure 13-7. A sample program with no documents open (top); a blank document open (middle); and two documents open (bottom)

Figure 13-8, on the other hand, shows what happens when more room is given to the application to start with—1000K in this case. The first bar shows it with no documents open; as in the previous figure, there's about 350K used up. The second bar shows what the memory usage is like when *five* average-size documents are open—there's still room to spare.

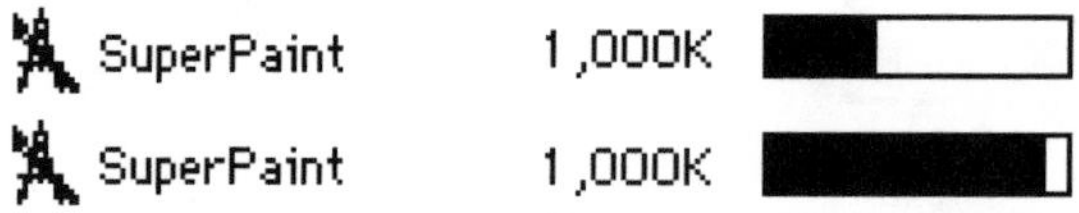

Figure 13-8. A sample program with no documents open (top); and five documents open (bottom)

Figure 13-9 shows four popular applications with their suggested memory sizes, and with sizes that are more reasonable for anything beyond minimal documents. As you can see, the 2M (2048K) of memory in a basic Mac won't go very far, especially when you have to start by handing over about half of it to the system software.

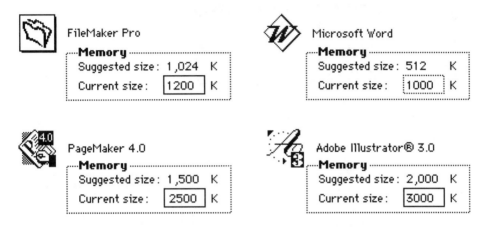

Figure 13-9.   Suggested and practical memory partition sizes

Fragmented Memory

As you open and close applications during a work session, portions of RAM are used and then freed up. But the Mac's memory isn't stored in some electronic tureen from which the right amounts can be ladled out and the extra thrown back in. RAM is one long continuous line, and pieces of it are portioned out, in order, as needed; when it's no longer needed, that specific portion is freed to be used again. But programs need *contiguous* memory for operation—they can't use pieces of RAM from different areas.

   Imagine you have four pictures, as shown in Figure 13-10: Microsoft Word, Symantec's More, Adobe Illustrator, and Aldus's PageMaker. You want to hang them in a horizontal line, but you have a limited amount of wall space. Figure 13-11 shows what happens if you hang Word first, then More, and then Illustrator: There's not enough room left for PageMaker.

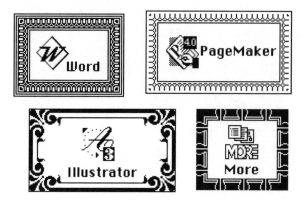

Figure 13-10. The four "pictures"

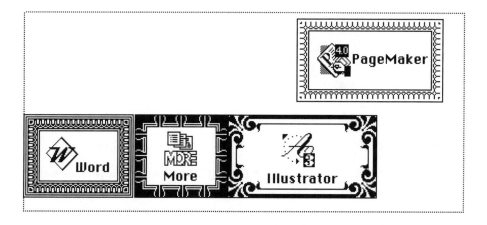

Figure 13-11. All four pictures can't fit on the wall at the same time.

Figure 13-12 shows what happens if you try to make room for the fourth picture by taking down one of the pictures already hanging. If you remove the More picture, PageMaker still doesn't fit, despite the fact that's there's enough total wall space; the space is divided into two areas, neither of which is big enough to hold the picture. But if you remove Illustrator instead, there's plenty of room to hang PageMaker.

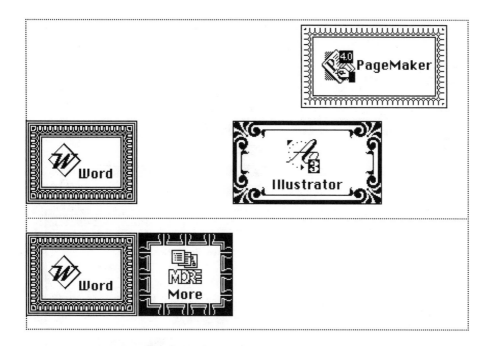

Figure 13-12. Removing More (top) doesn't make enough room for PageMaker, but removing Illustrator (bottom), does.

Of course, the example of hanging and removing pictures is analogous to opening and quitting programs. If you regularly open and close several applications during a work session, the computer's memory can become *fragmented*—the free RAM may be in several small pieces instead of one large piece.

As you work, you can check how much "wall space" you have left by using the About This Macintosh command from the Finder's Apple menu. Figure 13-13 shows how the window would look before and after quitting out of More; note that the Largest Unused Block report doesn't change even though there's obviously less memory in use when only the two applications (Word and Illustrator) are running.

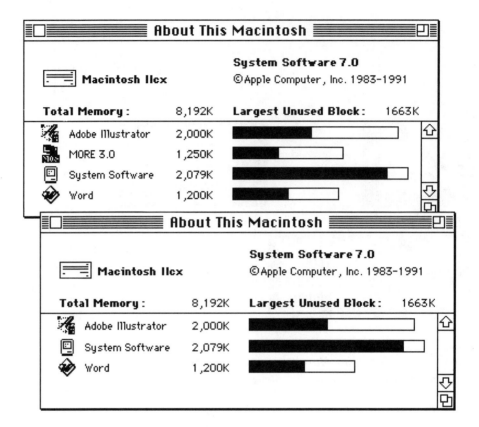

Figure 13-13.   Quitting a program doesn't always change the size of the largest unused block of memory.

Quitting the program that's last in line (taking down the Illustrator picture in Figure 13-12) isn't always the solution to the memory problem, because you may need to use that program. In the scenario used so far, what if you wanted to use Word, Illustrator, and PageMaker at the same time? Figure 13-14 shows the shuffling you have to do sometimes. If you take down (quit) both More and Illustrator, it frees up everything after Word's partition; starting Illustrator again gives it the space right after Word, and now there's plenty of room for PageMaker.

Figure 13-14. Quitting More and Illustrator and then reopening Illustrator gives it a partition next to Word and makes room for PageMaker.

Quickies

▪ The About This Macintosh window lists items in alphabetical order, not the order in which they've been assigned RAM partitions. When you have to quit programs in order to defragment memory, you'll have to remember which ones were opened first.

▪ If there's a program that you use almost constantly, open it first; it's less likely that you'll quit out of it, leaving a "hole" and fragmenting the memory.

▪ The amount of space an application takes on a disk and the amount of memory it needs to run are two entirely different figures. (Generally, though, the larger a program is on the disk, the more memory it will need to run properly.) Figure 13-15 shows the disk sizes and the recommended memory sizes for several applications.

		Disk space	Recommended memory
	TeachText	38K	192K
	PageMaker	1525K	1500K
	More	927K	1250K
	Word	672K	512K
	HyperCard	674K	1000K
	Illustrator	954K	2000K

Figure 13-15.   The amount of disk space an application requires is different from the amount of memory it needs.

VIRTUAL MEMORY

Basics

You can set aside a portion of a hard drive to act as RAM; this pseudo-RAM is called *virtual memory*.

Only certain Mac models can take advantage of this system capability. Neither the Classic nor the LC can provide virtual memory; all other current models, and any previous model with a 68030 processor chip, can use virtual memory.

Activating Virtual Memory

You use the Memory control panel to set the amount of virtual memory that you want. It's essentially a three-step process, as illustrated in Figure 13-16.

1. Click the On button. (This activates the popup menu.)
2. Use the menu to select the drive you want the virtual memory stored on.
3. Use the arrows to adjust the *total amount* of memory you want. The number represents the total of standard RAM and virtual memory together. (In the figure, the total is 12 megabytes: 8M of regular RAM and 4M of virtual memory.)

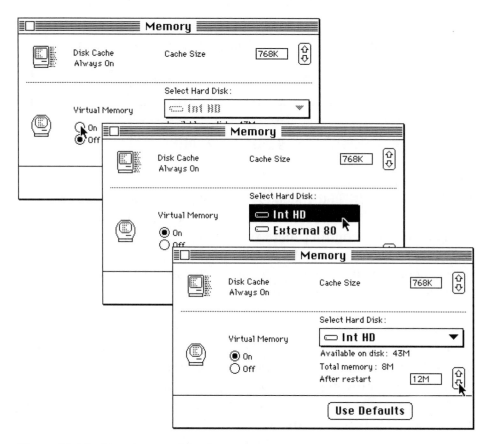

Figure 13-16. Turning on virtual memory

The virtual memory won't be available until you restart the Mac. When you do, the About This Macintosh memory report includes four items instead of two, as shown in Figure 13-17. The dialog shows both the built-in memory and the total memory (including virtual); it still shows the Largest Unused Block, and it also shows how much disk space (and which disk) is used to run the virtual memory.

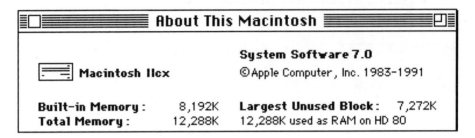

Figure 13-17.   The About This Macintosh dialog when virtual memory is on

DISK SPACE

The disk you specify in the Memory control panel needs enough room on it to store all the virtual memory information; in fact, if there's not enough room, the control panel won't let you select the disk.

The space you need on the disk is more than just the amount of virtual memory you've chosen: The disk space needed is the *total* memory—virtual memory and built-in RAM together.

VIRTUAL MEMORY LIMITS

Available disk space isn't the only thing that will stop you from creating as much virtual memory as you want; different Mac models have limitations as to how much memory they can address.

For the Mac IIsi, IIci, and IIfx, the sky is the limit: You can use more than a *gigabyte* (1024 megabytes) of virtual memory—assuming, of course, you have that kind of disk space available.

Mac models prior to the IIci that have a 68030 chip and can handle virtual memory are limited to 14M of total memory, *minus 1M for each NuBus slot in use.*

In any case, the control panel won't let you set an amount of virtual memory that's greater than your machine can use.

Physical Memory vs. Virtual Memory

Virtual memory provides two benefits. First, it lets you break the RAM barrier: Mac models are limited to using (*addressing*) specific amounts of *physical memory,* but most can address additional virtual memory.

The second benefit is price: Virtual memory is cheaper. At current prices, a megabyte of physical RAM costs about $40 while a single megabyte on an 80-megabyte hard drive costs about $6.

But virtual memory has its disadvantages, too. In most cases, you won't be able to tell the difference between the RAM installed in your machine and the virtual memory. But virtual memory is slower than true, physical RAM. If you assign more virtual memory than you have physical memory, you'll start to see the slowdown (although it's still faster than regular disk access). Virtual memory is used more efficiently in situations where you need it to run lots of little programs than in those where you need a very large portion of it to handle a complex document in a single application.

Quickies

- The reason a 68030-based machine can use virtual memory is because it includes a special chip called a *PMMU (paged memory management unit)*. A 68020 machine that's been upgraded to include a PMMU can also use virtual memory.

MEMORY UPGRADES

Basics

You're not forever limited to the amount of RAM that came with your Macintosh; most models can be easily and inexpensively upgraded to include larger amounts of memory. But different models have different overall RAM limitations and different configuration possibilities along the way to their maximum amounts.

In the modular Macs, it's relatively simple to remove and replace
memory chips, changing the amount of RAM in your Mac. The actual
chip replacement isn't much of a problem in the compact Macs, either,
but opening the case is difficult without the correct tools—and if you do
it yourself, you may void whatever warranty you still have with Apple.

How Much Do You Need?

You need a minimum of 2 megabytes of RAM to run System 7. That 2M
gives you enough room to run a single average-size application and a few
small desk accessories at the same time. To run bigger applications,
additional applications, or to work with very large documents, you'll
need more memory.

While 3 megabytes of memory might be a comfortable practical minimum to work with, most Mac models can't be configured for 3M of
memory. So, 4M is the recommended amount; with that, you'll be able to
"soup up" your system with extensions that make life easier and run two
or three average-to-large applications at the same time.

SIMMs

To increase the memory of your computer, you use *single inline memory modules—SIMMs* (pronounced as a single word, not as initials).

A SIMM is a small (about 3 1/2-by-1-inch) board with memory chips
installed on it; Figure 13-18 shows what a basic SIMM looks like. The
dark rectangles are the memory chips, and the half-ovals along the
bottom edge are the metal teeth that make the contact when you install
the SIMM in its special slot in the computer.

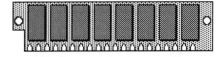

Figure 13-18.   A SIMM

The amount of memory in each of the chips on a SIMM determines the size, or *density,* of the SIMM. ("Size" refers to the amount of memory, not the physical dimensions.) The most common sizes of SIMMs right now are 256K and 1M, but they're also available in 512K, 2M, and even 4M densities.

Memory Configurations

Memory chips can be permanently attached to a board in the computer, or SIMMs can be installed in special slots. Since there are rules that govern what size SIMMs can be in which groups of slots, there are specific memory configurations available for each Mac model.

Here are two examples of how SIMM installation rules govern memory configurations:

The Mac Classic that comes with 1 megabyte of memory in it has the RAM on its main board. You can get an upgrade for the memory that consists of an add-on board with another 1 megabyte of RAM installed and two empty slots. If you use the slots, you have to fill both of them, and the SIMMs have to be the same size. So, installing two 256K SIMMs adds another half-megabyte of memory, while adding two 1-megabyte SIMMs would add two megabytes of memory. Table 13-1 shows the possibilities for a Classic's memory configuration.

Table 13-1. The Four Memory Configurations for the Mac Classic

Main Board	1M	1M	1M	1M
Add-on Board	none	1M	1M	1M
In Slots	none	none	two 256K	two 1M
Total RAM	1M	2M	2.5M	4M

The SE/30, on the other hand, has 2 *banks* of four slots for memory chips. The rules are that a bank must be completely filled or completely empty, and every slot in a filled bank must have SIMMs of the same size. Table 13-2 shows the memory configuration possibilities using 256K and 1M chips.

Table 13-2. The Five Memory Configurations for the SE/30

Bank 1	four 256K	four 256K	1M	1M	1M
Bank 2	empty	four 256K	empty	four 256K	four 1M
Total Memory	1M	2M	4M	5M	8M

Table 13-3 shows the memory configurations available for each of the current Mac models using, at most, the 1M chips available from Apple. The second row shows the maximum amount of RAM each model can use if there are 4M SIMMs available for its slots. (Note that the Classic and the SE/30 can't make use of 4M chips.)

The figures in the second row are the maximums if only the available SIMM slots are used. It's also possible to have memory on a separate card that's installed in a NuBus slot inside the computer; the IIsi, IIci, and IIfx can each address up to 128 megabytes of RAM if you can supply it.

Table 13-3. Possible and Maximum Memory Configurations

	Configurations	Maximum
Classic	1, 2, 2.5, 4	4
SE/30	1, 2, 4, 5, 8	8
LC	2, 4	10
IIsi	3, 9	17
IIci	1, 2, 4, 5, 8	32
IIfx	1, 2, 4, 5, 8	32

Quickies

▪ The RAM used in most Macs is *dynamic* RAM, or *DRAM* ("dee-ram"), that needs constant electrical refreshing to keep its switches in place. The Mac Portable uses *static RAM* chips that don't need the constant electrical flow, but they are significantly more expensive.

▪ A SIMM chip is rated not only according its density, but also by the speed with which its memory can be accessed. The speed is measured in *nanoseconds*, or *ns*. The lower the speed rating, the faster the chip works—so a 100ns chip is faster than a 120ns chip. Different Mac models need different SIMM speeds, so make sure the SIMMs you buy are rated for the machine you have. (You can put in a SIMM that's faster than you need, but the computer won't take advantage of it.)

- Apple's SIMM prices have always been significantly higher than those of other manufacturers. Unless you need a special upgrade board, as for the Classic, buy your memory elsewhere.

- If you install more than 8 megabytes of RAM in your machine, you have to activate the *32-bit addressing* option in order for your Mac to see the additional memory. If your machine is capable of 32-bit addressing, there will be On and Off buttons for 32-bit addressing at the bottom of the Memory control panel.

SUMMARY

Now you know everything you need to (and then some) about the memory in your Mac—how it's used, how to make the most of what you have, and when what you have isn't enough and how to arrange for more.

The next chapter covers the other aspect of computing where how many megabytes you have and how you use them counts for so much: disks.

Disks and Drives

ABOUT THIS CHAPTER

DISKS

Basics
How a Drive Works
Initializing Disks
Invisible Files
Making Backups
Startup Disks
Quickies
Also See . . .

FLOPPY DISKS AND DRIVES

Basics
Three Disks and Drives
Initializing Floppies
Locking Disks
Erasing Disks
Quickies
Also See . . .

HARD DRIVES

Basics
Formatting a Hard Drive
Fragmentation
Quickies
Also See . . .

SUMMARY

ABOUT THIS CHAPTER

Creating the most superb document ever generated in the history of computing won't do you much good if it disappears when you turn off the machine. The disks that provide storage, and the drives that let the computer "read" and "write" to the disks, are an integral part of your computer system.

DISKS

Basics

When you're using floppy disks, it's easy to see the difference between the *disk* that's the storage medium and the *drive,* the mechanism that lets the computer access it. A hard disk, however, is the storage medium and the drive mechanism rolled into one, which is why it's variously referred to as a *hard disk* or a *hard drive*.

Information is stored on computer disks by magnetizing the coating on the disk. The binary language of computers that deals with only ones and zeroes happily coincides with the north/south options of magnetized material.

Different size disks store different amounts of information, but it's not just the size of the disk that matters—how the information is packed onto the disk also counts. That's how the capacity of the 3 1/2-inch floppy disk has increased from the original 400K when the Mac first came out through the popular 800K in use today to the 1.4M disk that's also available.

How a Drive Works

When the computer is putting information onto a disk, it's *writing* to the disk; when it's getting information from the disk, it's *reading* the disk.

When you insert a floppy disk into a drive, it's sandwiched between a pair of *read-write heads*. These mechanisms check and change the charges of the magnetic particles on the disk surface. Since the disk spins around and the read-write heads move in and out, every spot on the disk can be accessed (see Figure 14-1).

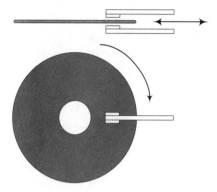

Figure 14-1.   The read-write head moves in and out and the disk spins, so every part of the disk can be reached.

A hard drive uses basically the same mechanism, but it usually consists of a series of stacked platters, with a set of read-write heads for each platter. Because the information on a hard disk is packed so tightly, a speck of dust is more disastrous on a hard drive than on a floppy; hard drives, therefore, are completely sealed.

Initializing Disks

When you insert a new, blank floppy disk into a drive, you'll get a dialog telling you that it's not a Macintosh disk and asking you if you want to *initialize* it.

A disk is not inherently a Macintosh disk, or any other kind of computer disk. But different computers store and retrieve information from disks in different ways, and if the information isn't organized correctly, the disk can't be read.

Information on a disk is stored in *sectors,* which are segments of concentric rings called *tracks*. Figure 14-2 gives an idea of the track/sector setup, but the actual number of tracks and sectors depends on the type of disk; high-density floppies, for instance, have 80 tracks of 18 sectors each.

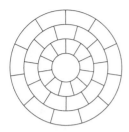

Figure 14-2. The concentric rings on a disk are tracks; *the divisions of a track are* sectors.

There are no actual divisions on the disk; initializing, or *formatting,* a disk builds the magnetic fences that define the tracks and sectors. The correct fences make the disk recognizable as one used by a specific computer system.

Invisible Files

The Mac reserves part of each disk for its own use and stores informa-tion in invisible files—you won't see any icons for them on the Desktop, although special utility programs let you see, and even manipulate, them.

Figure 14-3, for instance, shows an empty floppy disk. Although the header says there are no files on it, it still reports that 1K of information is in the disk.

	Pictures	
0 items	1K in disk	1.3 MB available

Figure 14-3. This "empty" disk with no files on it still reports 1K of the disk in use.

THE DIRECTORY

One of the many little housekeeping details taken care of when you initialize a disk is the creation of a *directory*—a file that keeps track of what's stored where on the disk.

From your point of view, files are kept in folders on the disk. But the folders are basically a figment of the Finder's imagination, because a file can be stored anywhere on a disk—and is often stored in bits and pieces instead of all in one spot. The directory lets the computer find out the location of a file (or its parts). The more files you store on a disk, the more information is stored in the directory, so a directory file on a hard disk is much larger than one on a floppy.

Another invisible file, the *volume bitmap,* works in concert with the directory; it keeps track of which sectors on the disk are in use and which are free.

Neither of these files is included in the "in disk" count in the disk window's header; that's one reason the amounts reported in the header don't add up to the total capacity of the disk. Figure 14-4, for example, shows the disk window from an 80-megabyte hard drive; it reports 76.1M in use and 2.5 still available, for a total of 78.6M. Even allowing for the loss of a few hundred K due to the rounding of numbers in the conversion to megabytes, there's still 1.4 megabytes, or more than 1400K, unaccounted for.

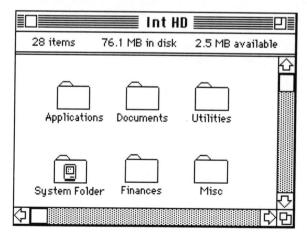

Figure 14-4. The "in disk" and "available" sizes for this disk don't add up to the 80M capacity of the drive.

THE DESKTOP FILE

The Desktop file is another, very important, invisible file. One of the things it keeps track of is the location of any applications that are on the disk, so that when you double-click on a document, the application can be found. It also catalogs any icons that are needed for the files on the disk—that's why a document icon can look the way it's supposed to even if the application isn't around.

The Desktop file goes through constant changes as you add and delete files from the disk. Sometimes the file winds up storing information you don't need any more—like icons of programs and documents that are outdated. Figure 14-5, for instance, shows a disk with six items, and six different icons, for a total of 73K in the disk. After the files are trashed, the header reports that there are zero items in the disk, yet there's 30K of information stored—the Desktop file has stored the icons for future use.

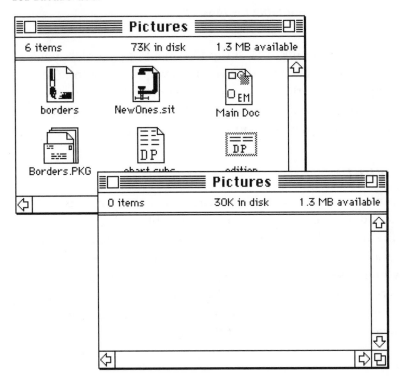

Figure 14-5. After the six items are trashed, there is still 30K of information left on the disk.

You can make the Mac rebuild the Desktop file for a floppy disk by holding down the Command and Option keys when you insert it. You'll get a dialog (shown in Figure 14-6) asking if you want the Desktop rebuilt. Click OK. Rebuilding the Desktop for the disk shown in Figure 14-5 will return it to having only 1K of "invisible" information, as shown in Figure 14-3.

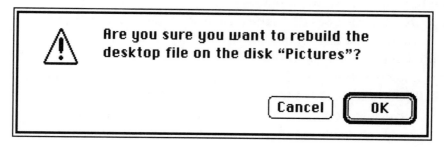

Figure 14-6. The dialog for rebuilding the Desktop

It's not necessary to rebuild a Desktop file on a floppy, unless you're really short of disk space. On a hard drive, however, the Desktop file undergoes changes constantly, so you should plan to rebuild it every month or so. To rebuild the Desktop of a hard drive, hold down the Command and Option keys when you start the computer.

Making Backups

The most important preventive medicine there is in computing is *backups:* a second, or even a third, copy of every file you use. If something ruins the original file or disk, your backup will save the day.

Sometimes a file becomes corrupted and can't be opened, even though everything else on the disk is fine. Making an extra copy of an important file right on the same disk as the original is an easy strategy for keeping a corrupted file from becoming a major disaster. (Just make sure you update the copy each time you edit the original.)

But you should also backup important files to another disk, because entire disks—and even hard drives—can fail. Sometimes the failure isn't one that requires mechanical repair, but it's not much consolation that your hard drive is working if you can't recover any of the information on it.

Backing up 40 or 80 megabytes of information is time-consuming, but it's worth it. The files that need to be backed up can be copied to floppy disks manually (a Desktop drag operation) or automatically (with the help of commercially available backup utility programs).

If you're backing up manually, don't bother copying the system software and applications—they can be reinstalled from their master disks if necessary. You also shouldn't bother backing up anything that you haven't changed since the last time you backed up your drive; use the Desktop's Find command to search for all the files modified after a specific date to round up your altered files.

One backup problem you can't deal with when you do it manually is that some files may be too big to fit on a floppy disk. Most backup programs can compress files to make them smaller or even split a file between two disks if necessary. Another advantage to a backup program is that using it is generally much faster than doing backups manually.

Startup Disks

When you turn on the Mac, it looks for a startup disk (one with a System on it) so it can get going. This is the scan order it uses in its search:

1. internal floppy drive
2. second internal floppy drive
3. external floppy drive
4. device identified in Startup Disk control panel
5. internal hard drive
6. external SCSI devices, starting with the one with the highest ID number

At this point the Mac checks the internal hard drive again, and then the internal floppy drive. If, after all this, it hasn't found a startup disk, you'll get the blinking question mark on the floppy disk icon on the screen.

You can control which of several chained hard disks will be the startup by setting its SCSI ID number and/or by using the Startup Disk control panel to identify it. No matter which drive you normally start up with, inserting a floppy startup will always take precedence.

Quickies

▪ When you erase a file from a disk, the information that was in the file is not actually removed from the disk; instead, the file's name is deleted from the directory and the sectors it was stored in are labeled as free to be used again. There are utility programs that take advantage of this strategy and let you recover files that you've trashed. Even if some of the information has been overwritten, a partial file can often be recovered.

▪ The same strategy that lets you recover a trashed file can wreak havoc with security if you *think* you've erased confidential information from a disk but it's still there. There are utilities that actually erase the information, not just change the directory, when you want a file deleted. Reinitializing a disk also erases all the information on it.

▪ Other programs besides the Mac's operating system place invisible files on disks; utilities like those that help you recover deleted files keep track of the deletions in an invisible file.

▪ Although a disk formatted for one computer system is not normally readable by another, the Apple File Exchange utility that comes with your system software lets the Mac read an IBM-formatted disk. (What it can do with the information on the disk is another matter entirely; some files are compatible with programs on different computers.)

Also See . . .

▪ Chapter 18 discusses some of the things you can do to recover information from damaged disks.

FLOPPY DISKS AND DRIVES

Basics

The Mac's floppy disks don't seem all that floppy, since they're encased in a hard plastic case. But the basic media is very floppy: It's a circular disk that's a lot like the material used in audio and video tapes.

The metal shutters on floppy disks open automatically when you insert them into a drive, and they snap shut again when they're ejected; this is to keep dust and other dirt (and your fingers) off the media itself.

Since the information on a disk is stored magnetically, magnetic fields can ruin the data. Telephones, halogen lamps, and electric motors all have magnetic fields that can potentially harm your disks. The Mac Classic's power supply gives off enough of an electromagnetic field that you shouldn't leave disks (or an external floppy drive) on the Classic's left side, where the power supply is installed.

Extreme heat and cold aren't kind to floppy disks, either. If your disks are exposed to inclement temperatures, let them return to room temperature before using them.

Three Disks and Drives

The original Macs had *single-sided drives* that could read and write to only one side of a disk. The *single-sided disks* it used stored 400K of information. It's been years since Apple produced a machine with a single-sided drive, and 400K disks aren't much in use or even readily available for purchase any more, but you may wind up with some if you exchange disks with someone who's been into Mac computing for a long time.

The next floppy drive in the Mac's evolution was a *double-sided drive* that used both sides of a *double-sided disk* to store a total of 800K of information. (The drive itself is usually referred to as an 800K drive.)

Current models of the Mac use a drive called the FDHD *(floppy drive high density)*, or more familiarly, the SuperDrive. It uses both sides of a *high-density disk* to store 1.4 megabytes of information. (The disk is sometimes referred to as a superfloppy.) High-density disks can store more information than other disks of the same physical size because they have a different coating on the disk media: The smaller magnetic particles allow information to be packed in more tightly.

How can you tell the difference between the disks, since they're in the same 3 1/2-inch case? When 800K disks were just coming into general usage, they were all marked, someplace on the disk case or the shutter, as "double-sided" or "800K." Most are still labeled, although since 800K is such a standard, many aren't. An unmarked disk might be 400K, but at this point in Mac history, it's almost sure to be 800K.

A high-density disk is easy to identify: It has an extra square hole in the case, across from the locking tab, as shown in Figure 14-7. The SuperDrive uses this hole to recognize a disk as high density when you insert it.

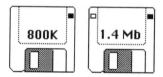

Figure 14-7. Both disks have locking tabs in the corner, but the high-density disk also has an extra square hole in it.

MIXING DISKS AND DRIVES

You're not limited to using only one type of disk in the drive you have; you can use any lower-capacity disk in it, too. So, a SuperDrive can handle 400K (if you have any), 800K, and its own 1.4M floppy disks.

But if you put a high-density disk in an 800K drive, the drive won't recognize the higher form of technological life that the disk represents. You'll get a dialog that says "*This disk is unreadable; do you want to initialize it?*"

(Note: Don't panic when you see this dialog, and *don't* click OK to initialize the disk—initializing erases everything on the disk.)

How much information a disk can store depends on both the disk itself and how you format it during the initialization process. You can format a disk in a lower form if you want to—you can use a 1.4M floppy as an 800K disk, for example. You might want to do this if you have no 800K disks around and you need to put some files on a disk for someone who doesn't have an FDHD drive to read the higher format.

Initializing Floppies

When you insert a new, blank disk into a drive, you'll get one of the dialog boxes shown in Figure 14-8. The dialog at the top is for high-density disks, and the one at the bottom is for 800K disks. (The one on the bottom is also the dialog that appears for *any* disk inserted into an 800K drive.)

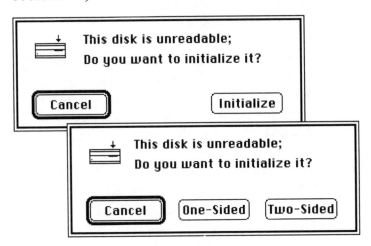

Figure 14-8. The dialog for a high-density disk (top) and the dialog for an 800K disk (bottom)

With a SuperDrive, a high-density disk is automatically formatted for 1.4M—that's why the dialog gives you only Cancel and Initialize options. An 800K disk, however, can be formatted for either 400K (single-sided) or 800K (double-sided)—that's why there are more button options in the second dialog.

With an 800K drive, you have the choice of initializing one or both sides of any disk you insert; a high-density disk isn't recognized as anything special and is treated the same as an 800K disk.

Table 14-1 shows the combinations of disks and drives, and the resulting capacity of a formatted disk.

Table 14-1. Disk Capacity

	800K Drive		1.4M Drive	
	Single-sided	*Double-sided*	*Single-sided*	*Double-sided*
800K Disk	400K	800K	400K	800K
1.4M disk	400K	800K		1.4M

HIGH-DENSITY DISKS FORMATTED AS 800K

You can't format a high-density disk as 800K in a SuperDrive because the drive detects the extra hole in the case and automatically formats it to 1.4 megabytes.

You might, however, come across a high-density disk that was formatted as 800K in someone's 800K drive. This causes a big problem: If you insert the disk into your SuperDrive, the drive detects the hole in the disk's case but doesn't see any high-density formatting. As a result, it gives you the dialog: *"This disk is unreadable; do you want to initialize it?"*

If you absolutely need the information from that kind of a disk and don't have access to an 800K drive, cover the hole in the disk case with a piece of masking tape to fool the drive into thinking that it's a standard disk. (Don't use this as a long-term solution, however; the tape will eventually come off, and it's likely to come off in the drive.)

Locking Disks

You can lock and unlock a floppy disk by sliding the plastic tab in its corner. When the tab covers the hole, the disk is *unlocked;* when the hole is closed, the disk is *locked*.

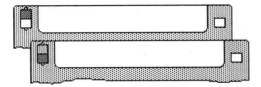

Figure 14-9. A locked disk (top) and an unlocked disk (bottom)

Any Desktop window that belongs to a locked disk is marked with a padlock in its header, as shown in Figure 14-10.

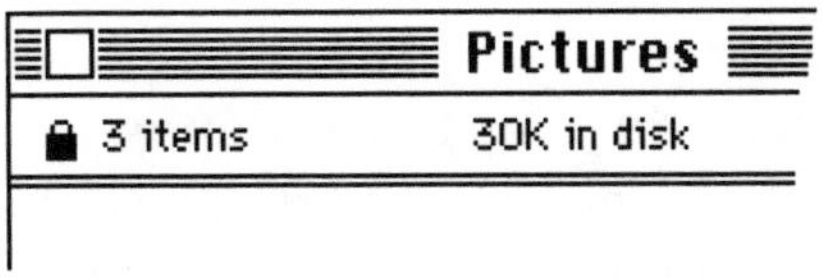

🔲 Pictures
🔒 3 items   30K in disk

Figure 14-10. Windows from locked disks are marked with padlocks.

You can't change anything on a locked disk. You can open windows and even move icons around or change how you view the window's contents, but the changes won't be "remembered" for the next time you use the disk. You can't erase anything from the disk, nor can you erase the disk itself.

You can open a document that's on a locked disk, but if you make any changes to it, you'll have to save the edited version on a different disk.

Erasing Disks

You can erase a disk at any time by selecting it on the Desktop and choosing Erase Disk from the Special menu. Erasing a disk reinitializes it; in fact, when you use the Erase command, you'll get the same basic dialog you get when you insert a blank disk (see Figure 14-11).

Erasing a disk takes longer than just dragging its contents to the Trash, but there are advantages to reinitializing: Everything on the disk is erased (including invisible files), the Desktop file is rebuilt (with old icons purged from it), and the initialization process checks the integrity of the media so that you can be sure the entire disk is still reliable.

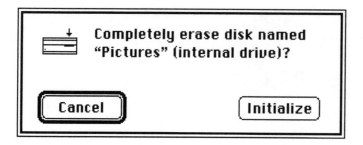

Figure 14-11.   Erasing a disk reinitializes it.

Quickies

▪ Despite the fact that the Mac is produced with only FDHD floppy drives now, the 800K disk is still the standard—manufacturers have to be sure their products are usable by everyone in the marketplace, and 800K drives are still in abundance.

▪ Sometimes you'll get a report that the initialization process for a disk failed. If that happens, try it again—sometimes it works the second time. If it fails the second time, get rid of the disk—even if the third try worked, the reliability of the disk is questionable.

▪ In addition to ejecting floppy disks by any of the methods described in Chapter 4, you can also use Command-Shift-1 to eject a floppy from an internal floppy drive and Command-Shift-2 to eject one from an external, or second internal, drive.

▪ If none of the Desktop or keyboard commands works for ejecting a floppy, inserting a straightened paper clip (or other similar item) into the small hole next to the disk slot will mechanically eject the disk. If the disk is stuck so that even that doesn't work, don't force it: Take the computer to a dealer who can open the unit and extract the disk.

Also See . . .

▪ Chapter 4 discusses disk icons and Desktop operations.

HARD DRIVES

Basics

Although hard drives were always highly recommended for Mac systems, they weren't an absolute necessity until the advent of System 7. You need a hard drive when you run System 7 because it takes so much room, but storage space isn't the only hard drive advantage.

Hard drives are much faster than floppy drives, for several reasons. A floppy disk sits still until you want something from it; at that point, it starts spinning, but you can't use it until it's up to speed. A hard drive is always spinning, so you don't have to wait for it to spin up. The disks spin at different rates, too: A high-density floppy makes about 300 revolutions per minute in a SuperDrive, but a hard drive's platters whirl around at about 3600 revolutions each minute. Finally, information is packed more closely on a hard drive platter, so it takes less time for a read-write head to get to it.

In addition to more speed and storage capacity, a hard drive offers the advantage of having all your files in one place. Aside from the convenience of not having to keep track of errant floppies, having all your applications and documents in one place makes it much easier to transfer information from one document to another.

Formatting a Hard Drive

When you have a blank floppy disk, you can just put it in a drive; the Mac knows there's something there even if it's not entirely sure what it is (*"this disk is unreadable"*) and lets you initialize it.

When you have a new, blank hard drive, however, you're faced with a different problem: If you boot up the system with an unformatted hard drive attached, the Mac won't even know it's there.

Most hard drives are formatted at the factory, so you don't have to worry about this; if the drive's icon shows up on the Desktop, it's already been initialized.

If you have a new, unformatted drive, however, you can use Apple's HD Setup to initialize it. (Most hard drive manufacturers provide their own formatting software.) Working from a floppy System disk, or from another hard drive, you run the HD Setup program.

In HD Setup, you click in the Drive button to make the program look for any SCSI drives attached to the computer. When you find the new drive, you click the Initialize button.

Once a hard drive's icon is available on the Desktop, you can reinitialize it at any time with the Erase Disk command in the Special menu.

INTERLEAVE FACTOR

Since different Macs "think" at different speeds, some can digest information from a disk more quickly than others.

All current Macs except the Classic can read a disk fast enough as it spins around so that it can read the sectors in order. By the time the Classic transfers what it reads from a sector into its memory and goes back for the next sector, however, the disk has spun far enough that the *third* sector is in position to be read.

To keep the Classic from waiting for the disk to spin all the way around so the second sector is available again, hard drives used with Classics are formatted a little differently. Instead of numbering its sectors sequentially, the Classic's hard drive numbers its sectors *alternately:* The first sector is 1, the third sector is 2, the fifth is 3, and so on. All the sectors are used, with the higher numbers wrapping around and filling in the skipped sectors, as shown in Figure 14-12. This process is called *interleaving*, and the Classic, with alternate sectors numbered sequentially, has an *interleave factor* or *interleave ratio* of 2 to 1. With this special interleave factor on its drive, the Classic can access it at optimum speed because the setup matches its reading ability.

When you use HD Setup to format a drive, it knows what computer you're using and formats the drive accordingly. If, however, you use a drive that was originally set up for another model, reinitializing the disk on your own system will optimize its speed.

All Mac models with 68020 and 68030 processors use interleave factors of 1:1, the Classic and the SE (not the SE/30) use 2:1, and the Mac Plus uses a 3:1 ratio.

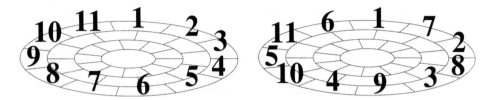

Figure 14-12. An interleave factor of 1:1 (left) and the Classic's 2:1 interleave (right)

Fragmentation

Although *fragmentation* occurs on both floppy and hard disks, it's really only a concern on hard drives because of how often you change and delete files when you're working with a hard disk.

Most files are stored in more than one sector on the disk; when the disk is relatively empty, it's easy to store them in contiguous sectors. But if you edit a file so that it's larger than it was originally, the sectors next to its current storage spots may no longer be available. So, parts of the edited file get stored elsewhere on the disk.

When you delete a file, its sectors are freed up to be used again. But a new file isn't often the same size as a deleted one and won't fit exactly into those sectors; it, too, will be divided up among several available sectors.

What you wind up with is files saved in pieces all over the disk in available spaces, as shown in Figure 14-13. Although it's the files that are fragmented, this mess is referred to as *disk fragmentation*.

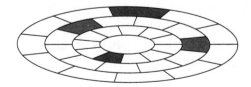

Figure 14-13. A single file may be stored in several noncontiguous sectors on a disk.

When your disk is heavily fragmented, operations begin to slow down—after all, the Mac has to jump around to find all the pieces of a file just to open it for you.

Defragmentation software is available commercially, and it's a good idea to buy some and plan to use it at monthly intervals.

Quickies

▪ An external hard drive needs anywhere from 10 seconds to a minute to get up to speed; if you start your system before that, the Mac won't know that the drive is there.

▪ Many external hard drives are designed to sit beneath a compact Macintosh, but you can put a hard drive almost anywhere, if the connecting cable's long enough. Some are designed to sit flat on a surface, and others stand vertically to take up less room. If your model wasn't designed to stand vertically, keep it flat.

▪ Despite manufacturers' warnings about the delicate nature of hard drives, most are very sturdy units that survive shipping and backpacking through airports with all their data intact. But treat a drive gently—and don't move it at all—when it's turned on.

▪ You can get the Mac to ignore an internal hard drive by holding down Command-Option-Shift when you start up the machine.

▪ There's a whole class of convenient storage media called *removable hard drives* that use hard drive technology, but the platters are in removable cartridges that store 40 to 80 megabytes of information.

▪ Some software lets you *partition* a hard drive so it can be used as separate *volumes*—in effect, separate disks on your Desktop. Apple's HD Setup's *Partition* button is only for partitioning a drive that's going to be divided between the Mac and a "foreign" operating system.

Also See . . .

▪ Most hard drives are SCSI devices; Chapter 12 discusses SCSI concerns.

▪ The HD Setup utility also provides some testing capabilities to check your hard drive for problems; Chapter 18 discusses problems and troubleshooting.

SUMMARY

Now that you know all about your disks (what goes on them and how it gets there), it's time to discuss what goes on paper and how it gets there: The next two chapters discuss printing and printers.

PART VI

More About Using Your Mac

CHAPTER 15

Fonts

ABOUT THIS CHAPTER

FONT FACTS

Basics
Font Terminology
Font Guidelines

FONT TECHNOLOGIES

Basics
Bit-Mapped Fonts
Outline Fonts
TrueType Fonts
Quickies

FONTS AND YOUR SYSTEM

Basics
Standard Fonts
Installing Fonts
*Using Multiple Font
    Technologies*
Also See . . .

SUMMARY

ABOUT THIS CHAPTER

The Mac introduced the world of personal computers to the wonder of fonts. Mac-generated documents were always easy to identify because they used typefaces other than the boring typewriter-like look of computer-generated printing. The Mac has grown beyond its initial font technology, and while that provides you with more choices, it also means there's more information you need to make the correct ones.

FONT FACTS

Basics

In the Macintosh world, a *font* refers to a certain typeface, no matter what its size or style. (In traditional typography, each size and style of a typeface design is considered a separate font.) Your system software came with certain fonts, your printer may have come with additional ones, and you can obtain even more fonts from commercial and even free sources.

But whether you're using the fonts that came with your system or font-shopping to add to your collection, knowledge of some basic font terminology and design issues is helpful.

Font Terminology

As word processors and page layout programs grow increasingly sophisticated, even the most casual of Mac users run into many terms that were previously familiar only to typographers.

Fonts are measured in *points;* a point is about ½ of an inch.

Baseline, cap height, x-height, ascender, and *descender* are measurements and parts of a character in a font, as shown in Figure 15-1.

The characters in a *serif* font have little caps or hooks at the end of all their lines; those in a *sans serif* font don't (see Figure 15-2).

Figure 15-1. Measurements and parts of characters in a font design

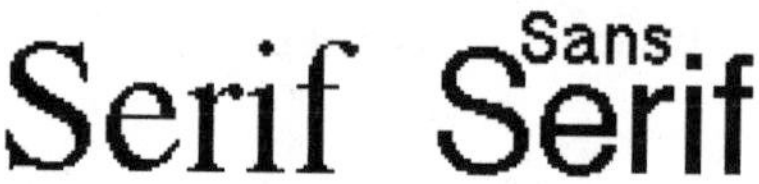

Serif Sans Serif

Figure 15-2. Serif fonts have caps at the ends of their lines and sans serif fonts don't.

Monospaced fonts give all their characters an equal amount of horizontal space no matter what the character's actual width. *Monofonts*, like Courier and Monaco (which are included with your Mac), tend to look computer-generated or typewritten. *Proportional fonts* give their characters horizontal space that depends on their widths; an *m*, for instance, gets about three times more space than an *i*, as shown in Figure 15-3.

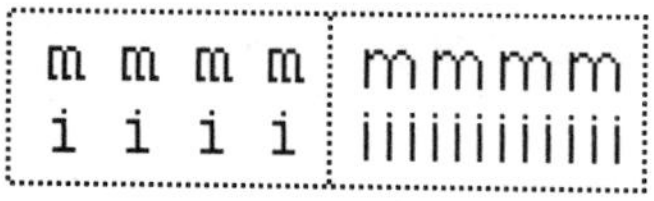

```
m m m m   mmmm
i i i i   iiiiiiiiiiii
```

Figure 15-3. Monospaced (left) and proportional (right) fonts

Kerning is changing the space between letters. Under normal circumstances, each letter occupies its own rectangular area, but some programs let you kern letters. Figure 15-4 shows how kerning can improve a word's appearance. In the words at the top, each letter occupies its own space; at the bottom, the *y* has been nested under the *T*'s overhang, and all three letters in the second word have been moved closer together.

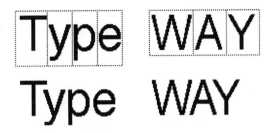

Figure 15-4.   Before kerning (top) and after kerning (bottom)

Leading ("ledding") is the space between lines; it's measured in points from baseline to baseline of the text in the lines, as shown in Figure 15-5. Most programs provide *auto leading* or *auto spacing* that adjusts the line spacing to accommodate the largest character in the line, but many also let you set a specific line spacing. Generally, line spacing is simply referred to as *single, space-and-a-half,* or *double-spaced,* using the point size of the font as the spacing for a line; programs that let you fine-tune line spacing usually refer to leading. When the leading measurement is different from the font size, the combination is referred to as, for example, *10/12 ("10 on 12"),* meaning 10-point type on 12-point leading. The text in this book, for instance, is 11.5/14.

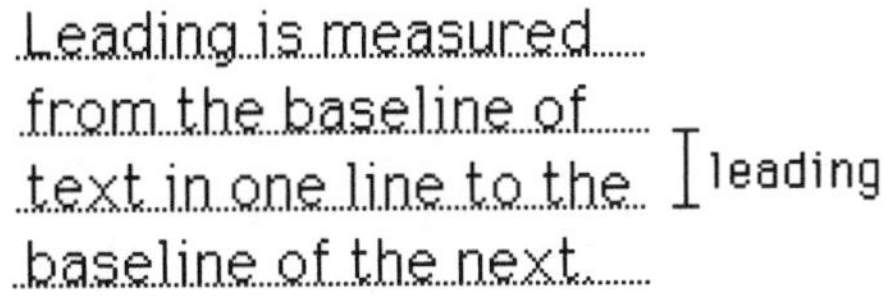

Leading is measured
from the baseline of
text in one line to the   ⏐leading
baseline of the next

Figure 15-5.   Leading is measured from one baseline to the next.

A *font family* is a group of related font designs that share the same basic name. Although the Mac can take any font and make it bold or italic, it does so in a very rough fashion. For italics, for instance, it merely shifts the top part of the character to the right and the bottom part to the left. Some fonts are designed specifically as italics, with their lines slanted; some fonts are designed with other styles built in. These kinds of fonts have their styles in their names, such as Geneva Italic and Times

Bold. The individually designed styles for a font are all considered a family: Times, Times Italic, Times Bold, and Times Bold Italic are all in one font family.

Font Guidelines

Faced with a menu full of font choices, most Mac users initially succumb to the temptation of using as many as possible in any given document. When the thrill has worn off, you can follow some general guidelines for font use:

- Use a serif font for body text; serif fonts are easier to read within a large block of type.

- Use a sans serif font for large-type headlines; serifs in large print are very distracting.

- Mixing a serif font for body text with a sans serif for headlines is fine; mixing different fonts in the body text, or as headline fonts, is something best left to professionals.

- Use a single style option for emphasis: **bold** or *italic*, for example, but ***not both***. Leave ugly <u>underlining</u> to typewriters, and avoid using ALL CAPITAL LETTERS for emphasis within text.

FONT TECHNOLOGIES

Basics

A *font file* contains information that the computer and/or the printer uses to draw the characters of the font. But because the Mac needs one kind of information to be able to display a letter on a screen that's no more than 90 dots per inch, and many printers use a different set of instructions to be able to print at resolutions that are 300 dots per inch, several font technologies have evolved.

The basic font technologies are *bit-mapped* fonts for the screen and *outline* fonts for high-resolution printers. Their different approaches are basically that of bit-mapped and object-oriented graphics, as described in Chapter 6. System 7's TrueType approach combines both technologies in one package.

Bit-Mapped Fonts

The characters in a bit-mapped font, as in a bit-mapped graphic, are defined by a series of dots. Figure 15-6 shows a magnified view of a bit-mapped letter.

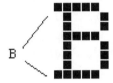

Figure 15-6. A bit-mapped character

The point size of a font defines how large a grid is available for character design: A 12-point font is 12 dots high, for example, but that has to include both full-height capitals and descenders. What you see as a single bit-mapped font in a menu is actually provided as several font files of different sizes, each specifically designed to look as good as possible with the number of dots available for a character. So, you'll find that your system contains six files for the New York font: New York-9, New York-10, New York-12, New York-14, New York-18, and New York-24.

Since the dots in a bit-mapped font are displayed as dots on the computer screen, there's no problem when you're displaying a font in a size that's in your system. But when you want a size other than one you have in your system, the Mac shrinks or enlarges an existing size, using it as a map to create the new size.

Figure 15-7 show what happens when you have only a 12-point font installed and try to create 24- and 48-point type from it. In the 24-point size, every dot from the original map becomes four dots on the screen;

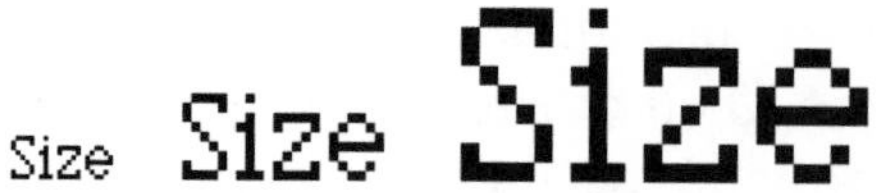

Size Size **Size**

Figure 15-7.   24-point and 48-point characters derived from a 12-point map

for a 48-point font, every map dot becomes 16 screen dots. As the size increases, what used to be an acceptable curve or diagonal becomes a series of stair steps informally known in the Mac world as *jaggies*.

The distortion of a bit-mapped font is even worse when you use something that's not a multiple of the installed size. In creating a 30-point font from a 12-point map, for instance, the Mac needs two and a half dots on the screen for every dot in the map. Since there's no such thing as half a dot on the screen, sometimes it's just left out, and sometimes it's represented by a full dot. As Figure 15-8 shows, this leads to unsightly blobs on some characters and erratic variations in the thickness of the lines that make up the character.

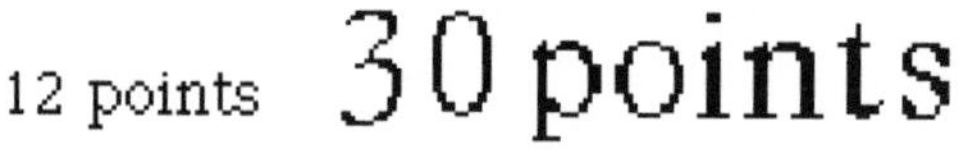

12 points   **30 points**

Figure 15-8.   Enlarging a bit-mapped font to a size that's not a multiple of the original

You run into similar distortion problems when you scale a font down from an existing font map. In addition, you run into the problem of trying to represent a letter shape with very few dots to work with; a 6-point font destined for a Mac screen is designed on a grid that's only 6 dots square.

The distortion you see on the screen will not always be echoed on a printer. The printed output depends on the printer's resolution and on the kind of font technology it uses.

Outline Fonts

Characters in outline fonts consist of a series of *instructions* instead of a map. The instructions refer to sets of coordinates and how lines and curves should connect the coordinates. The letter E in Figure 15-9, for

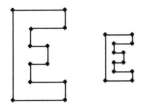

Figure 15-9.   Outline fonts are defined by coordinates and lines.

instance, consists of 12 coordinate points connected by straight lines.
When you need an E of a different size, the coordinate points are moved
closer together or farther apart and then the connecting lines are drawn.
So an outline font needs only a single file to create any size character.

POSTSCRIPT FONTS

PostScript is a "page-description" programming language from Adobe,
Inc., that is used by computers to generate high-resolution graphics.
PostScript fonts are outline fonts that conform to the PostScript language
and Adobe's specifications for font descriptions. Many other companies
besides Adobe produce PostScript fonts.

   The ability to interpret PostScript commands is built into many
printers. In fact, it defines a class of printers—PostScript-compatible
printers. Most PostScript printers have sets of outline fonts built into
them, the same way the Mac has permanent information in its ROM.

SCREEN FONTS

Except for Apple's own TrueType fonts, an outline font can't be displayed on the screen because the Mac doesn't know how to interpret
the information in the font file. So, an outline font intended for your
printer's use is always accompanied by a bit-mapped font, or *screen font,*
that will display on the screen.

   If you use a screen font but forget to install the printer font, the
screen font is used as a bitmap for the printer. If you install a printer font
but forget to install the screen font, you won't be able to access the
printer font because it's the screen font installation that puts the font's
name into the menu.

TrueType Fonts

While printers can interpret bit-mapped font information for their use, the Mac, until recently, wasn't able to interpret outline font information for *its* use.

Apple's font technology, TrueType, provides an outline font that the Mac can use for both the screen and any printer. Because it uses outline information, you can scale a font up or down without distortion; the information is converted to bitmaps of the correct size for display on the screen. Figure 15-10 shows a bit-mapped font in 12-, 24-, 30-, and 48-point sizes (with only a 12-point bitmap available) and the TrueType version of the font in the same sizes.

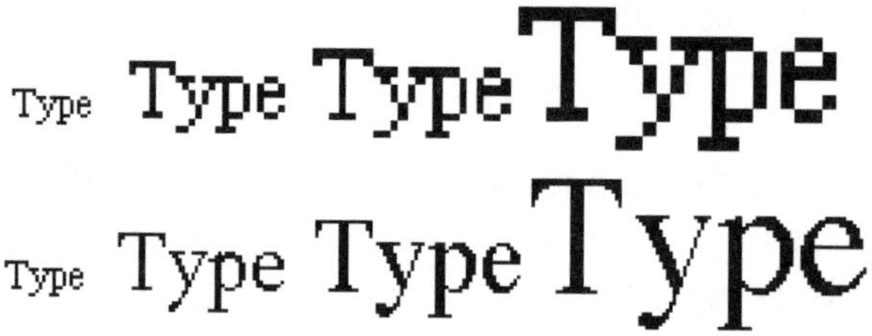

Figure 15-10.   A bit-mapped font in various sizes (top) and the TrueType font in the same sizes

BITMAPS ARE BETTER

Even when you're using a TrueType font, the screen always displays a bitmap; it's just a matter of whether the screen map is derived from a bit-mapped font description or from outline instructions. For screen displays, bitmaps designed in specific sizes are almost always better than their outline-derived equivalents—especially in sizes smaller than 18 points. Figure 15-11 shows 9-, 12-, 14-, and 18-point bitmaps for the Times font (on top) and the same sizes generated by TrueType; it isn't until the 18-point size that the TrueType rendering looks better than the hand-tuned bitmap design.

The magnified view in Figure 15-12 shows some of the design advantages to the bit-mapped version of the font. The 9-point TrueType font (on bottom) has lost all its serifs except for the top of the *i*. The 14-point TrueType *1, o,* and *i* are clunky compared to the true bitmap, the *i* and *n* are touching, and the *n* has a small piece missing.

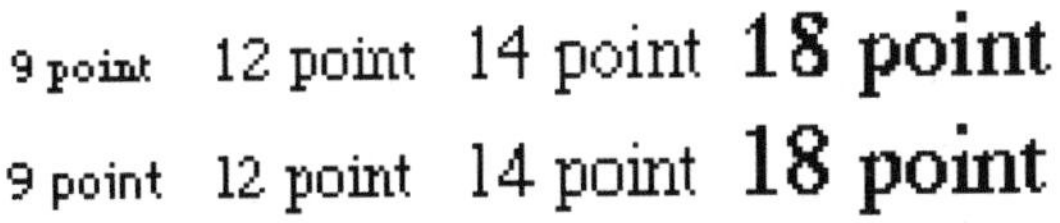

9 point   12 point   14 point   **18 point**
9 point   12 point   14 point   **18 point**

Figure 15-11. Bit-mapped (top) and TrueType (bottom) screen sizes

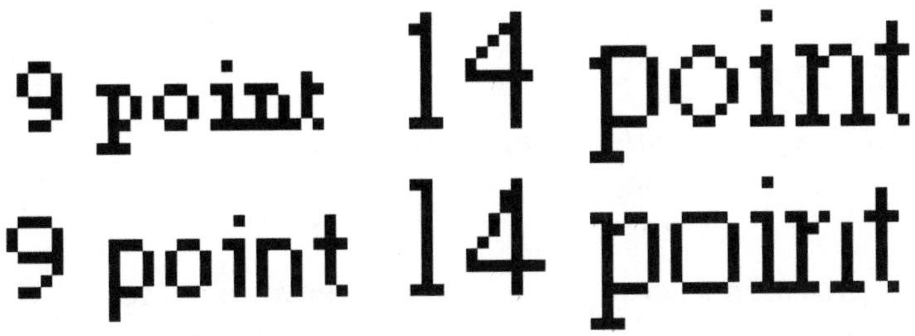

9 point   14 point
9 point   14 point

Figure 15-12. Magnified view of bit-mapped (top) and TrueType (bottom) screen fonts

While a bit-mapped version of the right size is superior for screen display, you can't have every possible size of a bit-mapped font in your system—they're not available, and they would take too much room. Besides, outline fonts are superior for printing on any high-resolution printer. Luckily, you can use both bit-mapped and TrueType versions of the same font, and the Mac will give precedence to the bit-mapped version of the correct size for screen display, and will switch to TrueType for odd-size screen display and for printing.

Quickies

▪ You can tell if a font of a specific size is available in your system by checking the point sizes listed in the Size menu of the application you're working in. Available sizes are outlined in the menu, as shown in Figure 15-13.

▪ A *printer* font is also referred to as a *downloadable* font because it's downloaded from the computer to the printer when it's time to print. Until TrueType came along, the phrase *outline font* was also synonymous with *printer font*.

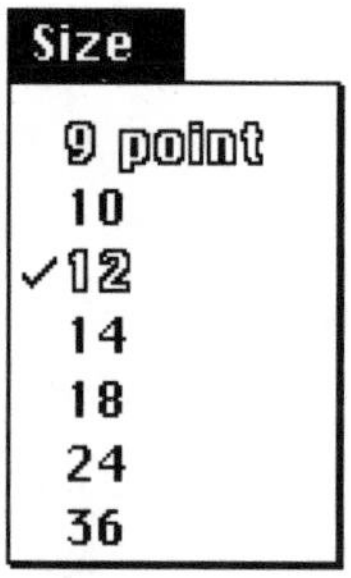

Figure 15-13.   Available sizes are outlined in the size menu.

■ The screen fonts provided as companions to printer fonts were designed to just represent the font on the screen, unlike bit-mapped fonts that were designed for optimum appearance on the screen. You'll find that although printer fonts look much better printed on a high-resolution printer, they don't look quite so attractive on the screen.

FONTS AND YOUR SYSTEM

Basics

Your basic Mac system software includes nine fonts (shown in Figure 15-14) that will appear in the Font menu of every application you run. If you've obtained more fonts with a printer or through other sources, you have to install them in your system before they will appear in any Font menu.

Standard Fonts

Of the nine fonts that come with your system software, there are five families of TrueType fonts: Chicago, Courier, Helvetica, Symbol, and Times. (The "relatives" are Courier Bold, Geneva Italic, Helvetica Bold, Times Bold, Times Italic, and Times Bold Italic.)

Geneva, Monaco, New York, and Palatino are bit-mapped fonts; most are supplied in five or six common sizes ranging from 9 to 24 points. Figure 15-14 shows the standard font menu and a sample of each font; the ones marked with the diamond shape are TrueType fonts.

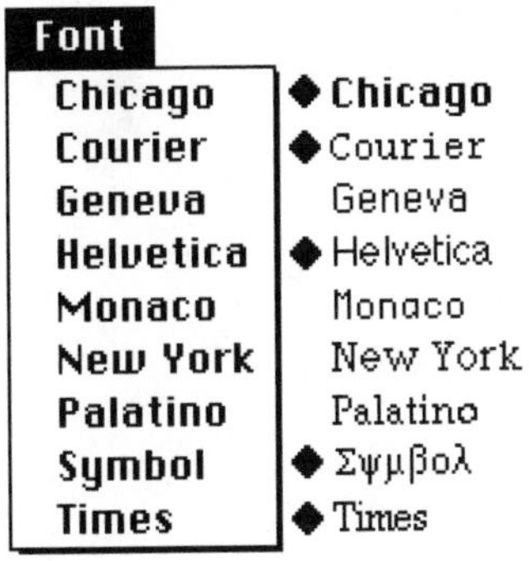

Font	
Chicago	◆ Chicago
Courier	◆ Courier
Geneva	Geneva
Helvetica	◆ Helvetica
Monaco	Monaco
New York	New York
Palatino	Palatino
Symbol	◆ Σψμβολ
Times	◆ Times

Figure 15-14.   The font samples marked with a diamond are supplied as TrueType fonts.

There's no way to tell by looking in a Font menu which fonts are TrueType or bitmaps. When you check the Size menu, however, you'll find that all the sizes are outlined for TrueType fonts, while only specific sizes are outlined for bit-mapped fonts.

LASERWRITER FONTS

If you have a PostScript-compatible LaserWriter, it came with built-in outline fonts and a disk of bit-mapped screen fonts for you to use. The standard LaserWriter fonts are shown in Figure 15-15.

Laser Fonts	
Avant Garde	Avant Garde
Bookman	Bookman
Courier	Courier
Helvetica	Helvetica
New Century Schlbk	New Century Schlbk
Palatino	Palatino
Times	Times
Zapf Chancery	*Zapf Chancery*
Zapf Dingbats	✱●□✲ ✦✦■✱✪●▼▲

Figure 15-15.   Standard LaserWriter fonts

Installing Fonts

There are three distinct kinds of font files that the Mac can use. Bit-mapped fonts and TrueType fonts have to be installed in your System file; printer fonts don't go in the System file, but they have to be in the right place or the Mac won't find them.

It's easy to tell the difference between a bit-mapped font file and a TrueType font file, because of their names and their icons, as shown in Figures 15-16 and 15-17. A bit-mapped font includes the font size in its name ("Courier 12"); its icon has a single *A* on it. A TrueType font has no size in its name ("Courier") and has three *As* of varying sizes on its icon.

If you double-click on a bit-mapped font icon, you'll get a sample of it; double-clicking on a TrueType font icon provides a sample of the font in several sizes.

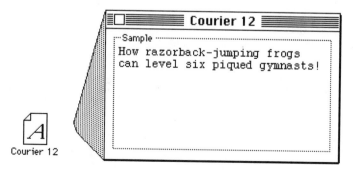

Figure 15-16.   A bit-mapped font icon, and its sample window

Figure 15-17. A TrueType font icon, and its sample window

Both bit-mapped and TrueType font files go into the System file; just drag the font icon into the System file icon, as shown in Figure 15-18, or into its open window.

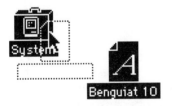

Figure 15-18. Installing a font into the System file

The icon for an outline font depends on the company that created it; Figure 15-19 shows an icon for an Adobe PostScript font. PostScript printer fonts usually have odd names, like the one shown in the figure; the first five letters of the printer file's name comes from the font name (Bengu for Benguiat) and the next three come from its style (Bol for Bold).

BenguBol

Figure 15-19. A PostScript font icon

Printer fonts go in the Extensions folder inside the System Folder. But you can simply drag the icon into the System Folder, and let the Mac take it from there: You'll get the dialog box shown in Figure 15-20.

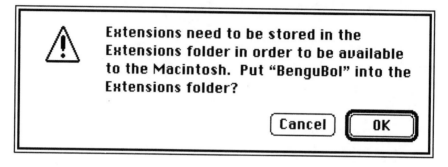

Figure 15-20. Dragging a printer font into the System Folder results in this dialog box.

If you have a LaserWriter with a hard drive attached, the printer fonts can be stored there instead of in the Extensions folder.

FONT SUITCASES

Previous versions of the Mac system software allowed files that contained multiple fonts; they were called *suitcases* because of their icons. You can easily transfer those fonts into your System file.

If you don't want all the fonts in the suitcase to go into your System file, double-click on the suitcase to open it. The window that opens will show all the fonts in the suitcase; select the ones you want and drag them into the System file (see Figure 5-21).

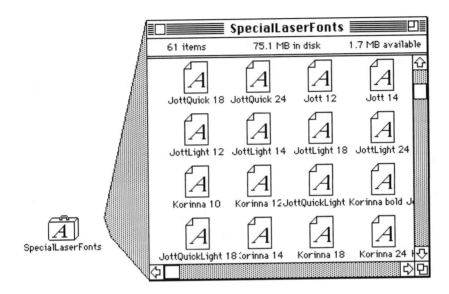

Figure 15-21. Double-click to open a suitcase of fonts.

If you want all the fonts from the suitcase to be put into your system, just drag the suitcase itself into your System file icon, as shown in Figure 15-22. All the fonts will be transferred into your system file; the suitcase itself disappears.

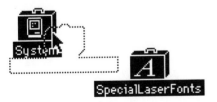

Figure 15-22. Dragging a suitcase into the System file

Using Multiple Font Technologies

TrueType fonts are an integral part of your Mac system; so are the separate bit-mapped fonts provided with the system software. You can also add printer and screen fonts, mixing all three technologies without any clashes because the Mac uses a simple hierarchical scheme when it's displaying a font or sending it to the printer.

For the screen, the Mac first looks for a bit-mapped font of the correct size; if it's not available, it uses the TrueType font.

For printing, the Mac first looks for the font in the printer itself; if it's not there, the Mac checks any hard drive attached to the printer and then it checks the Extensions folder for a downloadable font file. If the font doesn't exist in the printer or as a downloadable file, the Mac looks for a TrueType file and sends that information to the printer. Finally, if there's nothing but the bit-mapped versions of the font, the Mac sends the bitmap of the most appropriate size to the printer.

Also See . . .

▪ The Symbol font that comes with your system, and the Zapf Dingbats font that comes with most LaserWriters, are special-purpose fonts; Symbol is for mathematical typing, and Zapf Dingbats is used for all sorts of highlights in a document. The complete character sets for both these fonts are in Appendix E.

SUMMARY

In this chapter, you learned about various font technologies, how they differ, and how they work with your Mac. The next chapter discusses printer technologies and includes information about which fonts should be used with which printers.

Printers and Printing

ABOUT THIS CHAPTER

You wouldn't be too productive in or out of an office if you couldn't take the information you've generated with the computer and put it on paper to share with others. This chapter covers the basics of printer technology, Apple's printers, and how to print the things you've created on your Mac.

PRINTERS

Basics

There are three basic printer technologies, and Apple's line of printers provides something in each category: the ImageWriter is a dot matrix printer; the StyleWriter is an ink jet printer; and, there are four current LaserWriter models. Each technology has its advantages and drawbacks:

- The only plus to dot matrix technology is its low price; it's slow, noisy, and has low-resolution output. "Low resolution," however, is a relative term: If your printing consists basically of correspondence with few or no graphics, a dot matrix printer may be sufficient.

- Ink jet printers offer high resolution at low prices; the speed of ink jet printers vary, but Apple's is relatively slow.

- LaserWriters offer quiet operation and clean printouts at high resolution, but the benefits come with a high price tag.

All these technologies print by putting dots on paper. But the way the dots are put on the paper, the size of the dots, and how the dot positions are calculated are all factors that affect the quality of the output, or *hard copy*.

The ImageWriter

The ImageWriter is a *dot matrix* printer. Its *print head* incorporates moveable pins that can individually strike against a typewriter-like ribbon to put dots on the paper.

The ImageWriter prints at 72 dots per inch horizontally and 80 dpi vertically in one mode, and at 144-by-160 dpi in another. Although the size of the dots doesn't change from one mode to the other, the higher-resolution mode offers much more readable print because there aren't any gaps in the lines that form the characters.

The ImageWriter uses bit-mapped information from the computer to print its text and graphics; it can also use TrueType fonts.

Printing speed varies according to the print mode you've chosen. Draft mode prints a little over two pages per minute; Faster mode (at 72 dpi) prints about a page and a half per minute; in Best mode (at 144 dpi), you get one page a minute.

The ImageWriter can print in color if you use a color ribbon. Special ribbons with bands of colors can be used with software that knows how to send color information to the ImageWriter; by overprinting (printing a red dot and then a yellow dot on top of it to make orange), you can obtain many different colors. But because of the overprinting, the color bands don't last long, rendering the entire ribbon useless in a very short time.

The StyleWriter

The StyleWriter is an *ink jet* printer. The dots of ink it puts on the paper are shot in tiny spurts from nozzles in the print head.

Like the ImageWriter, the StyleWriter can print at two different resolutions. In Faster mode, it takes about a minute to produce a full page at 180 dpi. In Best mode, it prints at 360 dpi—higher than any of Apple's laser printers—but at a snail's pace of a half-page per minute.

The StyleWriter uses bit-mapped graphic information and both bit-mapped and TrueType fonts for printing.

LaserWriters

A *laser* printer is the top-of-the-line printer for personal computers. It puts information onto paper the same way a photocopy machine does; it melts tiny particles called *toner* onto the paper in areas it previously charged to attract the toner.

Apple currently has four LaserWriter models: the LaserWriter LS, the only non-PostScript printer; the Personal LaserWriter NT; the LaserWriter IINT; and the LaserWriter IINTX. All of the models print at 300 dpi and can use bit-mapped and TrueType fonts and bit-mapped graphics. The PostScript-compatible models can also print PostScript outline fonts and EPS graphics.

The main features of the LaserWriter models are summed up in Table 16-1.

■ *PostScript:* A built-in PostScript interpreter gives the printer the capability of printing PostScript fonts and EPS graphics. The PostScript printers have 35 outline fonts in 11 font families included in their ROMs.

■ *Memory:* One of the things a LaserWriter's RAM is used for is holding the font information from the computer. You can use more fonts in a document if you have more memory in your printer. The NTX's 2 megabytes of RAM is upgradable to 12M. The NTX also has a SCSI port for a hard drive that can be devoted solely to outline font files.

■ *Pages per minute:* Apple's official ratings (shown in Table 16-1) for pages per minute for each of its printers is misleading. The ratings are for how fast the page itself can be printed and cycled through the machine, but they don't take into account the processing time for *imaging* the document—taking the information from the computer and figuring out how it should look on the page. Imaging time varies from one printer to the next, and even from one document to the next. Text documents process more quickly than those with graphics in them, and complicated graphics take more time than simple ones.

■ *Network:* The LS is designed to work with only one Macintosh; the others can be shared by more than one machine.

- *Upgrade:* You can upgrade the NT to an NTX by trading in its controller board and buying the more sophisticated one. Apple's first non-PostScript LaserWriter, the LaserWriter SC (not included in the chart because it's no longer available) is upgradable to either an NT or an NTX.

Table 16-1. LaserWriter Features of Various Printers

	LS	Personal NT	IINT	IINTX
PostScript	no	yes	yes	yes
Memory	512K	2M	2M	2 to 12M
Pages per Minute	4	4	8	8
Network	no	yes	yes	yes
Upgrade	no	no	to NT	n/a

Quickies

- Slightly used ImageWriter ribbons are better for Best mode printing; the extra ink in new ribbons tends to smear.

- You should use high-quality paper in the StyleWriter so the ink won't soak in and spread before it dries. (And even after it's dry, it will smear if you dampen it.)

- A LaserWriter toner cartridge is usually good for 4000 to 5000 pages, but you don't have to buy a new cartridge every time you run out of toner. You can recycle a cartridge by having it recharged and filled with more toner.

PRINTING COMMANDS

Basics

Most applications have two commands directly related to the printing of documents: Page Setup and Print. Both these commands are available from an application's File menu.

```
┌─────────────────────────┐
│ █File███████████████████ │
│   New...           ⌘N    │
│   Open...          ⌘O    │
│   Close                  │
│ ························ │
│   Save             ⌘S    │
│   Save As...             │
│ ························ │
│ ██Page Setup...█████████ │
│ ██Print...█████████⌘P███ │
│ ························ │
│   Quit             ⌘Q    │
└─────────────────────────┘
```

The dialog box that you see when you choose either of these commands depends on the kind of printer you're using, since each printer provides some special printing options.

The Mac knows which printer you're using by checking what you've selected in the Chooser desk accessory. (Using the Chooser was covered in Chapter 10.) The icons that appear in the Chooser desk accessory are the *printer drivers* that you have in your Extensions folder inside the System Folder; the drivers are placed in the folder when you install your system software.

A printer driver translates information from an application into instructions that a particular printer will understand. With printing operations organized this way, an application doesn't have to include instructions for every possible printer; instead, it sends out a single set of instructions and the driver translates it into the appropriate commands for the printer.

The Page Setup Command

The Page Setup command in an application's File menu lets you set some overall parameters for printing a document. The options you have depend on the printer you're using, but they fall into four categories: paper size, orientation, printout size, and special effects.

Figure 16-1 shows what the Page Setup dialog boxes look like for the ImageWriter, the StyleWriter, the LS, and a PostScript-compatible LaserWriter.

ImageWriter			OK
Paper:	⦿ US Letter	○ A4 Letter	
	○ US Legal	○ International Fanfold	Cancel
	○ Computer Paper		
Orientation	Special Effects:	☐ Tall Adjusted	
		☐ 50 % Reduction	
		☐ No Gaps Between Pages	

StyleWriter		OK
Paper:	⦿ US Letter	○ A4 Letter
	○ US Legal	○ Envelope (#10)	Cancel
Orientation:		Scale: 100%

LaserWriter LS			OK
Paper:	⦿ US Letter	○ A4 Letter	
	○ US Legal	○ B5 Letter	Cancel
	○ No. 10 Envelope		
Orientation	Size:	⦿ 100%	☐ Exact Bit Images (Shrink 4%)
		○ 75%	☐ Text Smoothing
		○ 50%	

LaserWriter Page Setup			OK
Paper: ⦿ US Letter ○ A4 Letter		○ [Tabloid ▼]	Cancel
○ US Legal ○ B5 Letter			
Reduce or Enlarge: [100] %	Printer Effects:		Options
	☒ Font Substitution?		
Orientation	☒ Text Smoothing?		
	☒ Graphics Smoothing?		
	☒ Faster Bitmap Printing?		

Figure 16-1.   The Page Setup dialog depends on the printer you're using.

PAPER SIZE

Each printer provides several different standard paper sizes; some
LaserWriters offer additional paper choices in a popup menu, as shown
in Figure 16-2. Table 16-2 shows the sizes of the papers referred to in the
dialogs. (The sizes for Computer Paper and International Fanfold don't
include the tear-off edges used to guide the paper through the
ImageWriter's tractor-feed mechanism.)

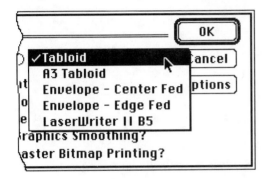

Figure 16-2. The Page Setup popup menu for some LaserWriters

Table 16-2. Common Paper Sizes

Paper	Size (in inches)
Computer Paper	8.5 by 11
International Fanfold	8.3 by 11.7
U.S. Letter	8.5 by 11
U.S. Legal	8.5 by 14
A4 Letter	8.3 by 11.7
B5	7.2 by 10.1
B4	10.1 by 14.3
10 Envelope	9.5 by 4.125
Tabloid	11 by 14
A3 Tabloid	11.75 by 16.5

ORIENTATION

Each printer allows you to print in the normal *portrait* orientation or
sideways, in *landscape* mode. The landscape mode is particularly
convenient for printing spreadsheets that contain so many columns that
they would be split across two pages if printed in portrait mode, as
shown in Figure 16-3.

Choose the orientation you want by clicking on the appropriate icon.

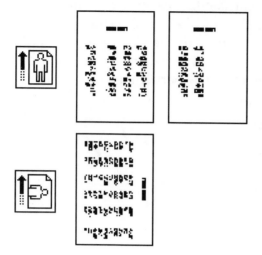

Figure 16-3. The portrait orientation (top) prints vertically on the page; the landscape orientation (bottom) prints sideways and is often better for some types of documents.

PRINTOUT SIZE

Regardless of the paper size you've chosen, each printer gives you some control over the size of the *image* on each page.

- The ImageWriter, in its list of special effects, has a checkbox that lets you choose a 50% reduction in the printout.

  ☐ **50 % Reduction**

- In the StyleWriter dialog, you choose the printout size by clicking in the arrows labeled *Scale*. It allows choices of 20%, 40%, 60%, 80%, or 100%.

  Scale: 100% ⬆⬇

- Non-PostScript LaserWriters allow you to choose from full size (100%), or 75% or 50% reductions by clicking in a radio button.

Size: ⦿ 100%
      ○ 75%
      ○ 50%

- PostScript LaserWriters let you specify a reduction or enlargement of the page by typing in the percentage you want—up to 400% of the original size. (A 400% enlargement would quadruple the size of the page image and use *16* pieces of paper because the image is four times its original size both horizontally and vertically.)

Reduce or [100]%
Enlarge:

When you choose an image size that's smaller than the actual page, you don't get multiple miniature pages on a sheet of paper. Each page is printed individually, with its image positioned at the upper-left corner of the paper. (If you shrink a page by 50%, as shown in Figure 16-4, the image will take only a quarter of the page because it will be 50% smaller in both its horizontal and vertical measurements.)

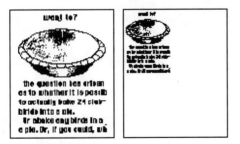

Figure 16-4. Printing at 50% reduction reduces the image to a quarter of the page.

IMAGEWRITER SPECIAL EFFECTS

The ImageWriter provides three special effects choices.

Special Effects: ☐ Tall Adjusted
☐ 50 % Reduction
☐ No Gaps Between Pages

▪ *Tall Adjusted:* Because the Mac screen has an equal number of dots per inch vertically and horizontally but the ImageWriter prints at 72-by-80 dpi or 144-by-160 dpi, the printout doesn't always match what you see on the screen. The 11% vertical distortion tends to turn circles into ovals. If you check the Tall Adjusted option, everything in the printout is expanded horizontally to make up for the distortion. (But that means that a block of text that was 5 inches wide becomes a little over 5½ inches wide with the option turned on.) Figure 16-5 shows a picture printed with and without the Tall Adjusted option.

Figure 16-5.   Before applying the Tall Adjusted option (left) and after using Tall Adjusted option (right)

▪ *50% Reduction:* Reduces the size of the page image, as just described.

▪ *No Gaps Between Pages:* The ImageWriter driver normally allows for the fact that tractor-feed paper has perforations between one page and the next that shouldn't be printed across, so it advances each page slightly before it starts printing. If you're using single sheets of paper, or special tractor-feed printing material like mailing labels, you should check the No Gaps Between Pages option.

LASERWRITER LS SPECIAL EFFECTS

The LaserWriter LS (the non-PostScript model) offers two special effects—one for text and the other for graphics.

☐ **Exact Bit Images (Shrink 4%)**
☐ **Text Smoothing**

▪ *Exact Bit Images (Shrink 4%):* Bit-mapped images (both graphics and text) are somewhat distorted on a LaserWriter because its 300-dpi resolution is not a multiple of the 72-dpi bit-mapped image. When you check the Exact Bit Images box, a graphics image is reduced by 4%, which increases its resolution to 75 dpi. Since 300 is a multiple of 75, the graphic prints without any distortion. Figure 16-6 shows the same graphic printed with and without the 4% reduction. The overall size change is minimal, but if you look at the gray area of the hat, you'll see that the pattern is distorted in the unadjusted version at the left.

Figure 16-6. Without the Exact Bit Images option, the gray pattern of the hat in the figure on the left is distorted. On the right, the 4% reduction has aligned the dots in the pattern properly.

▪ *Text Smoothing:* This option does not affect outline fonts, but it does improve the look of bit-mapped fonts by adding extra dots along the 45° and 90° lines of the characters. Figure 16-7 shows LaserWriter output of bit-mapped fonts with and without smoothing.

```
This is a bit-mapped        This is a bit-mapped
font printed with           font printed with
smoothing turned on.        smoothing turned off.
```

Figure 16-7.   Bitmapped font output with and without the Text Smoothing option

POSTSCRIPT LASERWRITER SPECIAL EFFECTS
Because the PostScript language provides so many ways to easily manipu-late a page image, PostScript LaserWriters have an abundance of printing options. Four of them are listed in the Page Setup dialog; others are available in a separate dialog that appears when you use the Options button in the Page Setup dialog.

Printer Effects:
☒ **Font Substitution?**
☒ **Text Smoothing?**
☒ **Graphics Smoothing?**
☒ **Faster Bitmap Printing?**

▪ *Font Substitution:* If you check this box, certain bit-mapped fonts in your document will be automatically converted to outline fonts for printing. Helvetica replaces Geneva, Times replaces New York, and Courier replaces Monaco, as shown in Figure 16-8. (Courier, of course, looks nothing like Monaco; the logic behind the substitution is that both are monofonts.)

```
Geneva    ———>  Helvetica
New York  ———>  Times
Monaco    ———>  Courier
```

Figure 16-8.   Font substitutions

■ *Text Smoothing:* The Text Smoothing option works the same way as it does with non-PostScript LaserWriters.

■ *Graphics Smoothing:* You can smooth the lines of a bit-mapped graphic the same way bit-mapped text is smoothed. But keep in mind that although smoothing always changes the look of a graphic, it doesn't always *improve* it. Graphics that are basically line drawings that include curves generally look better when smoothed, but bit-mapped graphics whose look depends on the textural quality of the artwork tend to lose the texture and become less attractive. Figure 16-9 shows images printed with and without smoothing. The ice cream looks better in the smoothed version, but the fish looks better unsmoothed.

Figure 16-9. Unsmoothed bit-mapped images (left) and the smoothed versions (right)

■ *Faster Bitmap Printing:* While this option speeds printing of documents that include bit-mapped fonts or graphics, sometimes it doesn't work at all. If your document fails to print, uncheck this option.

When you use the Options button in the Page Setup dialog, another dialog box appears (see Figure 16-10), providing further printing options. As you check these options, the sample page in the dialog changes to reflect the options you've chosen.

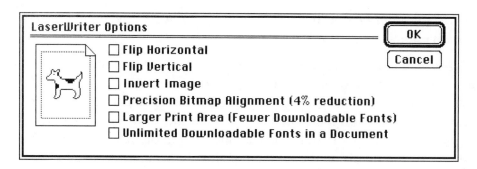

Figure 16-10. The Options dialog

■ *Flip Horizontal, Flip Vertical,* and *Invert Image:* These options are self-explanatory. The images on the left side of Figure 16-11 show their results.

■ *Precision Bitmap Alignment (4% reduction):* This is the same as the *Exact Bit Images* option for the non-PostScript LaserWriters.

■ *Larger Print Area (Fewer Downloadable Fonts):* The LaserWriter must hold an image of the entire page in its memory, but part of its RAM is reserved for the information it needs to print downloaded fonts. As a result, there's not enough memory available to print all the way to the edges of an 8½-by-11-inch piece of paper. If you don't use too many fonts in a document, you can shift some of the memory usage over to the page image, making the page margins a little smaller.

■ *Unlimited Downloadable Fonts in a Document:* You can trade in some printing speed for unlimited font handling. The LaserWriter normally retains font information that's downloaded to it in case you use the font again. If you check this option, a font is flushed from memory when room is needed for another one, which means the flushed font has to be downloaded all over again if it's used again. (As Figure 16-11 shows, this option has no effect on the look of the printed page.)

Because all these options are checkboxes, you can turn them on in any combination. Figure 16-12 shows what happens when the first three are turned on together.

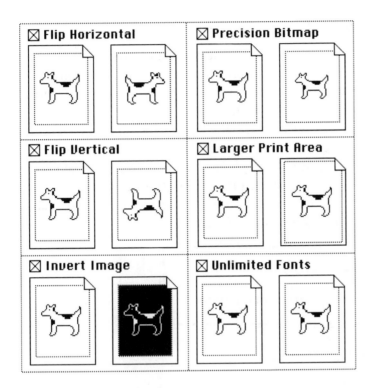

Figure 16-11.   The results of using various printing options

Figure 16-12.   You can combine special effects.

The Print Command

To print a document, you choose the Print command from an application's File menu, select the options you want from the Print dialog, and then click the Print button. (Or, if you change your mind, you can click the Cancel button to put the dialog away.)

During the printing process, there will be a dialog box on the screen to let you know what's going on. The exact dialog depends on the application that you're printing from. Some "progress report" dialogs have Cancel buttons in them, or even Pause and Restart buttons; some, like the one shown in Figure 16-13, have no buttons at all, but you can cancel the printing with a keyboard command.

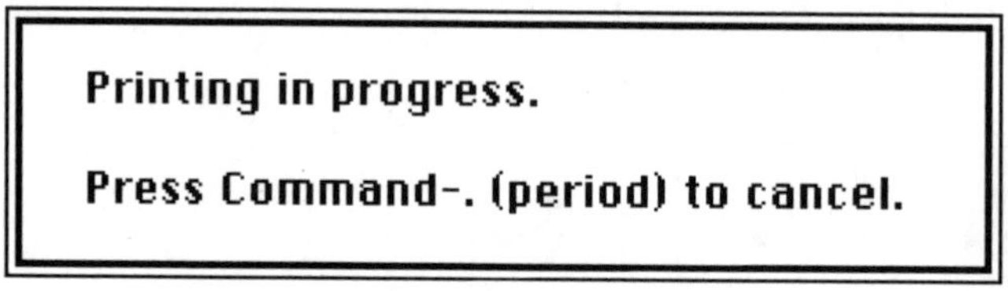

```
Printing in progress.

Press Command-. (period) to cancel.
```

Figure 16-13.   A printing progress report

The printing process is actually a two-way communication between the printer and the computer; for instance, the printer can inform the computer when it's ready for more information. Some printers, like LaserWriters, also send signals to the computer if something's wrong—if there's no more paper, or the paper has jammed, or the paper tray isn't in position. In these cases, the computer will beep to get your attention and you'll see a dialog box that explains the problem, like the one shown in Figure 16-14. These status reports seldom have any buttons in them; when you attend to the problem, the dialog goes away and printing resumes.

```
Printer has no paper tray
```

Figure 16-14.   A printing error report

As with Page Setup dialogs, the Print dialog that appears when you use a Print command depends on the printer you're using; Figure 16-15 shows some samples. Each printer provides certain special options, but they all have certain things in common.

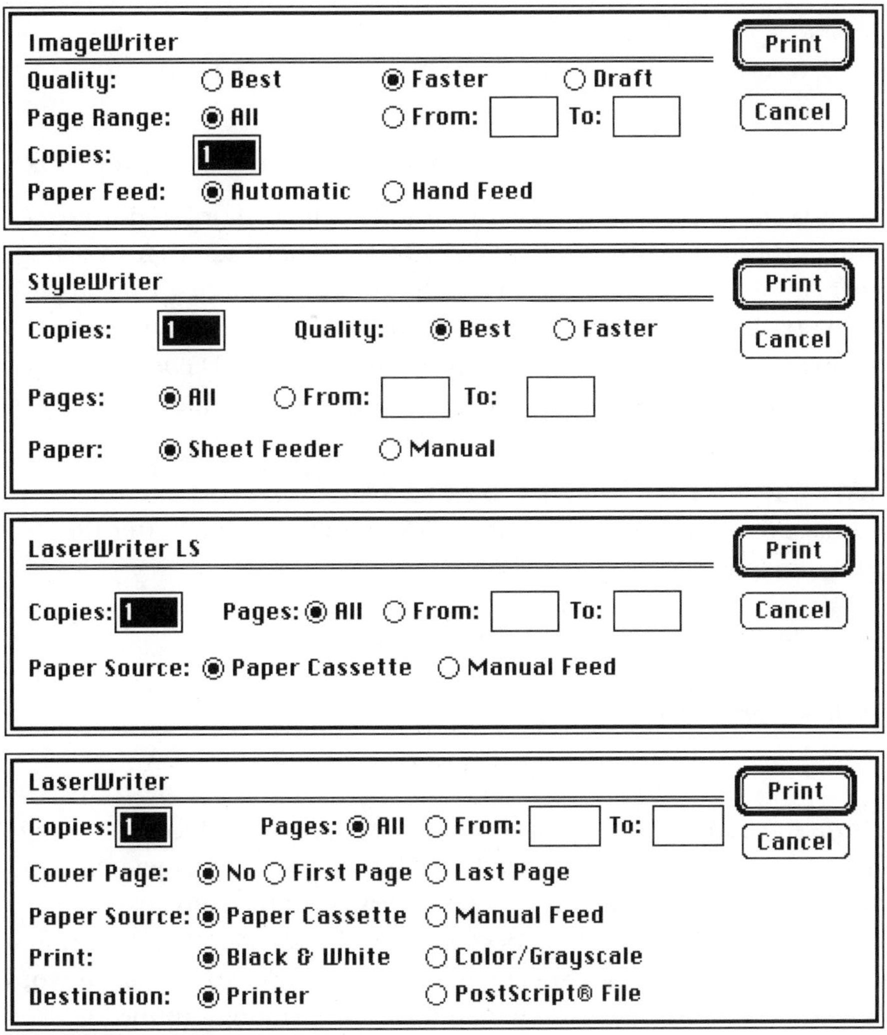

Figure 16-15. Print dialogs

COMMON OPTIONS

Although the choices in various Print dialogs may have slightly different names, they all offer options for Page Range, Number of Copies, and Paper Source.

- *Page Range:* Click the All button for the entire document to be printed, or click the From button and type the start and end page numbers in the From and To text boxes.

- *Copies:* Type the number of copies you want printed in the text box.

- *Paper Source:* Clicking the Manual (or Manual Feed or Hand Feed) button in this dialog prints one page at a time. After each page, a dialog appears on the screen so you can tell the printer when to go ahead with the next page. This gives you time to feed the next piece of paper or envelope to the printer. Using the Automatic (or Sheet Feeder or Paper Cassette) button causes the printer to print pages continuously.

IMAGEWRITER PRINTING OPTIONS

The ImageWriter prints text in three different modes; the better the output, the longer it takes to print.

| Quality: ○ Best   ⊙ Faster   ○ Draft |

ImageWriter printing modes

- *Draft:* In Draft mode, the ImageWriter uses its internal font, ignoring bitmaps (both fonts and graphics) from the computer. You get a low-quality text-only printout, but you get it very quickly. Word spacing in draft mode is very odd looking because, despite the fact that the printer is using its internal font for speedy output, it still tries to start each word on the same spot in a line as it would if it were printing proportional, formatted text. Since your document won't look at all like it did on the screen, draft printing is used only to proofread the text content, not to check its formatting.

- *Faster*: In Faster mode, the ImageWriter prints all the bitmaps as sent from the computer, at a 72-dpi resolution.

- *Best:* In Best mode, the ImageWriter uses its 144-dpi resolution, making two passes with the print head for every line, offsetting the second line slightly from the first to minimize any jagged lines. Since the bit-mapped image from the document is only 72 dpi, however, the ImageWriter driver first creates a bit-mapped image that's twice the size of the page and uses that as a map to create the standard-size page at 144 dpi.

Figure 16-16 shows sample ImageWriter printouts in the three modes.

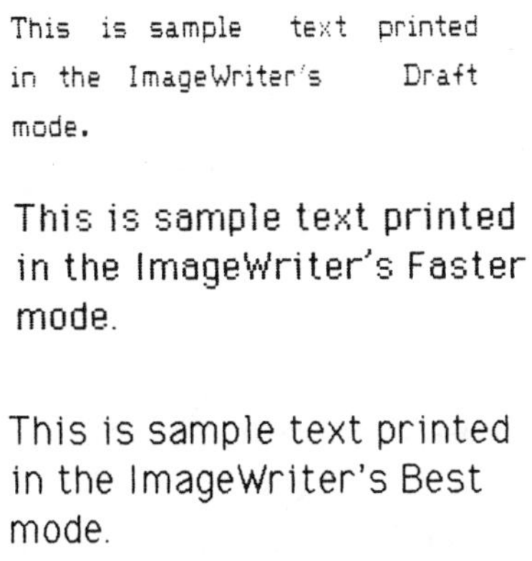

```
This  is  sample   text  printed
in  the  ImageWriter's    Draft
mode.
```

```
This is sample text printed
in the ImageWriter's Faster
mode.
```

```
This is sample text printed
in the ImageWriter's Best
mode.
```

Figure 16-16.   The ImageWriter's three printing modes: Draft (top), Faster (middle), and Best (bottom).

STYLEWRITER OPTIONS
The StyleWriter offers two print modes; as with the ImageWriter, the better output takes longer.

| Quality: | ○ Best | ◉ Faster | ○ Draft |

StyleWriter printing modes

- *Faster:* In Faster mode, the StyleWriter prints about a page a minute at 180 dpi.

- *Best:* In Best mode, the printout is 360 dpi, but it takes a full two minutes for even an uncomplicated page to be printed.

Figure 16-17 shows Best and Faster mode StyleWriter printouts.

This is sample text printed
in the StyleWriter's Faster
mode.

This is sample text printed
in the StyleWriter's Best
mode.

Figure 16-17.   The Style Writer's two printing modes: Faster (top) and Best (bottom)

GRAYSCALE PRINTING

One of the two special options provided in a PostScript printer's Print dialog is the choice between printing a black-and-white graphic or something more representative of the color or grayscale image on your screen.

Print: ⦿ Black & White   ○ Color/Grayscale

Special printing options for PostScript printers

The LaserWriters, of course, can print only in black, but at 300-dpi resolution it's easy to use *dithered patterns* (combinations of black and white dots) to represent shades of gray—or to use the dithered grays to represent the different hues of a color picture.

Figure 16-18 shows a grayscale image the way it looks on the screen; Figure 16-19 shows how it looks printed with each option. With Black & White, all the grays lighter than a certain shade are white and the rest are

Figure 16-18. A grayscale picture as it appears on the screen

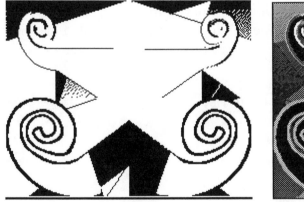

Figure 16-19. A grayscale picture printed in Black & White (left) and Color/Grayscale (right)

black; this results in the loss of parts of the image. With Color/Grayscale, the differing shades of gray are represented by dithered patterns, giving a better idea of how the actual picture looks. (While you wouldn't want to use even the dithered version as final output, many documents created on the Mac are printed on very-high-resolution devices that print grayscales and color; to some extent you can proof these documents using this LaserWriter option.)

CREATING POSTSCRIPT FILES

The Destination option in the LaserWriter dialog box shows where you
want the printing instructions to go: to the printer or into a disk file.

| Destination: ⦿ Printer   ○ PostScript® File |

PostScript output can go to the printer or to the disk.

If you click the Printer button, the document will be printed normally.

If you choose the PostScript File button, a file is created that contains
the PostScript commands that the printer needs to image the document.
But instead of sending the information to the printer, the file is saved to
the disk. (You'll get a Save dialog asking you to name the file.)

Since PostScript is a programming language, a PostScript file is a text
file that contains commands (unlike EPS—Encapsulated PostScript—
documents, which contain both PostScript commands and a screen
representation of the information). Figure 16-20 shows the first part of a
file that contains the PostScript commands to reproduce a page from a
graphics program that had a single, simple box drawn on it.

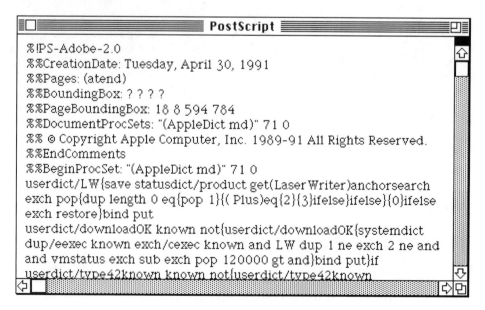

Figure 16-20.   A file of PostScript programming commands

A PostScript file can be altered by someone who knows the PostScript programming language, changing the final output of the file. PostScript files are more often used as is—but they're used for another printer, or by another computer (even a non-Macintosh) that's connected to a PostScript output device.

PostScript files can't be printed in the normal fashion; instead, they have to be *downloaded* to the printer. This is described in the last section of this chapter, "The LaserWriter Font Utility."

Quickies

- Many applications add their own options to both the Page Setup and Print dialogs.

- In the Print dialog, you don't have to click the From button; if you specify a page range by typing numbers in the boxes, the From button is automatically selected.

- If you specify a starting page number for the page range to be printed and don't put anything as the end page, everything from the starting page to the end of the document will be printed.

- If you buy a printer whose software wasn't available when you installed your system software, it will come with its own software. All you have to do is put its driver into the Extensions folder in your System Folder.

PRINTING CONSIDERATIONS

Basics

In the early days of the Mac, printed output was *WYSIWYG—What You See Is What You Get*. (It's pronounced "whizzy-wig.") The resolution of the screen matched the resolution of the printer, and both used bitmaps to create images.

Now most printers have much higher resolutions than screens have, and different sets of information may be used to generate the screen display and the printed output of the same text or graphic. As a result, there are several strategies you need to keep in mind in order to get the best possible output from your printer.

Printing Bit-Mapped Graphics

Bit-mapped graphics have a resolution of 72 dots per inch. The ImageWriter's Faster printing mode has the same resolution, so there's no problem. But its Best mode is 144 dpi, the StyleWriter prints at 180 dpi and 360 dpi, and the LaserWriters print at 300 dpi. A 72-dpi graphic can't automatically take advantage of a printer's higher resolution, and it's often distorted slightly in the printing process.

INCREASING THE GRAPHIC'S RESOLUTION

If you take an image in a paint-type graphics program (types of graphics programs were covered in Chapter 6) and reduce it to 50% of its original size, every other dot that made up the image is thrown out. You started with an image that had a resolution of 72 dots per inch, and you ended with an image of the same resolution—just smaller in size, and difficult (if not impossible) to interpret.

But if you're working in a program that treats a bit-mapped image as an *object* that retains an internal definition of what it should look like no matter how you manipulate it on the screen, you don't lose any information when you reduce its size. (Object-oriented graphics were also covered in Chapter 6, which also noted that bit-mapped images are treated as objects once you import them into an object-oriented graphics program, a word processor, or a page lay-out program.)

If you take a bit-mapped object (which still begins at 72 dpi) and shrink it to 50% of its original size, you've squeezed the 72 dots that used to make an inch into a half-inch space. The resolution of the graphic becomes 144 dpi because that's how many dots you can fit in an inch—but each dot is now half its original size. Of course, you can't see that on the screen, since Mac screens don't go much above 72 dpi, but when you print out the image, you'll see the graphic without the screen distortion.

Figure 16-21 shows a bit-mapped image at its original size (left) and at the 50% reduction on screen (top right) and in the printout (bottom right). By shrinking the image, you've increased its resolution, and that's the basis for getting good graphic output; you just have to be sure that you shrink it to the right percentage to take advantage of your printer's resolution.

Figure 16-21. The original image (left); the reduced screen image (top right); the reduced printed image (bottom right)

THE IMAGEWRITER
Since the ImageWriter's Best printing mode is 144 dpi, scaling a graphic by 50% takes the best advantage of the printer's resolution.

THE STYLEWRITER
Because the ratio of the StyleWriter's 360-dpi resolution to a 72-dpi image is 5 to 1, reducing an image to 20% of its original size will give you the best possible output. (Of course, the picture is a lot smaller, but if you know you're going to reduce to 20%, you can start by creating a much larger picture.)

You can increase the resolution of a bit-mapped object that you're printing without distorting it by printing it at 80%, 60%, or 40% of the original size. It's not coincidental that these are the choices in the StyleWriter's Page Setup dialog for page reduction, but remember, that option reduces the entire page.

THE LASERWRITERS

The ratio of the LaserWriter's 300-dpi resolution to a bit-mapped images's 72-dpi resolution is not an even one, so there's always a little distortion when you print a bit-mapped graphic on a LaserWriter. However, if you use a 96% reduction before printing, the overall size of the graphic won't change much, but its proportions will be correct. (This is exactly what happens when you use the Shrink Bitmaps option in the Page Setup dialog.)

For greater reductions to further increase the resolution of the image, use 72%, 48%, or 24% to keep the correct ratio between the image and the printout.

As with other reduced images, the screen version of the graphic is not representative of the printed output. Figure 16-22 shows an original bit-mapped graphic and four reduced sizes. Although the 96% reduction is not remarkable, you can see how the other reductions in size increased the resolution, making all the lines finer and all the curves less jagged.

Figure 16-22. The original image (top left) and 96%, 72%, 48%, and 24% reductions

Printing EPS Graphics

For PostScript LaserWriters, printing EPS graphics is a breeze. You can resize them to any proportions and they'll still print beautifully. In fact, unlike bit-mapped images, you can make an EPS graphic *larger* than its original version and it will still print clearly.

As explained in Chapter 6, EPS graphic files have one set of information for the screen and another for the printer. Figure 16-23 shows what an EPS image looks like on screen; Figure 16-24 shows a printout at both reduced and enlarged sizes.

Figure 16-23. A screen version of an EPS graphic

Figure 16-24. Reduced and enlarged versions of an EPS graphic

Printing Text

The considerations for the best possible text output are much like those for good graphics output because the basic factors are the same: there are several types of fonts, several types of printers, and the font and printer resolutions don't match.

BIT-MAPPED FONTS

Bit-mapped fonts are designed at 72 dots per inch, no matter what their point size.

When you want to print at the ImageWriter's highest resolution of 144 dpi, you need a font in the system that's *twice* the size of the one you're printing; for instance, if you're printing a 12-point font, you should have the 24-point version in your system. The ImageWriter uses the large version as a map for the printout; and, just as a graphic's resolution is doubled when you shrink it by 50%, the resolution of the 72-dpi text is increased to 144 dpi.

StyleWriters can also print bit-mapped fonts, but it's practically impossible to work with the correct size for the best printout. The StyleWriter's resolution is 360 dpi—*five times* that of a 72-dpi font. That means that for the best output of a 12-point font, you'd need a 60-point version in your system. This is unfeasible both because few bit-mapped fonts come in such large sizes and because they would take up too much room on your disk.

You have the same problem with bit-mapped fonts on LaserWriters— with the additional problem that the 300-dpi LaserWriter resolution is not a multiple of a 72-dpi font.

So if you're using a StyleWriter or a non-PostScript LaserWriter, stick with Apple's TrueType fonts.

TRUETYPE AND POSTSCRIPT FONTS

Outline fonts are scaled to whatever size is needed for the best output. While the ImageWriter can use TrueType fonts, the StyleWriter and LaserWriters are designed to really take advantage of the technology.

If you want to use a TrueType font, just install it in your system. From there, the Mac can use it for both the screen display and the printer output.

Although PostScript LaserWriters can use the TrueType fonts, there is a much larger variety of PostScript fonts to choose from at this point; in fact, there are more PostScript fonts built into your LaserWriter than there are TrueType fonts in your system software.

You usually need two versions of each PostScript font that you use. One, the screen font, has to be installed in your System file so it will appear on the screen and in Font menus. The second version is the printer font; if it's built into the LaserWriter (for a list, see Chapter 15), you don't need anything else. If it's not built in, you need the printer, or *downloadable,* font. The printer fonts can be on a hard drive attached directly to the printer, or in the Extensions folder in the System Folder.

SPECIAL PRINTING OPTIONS

Basics

Regardless of the type of printer you're using, you don't have to run an application before giving a Print command for one of its documents: There's a way to do it right from the Desktop.

And if you're using a LaserWriter, you have another special printing option available, one that lets you keep working while your printer churns out hard copy.

Printing from the Desktop

To print a file from the Desktop, select its icon and then choose Print from the File menu. The document and its application will open, and the Print dialog appears so that you can select options. When you click the Print button, the document will print; when it's finished, the application automatically quits.

The advantage to this method is that you can select several documents on the Desktop and the Print command will apply to all of them (see Figure 16-25). (Few applications give you a way to print more than one document at a time.) When you're printing multiple documents, the application that created them opens and displays the Print dialog. After you choose the options in the dialog and click Print, each document will open in turn and be printed, using the same printing options; you won't see the Print dialog again.

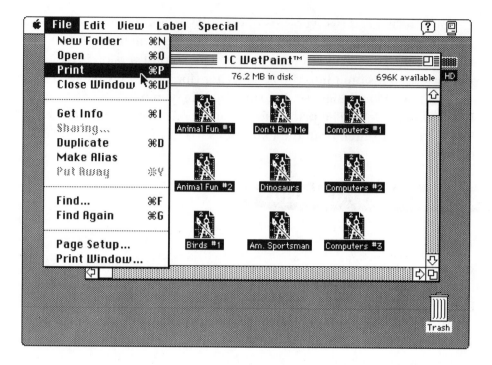

Figure 16-25. Printing documents from the Desktop

You can also choose multiple documents and print them even if they don't belong to the same application. Each application will open, print its documents, and quit in turn. You'll only have to attend to a single Print dialog for each application.

Background Printing

During normal printing operations, the computer feeds information to the printer a little at a time; the printer processes and prints it, and the computer passes on the next chunk of information. This means your computer is tied up during the entire printing process, even though it's not actively involved in the printing during the time that the printer is processing a page.

LaserWriters have the capability to do *background printing:* They can keep printing while you keep computing. When you set up background printing, the information that is normally sent to the printer a little at a time is instead compiled into a file that's saved on the disk. The first part of the file is sent to the printer, and while it's being processed there, you can keep working. When the printer is ready for the next round of information, it tells the computer to send it; your work is interrupted for a few seconds during this communication process, but the interruption is usually brief. (The faster your Mac model, the shorter the interruption.)

The program that controls this background printing process is called PrintMonitor, and it's installed in your Extensions folder during system installation.

PrintMonitor

You turn background printing on and off through the Chooser desk accessory: Open Chooser, select your LaserWriter driver icon, and then click the On or Off button for background printing (see Figure 16-26).

While PrintMonitor is working, it will be listed in the Application menu, like any other open program. If you choose PrintMonitor from the menu, you'll get a window (shown in Figure 16-27) that tells you what document is being printed and how many pages are left. You can close the window by clicking in its close box or by simply moving to another program; unlike other applications, the PrintMonitor closes its window if it's not the active one.

If you want to cancel a print job, use the Cancel button in the PrintMonitor window.

The Set Print Time button in the window opens the dialog shown in Figure 16-28; it lets you specify a time (including the date, although the current date is entered by default) for the printing to begin; if you don't specify a time, the printing begins immediately.

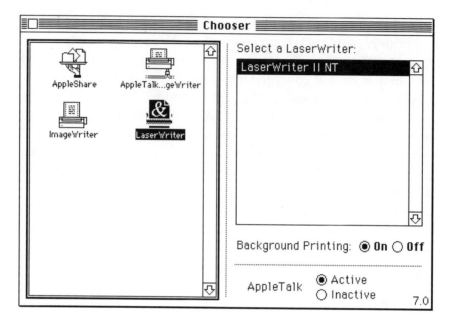

Figure 16-26. If you select a LaserWriter driver, the Background Printing buttons become available.

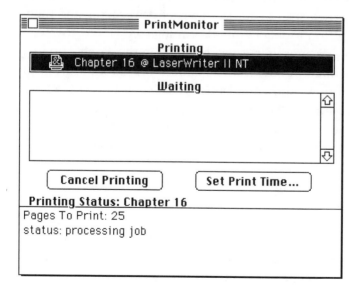

Figure 16-27. The PrintMonitor window

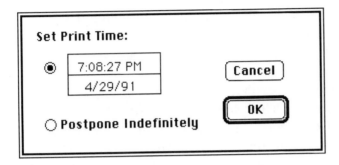

Figure 16-28. The current time and date are suggested as the printing time.

MULTIPLE DOCUMENTS IN PRINTMONITOR

You don't have to wait for PrintMonitor to finish with one document before you send the next; issue the Print command for as many documents as you want, and they will be lined up in a queue for printing. If you open PrintMonitor when there are documents waiting to be printed, you'll see them listed in the window. Selecting one in the list gives information about it: how many pages it is, what application created it, and when it was sent, or *spooled,* to PrintMonitor (see Figure 16-29).

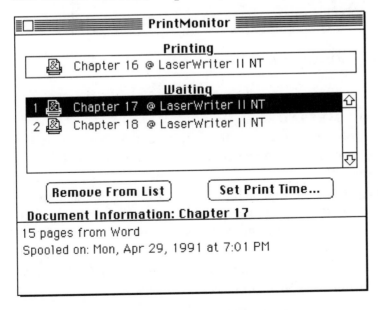

Figure 16-29. Queued documents in PrintMonitor

If you select an item in the list and click the Remove From List button, it won't be printed.

THE PRINTMONITOR FOLDER

When you use PrintMonitor, an extra folder is created inside the System Folder to hold the printer files. The folder is named, straightforwardly enough, *PrintMonitor Documents,* and it contains an icon for each of the documents waiting to be printed (see Figure 16-30). The icon marked through with an X is the one that's currently being printed, so it can't be thrown away. If you put any of the other icons into the Trash and empty it, the file will be removed from the print queue.

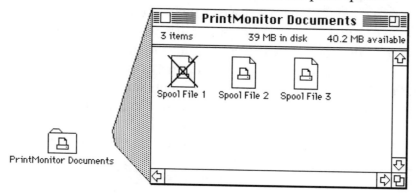

Figure 16-30. The PrintMonitor folder

PRINTMONITOR MESSAGES

During the course of normal printing, the computer may beep to alert you of a printing problem, placing a dialog on the screen to let you know what's wrong.

When printing is done in the background, all the warning dialogs go through PrintMonitor. If there's a message from PrintMonitor for you, the icon at the top of the Application menu will start flashing, alternating with the PrintMonitor icon. Selecting PrintMonitor from the menu opens its window and gives you the message that's waiting. Figure 16-31 shows the PrintMonitor window with a "no paper tray" message.

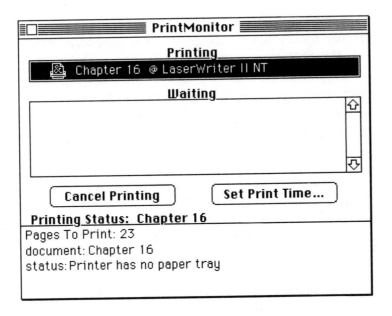

Figure 16-31.   A PrintMonitor status message

THE LASERWRITER FONT UTILITY

Basics

The LaserWriter Font Utility is a program that lets you check and change
several options for a LaserWriter. The program is placed in a folder
named Utilities when you install your system software.

LaserWriter Font Utility

*The Font Utility program is placed in the Utilities folder during system
installation.*

To run the LaserWriter Font Utility, double-click on it. You'll get a dialog (shown in Figure 16-32) that describes the basic functions of the utility. When you click the OK button, the dialog goes away and there are three menus available: File, Edit, and Utilities. There's nothing on the screen that belongs to the Font Utility, which can be a little disconcerting, but you can tell that you're in the program by its menus and, of course, by its icon on the Application menu.

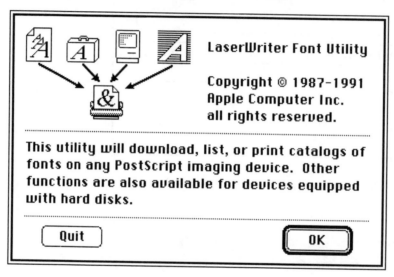

Figure 16-32. The LaserWriter Font Utility's opening screen

The Start Page

Each time you start your LaserWriter, it prints a test page, called the *start page,* that identifies which LaserWriter it is and how many pages it has printed so far in its lifetime.

Assuming you already know which LaserWriter you have, and you don't care enough about the page count to want to check it every time you turn the printer on, you can turn off this test page.

To control the test page, choose Start Page Options from the Utilities menu. In the dialog box that opens, you can turn the start page on or off by clicking in the appropriate button and then clicking OK (see Figure 16-33).

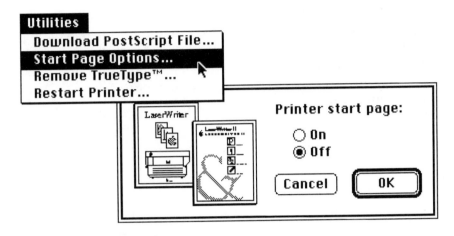

Figure 16-33. The Start Page Options dialog

Downloading Fonts

PostScript LaserWriters have 35 fonts built into them. When you want to use an outline font that's not built in, you simply use it in your document, assigning the font from the Font menu. When a document is being printed and the Mac discovers that the font it needs isn't in the printer, it looks for a printer font file that it can *download,* or send, to the printer.

You can use the LaserWriter Font Utility to "manually" download fonts, too. This is useful when you want to use a font that you don't normally keep on your hard drive (although its screen font will have to be installed in your system). You can manually download the font from a floppy disk directly to the printer's memory, where it will remain until you turn off the printer.

To download a printer font:

1. Choose Download Fonts from the File menu.
2. In the dialog that opens, shown in Figure 16-34, click the Add button.
3. In the Open dialog that appears (shown in Figure 16-35), you can find and select the fonts that you want to download. If you select a font and click the Add button (or just double-click on the font), the dialog doesn't go away; you can find and select additional fonts before closing the dialog with the Done button.

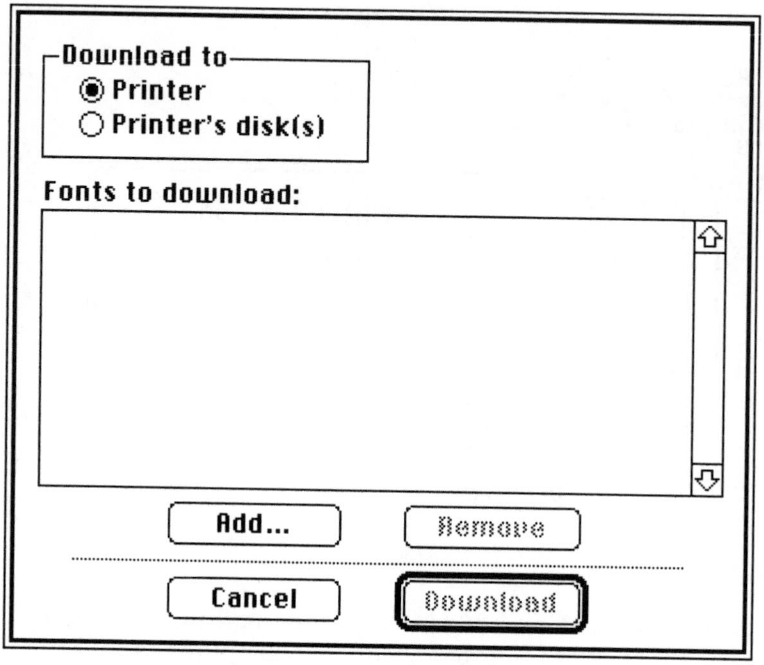

Figure 16-34. The Download Fonts dialog

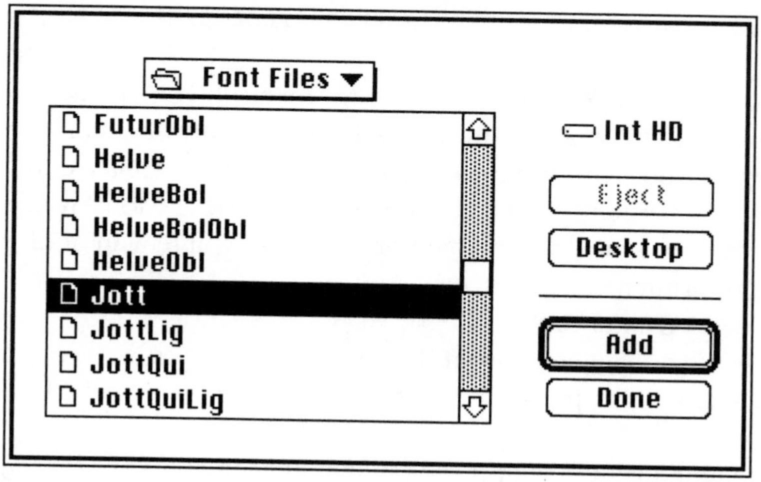

Figure 16-35. Selecting a downloadable font

4. Click the Done button. The Open dialog closes and you can see your list of fonts to be downloaded in the main dialog, as shown in Figure 16-36.

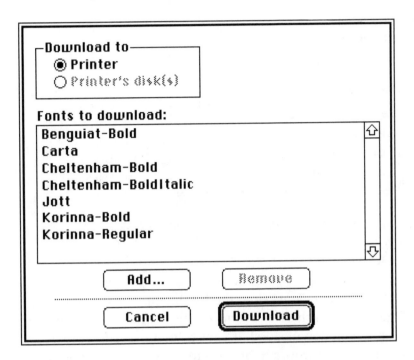

Figure 16-36. A list of fonts ready to be downloaded

5. With the Printer button at the top of the dialog box selected, click the Download button to send the font information to the printer. During the downloading (it takes about a half-minute per font), you'll get a progress report on the screen. When it's finished, you'll get a confirmation dialog (see Figure 16-37).

Before the downloading begins, you can select a font in the list and click the Remove button to delete it. You can cancel the Download dialog, or the downloading process itself, by clicking the Cancel button.

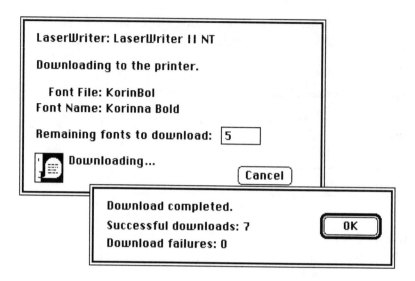

Figure 16-37.   The progress report and the final confirmation

CHECKING RESIDENT FONTS

You can see what fonts are available in the printer at any time by choosing Display Available Fonts from the File menu. The dialog that opens (see Figure 16-38) lists all the fonts in the printer: the built-in ones and any that have been downloaded. If your printer has a disk or special font card attached, the appropriate buttons in the window will be active so that you can check what fonts are installed in those places.

RESETTING THE PRINTER

When you turn off your printer, all the downloaded fonts are erased from memory. If you run out of room and can't download another font that you need, you can restart the printer without turning it off and back on again by choosing Restart Printer from the Utilities menu.

Because restarting the printer will erase all the downloaded fonts, you'll get an alert dialog (shown in Figure 16-39) before the printer is restarted, or *reinitialized.*

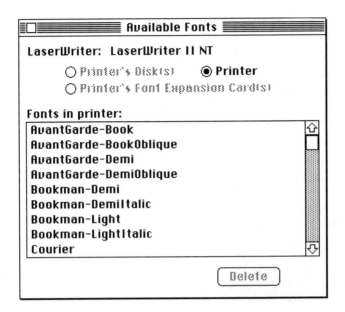

Figure 16-38. The Available Fonts listing

Figure 16-39. Using the Restart Printer command

Printing Catalogs and Samples

You can print a list of the fonts in your LaserWriter (resident and downloaded) by choosing Print Font Catalog from the File menu.

If you want a printed list of font *samples,* choose Print Font Samples from the File menu. You'll get a list of resident and downloaded fonts, and a sample sentence (the typist's standard *the quick brown fox...*) printed in each font.

```
┌─────────────────────────────────────┐
│ File                                 │
├─────────────────────────────────────┤
│ Download Fonts...              ⌘D    │
│ Display Available Fonts...     ⌘L    │
│ Initialize Printer's Disk...         │
│·····································  │
│ Page Setup...                        │
│ Print Font Catalog...          ⌘P    │
│ Print Font Samples...                │
│·····································  │
│ Quit                           ⌘Q    │
└─────────────────────────────────────┘
```

Downloading a PostScript File

A PostScript file contains all the PostScript commands needed to create a document on a PostScript printer. (The "Printing Commands" section earlier in this chapter described how to save a document as a PostScript file.)

When you want to send a PostScript file to the printer, you can't just open it in an application and print it, or you'll get a printout of the PostScript commands themselves (see Figure 16-20).

Instead, a PostScript file has to be *downloaded* to the printer in order for it to be printed correctly. Use the Download PostScript File from the Utilities menu to identify the file you want downloaded and printed.

Working with a Printer's Hard Drive

The LaserWriter NTX can have a hard drive attached to it to hold font files. The LaserWriter Font Utility provides several commands and controls for the printer's drive:

- Prepare the drive for this specialized use by using the Initialize Printer's Disk command from the File menu.

- To put fonts on the drive, use the Download Fonts command as just described, but select the printer's Drive button in the dialog before downloading.

- To check what printer fonts are on the disk, use the Display Available Fonts command as just described, but click the Printer's Disk button.

- Remove all the TrueType fonts from the printer's drive by using the Remove TrueType command in the Utilities menu.

SUMMARY

In this chapter you learned about the printing process: the technology of the printer itself, how Mac applications let you control printing, and how to make the most of a printer's capabilities. In the next chapter you'll learn about all the different kinds of software available for your Mac.

CHAPTER 17

Software

ABOUT THIS CHAPTER

CHOOSING AND USING SOFTWARE

Basics
System 7 Compatibility
How to Choose Software
Getting the Most Out of Your Software
Calling for Help
Quickies

STANDARD SOFTWARE

Basics
Word Processor
Database
Spreadsheet
Graphics
Page Layout
Communications
Quickies

OTHER SOFTWARE CATEGORIES

Basics
HyperCard
Outliner
Financial
Macro Programs
Quickies
Also . . .

SUMMARY

ABOUT THIS CHAPTER

You could have the best stereo equipment in the world, but it won't do you any good unless you have music to play on it. And, without software, you can't do anything with your computer.

This chapter discusses how to choose your software and how to make the most of the programs you buy. And, since it's difficult to choose software if you're not exactly sure what, for instance, a spreadsheet actually *does,* you'll also find descriptions of major (and even not-so-major) categories of software: what they are, what they do, and some of the special terms and concepts they use.

CHOOSING AND USING SOFTWARE

Basics

While choosing the right software package in a given category isn't always easy—and it's far from an exact science—there are some ways to increase your chances of finding the right product. And, once you have it, there are lots of ways to make sure you get the most out of it.

System 7 Compatibility

When Apple upgrades its operating system, some applications don't work correctly (or at all) under the upgrade. For the most part, it's the application's fault; when programs are written to Apple's guidelines, they should work under new system software.

But System 7 is more than just an update; it takes a new approach and includes entirely new features. As a result, even applications that were written "cleanly" and can run without problems still won't be able to take advantage of special features like publish and subscribe. There are several levels of System 7 compatibility, beginning with total incompatibility, which means that the program crashes when you try to open it or work with it. Then there's the level that means a program will run, but it's not "aware" of System 7; for instance, it will store its special files loose in the System Folder instead of neatly away in the Preferences folder. Complete compatibility means the program runs, knows how to "behave," and incorporates System 7's special features like publish and subscribe and help balloons.

As long as an application isn't crashing, you don't have to worry too much about the lack of neatness or special features; keep in touch with the manufacturer and get the program's update when you can.

How to Choose Software

At first glance, picking the right program seems a simple matter: Find one that has capabilities that meet your needs and a price tag that meets your budget. But even if you've managed to identify your needs, you'll probably discover that there are several programs that meet them, and the programs are all in the same price range. So you're back where you started, trying to figure out which software package to buy.

First, what should you look for in a piece of software? Here are some items to consider:

- Is it free from bugs that would keep it from running smoothly?

- Is it easy to learn? Does it have good, clear documentation?

- Is it easy to use? There's always a trade-off between ease-of-use and power, but that's no reason for a powerful program to make things even more difficult by bad interface implementation or poor design decisions.

- Is it powerful enough? It should have all the features you need, and then some, so you'll have room to grow.

- Is it compatible with the other software you use?

- Is the manufacturer a reputable company that's been around for a while and gives every indication that it will be around in the future? (But don't ignore a new company if it has a terrific product.)

- Does the publisher provide support—free or inexpensive upgrades, a telephone help line?

Those are helpful guidelines, but how do you find the answers—other than the hard way, which is buying the program and finding out that it *doesn't* meet all of those criteria. Here are a few ways to find out the details *before* you buy:

- Read product reviews in the major magazines (you'll find some listed under Special Resources in Appendix G).

- Talk to other people. Start at your Apple dealer or software store, but don't limit yourself to store personnel—strike up conversations with other customers. Find a user group and ask questions there.

- Ask a dealer for a hands-on demonstration.

- Check with the manufacturer to see if there's a demo version of the program available. (Some programs have demonstration versions that do everything but save or print a document.)

▪ Find a book about the product at a computer or book store. A major program may have several how-to books written about it, and you'll get more information about the product's features than can be squeezed into a 2500-word magazine review. If you're considering purchasing a $600 program, a $20 book is a wise investment.

▪ If you're in the vicinity of a Macintosh show—major ones are held in Boston and San Francisco every year (see Special Resources in Appendix G), and hundreds of smaller and special-interest shows are held around the country—stop in and watch some demos and ask questions.

Once you've decided on the package you want, where do you buy it? If your Apple dealer sells the package and can provide some support in the way of hand-holding while you're learning or troubleshooting later when you run into problems, it's worth buying retail. The best prices, however, are usually through reputable mail-order houses. (Again, check Special Resources in Appendix G.)

Getting the Most Out of Your Software

Once you have the program you need, it's time to learn how to use it. There are some definite strategies you can use to make sure you get the most out of your software. The most important rule is to avoid the trap of learning just enough to use a program on its basic level and never making the time or taking the effort to learn it more thoroughly.

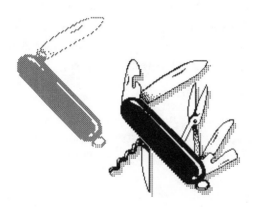

Take these steps with a new piece of software:

1. Register with the publisher. As a registered user, you may get any or all of the following benefits: notices of available upgrades to the product; free or inexpensive upgrades, or preferential prices for it; and a newsletter devoted to the product. Some publishers reserve their telephone support for registered users only.
2. Read through the tutorial (step-by-step) part of the manual and follow along on your computer.
3. Read through the manual. Even a well-written manual can be overwhelming if you don't yet fully understand the product, but you'll get a thorough grounding in the basics and a good overview of the program's capabilities. Even if you don't remember *how* to do something, you'll remember that the feature is available.
4. Use the program; dive in and do some real work with it.
5. After two or three months of using a program, go back and read the whole manual again—you'll understand all the references, and you'll be surprised at how much you learn the program can do beyond what you've been doing with it.

In between these steps, anywhere along the line and as long as you use the program, read through magazines, which provide many hints and tips for using the most popular programs. And (as usual) find a user group in your area and join it; you'll find others there who are using the same program and can share their expertise.

Calling for Help

Many manufacturers provide telephone technical support for their products, although the degree of expertise and helpfulness certainly varies from one company to the next. When you're stumped by a problem with your program and can't find a solution in the manual or from any other immediate source (like the suggested troubleshooting steps in Chapter 18), call the manufacturer. When you call, be ready with a list of information so the tech support person can better understand what the problem might be. You should know:

▪ Your serial number, if the program has one; some companies provide support only to users who have purchased a legitimate copy of the program (a reasonable enough restriction).

▪ What version of the program you're using. It's usually available in the About dialog from the Apple menu, or in the application icon's Get Info window. (Check for the decimal numbers: PerfectProgram 2.1 may have a different set of problems than PerfectProgram 2.0.)

▪ What version of the system software you're using. (Again, decimals are important; there will be differences between System 7.0 and System 7.01.)

▪ What extensions you have in your system, especially the non-Apple extensions like init programs that run automatically on startup.

▪ The specifics of the problem. "It keeps crashing" or "I can't print this document" aren't very descriptive or helpful. But "The program crashes every time I have a lot of material on the Clipboard and then try to create a new document" or "I can't print this document, but all the other documents I created can be printed with no problem and the only difference seems to be the extra fonts" can help the technician pinpoint the problem more easily.

Quickies

▪ A total reworking of a product generally results in its getting a new name: The database FileMaker, for instance, became FileMaker Plus, FileMaker II, and, in its current incarnation, FileMaker Pro. But you also can tell the extent of an upgrade by its version number. A new whole number is as major an upgrade as a new name: Excel 1.0, Excel 2.0, and Excel 3.0, for instance. A new *decimal* number tacked onto a version number is more minor: HyperCard 2.1 or PageMaker 3.01, for instance.

Whether the number is a tenth or a hundredth is usually indicative of how many changes were made—and how much you'll pay for the upgrade. Some minor upgrades are to fix obscure (and sometimes not-so-obscure) bugs; some update the program so that it stays compatible with another upgraded program or with new system software.

- *Copy protection* is any scheme used by a software manufacturer to prevent *piracy*—the unauthorized copying and distributing of its software. Due to consumer complaints, restrictive copy protection schemes—like having to insert a master "key" disk every time you launch a program from a hard drive—are seldom used.

STANDARD SOFTWARE

Basics

There are six major categories of software and it's safe to say that every user works extensively in at least one category; most users have two, or even three, categories covered.

Word Processor

A word processor is far more than an electronic typewriter. Chapter 6 showed the ease with which you can enter and edit text in any program and apply text and paragraph formats, but a word processor can also offer a wealth of specialized features. (If all you need is something to type memos and other correspondence, don't get carried away by a features list.)

Search commands let you find an occurrence of a specific string of text anywhere in the document. *Global changes* let you replace every occurrence of one word ("him") with another ("her"). You can add *headers* and *footers* at the top and bottom of every page; they can include a page number, the current date, and the document name, as well as any other text and sometimes even a graphic.

Spelling checkers are included in many word processors to catch not only typos ("hte") but also true misspellings ("mispellings"). Most word processors let you add footnotes to a document, automatically adjusting their numbers as you go along; many also let you mark words for automatic indexing or compiling a table of contents. Most programs include character-, word-, and paragraph-counting features, and some will even number lines or paragraphs.

Style sheets let you assign a combination of character and paragraph formatting with a single command—and change the look of every paragraph that's been assigned a style by merely changing the style's definition.

You can even do basic page layout in many word processors, arranging text in multiple columns and incorporating graphics into specific spots on a page.

Database

A database program is basically an electronic index-card filing system. Each "index card" is a *record;* records hold information in *fields* like "name" and "phone number"; the "box" that holds the cards is the database *file*.

The main advantage of an electronic filing system over its paper counterpart is the ease with which you can manipulate information. In a library-card catalog system, for instance, you need three cards for each book so that you can sort them by author, subject, and title. In a database file, there's only one record for each book because it takes only seconds for them to be sorted into a different order.

The ability to quickly select a group of records that match specific criteria is another important advantage of electronic filing systems: You can ask for records that show an outstanding amount of money owed—but only if it's over $300 and more than 60 days overdue.

Most databases use *calculated fields* to perform mathematical operations on the information in other fields in the record. You can generate *reports,* lists of information from the records in the file; there are mathematical functions available on the report level, too, so that you can do calculations *across* a group of records as well as within a record.

A *relational database* links its files so they can exchange information automatically. You could, for instance, create an invoice for a customer and the items listed in it would be automatically deleted from a separate file that handles your inventory. A database that doesn't have relational ability is a *flat-file* database.

Databases let you construct different *views* of your information; a record may include dozens of items of information, but you can create a view that includes only a person's name and address so that you can print mailing labels.

Mac databases offer many kinds of graphics abilities, both for creating professional-looking forms and to make the data-entry process and record manipulation easier. Many also let you automate procedures by creating *scripts,* lists of commands that are executed when you make a menu selection or click on an icon or button on the screen. Figure 17-1, for instance, shows a screen from a database designed in Claris's FileMaker Pro; it provides checkboxes and popup menus for data entry and icons that act as buttons for easy execution of commands.

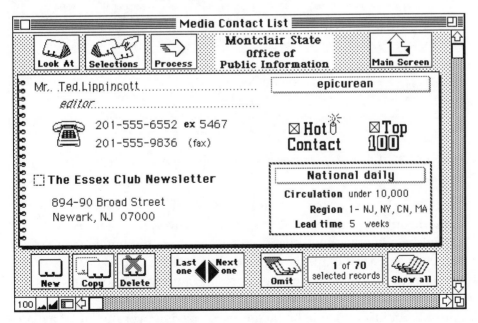

Figure 17-1. A FileMaker Pro database screen

Spreadsheet

The power of a spreadsheet lies in its ability to speedily calculate formulas applied to rows and columns of numbers, and recalculate them whenever a change is made to a number in any *cell*. A typical spreadsheet setup is shown in Figure 17-2. Each column represents a different category in a budget; the final column gives monthly totals, while the bottom three rows give the total, average, and maximum monthly amounts for each category over the course of a year.

	A	B	C	D	E	F	G	H	I
		Rent	Heat	Elec	Phone	Income1	Income2		Total
1									
2	Jan	385.00	75.00	65.00	75.00	1500.00	2200.00		3700.00
3	Feb	385.00	75.00	75.00	84.00	1500.00	2200.00		3700.00
4	Mar	385.00	75.00	57.00	65.00	1500.00	2200.00		3700.00
5	Apr	385.00	0.00	65.00	32.00	1500.00	2200.00		3700.00
6	May	385.00	0.00	70.00	84.00	1500.00	2200.00		3700.00
7	Jun	385.00	0.00	65.00	95.00	1500.00	2200.00		3700.00
8	Jul	385.00	0.00	72.00	87.00	1500.00	2200.00		3700.00
9	Aug	425.00	0.00	56.00	54.00	1500.00	2200.00		3700.00
10	Sept	425.00	50.00	87.00	54.00	1500.00	2700.00		4200.00
11	Oct	425.00	75.00	65.00	54.00	1500.00	2700.00		4200.00
12	Nov	425.00	125.00	89.00	84.00	1500.00	2700.00		4200.00
13	Dec	425.00	130.00	65.00	54.00	1500.00	2700.00		4200.00
14									
15	Total	4820.00	605.00	831.00	822.00	18000.00	28400.00		46400.00
16	Avg	771.25	94.58	133.08	130.75	2875.00	4550.00		7425.00
17	Max	425.00	130.00	89.00	95.00	1500.00	2700.00		4200.00
18									

Figure 17-2.   A typical spreadsheet arrangement of rows and columns of numbers

But you're not locked into situations where the information is numeric only and needs to be calculated in rows and columns. A spreadsheet handles any situation where interrelated numbers are used and changed. Any computer user can find uses for a spreadsheet—from keeping track of bowling league scores to figuring out how much of a car payment, or mortgage, can be squeezed out of a budget. (And figuring out just how much you are *really* paying over the life of a loan or getting back on an investment.)

Most spreadsheets can also take your numbers and turn them into graphs and charts. A simple pie chart made from the numbers in Figure 17-2 is shown in Figure 17-3; some spreadsheets offer built-in graphics tools to make the charts really eye-catching. And the high-end (that means full of features and with a high price tag) spreadsheets even incorporate database features so that you can manipulate rows, columns, or blocks of information as if they were records in a database.

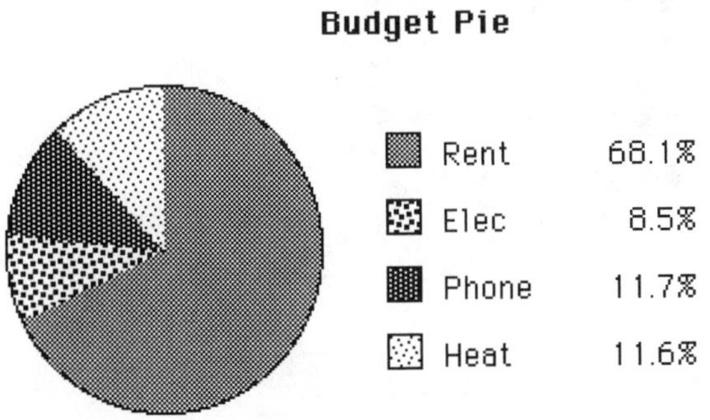

Budget Pie

▨	Rent	68.1%
▨	Elec	8.5%
▨	Phone	11.7%
▨	Heat	11.6%

Figure 17-3. A pie chart created from spreadsheet data

Graphics

Chapter 6 explained the basics of Mac graphics programs—the difference between paint and draw graphics and what an EPS graphics program can do, for example. But those explanations barely hinted at the flexibility and power available in some programs, or at the capability of working in color. Figure 17-4 shows a screen from Silicon Beach's SuperPaint 3.0, a combination color paint-draw program; you can see the wealth of tools available—and they're not all showing.

Mac graphics capabilities go far beyond the three basics. *CAD* programs (*computer-aided design*) replace the draftsman's pencil and triangle with tools that are not only far more accurate but are also easier to use and capable of rendering three-dimensional objects effortlessly. *3-D modeling* programs let you define an object and then view and

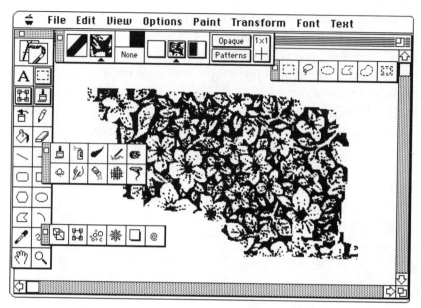

Figure 17-4. SuperPaint 3.0, a color paint-draw program

manipulate it as a wire frame or a solid, even rotating it to view it from any angle. *Animation* programs let you design a serious presentation, a light-hearted cartoon, or anything in between; some animations can even be *interactive,* responding to a mouse click on a specific item.

Page Layout

Page layout programs are the cornerstone of the *desktop publishing (DTP)* boom. They let you organize and arrange text and graphics on a page with a freedom not usually supplied by a word processor.

Some page layout programs provide standard word processor functions as well as some more advanced ones like spelling checkers and style sheets. But page layout programs go far beyond word processors—not only in flexibility, but also in accuracy. It's also easier to use a page layout program for many projects, because in addition to a wealth of rulers, grids, and guidelines, you can usually set up *master pages* whose elements will appear on every page of the document.

Although page layout programs offer built-in word processing and even certain graphics capabilities, they're generally used in conjunction with a word processor program and one or more graphics applications: You create the text and graphics in their own applications and then import them to the layout.

Communications

A directly wired network is not the only way your Mac can communicate with other computers in the world. With a *modem* to connect the Mac to a telephone, and communications software to control the modem, your Mac can talk to any other similarly equipped computer. Once you're connected to another computer, you can exchange information by straightforward typing or by sending or receiving files.

Most electronic communications (or *telecommunications*), however, are not one Mac talking to another—the equivalent of a "person-to-person" call. There are *online services* that provide a central computer that you can call, as do thousands of other customers, to *upload* (send) files or *download* (receive) them or to leave messages for other users. The messages you send and receive can be posted for the general membership to read and reply to, or you can direct your comments privately to a specific person. This messaging system is referred to as *electronic mail* or *Email*. The largest and most reputable of the online services are CompuServe, and America Online; you'll find their addresses in Appendix G if you want to contact them.

While the commercial online services are for-profit businesses that charge you for the time you're connected to them, there are also *bulletin board systems (BBS)* that are usually free (except, of course, for your phone bill). Many user groups have bulletin boards, and most offer message centers and files for downloading.

The kind of network used by many offices falls into another category of communications. Email programs on a network let you send messages and files to other users on the network. If the "addressee" is currently *logged on,* he or she will be notified of incoming mail by a beep or a dialog box on the screen; if the addressee is not there, he or she will be notified of a waiting message the next time the computer is turned on. Figure 17-5 shows a message screen from CE Software's QuickMail.

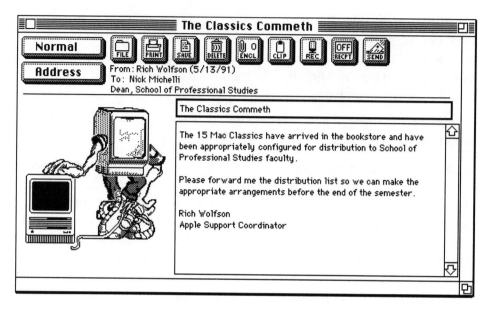

Figure 17-5.   A QuickMail Email message

To save time (and, in many cases, money) in sending files in any communications session, you can shrink the size of the file with a *file compression* utility program. (The compressed file can't be used until it's been decompressed, or *expanded.)*

Quickies

▪ *Integrated software* is a single application that provides two or more programs from different categories in the same package. Because the Mac makes short work of exchanging information between applications, integrating independent programs is easy; but the price and convenience of integrated packages make them worth considering.

OTHER SOFTWARE CATEGORIES

Basics

There are hundreds of other types of programs for the Mac. Some are *vertical market* programs that are of interest to only a small number of users. But this section describes a few more categories that are useful to the general user population.

HyperCard

What is HyperCard? is a question that's never quite been answered. Apple refers to it as system software; you get it with your computer, though you never need to use it. HyperCard's creator refers to it as a *software construction set,* and, indeed, you can use it to create your own "programs."

HyperCard uses a metaphor that refers to each screen as a "card" and each file of information as a "stack." You can put graphics, fields of texts, and even buttons on any card. Fields, buttons, and even the cards themselves can have *scripts* embedded in them—a series of instructions in a programming language called *HyperTalk.*

On its basic level, HyperCard is quite easy to work with; you can create your own simple stacks with very little effort, and you can even make buttons that will jump the user from one card or stack to another. But on any other level, be prepared to put in a lot of time and effort— HyperCard at its highest levels is a programming environment and a programming language (despite Apple's reluctance to label the program as such), and creating anything beyond simple stacks requires programming knowledge and skill.

Still, many companies release their products with stacks that explain how to use them, and the HyperCard application that came with your system software lets you run those stacks.

Outliner

An *outliner* is somewhat like a specialized word processor. You enter lines of text, variously referred to as *topics* or *headlines,* and you enter subtopics or subheadlines beneath them, creating as many levels as you need to organize your information. Any topic can have paragraphs of text and/or graphics "attached" to it.

Where an outliner departs from a word processor is in the ways you can view and reorganize topics in the outline. You can look at the entire outline branched out with all its levels displayed, or you can collapse it to look only at the major topic; expanding and collapsing can also be done separately on any section. (This is the same approach provided by list views in Desktop windows, where you can expand and collapse the contents of any or all of the folders in the list.) Reorganizing the topics isn't a matter of cutting and pasting, as it would be in a word processor; instead, you drag a topic into its new position and all its subtopics obediently move with it.

Financial

Financial programs include all sorts of applications that help you handle your finances. Simple but elegant checkbook programs can keep your records and even print your checks. (At first glance, entering all that information on the computer may seem a waste of time, but the first time you have the program compile lists for you at tax time—child-care expenses, home-office expenses, medical payments—you'll see what a timesaver it can be.)

There are accounting packages available, too, for small to mid-size businesses. They can track anything you can enter, and they take care of everything from a checkbook to payroll deductions.

You can even find software that can help you manage your stock portfolio.

Macro Programs

A *macro* is a series of commands executed by a single key combination or menu selection. A *macro program* is a utility that lets you create macros to play back at any time you need them.

A macro can be as simple as a string of menu commands, such as Save, Print, and Quit, that you can execute in one fell swoop. Or, if you find yourself repeating certain procedures over and over, a macro can do it for you. Consider, for instance, saving something in the Scrapbook: First you make a selection, then you copy it to the Clipboard, select the Scrapbook from the Apple menu, choose Paste, and then close the Scrapbook. After you do the initial selection, a macro could take over— and it could do it all in less time than it takes you to do it.

Most macro programs give you several ways to define the macros themselves. You usually start by activating the program and then do whatever it is that you want turned into a macro; the program watches you work and records your actions, and then plays them back when you use the key combination you've assigned to the procedure.

Quickies

- A *utility* program is a slippery thing to define; generally, it's a small program that doesn't create any documents but enhances your system or other applications in some way, or performs some small or useful job on a systemwide basis. *Screen capture* programs are utilities that let you take pictures of parts of your screen. File-compression and macro programs are generally regarded as utilities, as are backup and recovery programs (discussed in Chapter 18).

- The terms *public domain* and *shareware* are often confused in general usage and perception. Public domain software is free; it's created by a programmer who wants to share a nifty utility with the Mac world, and it's distributed through user groups and electronic services. *Shareware* is distributed through the same channels, but it's not free; its users are on the honor system. The author distributes the software and asks that after you try it, if you like it enough to keep using it, send a payment.

Also...

Project management software lets you manage large projects by breaking them down into tasks that take a certain amount of time and are either dependent on the completion of another task or can be done concurrently. You can see at a glance how long the project will take and, should any task take longer than anticipated, you can enter its new time factor and see immediately what effect it will have on the project completion date.

Forms generators let you design forms in a more specialized environment than a basic drawing program would afford. You can, for instance, stipulate that you need 20 lines of fill-in space preceded by checkboxes, and four lines in a grayed box "for office use only," or dotted lines for "cut along the dotted line." Everything is automatically spaced and can be easily moved in blocks and edited. Although forms generators look somewhat like databases, they're not meant for information entry—at least not on the computer. The forms made by these programs are meant to be printed out and reproduced by the hundreds or thousands, and filled out by hand.

Presentation software, at its simplest, lets you turn an outline of text into a bullet or tree chart. But most presentation software assumes that you're going to be giving a presentation with a slide projector at a business or educational meeting, so it gives you a graphic environment to work in. You create a frame for the slide that can set a common theme, and then add the contents (maybe those bullet charts). The program outputs one or several files that can be taken to a service bureau so slides can be made from them. In addition to the slides themselves, a good presentation program will print out miniatures of the slides along with comments that don't appear in the presentation itself; these can be used as speaker's notes and/or audience handouts.

There are also hundreds of programs that fall into the educational category from preschool reading and math preparation to university-level physics. While many of those programs are disguised as games, there are also plenty of *real* games available, running the gamut from arcade-style shoot-'em-ups to fantasy role-playing text adventures to erudite strategy games.

SUMMARY

Now that you have some idea of which software packages provide what capabilities, and some guidelines as to how to choose the right one, it's time to start, or add to, your software library. In no time at all, you'll need the information in the next chapter: what to do when you run into problems with your software or hardware.

Problems and Prevevntions

ABOUT THIS CHAPTER

This chapter covers some of the ways you can avoid problems with your Mac. And, since avoiding *every* problem is impossible, it also describes how to deal with the most common problems, describing trouble-shooting and fix-it strategies.

PREVENTIVE MEASURES

Basics

The best way to deal with a problem is to keep it from occurring. There are many things you can do to avoid common computing problems, from general system maintenance to protecting yourself from "viruses" and having backup and recovery software handy.

Hardware Maintenance

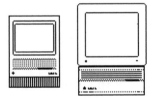

Avoiding hardware problems consists mostly of *not* doing certain things, such as:

- Don't connect or disconnect any equipment or devices while the computer is on. This includes major peripherals like hard drives as well as ADB devices like the mouse and keyboard. (This restriction doesn't apply to cables plugged into the modem or printer ports; you won't cause any hardware damage adjusting those cables while the computer's on, although you may interrupt data transmission.)

- Don't block any cooling vents.

- Don't leave the computer equipment on, or even plugged in, during an electrical storm. Unplug a modem not only from the power supply, but also from the telephone line.

- Don't put disks near magnetic fields. This includes not only magnets (like the ones in many paper clip holders), but also telephones, halogen lamps, and even vibrating phone beepers.

- Don't move a hard drive while it's on.

- DON'T LEAVE ONE DEVICE TURNED OFF IN A CHAIN OF SCSI DEVICES. One possible side effect of this seemingly minor mistake would be to make all the information on another device in the chain (such as your internal hard drive, for instance) totally unreadable.

- Don't assign the same identification number to two SCSI devices in a chain.

- Don't forget to properly terminate SCSI devices.

- Don't roll the mouse on a dirty surface—the dirt will wind up inside the mouse. Using a "mouse pad" is the best approach.

Keeping your equipment clean and dust-free can help prevent problems. (The best method for cleaning the mouse was described in Chapter 12.) When you're cleaning:

- Don't use a Dustbuster-type vacuum to clean out the inside of a modular Mac. The static charge that might result can ruin the circuit boards inside.

- Don't use an abrasive cleaner on the screen; the special anti-glare coating is plastic and will be ruined.

- Don't spray a cleaner directly on the keyboard; it can drip down past the keys into the casing. Spray the cleaner on a cloth instead.

The *do's* of hardware maintenance are pretty specific to the equipment. Printers, especially, need regular care and maintenance; you'll find the proper procedures described in the manual that came with the printer.

System Software Maintenance

There are two important *don'ts* when it comes to system software:

▪ Don't just shut off the computer: Use the Shut Down command from the Finder's Special menu. This gives the Mac a chance to make sure that everything is on the disk that should be there, instead of, perhaps, still stored in RAM. In addition, using Shut Down gives the Mac a chance to double-check that there aren't any open, unsaved documents around.

```
┌─────────────────────────┐
│ Special                 │
│  Clean Up Window        │
│  Empty Trash...         │
│ ......................... │
│  Eject Disk        ⌘E   │
│  Erase Disk...          │
│ ......................... │
│  Restart                │
│  Shut Down        ▶     │
└─────────────────────────┘
```

▪ Don't keep multiple System Folders on your hard drive. They tend to sneak up on you when you install new software (as explained in Chapter 7) and can cause system crashes.

There are several things you should do on a regular basis to keep your system working at top speed.

First, plan to rebuild the Desktop file on your startup drive on a monthly basis. (This was discussed in Chapter 14.) When you streamline the file by rebuilding it, it takes less time for the Mac to build your Desktop when you start the machine.

The second regular maintenance procedure is *defragmenting* the hard drive every two or three months. (This was also discussed in Chapter 14.) When you defragment the files on your drive, they'll be written to contiguous sectors on the disk; and it will take less time to retrieve them than when they're stored in bits and pieces. Defragmenting software (also referred to as *disk optimizing* software) is available commercially.

You should also use disk diagnostic software regularly to check your drive for problems that are in only their early stages. Disk First Aid, supplied with your system software, can check for problems (and fix some of them) if you've formatted the hard drive with the HD Setup utility.

Disk First Aid

SYSTEM UPDATES

Keep informed (through reading and/or a user group) about system software updates. Most minor updates (7.0 to 7.0.1, for instance) are to iron out small bugs in the current release. But since the *new* release may also have undiscovered bugs, the best strategy is to wait a month or so after the release (letting thousands of other people test it) and then get the update from your Apple dealer or a user group.

Viruses

A *virus* is a computer program that copies itself from file to file and disk to disk without your even knowing that it exists. Some viruses are designed to be destructive, corrupting files on your hard disk or slowing down network operations. But even the ones meant to be benign may unwittingly cause damage to your files or at least interrupt your work. (A "benign" virus might be designed to do something as simple as put a message on your screen on a certain date.)

Viruses hide themselves in other files. The virus spreads when you exchange disks with other users, or when you exchange files while telecommunicating or over a network; once an infected file is on a system, it can infect other files.

There are several anti-virus programs available both commercially and through user groups and electronic services. These programs are designed to read through the files on a disk and check them for viruses; some even automatically scan a floppy disk every time one is inserted into a drive.

It's not easy to tell when you have a virus, since they can cause all sorts of symptoms. Plan to run virus-checking software at regular intervals—weekly if you're on a network or if you exchange disks often, and monthly if your computer system is more isolated.

Insurance

There are several relatively easy things you can do to ensure that, even if you run into a problem, it won't be disastrous.

SAVE EARLY AND OFTEN

If you're working on a document and the program crashes or the power goes out, any work that you haven't saved to the disk is lost. Save a new document early in its creation, and very often thereafter—every 10 minutes or so; that way, you'll never lose more than 10 minutes' worth of work. There are utility programs available that will automatically save your work at preset intervals.

BACKUPS

No matter how careful you are, something can go wrong. If your hardware breaks down, it may need an expensive repair job, but it can be fixed or replaced. If you lose a hard drive's worth of files, however, there may be nothing you can do to get them back.

The most important procedure in computing is making *backups* of your files. You can make an extra copy of an important file right on the same hard drive, in case something happens to the file itself. But you should also plan for the fact that the entire drive might fail and all its files could be unrecoverable. Back up every important file onto a floppy disk; in fact, making two backup copies is often recommended for very important data.

Making backups is often ignored because it's a tedious and time-consuming procedure; invest in some good backup utility software that will make the task less of a chore.

REAL INSURANCE

There are insurance policies available (including AppleCare from your Apple dealer) that will insure your hardware against damage and failures. Few, if any, will also cover the cost of data recovery from a hard drive, so don't let hardware insurance lull you into a false sense of security about your data.

Recovery Tools

A *file recovery program* helps you recover files from a damaged disk. (In most cases, "damaged disk" means that the file directory, not the disk itself, has been damaged. File recovery utilities keep track of all your disk operations and make a second directory someplace on the disk. If the main directory is damaged (and that's what happens in a majority of "unreadable disk" problems), the recovery software, running from a floppy, can get at the second directory; with that information, it can find and retrieve files from the disk. You'll need another hard disk, or *lots* of floppies, for the recovered files. Some recovery software can also repair the damaged directory; if not, you can reinitialize the disk, giving it a new directory.

On a smaller scale, there are utility programs that let you recover a file that you've erased from a disk. The program keeps a log of where the file was stored; if, when you want to recover the file, the sectors it was stored in haven't yet been reused, the "undelete" program will piece it back together.

Another item to prepare ahead of time so you have it if you need it is a floppy startup disk. If your startup hard drive stops working, you can't start up the computer. Use the Installer program to create a *minimal system* on a floppy disk and keep it handy in case you can't get the hard drive to work.

Quickies

▪ If you're in an office environment where other people have access to your computer, you may want to protect your files—all of them, or some of them—from unauthorized use. Security software can protect your entire drive or folders or individual files by making them impossible to open without the correct password.

▪ You can keep a file from being erased accidentally by locking it through the Get Info window, as described in Chapter 4. You can lock an entire floppy disk to keep anything on it from being erased or changed; just slide the locking tab so you can see through the hole in the disk.

DEALING WITH PROBLEMS

Basics

Problems with your Mac can run from a piece of hardware breaking to a single file refusing to print to the entire system *crashing* or *freezing*.

A *crash*, or *bomb*, is the general term for when the system software misbehaves to the point of being unable to continue. You usually get an apologetic dialog (like the one shown in Figure 18-1) along with a picture of a bomb and sometimes an identification number for the problem. (You can't do much about the problem even if you know what the numbers mean, but make a note of the ID number if you're calling a tech support person for a solution.)

A *freeze*, or *hang*, is when the computer just stops working, refusing to acknowledge the keyboard or the mouse—and you don't even get a dialog.

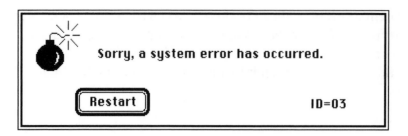

Figure 18-1.   A system error message

Probable Cause

Sometimes it's difficult to pinpoint a problem, since there are so many things involved with the procedure that's not working. If a document won't print, for instance, it might be a hardware-based problem (the printer or its cables) or a software-based one (the document, the application, the printer driver, or other system software).

Hardware problems are usually easier to identify than software problems, but you're less likely to be able to fix them by yourself.

When you run into a problem, the first thing to do is ask yourself: What changes did I recently make to my system? If you just added a new extension program, or changed printer drivers, or updated other system software, the new item is likely to be the culprit.

If you haven't made any system changes, try to isolate the problem. Consider all the components of the operation and change one at a time to see if you can find the root of the problem. If a document isn't printing, for instance, can you print other documents from the same application? Can you still print from other applications? Is the printer printing its test page?

Extension Clashes

Some system extensions are discrete programs that run only when they're needed—PrintMonitor, for instance, or any of the printer drivers. Others, however, run automatically at startup and sit around in RAM waiting to be used. These programs-in-waiting are called *inits,* which stands for *initialization resource*.

Apple's system software includes few inits, but there are many useful ones available from other sources. Macro programs and screen-capture programs run as inits; so do many interactive spelling checkers and utilities that let you quickly navigate through Open and Save dialog boxes; another popular init is one that automatically replaces straight quotes with the curly typesetter's quotes. It's very easy to collect a wide variety of inits in a very short time.

When you start your Mac, it checks the Extensions folder for any inits while it displays the opening Welcome to Macintosh dialog. The inits are loaded into memory, in alphabetical order; you'll usually see a series of icons representing the inits marching across the bottom of your screen after the Welcome dialog goes away and before the Desktop appears.

When you start having problems that you can't pinpoint, init programs are often to blame. Sometimes a single init can cause the problem; sometimes two inits work perfectly individually, but when you're using them both, they can cause problems.

Some extensions don't work well together.

To diagnose an init problem, run your system without any inits at all: Remove all of them from the Extensions folder and restart the computer. (Just removing them from the folder isn't sufficient—they're still in memory.) If everything runs as it should, you can be certain the original problem was caused by one or more inits. But which ones?

You can return the inits to the Extensions folder one at a time, restarting the computer after each addition to see when the problem recurs. Or, if you have an idea which program is causing the problem, put all the inits back except the suspect and see what happens. (It's usually safe to assume that the most recent addition is the one causing the problem.) If you find the problem, you should still check if it's causing the trouble all by itself or because it's clashing with another init; to do that, put *only* the problem file back in the Extensions folder and restart the computer. If everything works fine, you can start adding extensions to the folder (restarting the computer after each addition) to see which combination is causing the problem.

It may not be necessary to give up the functionality of an extension that's causing system crashes. First, check with the publisher to see if there's an update of the program that doesn't cause problems. And since the order in which inits are loaded is sometimes what causes clashes, you can change the loading order by changing the init's name. Force it to load first, or last, by adding a letter or other character to the beginning of its name. (Appendix D lists the alphabetization sequence for files.)

The Standard Procedures

There are four basic procedures used as "fixes" for many different software problems. Each was covered in earlier chapters under its topic area, but here's a roundup:

▪ *Resetting the computer:* Many software problems are the result of a program somehow misusing a portion of RAM so that the Mac, or another program, can't find it or do what it's supposed to do. When that happens, simply resetting the computer—either by switching it off and back on again, or by using the Reset button—cures the problem. But despite the fact that this is a sure cure in many cases, it should be your last resort. Resetting the Mac means everything that was in RAM is lost;

that includes portions of, or even entire, documents that haven't been saved, as well as any general information that hasn't been written to the disk yet. (The Reset button was covered in Chapter 12.)

- *Rebuilding the Desktop file:* To rebuild the Desktop file on a floppy disk, hold down the Command and Option keys while when you insert the disk. To rebuild the Desktop file on a hard drive, hold down Command and Option when you start the computer. (The Desktop file was discussed in Chapter 14.)

- *Zapping the PRAM:* To zap the PRAM, hold down the Command, Option, P, and R keys when you start the system. You'll know the PRAM's been reset if the computer starts and then restarts itself. (Chapter 13 discusses PRAM.)

- *Reinstalling the system software:* You reinstall the system software the same way you installed it originally—by using Apple's Installer program. But if you're reinstalling because you've been having problems, it's best to actually throw out the system files you already have on your drive; the installer *updates* existing files, and if one of the files is corrupted and is therefore causing a problem, simply updating it may not fix the file itself. To delete system files from a hard drive used as a startup, start the system with a floppy startup and erase the system files from the drive. Note, however, that throwing away the System file also throws away all the fonts and sounds you have installed on it. (Chapter 9 covered system software installation.)

Installer

General Hardware Problems

If the problem seems to be hardware-based, the first thing to check is that everything's plugged in—not just the power cord, but all the cables and cords as well. The best way to make sure that all the connections are firm is to unplug them and then plug them in again; make sure you do this while the computer is turned *off.*

- Check that the power cord is plugged into both the wall and the hardware.

- Check that cables are connected securely at both ends. A loose cable may work intermittently or not at all, since all its pins may not be aligned with the holes where they belong.

- Make sure that a cable is in good condition—check if any pins in the connector are bent. The wires within the cord may also be broken, but you won't be able to check that; however, using a borrowed or new cable will help diagnose a cable problem.

- See if the cables are connected to the correct port. Since most ports are different sizes and shapes on the Mac, it's only the printer and modem cables that are likely to be wrong.

Use the correct port.

If you have more than one SCSI device, make sure that each has a different ID number, that all of them are turned on, and that the chain is properly terminated.

If you're having trouble with the monitor and all its cables seem fine, check that the video card is firmly seated in its slot inside the case.

THE SAD MAC

If you start your Macintosh and get a black screen with an icon of a frowning Mac on it—the dreaded *sad Mac*—it's usually indicative of a serious hardware problem.

The sad Mac icon

If you can start up the Mac with an emergency floppy startup, then the sad Mac indicates a problem with the system files on the hard drive, and reinstalling the system software should take care of the problem.

But if you continue to get a sad Mac on startup, make a note of any code numbers on the screen and call your Apple dealer.

IF THE MOUSE STOPS WORKING...
Sometimes the mouse stops working even though keyboard input is still accepted. If that happens, try keyboard commands for saving any open documents—most applications use Command-S for Save. Then try Command-Q for quitting the application. If you're running multiple applications, the last one you used will then be activated and you can save any work in it and then quit that one also.

Sometimes the mouse stops working.

When you're at the Desktop, you can't get out of it or use the Shut Down command because there aren't any keyboard equivalents for those operations. At that point, you'll have to restart the computer with the Reset button.

A mouse freeze can be the result of a software error or a hardware problem. Once the machine is shut off, disconnect the mouse and reconnect it, then start up again.

General System Crashes

When you get a *Sorry, a system error has occurred* dialog box, all is not necessarily lost (although it usually is). Before you hit the Restart button in the dialog or the Reset button on the computer, try this:

Press the *Interrupt button* on the programmer's switch. (Chapter 12 discussed the switch and its buttons.) A dialog like the one shown in Figure 18-2 appears, with nothing in it except a > symbol. Type *G FINDER* (with a space after the *G)* and press Return. Sometimes this will return you to the Desktop; the application you were working in usually quits, but you'll have a chance to save the work you were doing in any other application. Then, since the contents of RAM are probably unstable, quit all the applications and restart the computer with Restart from the Special menu.

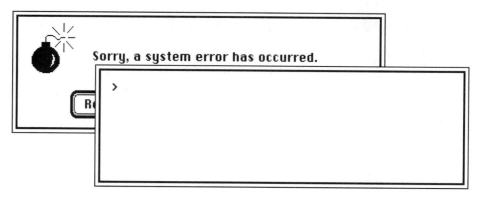

Figure 18-2.   Pressing the Interrupt button gives you a blank dialog.

When you seem to be having a lot of unexplained system crashes—things that you can't trace to a specific operation or application—there are two things to check:

- Check your system extensions and eliminate them as a source of trouble, as described under "Extension Clashes."

- Use the Find command on the Desktop to search your drive for multiple System Folders; if you find extras, erase them.

If neither of these situations caused the problem, it's time to generally clean up your act:

- Zap the PRAM.

- Reinstall the system software, first erasing the current system files from the hard drive so that any corrupted files won't be simply updated.

- Reinstall any applications in which the problems were occurring.

- Rebuild the Desktop file.

Disk Problems

Several problems you may run into with floppies or hard drives are not necessarily disastrous. (And major disasters can be mitigated by having backups of all your important files.)

MAKING MINOR REPAIRS

Sometimes when you insert a disk, you'll get a dialog that says *This disk needs minor repairs....* This usually means the Desktop file is damaged in some way; just click OK and the Mac will rebuild the Desktop file on the disk.

UNREADABLE DISKS

If you insert a floppy and get the message *This disk is unreadable; do you want to initialize it?*, and you know there's information on it, don't panic—and don't click Initialize unless you want the disk erased. Try any or all of these solutions:

- Try the disk in another drive in another computer, if one is available.

- Eject the disk and reinsert it. Sometimes a disk is simply misaligned. Also check that the metal shutter moves freely.

- If the disk has been recently exposed to extreme temperatures, let it return to room temperature and try again.

- Is it a high-density floppy that was formatted as 800K? If so, and you need the information on it, cover the extra hole in the disk case with a piece of masking tape to trick the SuperDrive into reading it as an 800K disk.

- Try rebuilding the Desktop file on the disk by holding down Command and Option as you insert it.

- Run a disk recovery program and insert the disk. Apple's Disk First Aid utility comes with your system software, but there are commercially available disk recovery tools, too.

WHEN A HARD DRIVE WON'T MOUNT

There are several reasons why a hard drive might not show up on the Desktop when it's connected to the computer (and formatted, and, of course, plugged in). Here are things to check and try:

- If you have more than one SCSI device connected to the computer, check that each has a unique ID number, that all of them are turned on, and that the chain is terminated properly.

- Zap the PRAM; sometimes a hard drive won't mount because there's corrupted information in PRAM—which keeps track of what the startup disk is supposed to be.

- Rebuild the Desktop file.

▪ Reinstall the system software; a startup drive won't mount if the System file or Finder are corrupted. (If the Mac starts with a floppy startup and you can see the hard drive on the Desktop, that usually indicates a problem with its system software.)

▪ Use the HD Setup program to reinstall the disk driver by clicking the Update button. *Don't* click the Initialize button or you'll erase the disk.

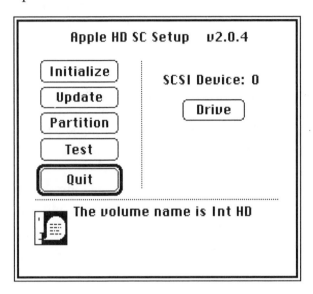

Figure 18-3. Use HD Setup's Update button to reinstall the disk driver.

▪ If you're using a removable hard disk cartridge, check that you have the correct driver in your Extensions folder; if it's there, try replacing it with a fresh copy.

▪ Run a file recovery program or a disk diagnostics tool.

FILES THAT WON'T COPY
Sometimes when you're copying a file to or from a floppy disk, you'll get a message that the file couldn't be read, or couldn't be written, and was skipped.

If the file couldn't be written, it's often due to a flaw in the disk media at a certain sector. You should reinitialize the disk; if it doesn't pass the initialization procedure, throw the disk away.

If the file couldn't be read, sometimes you can still open it from within the application that created it; if you can, do a Save As to make a new copy of the file and delete the original. Sometimes you can duplicate a problem file on the Desktop and work with that instead of the original.

Printing Problems

There are, of course, many problems mechanical in nature that you may have to deal with when you're printing—like paper jamming in the printer as it's fed through. But if everything seems fine on the hardware end, you'll have to consider the software problems that might be involved.

If you give a Print command and you get a dialog like the one shown in Figure 18-4, the printer is either not turned on, not connected to the computer, or not selected in the Chooser.

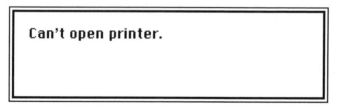

Figure 18-4. This dialog usually means that the printer's not turned on.

If your printing problems are not confined to a single document or application and the correct printer driver is selected in the Chooser desk accessory, try replacing the printer driver. Delete the one that's in the Extensions folder and then use its Customize option in the Installer program to reinstall the printer driver you need.

CHOOSER PROBLEMS

There are three basic problems you might run into with the Chooser desk accessory:

▪ If the icon for your printer is not in the left panel, the printer driver is not in the Extensions folder. Reinstall it with the Installer program.

▪ If you select a LaserWriter icon and the LaserWriter's name doesn't show up in the right panel, the LaserWriter isn't turned on. Or, if it is on, it hasn't warmed up yet. (Or it's the old standby problem—a cable is loose.)

▪ If you select the LaserWriter's name in the list and the Background Printing buttons don't appear or they remain dimmed, the PrintMonitor program is not in the Extensions folder.

DOCUMENTS PRINTING INCORRECTLY

If the document is printing but the text or graphics don't look correct, check that you've sized the graphic correctly for the printer and that you're using the correct font (see Chapter 16).

If other documents are printing, but one in particular won't print at all, or won't print something, check the settings in the software you're using and check the formatting of the document. Microsoft Word, for instance, allows *hidden text* formatting that shows text on the screen but prevents it from being printed. Silicon Beach's SuperPaint allows you to print from only one of the document's layers, if you prefer. Most spreadsheets let you print an entire spreadsheet or only a selected area.

LASERWRITER PRINTING PROBLEMS

LaserWriters have their own set of unique considerations for printing problems.

If blank pages are coming through the printer, check that you removed the protective strip from the toner cartridge when it was installed. Also check that the document was formatted correctly for printing. (Printing "hidden text," as just mentioned, can be a problem. And printing in grayscale when all the gray values in the picture are light results in nothing being printed at all.)

If nothing at all is printing although the printer itself seems fine:

- The document is may be too complicated for the printer's memory. The things that take up memory are complicated graphics and lots of fonts on a single page. The problem may also be just that a complicated page is taking a long time to process, and waiting it out will solve the problem. (Complicated pages, especially those printed with the gray-scale option turned on, can take 5 to 10 minutes to process; *very* complicated graphics can even take an hour.)

- Turn off the Faster Bitmap Printing option in the Page Setup dialog.

- If you're using background printing, the PrintMonitor may be set to print at a different date or time than the present.

If fonts are being printed incorrectly, make sure that you're using the correct fonts and that downloadable fonts are available. (Chapters 15 and 16 covered fonts and printing.) When there's no printer font available, the LaserWriter will create a bitmapped version of the font from the information in the screen font file. But if you find that Courier is being substituted for another outline font, that usually means that the LaserWriter ran out of memory and couldn't download the font information it needed.

Problems with Applications and Documents

Most of the problems you'll run into that are specific to applications and their documents are due to a bug in the application, an application file that's been corrupted, or memory problems.

APPLICATIONS QUITTING
When an application crashes, you'll usually get a polite dialog box like the one shown in Figure 18-5.

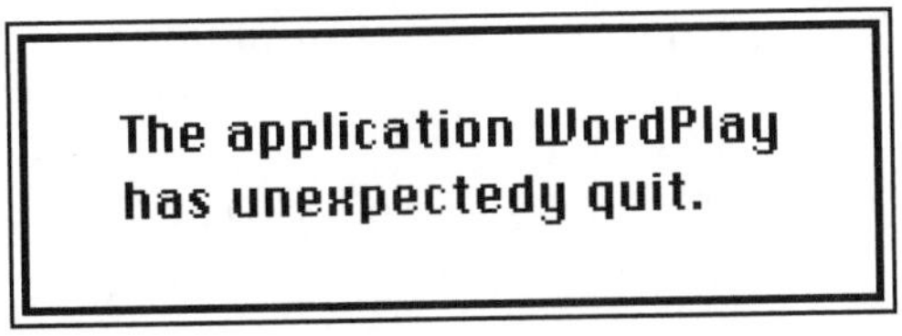

> **The application WordPlay
> has unexpectedy quit.**

Figure 18-5.   You'll see a dialog like this when a program crashes.

Here's what you can try to keep it from happening again:

■ The application may be clashing with some init program you're using; take them out from the Extensions folder and try again.

■ The application file may have been corrupted if it was open during a general system crash, so reinstall the application from its master disk.

■ There may not be enough memory allocated to the application. Change its memory partition size (as described in Chapter 13) and try again.

If the problem is a bug in the application itself, there's not much you can do; it might be unable to work under System 7, for instance.

MEMORY PROBLEMS
Figure 18-6 shows a dialog that will often appear to inform you of a memory shortage.

> **There is not enough memory
> available to launch this application.**

Figure 18-6.   There are several things you can do to avoid this dialog.

You can avoid this dialog by:

■ Allocating less memory, if possible, to the application.

■ Quitting another program that's running to free up more RAM.

- Quitting all the currently running programs to defragment memory and then trying to run them all again.

- If there's truly not enough memory no matter how you try to allocate it, consider a memory upgrade.

If you're in an application and can't open a document because there's not enough memory available, quit the application, allocate more memory to it, run it again, and then try to open the document. (Memory allocations and upgrades were discussed in Chapter 13.)

APPLICATION CAN'T BE FOUND

If you double-click on a document and get a message that says: *An application can't be found for this document,* the application isn't on any mounted drive. You can:

- Find the application and install it on your hard drive.
- Try to open the document in another, compatible application.

DAMAGED DOCUMENTS

If you double-click on a document to open it and you get a dialog that tells you it can't be opened because the document is damaged, try opening it from within its application. If it opens, do a Save As to make another copy of it. You can also try duplicating the damaged file on the Desktop and opening the copy.

Quickies

- There's a big difference between using the Reset button and using the Restart command from the Desktop's Special menu. Using the Restart command is basically the same as using Shut Down: The Mac has a chance to do its disk housekeeping before RAM is cleared. The Reset button—and any Restart button that's in a system error dialog— immediately clears RAM with nothing saved to the disk.

- If you're trying to start up the Mac with a floppy disk and it's ejected, that means it's not a startup disk.

SUMMARY

The solutions presented here won't work every time, and the chapter didn't cover every possible problem situation, but you did learn how to diagnose and cure some common problems.

Appendices

Desktop Shortcuts

ICONS

You can use the keyboard to select an icon in the active window:

- The arrow keys select icons in a specific direction from the current icon.

- Typing an icon's name (as many letters as required to uniquely identify it) selects it.

- The Tab key selects the item alphabetically after the currently selected icon. Shift-Tab selects the icon that alphabetically precedes it.

OPENING AND CLOSING WINDOWS

You can open and close windows with keyboard commands, manipulating not only the selected folder, but also its "parent"—the window that it's in:

- Command-down arrow opens a selected folder.
- Command-Option-down arrow opens a selected folder and closes its parent.
- Command-up arrow opens the parent of the active window.
- Command-Option-up arrow closes the active window while opening its parent.

EXPANDING AND COLLAPSING LIST VIEWS

You can expand or collapse the outline of a selected folder from the keyboard as well as by clicking on its arrow:

- Command-right arrow expands the first level of the selected folder.

- Command-Option right arrow expands all the levels of the selected folder.

- Command-left arrow collapses the selected folder; the level to which its inner folders were expanded will be remembered the next time you open it.

- Command-Option-left arrow collapses the selected folder and also collapses all the folders within it.

USING THE COMMAND KEY

There are some Command-key shortcuts on the Desktop:

- Holding down Command while dragging an icon reverses the current Snap to Grid setting.

- Holding down Command while pressing on a window's title opens its Path menu.

- Dragging an inactive Desktop window while holding down the Command key moves the window but does not activate it.

- Command-Shift-up arrow deactivates all the windows and activates the Desktop itself so you can use keyboard commands to select loose icons.

USING THE OPTION KEY

Adding the Option key to some Desktop operations often changes the result:

- Holding down Option while opening menus changes some commands: About This Macintosh becomes About the Finder; Close becomes Close All; Clean Up becomes Clean Up by [last sort criterion]; Empty Trash . . . becomes Empty Trash (or vice versa—the current Trash warning is reversed).

- Holding down Option while selecting from a window's Path menu closes the current window as you move to the selected window.

- Clicking in a window's close box while holding down Option closes all the Desktop windows.

- Clicking in a window's zoom box while holding down Option zooms the window open to the full size of the screen no matter how much is in the window.

- Holding down Option while clicking on a folder's arrow in a list view opens or closes that folder's outline to all levels.

- Holding down Option while you drag an icon from one folder to another on the same disk leaves a copy of the file in its original location.

Directory Dialog Shortcuts

There are several keyboard shortcuts available in Open and Save dialogs:

- In a Save dialog, use the Tab key to alternately activate the text box for the file's name and the list box.

- Select an item in the list by typing as many letters as needed to uniquely identify it.

- Select any item in the list by using the up and down arrow keys.

- Use the tilde (~) key to select the last item in the list.

- Use Return or Enter instead of the default Open or Save button.

- Use Command-N instead of the New Folder button.

- Use Command-D instead of the Desktop button.

- Use Command-period or the Esc key to cancel the dialog.

- Use Command-up arrow to move up one folder in the hierarchy. (Or click on the disk icon.)

- Use Command-left arrow and Command-right arrow to switch from one mounted disk to another, bypassing the Desktop level.

ASCII Codes

Every character you can type from the keyboard is assigned an ASCII code (from *American Standard Code for Information Interchange,* and pronounced "ask-key") to make it easy for different kinds of computers to exchange basic information. The first 31 characters are nonprinting characters, like Tab and Return, so Figure C-1 shows the codes and their letters starting with 32.

Code	Char	Code	Char	Code	Char	Code	Char	Code	Char	Code	Char	Code	Char
32	(space	64	@	96	`	128	Ä	160	†	192	¿	224	‡
33	!	65	A	97	a	129	Å	161	°	193	¡	225	·
34	"	66	B	98	b	130	Ç	162	¢	194	¬	226	‚
35	#	67	C	99	c	131	É	163	£	195		227	„
36	$	68	D	100	d	132	Ñ	164	§	196	ƒ	228	‰
37	%	69	E	101	e	133	Ö	165	•	197		229	Â
38	&	70	F	102	f	134	Ü	166	¶	198		230	Ê
39	'	71	G	103	g	135	á	167	ß	199	«	231	Á
40	(	72	H	104	h	136	à	168	®	200	»	232	Ë
41	)	73	I	105	i	137	â	169	©	201	…	233	È
42	*	74	J	106	j	138	ä	170	™	202	hard space	234	Í
43	+	75	K	107	k	139	ã	171	´	203	À	235	Î
44	,	76	L	108	l	140	å	172	¨	204	Ã	236	Ï
45	–	77	M	109	m	141	ç	173		205	Õ	237	Ì
46	.	78	N	110	n	142	é	174	Æ	206	Œ	238	Ó
47	/	79	O	111	o	143	è	175	Ø	207	œ	239	Ô
48	0	80	P	112	p	144	ê	176		208	–	240	
49	1	81	Q	113	q	145	ë	177	±	209	—	241	Ò
50	2	82	R	114	r	146	í	178		210	"	242	Ú
51	3	83	S	115	s	147	ì	179		211	"	243	Û
52	4	84	T	116	t	148	î	180	¥	212	'	244	Ù
53	5	85	U	117	u	149	ï	181	µ	213	'	245	ı
54	6	86	V	118	v	150	ñ	182		214	÷	246	
55	7	87	W	119	w	151	ó	183		215		247	˜
56	8	88	X	120	x	152	ò	184		216	ÿ	248	¯
57	9	89	Y	121	y	153	ô	185		217	Ÿ	249	˘
58	:	90	Z	122	z	154	ö	186		218	⁄	250	˙
59	;	91	[	123	{	155	õ	187	ª	219	¤	251	˚
60	<	92	\	124	|	156	ú	188	º	220	‹	252	¸
61	=	93	]	125	}	157	ù	189		221	›	253	˝
62	>	94	^	126	~	158	û	190	æ	222	ﬁ	254	˛
63	?	95	_	127	(none)	159	ü	191	ø	223	ﬂ	255	ˇ

Figure C-1. ASCII codes for printing characters

Alphabetization

Files are sorted alphabetically in list views on the Desktop and in list boxes in dialogs, with no differentiation between capital and lowercase letters. But you can also use nonalphabetic characters in file names—like punctuation (!, ?, and ;), symbols (*, >, and $), and even Option characters (•, ™, and ©).

All characters are sorted according to their ASCII codes, *except* the Option and Shift-Option characters that are foreign alphabetic characters. So, for example, å is sorted between A and B.

Character Sets

Figure E-1 shows the character set for the Symbol font included in your system software; Figure E-2 shows the Zapf Dingbats character set (it's built into LaserWriters). In both figures, the top picture shows the unshifted characters; the second shows the shifted characters; the third shows the Option characters; and the last shows the Shift-Option characters.

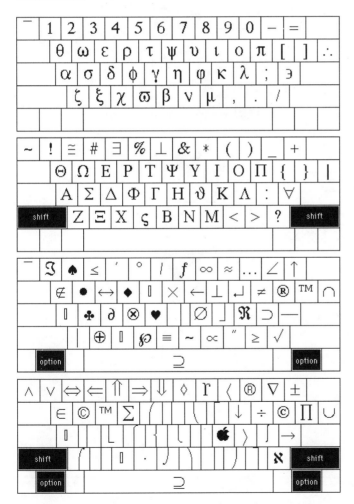

Figure E-1.   Character set for the Symbol font

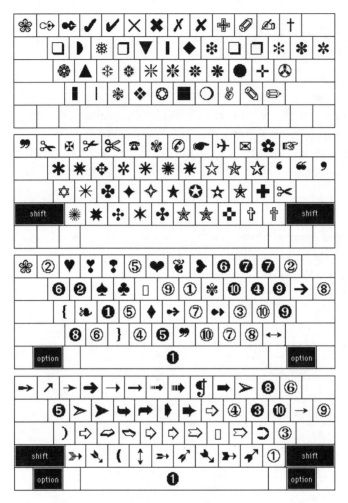

Figure E-2. Zapf Dingbats characters

System 6 Considerations

In the year or more it will take the Macintosh market to completely move up to System 7, you may run into several problems, or at least oddities, as you use disks on both systems or as you use programs or files designed for System 6.

▪ As discussed in Chapter 17, there are different levels of compatibility between a program and System 7, ranging from total incompatibility (where the program won't run at all) to total compatibility (where the program takes advantage of all of System 7's unique features).

▪ In System 6, fonts and desk accessories could be stored in files called suitcases. Under System 7, you can double-click on a font suitcase to extract the fonts you want to move into your System file, or you can drag the whole suitcase into your System file. To use a desk accessory from an old suitcase, double-click on the suitcase to open it and drag out the individual desk accessories that you want. (As with other programs, some may not work under System 7.)

▪ When you use a disk under System 7 that was previously used under System 6, you'll get a dialog that tells you the disk is being updated for use with System 7. This updating won't affect any of the files on the disk, but it can change the structure of the filing system on the old disk so that disk recovery software designed for System 6 won't work on it—even if you use it with System 6 again. (This doesn't mean that you can't use the disk or its contents under System 6; it just means that you shouldn't count on any old file recovery system that's installed on it.)

▪ When you use System 6 to look at disks that have been used under System 7, you'll see differences in the folders. Folders with icons, like the ones in the System Folder, will be plain; any icons you edited yourself will revert to their original look. There may be one or two extra folders on the disk: The Desktop Folder stores whatever was loose on the Desktop that belonged to that disk; the Trash Folder holds whatever was in the Trash and not emptied.

Special Resources

MAGAZINES

MacUser Magazine
Ziff-Davis Publishing
950 Tower Lane, 18th floor
Foster City, California 94404
415-378-5600

MacWeek
Ziff-Davis Publishing
Subscription inquiries:
JCI P.O. Box 1766
Riverton, New Jersey 08077-7366
609-461-2100

Macworld Magazine
502 Second Street, 5th floor
San Francisco, California 94107
415-243-0505

USER GROUPS

A good user group can be your most important single source of
information and education. Most groups meet monthly to exchange
information and see demonstrations of new products. Many publish their
own newsletters and provide disks of public domain software.

To find a user group in your area, call Apple's User Group hotline at
800-538-9696, ext. 500.

ONLINE SERVICES

America Online
8619 Westwood Center Drive
Vienna, Virginia 22182
800-227-6364

CompuServe
5000 Arlington Center Boulevard
Columbus, Ohio 43220
800-848-8199

NJMUG BBS
(Bulletin Board System for the New Jersey Macintosh User Group)
908-388-1676

BMUG BBS
(Bulletin Board System for the Berkeley Macintosh User Group)
415-549-BMUG

MAIL ORDER

MacAvenue
12303 Technology Boulevard
Austin, Texas 78727
800-926-6221

MacConnection
14 Mill Street
Marlow, New Hampshire 03456
800-334-4444

MacWarehouse
P.O. Box 3013
1690 Oak Street
Lakewood, New Jersey 08701-3013
800-255-6227

MAJOR MAC SHOWS

Macworld Expo
Mitch Hall Associates
260 Milton Street
Dedham, Massachusetts 02026
617-361-3389

CLIP ART

Following are addresses of the companies that provided some of the artwork in this book.

Claris Corporation
(HyperCard's Art Bits stack)
5201 Patrick Henry Drive
Box 58168
Santa Clara, California 95952
408-987-7000

Dubl-Click Software
9316 Deering Avenue
Chatsworth, California 91311
818-700-9525

3G Graphics
11410 NE 124th Street #6155 R
Kirkland, Washington 98034
800-456-0234

Index